INTELLECTUAL PROPERTY AND FREE TRADE AGREEMENTS

Intellectual Property and Free Trade Agreements presents the papers of the sixth IP conference organised by the Macau Institute of European Studies (IEEM) on intellectual property law and the economic challenges for Asia. The objective of the conferences is to provide up-to-date information on developments in global intellectual property law and policy and their impact on regional economic and cultural development. The current volume deals with the implications of free trade agreements for the international framework of intellectual property law, a topic of enormous economic and legal importance given the increasing number of free trade agreements in force or under negotiation.

International Intellectual Property Law: Volume 4

IEEM series on International Intellectual Property Law

The involvement of the Institute of European Studies of Macau (IEEM) in matters of intellectual property is based on annual conferences that take up topical issues of intellectual property from a comparative perspective with a particular focus on Asia and Europe. The first of these conferences was held back in 2000, and has meanwhile become an annual event complemented by an Intellectual Property School and IP Master Classes. All three venues serve as a platform for academic teaching and discussion on intellectual property awareness and the proper place and function of intellectual property law in the context of society and public interest.

From the very start, the intellectual property conferences, the IP Law School and the Master Classes have enjoyed the support, assistance and commitment of Mr Gonçalo Cabral, who is an advisor to the Government of Macau, of Ms Maria do Céu Esteves, past president of the IEEM, and the IEEM's current president Dr. José Luís de Sales Marques. The latter was also instrumental in setting up an IEEM chair for intellectual property law at the University of Maastricht, currently held by Anselm Kamperman Sanders, thereby further contributing to IEEM's academic commitment to the field of intellectual property law.

The conference papers, as revised and updated, are edited by Christopher Heath and Anselm Kamperman Sanders as an IEEM Intellectual Property Series the volumes of which are listed below:

1. Intellectual Property in the Digital Age—Challenges for Asia
   Christopher Heath and Anselm Kamperman Sanders (eds)
   Published by Kluwer Law International 2001
   ISBN 90-411-9847-4

2. Intellectual Property in the Bio-Medical Age—Challenges for Asia
   Christopher Heath and Anselm Kamperman Sanders (eds)
   Published by Kluwer Law International 2003
   ISBN 90-411-9926-8

3. New Frontiers of Intellectual Property Law
   Christopher Heath and Anselm Kamperman Sanders (eds)
   Published by Hart Publishing 2005
   ISBN 1-84113-538-0

4. Intellectual Property and Free Trade Agreements
   Christopher Heath and Anselm Kamperman Sanders (eds)
   Published by Hart Publishing 2007
   ISBN 978-1-84113-801-5

Intellectual Property and Free Trade Agreements

Edited by

Christopher Heath and
Anselm Kamperman Sanders

INSTITUTE OF EUROPEAN STUDIES OF MACAU
澳 門 歐 洲 研 究 學 會
INSTITUTO DE ESTUDOS EUROPEUS DE MACAU

•HART•
PUBLISHING

OXFORD and PORTLAND, OREGON
2007

Published in North America (US and Canada) by
Hart Publishing
c/o International Specialized Book Services
920 NE 58th Avenue, Suite 300
Portland, OR 97213-3786
USA
Tel: +1-503-287-3093 or toll-free: (1)-800-944-6190
Fax: +1-503-280-8832
E-mail: orders@isbs.com
Website: www.isbs.com

Hart Publishing, 16C Worcester Place, Oxford, OX1 2JW
Telephone: +44 (0)1865 517530 Fax: +44 (0)1865 510710
E-mail: mail@hartpub.co.uk
Website: www.hartpub.co.uk

British Library Cataloguing in Publication Data
Data Available

ISBN 978-1-84113-801-5

Typeset by Hope Services Ltd, Abingdon
Printed and bound in Great Britain by
Lightning Source UK Ltd

Preface

The editors hereby present papers of the sixth IP conference organised by the Macau Institute of European Studies (IEEM) on intellectual property law and the economic challenges for Asia.

The objective of the conferences is to provide up-to-date information on developments in global intellectual property law and policy and their impact on regional economic and cultural development. The current volume deals with the implications of free trade agreements for the international framework of intellectual property law, a topic of enormous economic and legal importance given the increasing number of free trade agreements in force or under negotiation. The interest the US and the EU have taken in inserting IP protection standards in such agreements uncomfortably show that WTO/TRIPS marked not the end, but rather the beginning of a spiralling upward trend towards more and stronger IP protection, often with a corresponding loss of commons contrary to public interest. Thus, most of the contributions in this book are rather critical not only regarding the coercion particularly developing countries are subject to when negotiating bilateral free trade agreements, but also with the level of IP protection and enforcement these agreements demand.

The success of the past IEEM intellectual property law seminars have turned the venue into an annual event that since the year 2005 has been coupled with the IP Law School and the IP Law Master Classes. The IP Law School is a unique initiative in Asia offering a taught programme in international intellectual property law and its relevance for Asian, European and global economic development and innovation policy. The Master classes are much more topical and are taught jointly by the regular IP Law School team and expert speakers at the IP Seminar. The IP Law School and Master Classes form a seamless companion programme to the Annual Intellectual Property Seminar. The seventh conference in 2006, whose proceedings are forthcoming, analysed the issues of spares, repairs and intellectual property rights, while the eighth conference in 2007 will look at intellectual property and the pharmaceutical industry.

The editors would specifically like to thank Mr. Gonçalo Cabral, who has been instrumental in organising both the IEEM annual seminars and the intellectual property summer school, and José Luís de Sales Marques, President of the IEEM, for his continuing support for both venues. The Netherlands Organisation for Scientific Research (NWO-ISW # 460-05-008) provided additional means to get the manuscripts in shape for publication. Moreover, the seminars would not have happened without the tireless commitment of Bentham Fong and the other staff members of IEEM in Macao. Last but not least, the editors would like to thank Richard Hart for having agreed to publish the proceedings of this and future conferences as a series on international intellectual property law.

Christopher Heath and Anselm Kamperman Sanders

Contents

Detailed Table of Contents

Part II Law and Policy of Multilateral v Bilateral Agreements

Part III FTAs and Patents

Part V FTAs and Antitrust

On the Authors and Editors

Maristela Basso is a Professor at the University of São Paulo and president of the International Trade Law and Development Institute, São Paulo, Brazil. Legal counsel, Basso & Vicenzi advogados, São Paulo.

She can be reached by e-mail at mbasso@usp.br

Edson Beas Rodrigues is a postgraduate student, University of São Paulo and member of the Working Group on Intellectual Property Policy of the International Trade Law and Development Institute. He served as legal consultant to the International Poverty Center of the United Nations Development Programme.

He can be reached by e-mail at edsonbeas@idcid.org.br

Andrew Christie is the Davies Collison Cave Professor of Intellectual Property at the University of Melbourne Law School. He is also the founding Director of the Intellectual Property Research Institute of Australia, a national centre for multi-disciplinary research on the law, economics and management of intellectual property.

He can be reached by email at a.christie@unimelb.edu.au

Daniel J Gervais is the Oslers Professor of Intellectual Property and Technology Law and holds a University Research Chair in Intellectual Property at the Faculty of Law of the University of Ottawa (Common Law Section), where he recently served as Acting Dean and Vice-Dean (Research). Prior to his teaching career, Prof. Gervais was successively Legal Officer at the GATT (now the World Trade Organization); Head of Section at the World Intellectual Property Organization (WIPO); and Vice-President, International of Copyright Clearance Center, Inc. (CCC). He also served as consultant to the Organization for Economic Co-operation and Development (OECD) and to various Departments of the Canadian Government. Dr. Gervais is the author of several articles, five books and a number of book chapters on copyright law and copyright management and international intellectual property law, published in six different languages, including a book on the history and interpretation of the TRIPS Agreement (2nd edition, Sweet & Maxwell, 2003). Since January 2007, he is the General Editor of the Journal of World Intellectual Property, now published by John Wiley & Sons (New York) and Blackwell's (Oxford).

He can be reached by email at dgervais@uottawa.ca

Christopher Heath (1964) studied at the Universities of Konstanz, Edinburgh and the LSE. He lived and worked in Japan for three years, and between 1992 and 2005 headed the Asian Department of the Max Planck Institute for Patent,

Copyright and Competition Law in Munich. Christopher Heath, who wrote his phD thesis on Japanese unfair competition prevention law, is a Member of the Boards of Appeal at the European Patent Office in Munich, co-editor of IIC and editor of the Max Planck Institute's Asian Intellectual Property Series published by Kluwer Law International.

He can be reached by e-mail at cheath@epo.org

Andreas Heinemann, Ref. iur. (Munich), Ass. iur. (Berlin), is Professor of Law at the University of Zurich. After having studied economics and law he participated in the 'Cycle International' of the *Ecole Nationale d'Administration* in Paris. He received his Ph.D. in Law and his 'Habilitation' from the Faculty of Law of University of Munich. The focus of his publications is European and International Economic law with special interest in antitrust and intellectual property law. He is co-editor of the project 'The Enforcement of Competition Law in Europe' ('Common Core of European Private Law') at the University of Trento and Member of the Scientific Advisory Board of the Munich Intellectual Property Law Center (MIPLC).

He can be reached by e-mail at andreas.heinemann@rwi.uzh.ch

Anselm Kamperman Sanders (1968), PhD (Lond), is Professor in European and International Intellectual Property Law at Maastricht University, The Netherlands. He was Marie Curie Research Fellow at Queen Mary and Westfield College, University of London and has held a research grant from the VSB fund and a Chevening Scholarship. Further research, teaching and advisory affiliations comprise the International Institute of Infonomics, the ETH in Zürich, Switzerland and the Institute of European Studies of Macau SAR, China. In 2003 he was adjunct professor at the Queensland University of Technology, Brisbane, Australia. He has acted as Rapporteur to an EC Commission DG Research working group on Strategic Use and Adaptation of Intellectual Property Rights Systems in Information and Communications Technologies-based Research. Anselm has worked in developing countries on WTO accession assistance projects for the EC/GTZ. His editorial and advisory board memberships comprise the Maastricht Journal of European and Comparative Law, Intellectuele Eigendom en Reclamerecht, International Journal of Intellectual Property Management, and the Intellectual Property Quarterly.

He can be reached by e-mail at A.KampermanSanders@pr.unimaas.nl

Roger Kampf is Counsellor at the Intellectual Property Division of the World Trade Organisation where he is responsible for the Secretariat's work in the area of the TRIPS Agreement as it relates to public health and enforcement, as well as the coordination and implementation of technical co-operation activities in the field of intellectual property. Previously he worked for the European Commission as Counsellor at the Geneva Delegation and as Deputy Head of Unit in DG TRADE, covering intellectual property and government procurement. He studied law at the Universities of Hamburg and Marburg and was a fellow at the Ecole Nationale d'Administration in Paris.

He can be reached by e-mail at roger.kampf@wto.org

Byung-Il Kim is a graduate of Yonsei University, Seoul. He was a Max-Planck Research Fellow between 1994 and 1999 and holds a PhD from Munich University. Currently, Dr Kim holds a chair as associate professor at Hanyan University, Seoul.

He can be reached by e-mail at hobyung1@dreamwiz.com

Dr Jakkrit Kuanpoth is currently a Senior Lecturer, Faculty of Law, University of Wollongong, Australia. Before coming to Wollongong, he taught at School of Law, Sukhothai Thammathirat Open University, Thailand. He holds LLB (Hons), Ramkhamhaeng University, Thailand; Barrister-at-Law, The Institute of Legal Education Thai Bar Association, Thailand; LLM, International Economic Law, University of Warwick, UK; PhD, University of Aberdeen, UK.

He can be reached by e-mail at jakkrit@uow.edu.au

Sophie Waller is currently practicing as a lawyer specialising in commercial and intellectual property law, and is completing a Master of Laws at the University of Melbourne. She was previously a researcher at the Intellectual Property Research Institute of Australia, a national centre for multi-disciplinary research on the law, economics and management of intellectual property. She holds a Bachelor of Science and a Bachelor of Laws with Honours, both from Monash University.

She can be reached by email at s.waller@pgrad.unimelb.edu.au

Kimberlee Weatherall is Senior Lecturer, TC Beirne School of Law, The University of Queensland, and Adjunct Research Fellow, Australian Centre for Intellectual Property in Agriculture. Her research focuses specifically on digital copyright issues and intellectual property enforcement.

She can be reached by email at k.weatherall@law.uq.edu.au

Ng-Loy Wee Loon, LLB (Sing), LLM (Lond), is an Associate Professor at the Faculty of Law, National University of Singapore. She is currently the Director of its LLM in IP & Technology program. She sat on the Board of Directors of Singapore's national IP office, the Intellectual Property Office of Singapore in 2001–2003.

She can be reached by email at loyweeloon@nus.edu.sg

Part I

General Issues

Chapter 1

The Development Agenda for Intellectual Property Rational Humane Policy or 'Modern-day Communism'?[1]

ANSELM KAMPERMAN SANDERS

I. INTRODUCTION

THIS CONTRIBUTION ADDRESSES the Development Agenda for the World Intellectual Property Organisation (WIPO) and the role of intellectual property rights (IPR) in fostering innovation and technology transfer. More in particular, the mounting pressure from developing nations to view intellectual property not just as a means to guarantee the interests of rightholders, but also to bring about economic development and welfare for the whole of global society. A balance of interest between IPR and the public domain features high on the agenda of new international initiatives aiming to harmonize and streamline IPR and procedures. Public interest concerns and a development dimension are key features in the search for this balance. This is why there is mounting pressure to make current discussions on a draft Substantive Patent Law Treaty (SPLT) and also the existing intellectual property framework subject to a so-called 'Development Agenda for WIPO'. This Development Agenda aims to bridge the gap that separates wealthy nations from the poor.

In the fall of 2004 Argentina and Brazil submitted a formal proposal to the WIPO relating to the establishment of a new development agenda within WIPO.[2] The proposal addresses the 'knowledge gap' and 'digital divide' that

[1] This is an updated version of the Inaugural Lecture, delivered on the occasion of the acceptance of the chair of European and International Intellectual Property Law at Maastricht University on 20 May 2005. The Institute of European Studies of Macau sponsors this chair. This sponsorship enables a number of selected Maastricht University students to attend the IEEM IP Law School, IP Master Classes and IP Seminar. This is testament to the IEEM's desire to build bridges between East and West for which the author is very grateful.

[2] WO/GA/31/11 of 27 August 2004.

separates wealthy nations from developing nations and calls for a case-by-case assessment of the role of intellectual property and its impact on development. Whereas in the previous years the prevailing trend has been to harmonise international legal norms through the World Trade Organisation's (WTO) Agreement on Trade Related Aspects of Intellectual Property (TRIPS Agreement), there is now a clear call for increased flexibility.

This flexibility should not only be exercised in respect of the existing obligations and their permitted limitations under the TRIPS Agreement, but should also prompt WIPO to act in consistence with the United Nation's Millennium Development Goals.[3] In this respect the development agenda places special emphasis on Articles 7 and 8 of the TRIPS Agreement. These provisions deal with the objectives of the TRIPS Agreement and point to the need for the international transfer of technology and to the promotion of public policy objectives of socio-economic and technological development. It is the aim of the WIPO Development Agenda to make sure that all future WIPO initiatives reflect these TRIPS objectives:

First, these provisions place the protection of intellectual property rights in the context of a balance of rights and obligations of producers and users of technical knowledge. This places a special emphasis on the promotion of technological innovation and the transfer and dissemination of technology in a manner beneficial to social economic welfare.

Second, these provisions recognise that WTO Members are entitled to a certain degree of flexibility when it comes to the protection of public health and nutrition, and the promotion of public interest in sectors of vital importance to their socio-economic and technological development.

Third, the provisions recognise that members may take appropriate measures to prevent the abuse of intellectual property rights or practices that restrain trade or adversely affect technology transfer.

II. PLAN

This contribution introduces the content of the Development Agenda and the role and place of the WIPO and the WTO in international standard setting for intellectual property. In this light the flexibilities that developing countries are seeking in implementing and interpreting the TRIPS Agreement are covered. This so-called 'rational and humane policy' should serve to meet the needs of developing nations when it comes to public and health policy, innovation and technology transfer. By means of examples involving compulsory licensing for essential drugs and recent enhancements of the copyright system, it exemplifies

[3] See www.developmentgoals.org/. The goals are: 1) Eradicate extreme poverty and hunger, 2) Achieve universal primary education, 3) Promote gender equality and empower women, 4) Reduce child mortality, 5) Improve maternal health, 6) Combat HIV/AIDS, malaria, and other diseases, 7) Ensure environmental sustainability, 8) Develop a global partnership for development.

how the Western world is undermining the Development Agenda by introducing so-called TRIPS-plus obligations through the WTO system and bilateral Free Trade Agreements (FTAs) and Bilateral Investment Treaties (BITs).[4]

In conclusion examples are provided on how, for the purpose of furthering investment in innovation and technology transfer to the benefit of developing countries, use can be made of the existing IPR framework and how minor amendments could even yield more results.

III. THE DEVELOPMENT AGENDA

The Development Agenda is about finding flexibility in the implementation of TRIPS obligations but also about balancing the monopoly of the intellectual property rightholder with the interests of third parties and of society as a whole. Flexibility is, however, something that sits uneasy with the current trend in intellectual property policy. This trend has been one of maximizing rights to stamp out piracy and one of harmonization to provide a one-size fits all level playing field of rights. Flexibility to curb the full exercise of the intellectual property monopoly to accommodate the interests of users, competitors or developing countries is not popular among industrialists. In a recent interview Bill Gates even went so far as to say that restricting intellectual property rights is tantamount to communism:

> . . . [O]f the world's economies, there's more that believe in intellectual property today than ever. There are fewer communists in the world today than there were. There are some new modern-day sort of communists who want to get rid of the incentive for musicians and moviemakers and software makers under various guises. They don't think that those incentives should exist.
>
> And this debate will always be there. I'd be the first to say that the patent system can always be tuned—including the US patent system. There are some goals to cap some reform elements. But the idea that the United States has led in creating companies, creating jobs, because we've had the best intellectual-property system—there's no doubt about that in my mind, and when people say they want to be the most competitive economy, they've got to have the incentive system. Intellectual property is the incentive system for the products of the future.' (Bill Gates, January 2005)[5]

This statement is testament to the idea that stronger IPR automatically lead to more innovation and that one uniform—read US—system of rights is superior.

A recent World Bank publication on Intellectual Property and Development,[6] however, shows that neither strong IPR, nor bilateral investment or free trade

[4] See www.bilaterals.org.

[5] Gates, 'Restricting IP rights is tantamount to communism', interview with Kanellos, CNET News.com, January 06, 2005, available at insight.zdnet.co.uk/software/windows/0,39020478, 39183197,00.htm

[6] Fink/Maskus (eds), Intellectual Property and Development—Lessons form Recent Economic Research (2005, New York, World Bank/Oxford University Press). See also Braga/Fink/Sepulveda, Intellectual Property Rights and Economic Development, World Bank Discussion Paper No 412 (2000, Washington, World Bank).

agreements automatically yield an increase in technology transfer and foreign direct investment (FDI).[7] Figures show that countries with weak protection or enforcement of IPR like Brazil and China have been more successful in attracting FDI than many developing countries that have made strong IPR central to their development strategy.[8] Brazil and China are high growth, large market economies with an increasingly adequate regulatory system involving taxes, investment regulations, production incentives, trade policies and even a hint of competition rules. The strength of IPR protection is clearly not the only factor in investment decision making. Empirical economic studies show that the relationship between IPR and FDI in developing countries varies highly in respect of industry type, the stage of economic development and the natural and labour resources of the country in question. Econometric evidence of positive effects of strong IPR on FDI and technology transfer is not conclusive.[9] Strengthening IPR is therefore mostly seen as a signal indicating that a country is willing to provide a more business-friendly environment. It is clear that IPR protection should not be detrimental to follow-on investors and creators. This requires careful definitions on the scope of protection provided by IPR, sensible fair use exceptions that allow certain uses related to teaching, research and private use of protected materials and a balanced compulsory licensing regime, making essential patents and protected works available to competitors and follow-on creators against reasonable royalty rates.

So far the likes of Bill Gates have been extremely successful in getting their point across. The protection of databases, the legal recognition of digital rights management that limit fair use,[10] the protection of gene sequences for the purpose of diagnostic testing, the patenting of business methods and software are but a few examples of new standard setting that may lead to the de facto protection of ideas and facts, as opposed to the protection of innovation and original expression.

Prior to this the entry into force of the TRIPS Agreement[11] had already strengthened the position of intellectual property rightholders by obliging Members to the WTO to adopt minimum standards for protection and provide effective enforcement measures. Since its adoption in 1994 the TRIPS Agreement has become the de facto norm that shapes multilateral, regional, bilateral and national intellectual property laws and practices. It is the basis for all current and future standard setting in the area of IPR.

[7] Correa, Bilateral investment agreements: Agents of new global standards for the protection of intellectual property rights? (2004, GRAIN) at 3, available at www.grain.org.

[8] Maskus, 'The Role of Intellectual Property Rights in Encouraging Foreign Direct Investment and Technology Transfer', note 6 at 54, where examples cited comprise Sub-Saharan Africa and Eastern Europe.

[9] *Ibid* at 63–6.

[10] Klein/Lerner/Murphy, 'The Economics of Copyright "Fair Use" in a Networked World', American Economic Review, May 2002 (Papers and Proceedings), 92(2), pp 205–8.

[11] The TRIPS Agreement was adopted as part of the Final Act of the Uruguay Round of Trade Negotiations in 1994. See www.wto.org for the full text of the Agreement.

Further development of IPR protection based on TRIPS Agreement obligations is controversial. A combination of multilateral and bilateral agreements is widening the scope of IPR even more. These BITs or FTAs permit developed countries to use their considerable economic leverage comprising foreign direct investment or market access to influence the domestic economy of developing countries. When IPR provisions are included, these agreements are referred to as TRIPS-plus agreements and they can have serious adverse effects on the public interests in developing countries.

An authoritative UK Government Commission on Intellectual Property Rights has noted that introducing higher standards of protection and enforcement of IPR already put a considerable strain on the resources and economies of developing countries.[12] Further increases could have a negative impact on agriculture, education, public health, innovation and technology transfer and commonly raise the cost of administration and enforcement for developing nations.

Still, TRIPS-plus standards are now a permanent fixture in international trade, as they are integral to many bilateral trade and investment agreements.[13] Furthermore, WIPO's efforts to develop and promote IPR have more TRIPS-plus overtones than mere TRIPS implementation assistance would require.[14]

From its inception in 1970 and subsequent status as an agency of the United Nations system of international organisations, WIPO has played a central role in the administration of intellectual property Unions and the promotion of the protection of intellectual property[15] and currently has 182 members. The arrival in 1994 of WTO as the new kid on the block has prompted WIPO to reassess its role. Gone was the possibility for members to pick and choose intellectual property regimes and enforcement standards that the WIPO had on offer. Gone was the possibility of membership without effective enforcement. The TRIPS Agreement galvanised both minimum norms of protection and enforcement. WIPO was in danger of becoming sidelined.

To provide a basis for a sensible division of tasks and competences, a cooperation Agreement was reached with the WTO in 1995. Under it, WIPO now also provides technical assistance for TRIPS implementation to developing country members of the WTO. Providing assistance is after all one of the areas in which WIPO is specialised. In many ways this has become a lifeline for WIPO, which is now able assist the WTO by offering expertise in the area of

[12] Commission on Intellectual Property Rights, Integrating Intellectual Property Rights and Development Policy (2002, London, Commission on Intellectual Property Rights). Bilateral agreements entered into between the EC and their Member States and various partners require these partners to ensure adequate and effective protection of intellectual property rights 'in conformity with the highest international standards', see Drahos, Developing Countries and International Intellectual Property Standard-Setting 14–18 (2002), study prepared for the UK Commission on Intellectual Property Rights, all available at www.iprcommission.org.

[13] Vivas-Eugui, Regional and Bilateral Agreements and a TRIPS-plus World: the Free Trade Area of the Americas (FTAA), TRIPS Issues Papers No 1 (2003 QUNO/QIAP/ICTSD, Geneva).

[14] Musungu/Dutfield, Multilateral Agreements and TRIPS-plus World: The World Intellectual Property Organisation (WIPO) (2003, QUNO/QIAP/ICTSD, Geneva).

[15] Vide Art 3 and 4 of the WIPO Convention.

intellectual property law so as to ensure a successful implementation of the TRIPS Agreement. It also enables WIPO to continue to be engaged in the spread of its own WIPO Copyright and Performances and Phonograms Treaties and the further development of new intellectual property initiatives, being most notably the overhaul of the Patent Cooperation Treaty and the before-mentioned inception of a Substantive Patent Law Convention.

Yet this newfound role of WIPO as the ambassador of the TRIPS Agreement has also made WIPO more vulnerable to criticism over all activities that they undertake in respect of furthering the acceptance and development of IPR. It is against this backdrop that international standard setting leads to international trade disputes.

All these developments have prompted a debate on the negative impact that raised IPR and TRIPS-plus agreements may have for developing countries. The issues are too numerous to cover within the scope of this lecture, but it suffices to say that TRIPS-plus will stretch the scarce resources of developing nations even further. I will just mention the issue of protection of Geographical Indications for wines and spirits, and other agricultural products or handicraft items,[16] the protection of traditional knowledge and folklore,[17] establishing collecting rights societies in developing countries,[18] protection of plant varieties and biodiversity,[19] and the patenting of biological material.[20]

Therefore this contribution is confined to two detailed examples illustrating the Development Agenda's concerns. First, the contentious issue of access to essential medicine by means of compulsory licensing, which still is a cornerstone of the WIPO Development Agenda.

[16] Heath, 'Geographical Indications: International, Bilateral and Regional Agreements'; Kamperman Sanders, 'Future Solutions for Protecting Geographical Indications Worldwide'; and Corte-Real, 'The Conflict Between Trade Marks and Geographical Indications—The Budweiser Case in Portugal', all in Heath/Kamperman Sanders (eds), New Frontiers of Intellectual Property, IIC Studies 25, Richard Hart Publishing Oxford/Portland 2005.

[17] Bachner, 'Back to the Future: Intellectual Property Rights and the Modernisation of Traditional Chinese Medicine'; Antons, 'Traditional Knowledge and Intellectual Property Rights in Australia and Southeast Asia'; Gray, 'Maori Culture and Trade Mark Law in New Zealand', all in Heath/Kamperman Sanders (eds.), New Frontiers of Intellectual Property, IIC Studies 25, Richard Hart Publishing Oxford/Portland 2005.

[18] Schlatter, 'Copyright Collecting Societies in Developing Countries: Possibilities and Dangers', in Heath/Kamperman Sanders (eds), New Frontiers of Intellectual Property, IIC Studies 25, Richard Hart Publishing Oxford/Portland 2005.

[19] Heath, 'Plant Varieties, Biodiversity and Access Rights'; Mo, 'Protection of Plant Varieties in Greater China'; Donavanik, 'Plant Varieties and Access Rights in Asia and the South', all in Heath/Kamperman Sanders (eds), Industrial Property in the Bio-Medical Age, Max Planck Series on Asian Intellectual Property Law vol. 8, Kluwer Law International The Hague/London/New York 2003.

[20] Llewelyn, 'Perspectives on Patenting Biological Material', Sherman, 'Biological Inventions and the Problem of Passive Infringement', all in Heath/Kamperman Sanders (eds.), Industrial Property in the Bio-Medical Age, Max Planck Series on Asian Intellectual Property Law vol. 8, Kluwer Law International The Hague/London/New York 2003; Hubicki/Sherman, 'Terminator Genes as "Technical" Protection Measures for Patents?', in Heath/Kamperman Sanders (eds), New Frontiers of Intellectual Property, IIC Studies 25, Richard Hart Publishing Oxford/Portland 2005 .

Second, the issue of how raised standards on copyright may negatively affect follow-on investment and creativity in downstream markets. This demonstrates that there is a more fundamental problem in international standard setting, namely that of raising IPR levels of protection, while omitting to also to address the issue of user rights and competition concerns.

IV. ACCESS TO ESSENTIAL MEDICINE

Compulsory licensing of patented pharmaceuticals has been a hot topic for quite some time.[21] Most notably the issue of providing access for the poor to drugs to combat AIDS made headlines in the global media and was subject of intense lobbying at the WTO. Governments of South Africa and Brazil, and major drug companies together with industrialized nations found one another on opposite sides of the fence. If anything, the media coverage has also made the general public aware that drug companies prefer to target the tourists rather than the developing nations they visit in increasingly greater numbers when it comes to making available much-needed medication for diseases such as malaria, tuberculosis and HIV. These three diseases alone kill 5 million people every year.[22] Although less than 5 per cent of the drugs on the World Health Organization (WHO) Essential Drugs List[22] are patented[24] and patent protection in many developing countries is less stringent than TRIPS otherwise requires,[25] the drugs are still not available. It is estimated that 2 billion people cannot get adequate treatment.[26] Lack of distribution channels and high cost of drugs relative to the gross domestic product (GDP) and average wage make up half of the explanation why this is so. When it comes to the availability of the latest, more effective, or complex drugs, patent rights and

[21] See also Kamperman Sanders, 'Patents—Antitrust, Compulsory Licensing and Research Exceptions', in Heath/Kamperman Sanders (eds.), Industrial Property in the Bio-Medical Age, Max Planck Series on Asian Intellectual Property Law vol. 8, Kluwer Law International The Hague/London/New York 2003, 163–84; and 'Compulsory Licensing and Public Health', 11 MJ 4 (2004) 337–46.

[22] See AIDS Epidemic Update December 2004, UNAIDS/04.45E (2004, UNAIDS/WHO), available at www.unaids.org.

[23] See www.who.int/medicines/organization/par/edl/procedures.shtml for the selection criteria of essential medicines, which do not include the patent status of the drug in question, but does give consideration to cost, thus potentially excluding therapeutically important, but expensive drugs, and for the list see mednet3.who.int/eml/eml_intro.asp; See also Velásquez, 'Phamaceutical Patents and Accessibility to Drugs', Revue Internationale de Droit Economique Special Edition: Pharmaceutical Patents, Innovations and Public Health (2001), 41 and Dumoulin, 'Patents and the Price of Drugs', Revue Internationale de Droit Economique Special Edition: Pharmaceutical Patents, Innovations and Public Health (2001), 49.

[24] IFPMA Press Release, Geneva, 20 December 2001, available at www.ifpma.org.

[25] The Doha WTO Ministerial Declaration on TRIPS and Public Health of 14 November 2001 (WT/MIN(01)/DEC/2) reiterates that the least developed members are exempted from implementing, employing and enforcing pharmaceutical product and test data protection and may refrain from granting exclusive marketing protection during the period patent protection is not provided until 1 January 2016, see www.wto.org.

[26] See www.europa.eu.int/comm/trade/issues/global/medecine/index_en.htm.

the lack of production facilities make up the other half. Increasingly traditional producers and suppliers of cheap generic drugs such as India, the world's leading supplier of generic medicines,[27] have been under pressure[28] to adopt TRIPS compliant patent acts that protect pharmaceutical products, processes, and products directly obtained by use of this patented process.[29] India is also a nation where as high as one in seven people may be infected with HIV.[30] A recently adopted[31] Indian patent act will provide heightened protection to medicines invented after the implementation date, but also those that have been patented outside of India since January 1, 1995. According to TRIPS[32] India was required to establish a 'mailbox' when it became a member of the WTO. Foreign applicants could already file patents between 1995 and 2005 for later consideration. There are some 4,000 patent applications for medicines that are now waiting to be examined by the Indian Patent Office. Patents eventually granted may affect generics currently available on the market, unless they are made subject to a compulsory licence.

V. COMPULSORY LICENSING AND THE FLEXIBILITY OF THE TRIPS AGREEMENT

The TRIPS Agreement offers WTO members a broad discretion on government use of compulsory licensing. There are no limitations on the grounds upon which a government can authorize use of a patent by third parties. Grounds explicitly mentioned in Art 31 TRIPS are national emergency, anti-competitive practices, public non-commercial use and dependent patents. Further grounds can be found in Art 8(1), which allows members to adopt measures necessary to protect public health and nutrition, and to promote the public interest in sectors of vital importance to their socio-economic and technological development. Furthermore Art 8(2) permits members to take necessary measures to prevent the abuse of IPR by right holders and practices that unreasonably restrain trade or adversely affect the international transfer of technology. There are, however, a number of procedural requirements that can be summarized as follows:

1. Cases have to be judged on their individual merits, thus excluding blanket advance approval for patents in a particular field of technology;[33]

[27] 66.7% of India's drug exports go to developing countries.

[28] See report of the WTO Dispute Settlement Body Panel on India—Patent Protection for Pharmaceutical and Agricultural Chemical Products, WT/DS79/R of 24 August 1998.

[29] Patents Bill (Bill No. 32-C of 2005), of which TRIPS compliance is still an issue.

[30] On the contentious issue whether India is the most HIV-dense country see www.theglobalfund.org and HIV is "out of control" in India', news.bbc.co.uk/1/hi/world/south_asia/4461999.stm and 'India rejects HIV infection claim', news.bbc.co.uk/1/hi/world/south_asia/4463899.stm See also Médecins Sans Frontières www.msf.org/countries India.

[31] The bill was passed by the Indian parliament in March 2005.

[32] Art 70(8).

[33] Further reinforced by Art 27(1), which states that patents shall be available and patent rights enjoyable without discrimination as to the place of invention, the field of technology and whether products are imported or locally produced.

2. Prior to authorizing third party use there should be an effort to negotiate a voluntary licence on reasonable commercial terms;
3. Government must provide for adequate remuneration, taking into account the economic value of the authorization; and
4. Use shall be authorized predominantly for the supply of the domestic market;
5. The scope and duration of the licence is limited to the purpose for which it was authorized, a requirement which is supplemented by the 'Intel clause', limiting the compulsory licensing of semiconductor technology to public non-commercial use and judicial remedies for anti-competitive behaviour;
6. Licences must be terminated if and when the circumstances, which led to it, cease to exist and are unlikely to recur.

Exemptions can be found in Art 31(b), which allows a waiver of the requirements for negotiation for a voluntary licence on reasonable commercial terms in case of

1. A national emergency or other circumstances of extreme urgency; or
2. In cases of public non-commercial use.

In short, the TRIPS rules on compulsory licensing seemingly already offer the necessary flexibility that proponents of the WIPO Development Agenda seek.

However, nations, most notably Brazil and South Africa, trying to use this flexibility for the purpose of supplying generic anti-retroviral AIDS drugs produced under (threat of) compulsory licences, found that their interpretation of this scope of the flexibility that TRIPS often differs from western notions for fair licensing.

The United States in particular were quick to point to the general nature of the compulsory licensing provisions in the patent statutes of these countries and in 2001 took action against Brazil before the WTO.[34] The USA complained:

> Brazil has asserted that the US case will threaten Brazil's widely-praised anti-AIDS program, and will prevent Brazil from addressing its national health crisis. Nothing could be further from the truth. For example, should Brazil choose to compulsory licence anti-retroviral AIDS drugs, it could do so under Section 71 of its patent law, which authorises compulsory licensing to address a national health emergency, consistent with TRIPS, and which the United States is not challenging. In contrast, Section 68—the provision under dispute—may require the compulsory licensing of any patented product, from bicycles to automobile components to golf clubs. Section 68 is unrelated to health or access to drugs, but instead is discriminating against all

[34] On 1 February 2001, a WTO panel was established to hear the case (WT/DS199/1). The US position was that the compulsory licensing provision for non-working is in violation of Art 27(1) TRIPS, which prohibits Members of the WTO from requiring the local production of the patented invention as a condition for enjoying exclusive patent rights. The United States asserted that the 'local working' requirement contained in the Brazilian Patent Act can only be satisfied by the local production—and not the importation—of the patented subject-matter. This position is fuelled by the impression that working of the patent needs to take place in the territory of Brazil. Furthermore, the US takes issue with the fact that failure to work the patent also comprises incomplete manufacture of the product or a failure to make full use of the patented process.

imported products in favour of locally produced products. In short, Section 68 is a protectionist measure intended to create jobs for Brazilian nationals.[35]

In the ensuing public relations battle Brazil put itself ahead of the game in that it capitalized on the AIDS drugs patent dispute in South Africa[36] and brought its successful national STD/AIDS programme to the attention of the world.[37] Brazil even managed to get a resolution adopted by the UN Commission of Human Rights on the right of access to medication.[38] The 53-member body passed the resolution by a 52-0 vote, with the United States abstaining.

At the WTO Doha Ministerial Conference of November 2001 in Quatar, consensus on the compulsory licensing issue was seen as imperative for the successful conclusion of a new round of world trade negotiations.[39] Ironically the Anthrax crisis in the USA and the reaction of the US government in face of this national emergency to obtain the drug CIPRO at the lowest price possible was a godsend for developing countries. They felt empowered to push within the WTO for a deal on compulsory licensing.

Due to the continuing media exposure of the lack of availability of antiretroviral AIDS drugs for the poor, of the fact that profit margins for Big Pharma are the highest of any industry,[40] and of the Anthrax crisis in the USA[41] a breakthrough was possible in the post 9/11 world. The result was a joint declaration on the TRIPS Agreement and Public Health.[42] The Ministerial Declaration amounts to an understanding that members will not bring action under the WTO Dispute Settlement Understanding over compulsory licensing of essential

[35] US Special 301 report, 2001, www.ustr.gov/enforcement/special.pdf on the dispute before the WTO with Brazil.

[36] See Seeman 'Patently Wrong', National Review, 21 March 2001, www.nationalreview.com/nr_comment/nr_commentprint032101a.html; Mutetwa, 'HIV/AIDS: is Zimbabe doing enough?', Financial Gazette 26 April 2001, www.fingaz.co.zw/fingaz/2001/April/April26/1429.shtml, Reuters, 'Cuba Backs Brazil in AIDS Drugs Patent Dispute', 3 April 2001, and 'Cuba Seeks Third World Challenge to Patent Rules', news.findlaw.com/legalnews/s/20010323/cubausapatents.html.

[37] See Commission on Intellectual Property Rights, Integrating Intellectual Property Rights and Development Policy (2002, London, CIPRs) at 43, available at www.iprcommission.org.

[38] See the resolution adopted by the UN Sub-Commission on the Promotion and Protection of Human Rights, Intellectual Property Rights and Human Rights, UN Doc. E/CN.4/Sub.2/Res/2000/7. See also UN Commission on Human Rights Resolution, Access to medication in the context of pandemics such as HIV/AIDS, UN Doc. E/CN.4/RES/2001/33, of 23 April 2001, which was proposed by Brazil. Available at www.unhchr.ch/.

[39] Moore, former director-general of the WTO, indicated in a statement that 'resolving the TRIPS and public health issue might be the 'deal-breaker' for a new trade round', see Banta, 'Public Health Triumphs at WTO Conference', 286 Journal of the American Medical Association, 2655 (2001), 2656, available at jama.ama-assn.org/issues/v286n21/fpdf/jmn1205.pdf.

[40] In terms of profit ranked by percentage return on revenues, pharmaceuticals rank first at over 18%. By means of comparison, commercial banks achieve rates of 14%, mining and crude oil production 9%, household and personal products 8%, and insurance and securities 7%. See 362 New Internationalist (2003), available at www.newint.org.

[41] See 'Double Standards', Nature, 1 November 2001, vol. 4141 at 1: 'The Bush administration . . . proceeded to extract agreement from Bayer to supply the drug at one-fifth of its previous price. The health secretary, Tommy Thompson, even boasted that the threat of compulsory licensing had helped to clinch the deal'.

[42] Adopted on 14 November 2001, WT/MIN(01)/DEC/2, 20 November 2001.

patented drugs.[43] It also reiterated that the least developed country Members[44] will not be obliged, in respect to pharmaceutical products, to implement the patent section[45] or to enforce rights provided for under these sections before 1 January 2016, thus alleviating any pressure on the compulsory licensing issue.[46] The Ministerial Declaration hinges on the interpretation of TRIPS Article 8(1) and its exception for the institution of measures necessary[47] to protect public health that are consistent with the TRIPS provisions.[48] In the face of adversity (the US and Big Pharma tried to limit the scope of the Declaration to drugs for the treatment of HIV/AIDS, tuberculosis and malaria) the WTO members took some two years to agree on measures that would lead to a satisfactory arrangement to give effect to the Declaration. The supply of essential drugs under compulsory licences to least-developed WTO members and WTO members with insufficient or no manufacturing capacity in the pharmaceutical sector was finally guaranteed in the WTO General Council Decision of 30 August 2003 on the Implementation of Paragraph 6 of the Declaration of the TRIPS Agreement and Public Health.[49] The Decision will see the WTO begin to routinely review the issuance of individual licences for pharmaceutical products and will look at the terms of individual licenses. It will evaluate the basis for deciding manufacturing capacity is insufficient, or review any of the new terms and obligations for the issue of compulsory licences of patents on medicinal products. The conditions for a compulsory licence will then also include measures to ensure tiered pricing and measures on parallel imports. This means that cheap medicine destined for developing nations is not imported back to developed nations to be sold at a premium price.

[43] Vandoren, 'Médicaments sans Frontières? Clarification of the Relationship between TRIPS and Public Health resulting from the WTO Doha Ministerial Declaration', 5 Journal of World Intellectual Property (2002); and Abbott, 'The TRIPS Agreement, Access to Medicines, and the WTO Doha Ministerial Conference', 5 Journal of World Intellectual Property (2002).

[44] For a list of least developed countries see www.unctad.org/Templates/webflyer.asp?docid=2929&intItemID=1634&lang=1.

[45] Section 5 TRIPS Agreement.

[46] On the issue of the role of the patent system as a motivator or hindrance to innovation in the pharmaceutical area see Muennich, 'Pharmaceutical Patents and Availability of Drugs', Revue Internationale de Droit Economique Special Edition: Pharmaceutical Patents, Innovations and Public Health 73 (2001) and Mossinghoff, 'The Importance of Intellectual Property Protection to the American Research-Intensive Pharmaceutical Industry', 31 Columbia Journal of World Business 38 (1996).

[47] See Canada, where stockpiling of drugs in the last six months of patent term was permitted. Rogers, 'The Revised Canadian Patent Act, the Free Trade Agreement, and Pharmaceutical Patents: An Overview of Pharmaceutical Compulsory Licensing in Canada', [1990] 10 EIPR 351. See WTO Dispute Settlement Body Panel Report in Canada—Patent Protection of Pharmaceutical Products WT/DS114/R of 25 April 2000. Canada had to comply with the DBS's rulings and recommendations by 12 August 2001, abolishing the stockpiling practice.

[48] See Art 27(1) TRIPS, which states that any measures adopted cannot discriminate as to the place of invention, the field of technology and whether products are imported or locally produced; and also Art XX of GATT 1994, indicating that any measures under TRIPS necessary to protect health also cannot amount to 'arbitrary or unjustifiable discrimination between countries where the same conditions prevail, or a disguised restriction on international trade'.

[49] WT/L/540 of 2 September 2003.

We are currently witnessing the first proposals on the implementation of the WTO Decision in the EU and Canada.[50] These proposals provide for a two-pronged approach to the issue of compulsory licensing. First, that essential medicine may be produced under compulsory licence in the EU and Canada for the purpose of export to WTO members with insufficient production capacity. Second, that these drugs are so distinctive that customs can easily detect illegal parallel re-importation. The EU and Canada seem intent on protecting their own pharmaceutical industry base by allowing production of generics in the EU and Canada under strict conditions by making use of the WTO system. European and Canadian production and control over distribution of drugs will after all prevent technology transfer to developing countries.

VI. DATA EXCLUSIVITY

The USA appears to regard the multilateral trade system with flexible standards on compulsory licensing of pharmaceuticals as being contrary to US interests. It bypasses the WTO system that it was previously a major advocate of by entering in bilateral trade agreements. Since the establishment of the WTO in 1995, the United States have entered into more than 40 BITs and FTAs,[51] most which contain a particular US-style interpretation on appropriate standards for exclusivity of data[52] necessary to obtain marketing approval test results for new drugs.[53]

In order to obtain marketing authorisation for a pharmaceutical product, regulatory standards attesting that the product is clinically proven to be safe and effective have to be met. Drugs are therefore subject to controlled trials that generate the data necessary to satisfy national or regional regulators. Medical trials are expensive and require substantial technical skill and expertise. According to the TRIPS Agreement, the investment and skill necessary to conduct medical trials has to be safeguarded and WTO members have to provide for the protection

[50] Proposal for a Regulation of the European Parliament and of the Council on compulsory licensing of patents relating to the manufacture of pharmaceutical products for export to countries with public health problems COM (2004) 737; Similarly see Canadian Bill C-9, An Act to amend the Patent Act and the Food and Drugs Act (The Jean Chrétien Pledge to Africa), 3d sess, 37th Parl, 2004 and the 'Regulations Amending the Food and Drugs Regulations, (1402—Drugs for Developing Countries', Canada Gazette Vol 138, No 40—October 2, 2004, pp 2748–60.

[51] Signed US FTAs comprise Jordan, Chile, Singapore, Guatemala, El Salvador, Nicaragua, Honduras, Costa Rica, Australia, Morocco, the Dominican Republic and Bahrain. A further FTA with the Central American states as a group (CAFTA) is in the process of being ratified by the US Congress.

[52] Art 39(3) TRIPS provides: 'Members, when requiring, as a condition of approving the marketing of pharmaceutical or of agricultural chemical products which utilise new chemical entities, the submission of undisclosed test or other data, the origination of which involves a considerable effort, shall protect such data against unfair commercial use. In addition, Members shall protect such data against disclosure, except where necessary to protect the public, or unless steps are taken to ensure that the data are protected against unfair commercial use."

[53] On data exclusivity see Brazell, 'A World United? The US Approach to the Protection of Regulatory Data', (2004/2005) 168 Patent World, 23–5.

of this data submitted to regulators. Producers of generic drugs also have to apply for marketing approval. The usual method of obtaining rapid marketing approval is by showing that the generic drug is bio-equivalent to the drug that has already been approved and that the generic producer is capable of producing the drug at consistent quality standards. The test for consistency in production requires the generic producer to breach any patent that may still be valid. Whether there is an exception for manufacturers of generic drugs to engage in clinical trials prior to patent expiry is not harmonised by the TRIPS Agreement and standards and procedures vary from jurisdiction to jurisdiction. The lack of harmonisation in the area of patent licensing for the purpose of clinical testing is compounded by the existence of data exclusivity, as this may force subsequent applicants for marketing approval to generate their own clinical data independently and at their own expense. Data exclusivity therefore not only raises the cost of the generic product, but serves as a protection mechanism in addition to patent protection, since there is limited value in holding a compulsory licence if the holder nevertheless has to spend time and money generating its own clinical trial data in order to obtain marketing approval.[54]

In most cases, a bilateral agreement with the United States obliges the other signatory to provide a period of data exclusivity of between five and ten years. A common element is that if medical trial information submitted in the first country of marketing approval is relied on to obtain marketing approval in another country, the term of data protection of the first country is recognized in the other. Furthermore, patent holders are usually to be notified if producers of generic drugs attempt to obtain marketing approval prior to patent expiry, enabling patent holders to take immediate infringement action should medical trials be conducted or production and stockpiling of generics be undertaken prior to patent expiry. This turns the regulatory authorities that deal with marketing approval for drugs into watchdogs for the pharmaceutical industry. Some FTAs even require signatories to provide for data exclusivity for all pharmaceutical products, even if these do not incorporate new chemical entities.[55]

What is worrying is that the EU also seems to have picked up on the possibility of using the provisions on data exclusivity as a means of mitigating the effects of compulsory licensing of pharmaceuticals. The EU is actively pursuing the issue of data exclusivity within the framework of the Cotonou Agreement with African, Caribbean and Pacific (ACP) countries.[56]

The fact that the issue of data exclusivity has not been included in the Doha Declaration now appears to be an oversight that is exploited to foreclose on the flexibility agreed to in the Doha Declaration. The scope for compulsory

[54] On clinical trials see A. Kamperman Sanders, 'Patents—Antitrust, Compulsory Licensing and Research Exceptions' in Heath/Kamperman Sanders (eds), Industrial Property in the Bio-Medical Age, Max Planck Series on Asian Intellectual Property Law vol. 8, Kluwer Law International The Hague/London/New York 2003.

[55] US–Singapore FTA, Article 16(8) and draft FTAA Section B(2)(j), Art 1.

[56] See the Third World Network Africa website at twnafrica.org/news_detail.asp?twnID=788

licensing remains severely limited if data exclusivity rules preclude a rapid response to a national emergency. No doubt Big Pharma[57] is following these developments with glee. With a global system of protection of data exclusivity in place they no longer need to rely on patents. Government regulators will ensure that suppliers of medical trial data retain a de facto market monopoly over the drug they have marketed. Government regulators will furthermore give Big Pharma early warning of any attempt at producing or marketing generic drugs close to patent expiry, so that patent infringement action can still be brought in time. The cost for all this extra work for regulators will be borne not by Big Pharma, but by nations under the obligation to provide data exclusivity.

VII. INCENTIVES FOR INNOVATION

In the domain of copyright similar developments take place. IPR create a market for inventions, artistic works, or distinctive signs. This market enables the rightholder to exercise control over the first sale of an industrial or intellectual creation, or a product that embodies or carries this creation, so that he is able to reap the rewards of his innovation, creation, or marketing effort. IPR also offer the possibility to control the use of the protected intellectual asset after the first sale. This form of licensing power over downstream markets may be detrimental to welfare,[58] because it may limit the development of downstream innovation.

A striking example of this problem is reflected in the discussion on the legality of filesharing technology, such as Kazaa, Morpheus, Grokster and other non-centralised peer-to-peer networks.[59] The US Supreme Court recently decided on the question of the legality of filesharing technology in the case of *MGM v Grokster*.[60] The discussion is similar to that on the legality of video recorders in the previous century,[61] namely whether producers of copyright content should be able to control the market of the technology used to reproduce and distribute this content even if this technology is innovative and also has non-infringing purposes. The example from the past concerned the use of the video recorder to

[57] The Big Pharma top 10 list comprises Pfizer, GlaxoSmithKline, Merck, AstraZeneca, Johnson & Johnson, Novartis, Bristol-Myers Squib, Pharmacia, and Weyth.

[58] Boldrin/Levine, 'The Case Against Intellectual Property', American Economic Review, May 2002 (Papers and Proceedings), 92(2), pp 209–12.

[59] *Metro-Goldwyn-Mayer Studios Inc. et al. v Grokster, Ltd, et al* 545 US (2005). In *MGM v Grokster*, 380 F 3d 1154 (9th Cir 2004), the Ninth Circuit found that P2P file-sharing software is capable of, and is in fact being used for, noninfringing uses. Relying on the Betamax precedent of *Sony Corp of America v Universal City Studios*, 464 US 417 (1984), the court ruled that the distributors of Grokster and Morpheus software cannot be held liable for users' copyright violations. See also *Grokster I*, 259 F Supp 2d at 1031–3.

[60] See in this respect also the opposing briefs by numerous law and economic professors in the Supreme Court case of *MGM v Grokster*, *ibid* on behalf of either the respondent (Grokster) or the petitioners. All available at www.eff.org/IP/P2P/MGM_v_Grokster/.

[61] *Sony Corp of America v Universal City Studios*, 464 US 417 (1984).

view recorded TV programmes at a time that better suits our busy lifestyles.[62] Now it is the use of software to find and disseminate information of any description using the least bandwidth and distributed computing power. The Supreme Court decided the issue on contributory or vicarious copyright infringement and held that:

> . . . [O]ne who distributes a device with the object of promoting its use to infringe copyright, as shown by clear expression or other affirmative steps taken to foster infringement, is liable for the resulting acts of infringement by third parties. . . . We are, of course, mindful of the need to keep from trenching on regular commerce or discouraging the development of technologies with lawful and unlawful potential. Accordingly, just as Sony did not find intentional inducement despite the knowledge of the VCR manufacturer that its device could be used to infringe, . . . mere knowledge of infringing potential or of actual infringing uses would not be enough here to subject a distributor to liability. Nor would ordinary acts incident to product distribution, such as offering customers technical support or product updates, support liability in themselves. The inducement rule, instead, premises liability on purposeful, culpable expression and conduct, and thus does nothing to compromise legitimate commerce or discourage innovation having a lawful purpose.

Increasingly, however, technical protection mechanisms affect what an end-user can or cannot do in respect of information that has been purchased legally, thus limiting previously established user rights, such as making copies for private or educational use. In effect these recognised exceptions and limitations to copyright are curtailed.[63] Current broadband access that indeed enables users to conveniently bypass the media industries' old fashioned distribution methods for music and films is predominantly available to 117,6 million households in industrialised nations. Although large-scale copyright infringement through file sharing networks is therefore a problem in the industrialised world, the global copyright system has already been tailored to meet the worries of media industries by means of the WIPO Copyright and Performances and Phonogrammes treaties. These treaties have introduced the right to control communication to the public of copyright works and provide rightholders with the possibility to act against the removal or alteration of digital rights management information, and technical protection mechanisms.

[62] Upon the introduction of Microsoft's Media Center software, Bill Gates suggested that the technical possibility offered by digital video recorders to automatically remove advertising from recorded content is infringing rights of broadcasters and advertisers. See his interview for the Hollywood Reporter on the way Microsoft will ensure that we will continue to receive advertising at www.hollywoodreporter.com/thr/new_media/article_display.jsp?vnu_content_id=1000671642

[63] See Gordon, 'Fair Use as Market Failure: A Structural and Economic Analysis of the Betamax Case and Its Predecessors', 82 Columbia Law Review, 1600–57 (1982), showing that the US Supreme Court decision in the Betamax case that the sale of Betamax video recorders did not constitute contributory copyright infringement made perfect economic sense because the video recorder has substantial non-infringing uses (like time-shifting) that do not adversely affect the market value of the original copyrighted work. Licensing control of the film studio's over the market for video recorders would stifle technical innovation.

Although not part of the WTO TRIPS Agreement, these WIPO treaties are fast becoming the de facto world standard, not because countries voluntarily sign up to these agreements, but through inclusion in BITs and FTAs. The United States is exporting its version of the WIPO treaties, the Digital Millennium Copyright Act (DMCA), not because it fulfils the needs of citizens and industry in developing nations, but because of economic and political pressure it can exert through BITs and FTAs.[64]

Criticism against the unilateral focus on strengthening of rights is rife.[65] The problem stems from the fact that international copyright harmonisation has focussed on the protection of copyright, not on establishing common standards on limitations and exceptions. National law predominantly determines the scope and number of these limitations and exceptions. Limitations and exceptions can be found in statute, as is the case in Europe, or in jurisprudence by means of an intricate case-by-case fair use analysis, as is the case in the USA.

The inclusion of IPR in BITs and FTAs means that countries that lack access to even the most elementary educational materials are confronted with the demand that their copyright statutes are tailored to meet the highest western norm. Exceptions and limitations enabling fair use of copyright works are, however, not part of that international standard setting to the same extent as heightening protection levels are. There is little guidance on the appropriate limitations and exceptions, let alone special concessions for developing countries, other than the WTO-endorsed mantra that the economic interests of rightholders should not be harmed.[66] The fact that the media industry has long been inapt and unwilling[67] to replace outdated CD and DVD disc technology by adequate internet distribution methods only reinforces the feeling that stronger IPR merely serve to preserve the stranglehold of western big media industry over new global distribution methods. It is not surprising therefore that developing countries feel they have been forced to adopt a copyright system that enables western media conglomerates to maintain a position of global dominance.

Apart from the fact that the United States of America appears to be intent on establishing a new status quo outside of multilateral WTO framework, the problem with this practice is that the DMCA itself is controversial. Many user interest groups in the USA itself, like the Electronic Frontier Foundation argue that the unilateral focus on strengthening IPR leads to the loss of the traditional balance between rightholders and users underpinning the intellectual property

[64] See Correa, n 7 above; Drahos, Expanding Intellectual Property's Empire: the Role of FTAs (2003, GRAIN), both available at www.grain.org.

[65] Boyle, 'A Manifesto on WIPO and the Future of Intellectual Property', 9 Duke Law and Technology Review (2004) 1.

[66] See the WTO Dispute Settlement Body Panel Report on United States—Section 110(5) of the US Copyright Act WT/DS160/R of 15 June 2000, providing interpretation on the Berne Three step test dealing with appropriate exemptions to copyright.

[67] See Alderman, Sonic Boom—Napster, MP3, and the New Pioneers of Music (2001, Perseus, Cambridge MA); Lessing, Free Culture: How Big Media Uses Technology and the Law to Lock Down Culture and Control Creativity (2004, New York, Penguin).

system. They advocate the curbing of IPR by means of enacting stronger user rights in relation to copyright, allowing for compulsory licensing for essential facilities in the media or medical domains, or simply excluding subject matter from patentability. Others simply defend the interest of righholders and claim that IPR are full property rights conferring an absolute monopoly that should not be subject to limitations harming the righholder's interests. The widely diverging beliefs held by either side in this debate can be seen in the briefs submitted to the court in support of the media industry or producers of filesharing technology in the recent US Supreme Court case in *MGM v Grokster*.[68] It is clear from these statements of support that even law professors, economics professors and authors of intellectual property treatises cannot agree on appropriate user rights.

VIII. THE DEVELOPMENT AGENDA AND IPR POLICY

The mandate of the Development Agenda[69] is to come up with a humane policy that takes into account the needs of developing nations. The recognition of access to medicine as a human right was seen as a first step in formulating this humane policy. Yet, the adoption by the UN Commission of Human Rights of a declaration on the right of access to medicine remains merely symbolic if the IPR system remains unclear on the appropriate balance of rights and interests. Rather than looking to other or higher legal principles like human rights[70] to

[68] See in this respect also the opposing briefs by numerous law and economic professors in *MGM v Grokster*, n 59 above, on behalf of either the respondent (Grokster) or the petitioners. All available at www.eff.org/IP/P2P/MGM_v_Grokster/. See also the opinion of Justice Breyer:

> Here the record reveals a significant future market for noninfringing uses of Grokster-type peer-to-peer software. Such software permits the exchange of any sort of digital file-whether that file does, or does not, contain copyrighted material. As more and more uncopyrighted information is stored in swappable form, it seems a likely inference that lawful peer-to-peer sharing will become increasingly prevalent . . ..
>
> And that is just what is happening. Such legitimate noninfringing uses are coming to include the swapping of: research information (the initial purpose of many peer-to-peer networks); public domain films (eg, those owned by the Prelinger Archive); historical recordings and digital educational materials (eg, those stored on the Internet Archive); digital photos (OurPictures, for example, is starting a P2P photo-swapping service); 'shareware' and 'freeware' (eg, Linux and certain Windows software); secure licensed music and movie files (Intent MediaWorks, for example, protects licensed content sent across P2P networks); news broadcasts past and present (the BBC Creative Archive lets users ìrip, mix and share the BBCî); user-created audio and video files (including 'podcasts' that may be distributed through P2P software); and all manner of free 'open content' works collected by Creative Commons (one can search for Creative Commons material on StreamCast). . . . Of course, Grokster itself may not want to develop these other noninfringing uses. But Sony's standard seeks to protect not the Groksters of this world (which in any event may well be liable under today's holding), but the development of technology more generally. And Grokster's desires in this respect are beside the point.

[69] Koury Menescal, 'Changing WIPO's Ways? The 2004 Development Agenda in Historical Perspective', (2005) 8 *J Of World Intellectual Property,* 761.

[70] Anderson/Wager, 'Human Rights, Development, and the WTO: The Case of Intellectual Property and Competition Policy', (2006) 9(3) Journal of International Economic Law 707–47;

forge humane IPR policy, the IPR system needs to internalise the recognition of the interests of all stakeholders. The recognition of interests of both developed and developing nations is therefore part of a wider concern on the fundamentals of the IPR system. Individual rightholders, consumers, citizens and society at large all share a common interest in innovation and development of and access to industrial and intellectual creativity. WIPO, as the UN's bureau on the development of IPR, should take a leading role in tailoring the IPR system to accommodate the needs of all stakeholders.

On 4 October 2004 the WIPO General Assembly agreed to adopt a decision to further examine the Development Agenda proposal originally presented by Brazil and Argentina and subsequently sponsored by many developing countries to integrate in a more systematic manner the development dimension in all of WIPO's work. Prior to the General Assembly meeting, hundreds of non-profit organizations, scientists, academics and other individuals had signed the 'Geneva Declaration on the Future of WIPO'[71] in support of the Development Agenda's aims to engrain in WIPO's policies the practice of using IPR as tools for the development of nations as opposed to the mere safeguard of the interests of individual rightholders. Despite the apparent support in the WIPO General Assembly for the Development Agenda no new bodies to discuss matters raised in the proposal were created, because after all: 'WIPO had always been sensitive to the concerns of developing countries'. The Development Agenda has not yet died a quiet death, but our patient is seriously ill.

An inter-sessional intergovernmental meeting in the Development Agenda for WIPO was held on 11–13 April 2005. Brazil, now heading the 'Group of Friends of Development', comprising Argentina, Bolivia, Brazil, Cuba, Dominican Republic, Ecuador, Egypt, Iran, Kenya, Peru, Sierra Leone, South Africa, Tanzania and Venezuela raised the stakes in a more elaborate proposal on the Development Agenda for WIPO.[72] This document reads as an indictment of all that is wrong within WIPO. The issue that stands out is WIPO's effort to standardize IPR to the highest norm at the expense of least developed and developing nations. The document reiterates that WIPO should be driven by a policy recognising that:

> Intellectual property should be regarded not as an end in itself, but as a means for promoting the public interest, innovation, and access to science, technology and the promotion of diverse national creative industries—in order to ensure material progress and welfare in the long run. Promotion of intellectual property protection alone is not sufficient if unaccompanied by policies that respond to the specific development needs of each country.[73]

Geiger, 'Fundamental Rights, a Safeguead for the Coherence of Intellectual Propery Law?' 35 (2004) IIC 268; Ostergard, 'Intellectual Property: A Universal Human Right?', 21 Human Rights Quarterly 1 (1999) 156.

[71] See www.cptech.org/ip/wipo/futureofwipo.html

[72] Proposal to Establish a Development Agenda for WIPO: An Elaboration of Issues Raised in Document WO/GA/31/11, WIPO document IIM/1/4/ of 6 April 2005, available at www.wipo.int.

[73] *Ibid*, p 4.

A proposal submitted for discussion by the United Kingdom[74] recognises the needs of least developed and developing countries and points to the burdens associated with TRIPS implementation on these countries. It indicates that there ought to be flexibility to the point of a clear opt out for least developed and developing countries to implement and reform of their IPR system at a pace in line with their rate of development. However, the UK submits that the WTO and not WIPO is the appropriate forum to address these complex issues of technology transfer.

Even more remarkable, given the fundamental criticism and sweeping proposals for change within WIPO that the Group of Friends of Development's paper contain, is the proposal[75] from the United States of America for the same meeting. It contains little more than a proposal for the 'WIPO Partnership Program'. This is an internet clearing house for development hosted by WIPO, which should bring together donors and recipients of IPR development assistance. The rationale for the WIPO Partnership Program is to provide more co-ordinated technical assistance in the area of IPR development. Could it be that the United States is talking about assistance to further the development of IPR, as opposed to IPR and development? I fear this is indeed the case.

Those who have signed the Geneva Declaration on the Future of WIPO, and I have seen that many colleagues have done so, have to rise to the challenge of making sure that the need for a Development Agenda for WIPO is not forgotten. The role of academics in the field is to teach students and to make policy makers aware of the possibilities to redress the balance of the IPR system. Possibilities are manifold and there is a lot of work still to be done.

IX. IN CONCLUSION

Four points stand out.

First, governments should be made aware of methods to provide equal access to publicly funded research by stipulating that participating academic and industry partners commit themselves to an 'open source' licensing regime. Such a regime should allow partners and third parties to make use of and innovate on the basis of the results stemming from this research on condition that these original results remain free from other IPR.[76] In combination with an active policy on technology transfer, open source licensing may be a valuable instrument in

[74] WIPO document IIM/1/5 of 7 April 2005, available at www.wipo.int.

[75] WIPO document IIM/1/2 of 18 March 2005, available at www.wipo.int.

[76] See the European Commission expert group reports on: IPR Aspects of Internet Collaborations (2001, EUR 19456); Managing IPR in a Knowledge-based Economy—Bioinformatics and the Influence of Public Policy (2001, EUR 20066); Role and Strategic Use of IPR in International Research Collaborations (2002, EUR 20230); Strategic Use and Adaptation of Intellectual Property Rights Systems in Information and Communications Technologies-based Research (2003, EUR 20734).

providing aid, especially when used to stimulate FDI in start-ups and joint ventures in developing countries.

Second, policy makers have to be made aware of the fact that strengthening and introducing new IPR like data exclusivity can have surprising and undesired effects. Unless the current IPR incentive structure is changed, access to medicine will continue to be subject to trade disputes over patent protection, compulsory licensing, tiered pricing, parallel importation and data exclusivity. The current WTO General Council Decision on the TRIPS Agreement and Public Health aims to provide tiered pricing of pharmaceuticals. This is a first effort to discriminate between the sale of highly priced commercial pharmaceuticals for the consumer in developed nations and the distribution of essential medicine for HIV/AIDS, malaria, tuberculosis and other tropical diseases to the needy in least developed and developing countries.

It is problematic that R&D spending for pharmaceuticals to combat many tropical diseases is not a priority, because the expected return on investment is low.

Until Big Pharma is offered real incentives to invest in R&D of drugs for the poor[77] and is offered a way to recoup the investment in patented medicine already on the market, it will continue to use all means to protect its market.[78]

We also need to accept that under spending in R&D for diseases affecting least developed and developing nations is comparable to the problems related to R&D into serious diseases that affect relatively few people. To provide incentives for research in medicine for the cure of rare diseases, so-called Orphan Drugs Acts were enacted in the US,[79] Europe,[80] and a number of other countries. It is questionable though whether the solution provided by these acts will provide a stimulus for R&D in tropical diseases where those suffering have severely limited means to purchase the drugs.

In addition to patent protection, Orphan Drugs Acts offer incentives to develop orphan drugs by providing tax benefits, government grants, and a

[77] Cohen, 'An Epidemic of Neglect: Neglected Diseases and the Health Burden in Poor Countries', 23 Multinational Monitor, No 6 (2002), available at multinationalmonitor.org.

[78] Weissmann, 'Victory and Betrayal The Evergreen Patent System Pharmaceutical Company Tactics to Extend Patent Protections', 23 Multinational Monitor, No 6 (2002), available at multinationalmonitor.org

[79] US Orphan Drug Act (January 4, 1983), Public Law 97-414; 21 USC 360ee.

This special designation of 'orphan drug' is granted if the disease in the population affects less than 200 000 people (approximately 0.1%) or if no profits cannot reasonable be expected. Benefits include:

— assistance to design research protocols;
— tax credits of 50% for clinical research for clinical trials undertaken in the US;
— seven years of marketing exclusivity following the marketing authorization;
— funding grants of up to US$ 200.000 for clinical research to support development;
— penalty for intentionally false statement of orphan status;
— process patents granted for biotechnology products;
— accelerated approvals.

[80] Regulation (EC) No 141/2000 of the European Parliament and of the Council of 16 December 1999 on orphan medicinal products, (2000) OJ L18/1.

period of 7 to 11 years of market exclusivity. This IPR is available irrespective of the research input actually required to develop and market Orphan Drugs. There is justified criticism that this lack of competition increases orphan drug prices unnecessarily.[81]

An incentive system for R&D in essential medicines for least developed and developing countries should result in low prices and maximum access to the drugs. It is possible to counterbalance a compulsory licence by means of a geographically limited patent term extension certificate for the licensor, provided that it addresses the issue of reasonable royalty payment only. Producers of compulsory licensed generic drugs are then able to reduce the price of drugs in least developed and developing countries further by spreading the payment of royalty fees over a longer period of time, even after the normal date of patent expiry. In return for a term extension the patent holder should be required to plough the proceeds of such a scheme back into R&D targeting diseases that affect least developed and developing nations most. These specific R&D programmes would them be much more identifiable for additional public funding by governments, or by aid organisations and charitable institutions. This would make them stakeholders in the development, production and marketing of essential medicine. Such public-private partnerships should be subject to the active policy on technology transfer and open source licensing mentioned above. IPR licensing can therefore be used to make sure that any new patentable invention that is the result of this research is part of a common patent pool to which all stakeholders have guaranteed access. On the basis of this jointly held IPR it is also possible to licence on the basis of tiered pricing regimes, or not to apply for patent rights in developing or least developed nations at all.

Third, patent offices, as keepers of public records, have to fulfil their obligation to society at large in making available up-to-date and current information to the World Health Organisation and recognised aid organisations (like Médécins Sans Frontières) on which medicines are patented, where, and for how long. This means that investment and technology transfer decisions can be made on locating production capacity for generic essential medicine in countries where patent rights are not in force. This brings both drugs and knowledge to the people in need and decreases the need for long and complex distribution channels.

Fourth, local communities in third world countries should be made aware of ways to using the IPR system to their advantage. A perfect example is the recent agreement[82] between six indigenous communities, represented by the Association for Nature and Sustainable Development (ANDES) and the International Potato Centre (CIP) in Peru. The agreement deals with the repatriation, restoration and monitoring of agro-biodiversity of native potatoes and associated community knowledge in growing and developing unique potato

[81] See the UK House of Commons Health Committee, The Influence of the Pharmaceutical Industry, Fourth Report of Session 2004–5, Volume I, HC 42-I of 05-04-2005, at 32.

[82] See www.grain.org for details on the agreement.

strains. The International Institute for Environment and Development in London and the Dutch Government supported this initiative. Its objective is to ensure that the genetic resources and knowledge remain under the custody of the communities and do not become subject to IPR held by others.[83] In effect this means the storing and making available of potato genome information through databases in an effort to destroy the novelty required for patenting genome sequences. The agreement contains provisions on the joint conservation and management of the genetic resources of native potato, equitable benefit sharing of the benefits gained from the use of genetic plant resources for food and agriculture and obligations to develop, record and protect indigenous knowledge related to these genetic resources. The agreement recognises that indigenous people hold a different view of property than westerners do, yet it relies on contract and the IPR system to provide a number of communities with the common ownership and stewardship of genetic resources and indigenous knowledge.

These are merely four exercises in flexibility that show that even the current IPR system can be used as a policy instrument for development. Common or joint ownership of IPR—or dare one say a little bit of modern-day communism-can go a long way in providing incentives for preservation, development and technology transfer.

X. POST SCRIPT

The Third Session of the WIPO Provisional Committee on Proposals Related to a WIPO Development Agenda[84] (19–23 February 2007) produced some common ground on WIPO's approach to intellectual property and development, leading to a number of recommendations in relation to Technical Assistance and Capacity Building, Norm-setting, flexibilities, public policy and public domain, Technology Transfer, Information and Communication Technologies (ICT) and Access to Knowledge, Assessment, Evaluation and Impact Studies, Institutional Matters including Mandate and Governance, and other issues.[85]

Central to the recommendation is the emphasis on development-oriented, demand-driven and transparent technical assistance, especially for developing countries, and for WIPO to intensify its cooperation on IP related issues with UN agencies (UNCTAD, UNEP, WHO, UNIDO, UNESCO) and other relevant international organizations, especially WTO. It is interesting to note that in this context WIPO should:

[83] On IPR and investment strategies for agricultural societies see Lele/Lesser/Horstkotte-Wesseler (eds), Intellectual Property Rights in Agriculture (2000, Washington, World Bank).

[84] Established at the 31st Session of the WIPO General Assembly (27 September to 5 October 2004).

[85] See http://www.wipo.int/edocs/prdocs/en/2007/wipo_pr_2007_478.html#pcda for the list of recommendations.

> [a]pproach intellectual property enforcement in the context of broader societal interests and especially development-oriented concerns, with a view that 'the protection and enforcement of intellectual property rights should contribute to the promotion of technological innovation and to the transfer and dissemination of technology, to the mutual advantage of producers and users of technological knowledge and in a manner conducive to social and economic welfare, and to a balance of rights and obligations', in accordance with Article 7 of the TRIPS Agreement.[86]

With Article 7 of TRIPS as guiding principle, the ball appears to be firmly in the court of the WTO again. FTAs are fast overtaking the multilateral WTO system, leading developing countries, according to Oxfam, to sign away their future:

> The USA, EU, and Japan are using trade and investment agreements to extend the influence of their leading companies, and reduce the ability of developing countries to gain a beneficial foothold in the global economy. [. . .] The USA is the most aggressive proponent of stricter intellectual- property rules, requiring developing countries to sign agreements that go far beyond the WTO Trade Related Intellectual Property Rights Agreement (TRIPS). The EU is following closely on its heels [. . .].[87]

It will be a real challenge for WTO Members to reclaim the initiative in finding multilateral solutions in the face of the onslaught of bilateral TRIPS-plus realities.

[86] *Ibid.* Annex, Cluster F: Other Issues, para. 24.

[87] Oxfam, Signing Away The Future—How trade and investment agreements between rich and poor countries undermine development, Oxfam Briefing Paper 101 of 20 March 2007, at p 6 and p 11 available at http://www.oxfam.org.uk/what_we_do/issues/trade/downloads/bp101_ftas.pdf

Chapter 2

TRIPS-Plus Rules under Free Trade Agreements: An Asian Perspective

JAKKRIT KUANPOTH

I. INTRODUCTION

TO DATE, THE United States has signed Free Trade Agreements (FTAs) with many countries including Chile, Jordan, Morocco, Panama, Bahrain, countries in Central America, the Andes, Southern Africa, and Asia (Singapore, Jordan, Vietnam, and Laos). Bilateral trade negotiations with Thailand are ongoing.

Negotiations for a bilateral agreement between the US and Thailand started in October 2003 when George W. Bush visited Bangkok for the summit of the Asia-Pacific Economic Cooperation (APEC) forum. While negotiations with Thailand are underway, the US is also looking at three other ASEAN countries (Indonesia, the Philippines, and Malaysia) as its next targets for bilateral FTAs. The US-Thailand deal will drive talks for similar agreements with other Southeast Asian nations.

This paper highlights important IP issues under the FTAs that the US has entered into or proposes to sign with other countries. It also assesses the impact of TRIPS-plus rules in various FTAs by focusing on the experiences of Asian countries. It explores major TRIPS-plus issues and considers the broad implications of such rules under various headings, including effects of TRIPS-plus rules on access to medicines, agriculture, and access to knowledge.

II. GENERAL BACKGROUND OF FTAS

The years from 2000 onwards saw the proliferation of free trade agreements (FTA). These arose after some WTO Member countries became weary of the slow progress in multilateral trade negotiations. Since trade liberalisation was getting more difficult under the WTO framework, some governments of developed countries, particularly the US, have used bilateral and regional trade fora to achieve what they could not achieve in the multilateral WTO forum, namely enforcing an inflexible, high level IP protection in developing countries. The US and some other developed countries have apparently changed their negotiation strategies by shifting the forum of negotiation from multilateral to bilateral and regional. Those countries are aware that it is difficult to swiftly implement their entire trade agenda on a multilateral level. Under FTAs, developed countries' trade negotiators can easily manage to set benchmarks with respect to all their trade objectives that will be difficult to achieve in WTO negotiations.

Under such bilateral free trade agreements, the US offers certain developing countries concessions in core trade areas like agriculture, textile and other market access preferences provided that those countries are committed to economic reforms and liberalisation of their markets. These FTAs are wide in scope and cover trade, services, investment, government procurement, environmental and labour rules, and IP protection. FTAs to which the US is a party also include an IP Chapter containing TRIPS-plus standards beyond what is already included in the WTO/TRIPS Agreement.

A successful conclusion of an FTA with one country (eg Singapore, or Australia) will serve as a model for other FTAs (eg with Thailand and others), and eventually for multilateral trade negotiations. The aim of the US to establish an acceptable international standard for IP protection is reflected in the provisions of the FTA between the US and Australia that contains for example a TRIPS-plus rule on data exclusivity although such protection is already available in Australian legislation. The inclusion of the exclusivity provision is necessary from the US trade negotiator's point of view as it can serve as a model for use by the US in negotiations with other countries. The international obligations will also prohibit Australia from changing its legislation if it so desires.

Although the proposed FTAs are in principle open to negotiation, the agreements concluded between the US and its trading partners are basically built on the basic rules embodied in US legislation. In fact, the real intention of the US Trade Representative (USTR) is to bring the law of the trading partner closer to US law. All FTAs signed by the US are quite similar to one another. It seems that the USTR is committed to the basic structure of the model treaty and will only accept minor changes.

The US unhidden agenda is reflected in the statement of objectives in the USTR's Letter of Notifications for FTA negotiations with Thailand:

> The United States concerns about intellectual property protection in Thailand. The United States has worked with Thailand on intellectual property rights issues under the Trade and Investment Framework Agreement (TIFA). While some progress has been made, bringing Thailand's intellectual property regime up to the standards set in other recent FTAs that the United States has negotiated will be a high priority of these negotiations.[1]

[1] Letter of Notification of USTR to US Congress of Intent to Initiate Free Trade Agreement Negotiations with Thailand, 12 February 2004.

The US also has clear objectives in negotiation on IP rights, as is reflected in the USTR formal notification letters to Congress:

— Seek to establish standards to be applied in Thailand that build on the foundations established in the WTO Agreement on Trade-Related Aspects of Intellectual Property Rights and other international intellectual property agreements, such as the World Intellectual Property Organization (WIPO) Copyright Treaty, the WIPO Performances and Phonograms Treaty, and the Patent Cooperation Treaty.
— In areas such as patent protection and protection of undisclosed information, seek to have Thailand apply levels of protection and practices more in line with US law and practices, including appropriate flexibility.
— Seek to strengthen Thailand's laws and procedures to enforce intellectual property rights, such as by ensuring that Thai authorities seize suspected pirated and counterfeit goods, equipment used to make such goods or to transmit pirated goods, and documentary evidence.
— Seek to strengthen measures in Thailand that provide for compensation of right holders for infringements of intellectual property rights and to provide for criminal penalties under Thai law that are sufficient to have a deterrent effect on piracy and counterfeiting.

The costs and benefits of FTAs to developing countries are an issue of controversy. The countries that enter into FTA negotiations with the US expect that the bilateral deal will increase the volume of international trade and investment. It is, however, argued that the economic activities on a bilateral and regional level do not suit the need of developing countries. Rather, such trade deals will bring about the opposite result: The economic and social costs for those countries are enormous despite short-term benefits. The prospective costs of the bilateral trade treaties include various problems relating to monopolisation, public health, education, food security, environment, labour rights, technology transfer, biodiversity management, etc.[2]

FTA negotiations with the US are generally carried out in a non-transparent manner. Negotiations of FTAs reflect a failure of sound and transparent policy making of the countries that enter into such trade talks. In Thailand, for example, the government has not conducted consultations across the community in relation to the proposed FTA. There is also a lack of official information about what the legal effect of the FTA will be because negotiations are not public. So far, the trade liberalisation policy of the Thai government has been criticised for deepening inequalities between different interest groups within the country. Most key decisions are worked out by a group of bureaucrats and business people. The vast majority of the population has very little real say in trade negotiations. The Thai government has never allowed the poor to participate in the many formal and informal meetings to which business people and trade councils are invited. As a result, the issues put up for negotiation, and the

[2] Oxfam Canada 'Let's Harness Trade for Development: Why Oxfam Opposes the FTAA', 2001. http://www.oxfam.ca/news/Peoples_Summit/intellectualProperty

decisions made by the government, tend to be biased against grass-roots interests.[3]

III. TRIPS-PLUS RULES AND THEIR IMPACT ON ACCESS TO MEDICINES

Since the late 1980s, the world's producers and exporters of medicines raised concern about the absence of patent protection for pharmaceuticals in a number of developing countries. The pressure by a number of developed countries led to signing of the TRIPS Agreement which demands for adequate and effective worldwide protection of pharmaceuticals and effective enforcement of patent rights throughout the world. The TRIPS Agreement thereby established a new area of trade regulation in the WTO. TRIPS contains new multilateral rules and minimum IPR protection standards that all WTO Members must implement. WTO Members are required to provide patent protection for pharmaceuticals, balanced by various legal measures that WTO Members may take if IPRs are abused.[4]

While TRIPS demands for patent protection for pharmaceuticals, a number of developing countries have expressed concern that exclusivity under patents is leading to substantially higher drug prices, with adverse effects on healthcare services. The experience of some countries (South Africa, Thailand, Brazil) regarding the actual impact of patent rights on access to medicines, led to the WTO Doha Declaration on the TRIPS Agreement and Public Health.[5] The Doha Declaration, which was adopted on 14 November 2001, expresses concern of Member countries over 'the gravity of the public health problems afflicting many developing and least-developed countries, especially those resulting from HIV/AIDS, tuberculosis, malaria and other epidemics.' The declaration clarifies some of the ambiguities with respect to the relationship between the TRIPS Agreement and Members' rights to protect public health, and reaffirms the 'right of WTO Members to use, to the full, the provisions in the TRIPS Agreement', including taking advantage of TRIPS' compulsory licensing provision.

The Doha Declaration stipulates that TRIPS 'can and should be interpreted and implemented in a manner supportive of WTO Members' right to protect public health and, in particular, to promote access to medicines for all.' The Declaration goes on to recognise that WTO Members are free to use the flexibilities under TRIPS, such as compulsory licensing, in order to promote access

[3] For critical opinions of the US-Thai FTA negotiations, see http://www.ftawatch.org

[4] Correa, CM, Integrating Public Health Concerns into Patent Legislation in Developing Countries, South Centre, Geneva, 2000. http://www.southcentre.org/publications/publichealth/toc.htm; Rein, J (2001) 'International Governance Through Trade Agreements: Patent Protection for Essential Medicines', 21 Northwestern Journal of International Law & Business 379.

[5] WTO Ministerial Conference, 4th Session, Doha, 9–14 November 2001, WT/MIN(01)/Dec/2, 20 November 2001.

to medicines, and are free to determine the grounds upon which to issue compulsory licenses.

The Doha Declaration instructed the WTO Council to recommend a solution to the problem faced by countries with insufficient or no manufacturing capacities. The problem concerns Articles 31(f) and (h) of the TRIPS Agreement which permits Members to grant compulsory licenses to supply foreign markets but limits exports to less than half of the production and requires payment of adequate remuneration to the patent holder when such licenses are issued. The WTO General Council adopted a decision on 30 August 2003 implementing interim waivers with regard to the obligations set out in paragraph (f) of Article 31 permitting a production for export under a compulsory license, and in paragraph (h) of the same article waiving the payment requirement in the eligible importing Member to prevent duplication of royalty fee payments.[6]

TRIPS, as reaffirmed by the Doha Declaration on the TRIPS Agreement and Public Health, leaves plenty room to manoeuvre for developing countries as regards to the protection of public health interests and improving access to medicines. The feasible options include:

- — The adoption of the principle of the international exhaustion of rights so as to facilitate parallel imports of cheaper drugs (Article 6);
- — Flexible interpretation of each provision of TRIPS in light of the objectives and principles stipulated under Articles 7 and 8;
- — Exclusion of certain biotechnological inventions, as well as medical methods for the treatment of human and animals (Article 27);
- — Provision for limited exceptions to patent rights such as a research exemption, prior users' rights, etc. (Article 30);
- — The use of compulsory licences for making available patented drugs (Article 31).

When the USTR submitted the draft IP text to Thailand in the sixth round of FTA negotiations (January 2006), the text contained TRIPS-plus patent rules that circumvented the flexibilities and options that Thailand has under TRIPS and the Doha Declaration.[7] If Thailand signed an FTA with the US, the TRIPS-plus commitment would have negative implications for access to medicines. It would undoubtedly limit generic competition and impose restrictions on the flexibilities contained in the TRIPS Agreement, as the following discussion explains.

[6] WT/L/540, 2 September 2003, Implementing of paragraph 6 of the Doha Declaration on The TRIPS Agreement and Public Health, Decision of the General Council of 30 August 2003. See also Correa, CM (2002) Implications of the Doha Declaration on the TRIPS Agreement and Public Health, WHO/EDM/PAR/2002.3, (Health Economics and Drugs EDM Series No.12, WHO).

[7] Available at: http://www.bilaterals.org/article.php3?id_article=3677

1. TRIPS-plus rules on pharmaceutical patents

a) Patentable subject-matter

The IP text that the USTR proposed to Thailand, for example, provides that:

> Each Party shall make patents available for the following inventions:
>
> (a) plants and animals, and
> (b) diagnostic, therapeutic, and surgical procedures for the treatment of humans or animals.
>
> In addition, the Parties confirm that patents shall be available for any new uses or methods of using a known product.

This means that effective and adequate protection must be given to inventions in all technological fields, including plants and animals that under TRIPS Article 27.3(b) can be excluded from patentability. The US FTA also prohibits trading partners to exclude patentability to medical practices, such as diagnosis, therapy, and surgery on the human or animal body. The exclusion of methods of treatment is based on the ground of ethical and social policy in order to protect medical practitioners from the restrictions of monopoly privileges, and at the same time allowing for healthy competition to enhance the well being of the public. The obligation to protect medical treatment imposed on Thailand by the USTR raises a number of ethical questions, including the question of whether the State should enforce monopoly rights in procedures of medical treatment, which directly affect the human health care, by making them a means of profiteering. Public well-being would undoubtedly be denied where a physician cannot carry out the required medical treatment, due to the restrictions of exclusive monopoly.[8]

The USTR also demands from Thailand patent protection for any form of pharmaceutical inventions including new uses or methods of a known product for the treatment of humans and animals (second medical indication). This is in contradiction with Article 27.3(a) of the TRIPS Agreement which permits WTO Members to exclude these types of invention from patentability.

There are two issues relating to the patenting of a known pharmaceutical in the forms of new uses or new methods. When a pharmaceutical substance has been already known to the public, the claims to the product as such are no longer patentable. Alternative solutions for the pharmaceutical company are: (i) to claim new pharmaceutical compositions, or (ii) to claim a new use of the product that is already known.

First, it is common for a research-based pharmaceutical company to broadly claim pharmaceutical compositions containing the active ingredient (ie a formulated product containing a known active ingredient and appropriate

[8] The issue is certainly a complicated one that involves ethical as well as practical issues. An overview over the issue from a European aspect is provided by D. Thomas, Patentability Problems in Medical Technology, 34 IIC 847 (2003).

additives). Such a claim is advantageous as it is not limited to any specific pharmaceutical indication. The commercial use of the claimed compound for any use whatsoever would constitute a patent infringement. Yet, an invention used in one area may have applications in other areas. For example, an agrochemical substance may be used as a pharmaceutical product, or a well-known drug can have a new therapeutic application. Such second use may then be claimed either by the company that holds the patent over the substance as such, or by another company that has discovered such second use.

TRIPS does not require WTO Members to patent second use inventions. Some developed countries (eg US, EU and Japan) have permitted patenting of the use inventions.[9] The US FTA demands that the second use of known drugs be patented. This no doubt would limit the freedom of countries to determine what should be protected under product and process patents as provided by TRIPS. Medicines that are no longer patented as products could be patented as a second use, new dosages of existing drugs, or new combinations of existing drugs. Patents for the subsequent uses of a known drug would thereby unnecessarily prolong the monopoly and deprive consumers of essential medicines.

b) Compulsory licensing

Compulsory licensing refers to a non-voluntary license issued by the State to a third party to perform acts covered by the patent exclusive rights (eg manufacturing, selling or importing the patented product), on the condition that the licensee pays reasonable remuneration to the patent holder in return. The compulsory licensing system is the very cornerstone of the patent system. The experience of many countries including the US,[10] Canada[11] and

[9] In Europe, the issue was widely discussed in the first decisions of the EPO's Enlarged Board of Appeal, G 1/83, G 5/83 and G 6/83. The Board affirmed the patentability of a second medical use, yet it is relatively clear that this is based not strictly on a legal interpretation of the relevant provisions, but on the assumption that such protection is useful in order to advance technological progress in the field of pharmaceuticals, and not contrary to the provisions in the European Patent Convention. Refusing protection for second medical uses is absolutely compatible with the obligation to grant absolute protection to pharmaceutical products and not contrary to TRIPS. The decision is rather one of economic policy, and the answer may well differ between developed and developing countries.

[10] Consistent with a focus on innovation, the US government has used compulsory licenses to curb anti-competitive behaviour. By 1977, the Federal Trade Commission and Department of Justice had issued approximately 125 decrees over thousands of patents in the context of mergers, price-fixing, and the abuse of monopoly or market power. Compulsory licensing is also used as another form of price regulation. For example, in the 1960s and 1970s, the US government made and used tetracycline and meprobamate for the military without permission from patent holders, and in 2001 it also threatened to use a compulsory license against the patented drug Cipro which drove down the price of the drug by almost 50%. C Chien, *Cheap Drugs at What Price to Innovations: Does the Compulsory Licensing of Pharmaceuticals Hurt Innovation?*, 18 Berkeley Technology Law Journal 853 (2003).

[11] From 1969 to 1983, Canada issued a large number of compulsory licenses over medicines under sections 4(1) and 39(4) of its patent law. Almost 80% of the applications for compulsory licenses were granted, resulting in an average of approximately twenty compulsory licenses per year. The policy of issuing compulsory licenses for drugs allowed Canada to develop domestic generic drug industry. Chien, *Ibid.*

Brazil[12] has shown that compulsory licensing is an effective mechanism to limit abusive practices of the patent holder and helps to force prices down.

According to TRIPS, countries are free to use the compulsory licensing of patents, provided that certain conditions are fulfilled.[13] In practice, countries that intended to use the compulsory licensing have always been under considerable economic pressure. With the adoption of the Doha Declaration on TRIPS and Public Health, it now seems obvious that WTO member countries can legitimately employ this legal mechanism to improve access to medicines.

Limiting the right of a country to use compulsory licensing is probably the most significant constraint under the US FTAs. The TRIPS-plus rule attempts to make the compulsory licensing provisions difficult to apply, as it sets more stringent conditions than the TRIPS standards. The US-Singapore FTA, for example, confines circumstances under which compulsory licenses may be issued to (1) remedy anti-competitive practices, (2) the case of public non-commercial use, and (3) the case of national emergency or other circumstances of extreme urgency.[14]

Issuing a compulsory license on the ground of non-working or insufficient working of patents is thereby prohibited, despite the fact that the use of compulsory licenses for local working of patents is the cornerstone of most countries' patent law and explicitly enshrined in the Paris Convention.[15]

According to the US-Singapore FTA, a compulsory license may be issued to remedy an anti-competitive practice only after a judicial or administrative process.[16] This requirement would render the compulsory licensing practically unworkable against anti-competitive behaviour, as the patentee can contest any proceedings and grants of a license in court or before the antitrust authority.

In the case of public non-commercial use or national emergency, a compulsory license can be granted only in accordance with the following conditions:

[12] Under the Brazilian patent law, patent protection is provided on condition that the patent holder produces at least part of the patented good within Brazil. If the patentee fails to satisfy this 'local working' requirement, its patent rights may be subject to a compulsory license, which may be issued to Brazilian pharmaceutical companies so that they may produce generic copies of the drug to supply the local market. Because of this requirement, Brazilian pharmaceutical companies now manufacture generic versions of eight of the twelve drugs that compose the AIDS cocktail at a cost that is 70% below the market price. The Brazilian government defends its practices by asserting to Article 30 of the TRIPS Agreement which guarantees WTO Members' right to issue compulsory licenses during times of national emergency. Bass, N.A. Implications of the TRIPS Agreement for Developing Countries: Pharmaceutical Patent Laws in Brazil and South Africa in the 21st Century, 34 George Washington International Law Review 191 (2002).

[13] TRIPS Agreement, Art 31.

[14] US-Singapore FTA, Art 16.7(6).

[15] See the Paris Convention for the Protection of Industrial Property (1967), Art 5(A). C. Vaitsos, *Patents Revisited: Their Function in Developing Countries, Journal of Development Studies, Vol 9 No 1*, 1972, pp 71–97. Even the provision currently contained in the Paris Convention had been subject to intense lobbying efforts for their abolition by industrial interest groups: A. Koury Menescal, Those behind the TRIPS Agreement: The influence of the IIC and AIPPI on international intellectual property decisions, 2005 *Intellectual Property Quarterly* 155–182.

[16] US-Singapore FTA, Art 16.7(6)(a).

— It can be issued only to the public sector or third parties authorised by the government.
— The patent holder shall receive full compensation with reference to the TRIPS provision for compulsory licenses.
— There must be no requirement for the transfer of undisclosed information or for the disclosure of know-how without the consent of the right holder.[17]

The TRIPS-plus provisions under US FTA attempt to limit essential measures such as compulsory licensing to certain situations and make the procedures for issuing a compulsory license intricate and prolonged. The constraints imposed on developing countries will threaten to restrict the measures those countries can take to pursue affordable drugs, and will affect the ability of many countries to promote access to medicines. Yet access to medicines for ASEAN countries is largely dependent on the corresponding ability of their neighbouring countries. The limitation of a country to access essential medicines will have an adverse effect on the ability of other countries in the region. For example if Thailand signs an FTA with the US, this will result in limited access to medicines not only in Thailand itself but also in its neighbouring countries like Vietnam, Myanmar, Cambodia and Laos, which have been relying on Thailand as an important source of drug supply.[18] With the FTA in place, Thailand would not be able to issue a compulsory license and export the compulsorily licensed drugs to those countries that have no or insufficient capacity in drug production, thereby denying their rights as reaffirmed by the Doha Declaration on TRIPS and Public Health.

c) Revocation of patents

Unlike the Paris Convention, TRIPS does not set out any grounds or conditions for the revocation of patents. Any revocation will therefore be compatible with TRIPS. The TRIPS-plus standard introduced by the US prohibits a trading partner from revoking patents on other grounds than those that would have justified a refusal to grant the patent (eg lack of patentability, insufficiency of or unauthorised amendments to the patent specification, non-disclosure or misrepresentation of prescribed, material particulars, fraud, or misrepresentation).[19] Revocation of patents is not possible in the cases where compulsory licenses were not sufficient to curb abuses of patent rights or non-working as provided by the Paris Convention.[20] Limited compulsory licensing therefore becomes only one mechanism that a trading partner can use to curtail abusive practices of patent owners.

[17] *Ibid*, Art 16.7(6)(b).
[18] See J Kuanpoth and D Le Hoai, Legal and Trade Issues Related to Access to Affordable Anti-retroviral Drugs for People Living with HIV/AIDS in Vietnam, Report Commissioned by the Ford Foundation, Hanoi 2004.
[19] US–Singapore FTA, Art 16.7(4)
[20] See the Paris Convention, Art.5 (A)(3).

The TRIPS-plus treaties increase the monopolistic power of large companies by demanding for harsh penalties, criminal enforcement for IP violations, and imposing obstacles to the use of compulsory licensing and revocation of patents, restricting the leverage that has helped the patent-granting country to achieve monopoly control.

d) Parallel imports

The FTAs proposed by the US allow patent holders to prevent the parallel importation of patented products. Under the US FTAs, the trading partner must adopt a system of national exhaustion only, thus prohibiting the international exhaustion in which the first sale of an object embodying IP in a foreign country exhausts the right holder's exclusive rights.[21]

According to Article 6 of TRIPS, different systems of exhaustion may be applied by WTO Members: national exhaustion, regional exhaustion (notably the European Union), or international exhaustion. According to the latter, the right owner cannot use his IP rights to prevent further distribution of the goods that have been placed into commerce anywhere by himself, or with his consent. Since the TRIPS-plus prohibits international exhaustion, parallel importation is regarded as an IP infringement and cannot be carried out without the authorisation of the right holder.

Note that the FTA between the US and Singapore does not explicitly prohibit the international exhaustion rule, but provides an opportunity for the patent holder to restrain parallel imports through contractual arrangements. Under the FTA, right holders are permitted to take legal action against imports or exports of patented products by a party who knows or has reason to know that such product has been distributed in breach of a contract between the right holder and a licensee, regardless of whether such breach occurs in or outside its territory.[22] In this way, the patent owner can impose restrictions on the resale of patented goods and thus limit the possibility of exporting the product from Singapore or importing the product to Singapore when it is sold in a foreign market. Although such restrictions have an anti-competitive character, Singapore is prohibited to void the restrictions on parallel imports.

Prohibiting parallel imports no doubt is an attempt to block the importation of cheap medicines and other goods, often in disregard of the humanitarian and economic needs of the country. For a number of years, developing countries like Thailand have been progressively promoting parallel imports through court cases and national legislation.[23] This attempt will turn out to be unsuccessful

[21] See US–Australia FTA, Art 17.9.4.

[22] US–Singapore FTA, Art 16.7(2).

[23] See Supreme Court decision, Case No. 2817/2543. See also Patent Act B.E. 2522, s 36(7). An overview is provided by V Ariyanuntaka, Exhaustion and Parallel Imports in Thailand, in C Heath (ed), *Parallel Imports in Asia, Max Planck Asian Intellectual Property Series vol 9*, London/The Hague/New York Kluwer Law International 2004, 95.

once Thailand signs the TRIPS-plus trade treaty with the US. Recent experiences regarding pharmaceutical patents and access to HIV/AIDS medicines should guide Thailand into being cautious about entering into any new commitments.[24]

e) Prohibiting pre-grant opposition

The USTR text prohibits Thailand from introducing a pre-grant opposition to a patent. The effectiveness of the patent system primarily depends on the quality of the technical examination. Even in developed countries, it is not uncommon to find a number of invalid patents being issued each year.[25] In view of the weaker patent examination system, it is thus logical to assume that the number of invalid patents granted in the developing countries like Thailand is even higher.[26] The case of ddI, where civil society organisations fought to cancel the invalid patents in court, reflects the significance of a pre-grant opposition which provides proceedings for the invalidation or amendment of patents before the patent office.[27] A straightforward administrative procedure is necessary because it would allow the patentee's competitors to challenge the validity of the patent at relatively low cost prior to an infringement action. The system would also reduce the excessive burden on the court and contribute to speedy proceedings of patent invalidation.

f) Term of protection

The twenty-year patent term under TRIPS is supposed to reward the inventor for his innovative efforts. Some products, such as pharmaceuticals and agrochemicals, require official authorisation before they can enter the market, and the approval process normally takes several years. The US FTA provides for extensions of these patents to provide compensation for unreasonable delays in issuing the patents or for the loss of patent term due to the approval process.[28] The rationale behind the patent term extension is to allow the patent holders to capture economic benefits that could not be obtained during the approval procedure.

[24] Thailand has had problems of accessibility to essential medicines, especially regarding antiretroviral drugs. It jointly proposed a draft text for a ministerial declaration on the TRIPS Agreement and Public Health in 2001. See the Submission by the African Group, Barbados, Bolivia, Brazil, Cuba, Dominican Republic, Ecuador, Honduras, India, Indonesia, Jamaica, Pakistan, Paraguay, Philippines, Peru, Sri Lanka, Thailand and Venezuela (IP/C/W/296).

[25] RM Sherwoon *et al* 'Promotion of Inventiveness in Developing Countries through a More Advanced Patent Administration', 39 IDEA 473 (1999).

[26] See for example L Tanasugarn, 'When Patent Rights may not be Enforceable: The Case of the Kwao Krua Patent' The Intellectual Property and International Trade Law Forum: Special Issue, 105 (1999).

[27] J Kuanpoth, 'Patents and Access to Medicines in Thailand—The ddI case and beyond', 2006 *Intellectual Property Quarterly* 149–159.

[28] The demand is based on US law, the Drug Price Competition and Patent Term Restoration Act of 1984, generally known as the Hatch-Waxman Act. See US–Singapore FTA, Arts 16.7 (7)(8) and 16.8 (4).

The extension of the patent term will allow multinationals to monopolise the market longer than under the conventional patent rule, despite the fact that those companies can utilise various marketing techniques, such as brand name advertisement and trade mark protection, to secure their monopoly position even after the expiration of the patent term. Extension of the patent term will delay the potential introduction of affordable generic medicines and defer the day when consumers can reap the benefit of generic competition.

g) Linkage of drug registration and the patent status of a drug

The text that the USTR has proposed to Thailand contains a provision obligating the Thai drug regulatory authority to inform the patent holder of any attempt to register a generic drug. The linkage of drug registration with the patent status will impose an unnecessary burden on the drug authority and unnecessarily restrains the entry of generic medicines. The TRIPS Agreement makes it very clear that IPRs, including patents, are private rights. The owner of those rights rather than the State must protect their interests. The practice of linking patent status to registration obviously provides legal protection for IPRs that are much stronger than any other rights of the private party. This sort of proposal therefore should be rejected by Thailand.

2. Data protection

Laws of most nations require pharmaceutical and agrochemical products to be registered before they can be put on the market. The company that seeks registration must submit data relating to the products' quality, safety and efficacy, the so-called test data, to the relevant regulatory authority. Since the compilation of these data involves considerable effort, international agreements demand protection for such data.

Article 39.3 of TRIPS stipulates that Members must protect the undisclosed data submitted for marketing approval of new chemical entities against 'unfair commercial use' and 'disclosure' of the data.[29] This has left WTO members with considerable leeway to determine rules for the protection of undisclosed test data. For example, countries may allow use of the test data as long as such use does not constitute 'unfair commercial use' or does not breach the 'non-disclosure' obligations in the framework of unfair competition law. In addition, the regulatory authorities may rely on the data submitted by the supplying company or on the evidence of a registration made in a foreign country to grant marketing approval for subsequent applications on a similar product.

Some developed countries, including the US, grant TRIPS-plus protection on the basis of data exclusivity in order to maintain technological and economic

[29] CM Correa, Protection of Data Submitted for the Registration of Pharmaceuticals: Implementing the Standards of the TRIPS Agreement, South Centre, Geneva, 2002.

superiority of their multinationals.[30] Multinational drug companies have long been pushing for Article 39.3 of TRIPS to be interpreted as requiring data exclusivity. The US is responding to the demand by requiring all its FTA partners to enforce data exclusivity for at least five years.

According to the US-Singapore FTA, for example, the parties are required to provide exclusivity for test data submitted to a government for the purpose of product approval, for a period of five years for pharmaceuticals and ten years in case of agricultural chemicals.[31] The trade agreement between the US and Vietnam demand the parties to prohibit third parties (ie generic companies seeking to introduce generic versions) from relying on the test data previously submitted by the first company (ie an originator company) in support of an application for product approval, for at least five years.[32] Like other US FTAs, the USTR text requires Thailand to enforce data exclusivity, which prevents the national drug regulatory authority from using the originator's clinical test data for a period of 5 years (in the case of new medicines) or 3 years (for the new use of known products) from initial regulatory approval of the original product. The drug regulatory authority is prevented from granting market approval to generic drugs on the basis of bio-equivalence or on the fact that the original product has got a marketing approval in a foreign country.

Furthermore, while TRIPS requires protection only for new chemicals, the US FTAs do not contain such a limitation. Exclusivity protection must be provided for all kinds of data submitted for marketing approval, including data with respect to compositions, dosage forms and new uses of a known drug. This TRIPS-plus commitment will limit the country's ability to flexibly implement Article 39.3 of TRIPS.

The provision on data exclusivity may delay the market entry of generic drugs, as generic companies will have to enter a long and costly testing process and complete the registration trials before the marketing approval of a generic drug can be obtained. It may also restrain the effectiveness of the compulsory licensing system, potentially preventing the drug regulatory authority from registering the generic drug produced under the compulsory license. Developing countries will be inhibited from using compulsory licensing to gain access to lower priced medicines.

IV. TRIPS-PLUS RULES AND THEIR IMPACT ON AGRICULTURE

TRIPS-plus rules under US FTAs require the patentability of all categories of life-forms, including plants, animals, biological processes, genes, and gene sequences. Patents on biological materials and methods still have various

[30] US laws adopt an absolute exclusivity regime for pharmaceuticals and a limited-exclusivity regime for pesticides. See Correa, *ibid.* at p 8.

[31] US–Singapore FTA, Art 16.8.

[32] US–Vietnam BTA, Art 9.6.

shortcomings and flaws and are still subject to different rules. Patent laws of developed countries such as the European Patent Convention, still exclude some forms of biotechnological inventions (eg plant and animal varieties) from patent protection. Under FTAs with the US, developing countries are obliged to patent the by-products of genetic engineering and other biotechnological methods without linking patentability to ethical, social, economic and environmental considerations.

The patenting of life when imposed through an FTA could have a considerable socio-economic impact on developing countries, especially countries like Thailand that rely on agriculture to sustain its economy. If Thailand adopts the TRIP-plus rule by granting patents on biological materials such as genes, it will cause a power shift in agriculture towards large biotechnology companies and will disrupt the access to essential products such as seeds or foodstuffs in the same way as patents may be unfairly restricting access to vital medicines for people in developing countries. Stricter IP protection would increase monopoly powers of the right holders, generally multinational firms, allowing them to gain a far greater control over the production chain of crops and food.

Moreover, gene patenting will have detrimental effects on the research environment and generate negative effects on downstream innovation. As pointed out by Heller and Eisenberg, the patenting of biological products and processes is regarded as 'anti-commons', in which 'individuals put fences around the peoples' private property and destroyed the commons'. This, according to the authors, could impede discovery and innovation in the fastest-growing field of technology.[33]

When a company is allowed to own patents on biotechnological inventions, such patents would act as a barrier to the transfer of technology to the developing countries. Patenting such products would override technological and economic requirements of the country as it will increase the cost of modern technologies and provide innovative disincentives for local research agencies.

With respect to plant variety protection (PVP), Article 27.3 (b) of TRIPS gives signatory countries the option to protect plant varieties by patents, an effective *sui generis* system, or both. The International Union for the Protection of New Varieties of Plants (UPOV) system is recognised to be one, but not the only means, of such *sui generis* system. The ambiguity of the term 'effective *sui generis* system' under TRIPS allows developing countries to avoid having to develop full IP law covering plant varieties. Some developing countries, such as Thailand and India, have flexibly implemented the TRIPS provision by incorporating the Farmers' Rights[34] and the access and benefit sharing (ABS) system under the Convention on Biological Diversity into their national legislation.

[33] M Heller and R Eisenberg 'Can Patents Deter Innovation?: The Anticommons in Biomedical Research', Science, 1998, pp 698–701.

[34] The concept of Farmers' Rights adopted by the Food and Agriculture Organisation (FAO) has the aim of compensating farmers who have been conserving plant genetic resources for the past centuries and thereby have contributed to the development of plant varieties.

Thailand has so far resisted ratifying UPOV or adopting it as the standard for its PVP law. This is because plants are vitally important for agriculture, still regarded as the backbone of the Thai economy. Thailand's current law, the Plant Variety Protection Act B.E. 2542, does not follow the UPOV model. Unlike the UPOV, the law aims at promoting not only the creation of new varieties of plant but also the conservation and encouragement of agricultural practices in the country. The law protects breeders' rights and recognises the rights of farmers and local communities over plant genetic resources. It also adopts legal requirements such as prior informed consent and ABS that allows individuals and communities to claim compensation for their contribution to the resources.

It seems that countries can adapt and change the PVP system to their local conditions, agriculture and farming sectors. The US FTAs limit this flexibility by requiring trading partners to join the UPOV 1991 Act. The UPOV system will leave Thailand and other FTA partners with no option regarding the scope of protection, as the 1991 Act provides the least discretion to the signatory states in choosing how to protect plant varieties.

According to Article 14 of the 1991 Act, protection must be extended to all plant varieties. The exclusive rights must cover vegetative or reproductive propagating material, and extend to essentially derived varieties and harvested material. The rights of farmers to save, use, exchange, or sell farm-saved seeds are constrained. Such full-scale monopoly right will adversely affect food and agricultural sectors, and cause adverse effects on the interest of poor farmers, in particular when their right to save seeds is removed. Moreover, the accession to UPOV 1991 will prohibit the inclusion of provisions requiring the applicants to prove that the plant variety is safe and does not have any harmful effects to environment, as currently enshrined under the PVP law of Thailand.[35]

As already mentioned, the Thai economy has been dominated by agriculture and will continue to rely on this important sector for export earnings. By ratifying a TRIPS-plus bilateral treaty, Thailand will open the door for the US biotechnology industry, the largest biotechnology industry in the world, not only to dominate Thailand's farming sector, but also to exploit Thailand's abundant biological resources. Although endowed with plentiful amounts of biological resources, Thailand will not be able to take advantage of the resources as a source of economic growth and poverty alleviation. The UPOV system would impose the mandatory components of PVP and restrain the country's sovereign rights over its biological resources and its ability to regulate access to the biodiversity. Under the TRIPS-plus and UPOV regimes, Thailand's attempt to balance IP protection with maintaining an alternative rights system would be reduced accordingly.

[35] See Thailand's Plant Variety Protection Act BE 2542, Section 13.

V. TRIPS-PLUS RULES AND THEIR IMPACT ON ACCESS TO KNOWLEDGE

1. Extension of the term of copyright protection

The US FTAs require trading partners to extend the term of copyright protection form 50 years from the death of the author to 70 years after the death of the author, bringing it into conformity with US law (ie the Sonny Bono Copyright Extension Act 1998).[36] It was observed that the extension of the general term of copyright protection was the result of an intense lobbying by the US copyright owner group which represents such heavyweights as the Disney Corporation, Sony Pictures Entertainment, MGM, Paramount Pictures, Twentieth Century Fox, Universal Studios and Warner Brothers. Of particular concern was the 2003 expiration of the Mickey Mouse character.[37]

The extension of the copyright term will be undertaken by US trade partners without any analysis as to the costs and benefits of the extension. Yet it is arguable that the extension will generate an adverse economic impact on libraries, universities, cultural institutions, and the public at large. The extension will particularly increase the costs of educational institutions for an extra twenty years, extend the payment of royalties, reduce the incentive to create more works, and alter the balance very much in favour of copyright owners at the expense of users.[38]

2. Digital Agenda under the US FTAs

The TRIPS Agreement does not deal with IP issues in cyberspace. In 1996, the WIPO has adopted two 'internet treaties': the WIPO Copyright Treaty and the WIPO Performances and Phonograms Treaty. They establish important international norms related to the right to make a work available to the public through interactive media. They also provide for the protection of rights management information and technological measures used to guard copyrighted and non-copyrighted works. Pressuring all trading partners to adopt the very dynamic digital agenda of the WIPO is one of the main objectives in current US trade policy.

The US digital agenda has focused on, inter alia, the following issues.

[36] See US–Singapore FTA, Art 16.4(4)(a).

[37] Australian Financial Review 'Mickey Mouse holds key to the future', 8 December 2003.

[38] Australian Intellectual Property and Competition Review Committee, Review of Intellectual Property Legislation under the Competition Principles Agreement, September 2000.

a) Anti-circumvention provisions

While TRIPS is absent on obligations concerning technological protection measures (TPMs), all FTAs proposed by the US stipulate that parties must provide adequate legal protection and effective legal remedies against acts of circumventing TPMs and against devices which could be used for circumvention, regardless of the intended use of the device.[39] It also limits the scope of exceptions in which TPMs may be used and extends the scope of criminal offences relating to the manufacture, distribution and use of circumvention devices. This means in effect that the US is now creating a new concept of copyright protection by extending the conventional economic rights of the author to the right to use and distribute circumvention devices.

This new area of IP protection will no doubt allow content owners to enjoy greater protection than conventional copyright rules would afford. The provisions on prohibition of circumventing TPMs and devices will enable the owners to extend greater control over access to and distribution of works that copyright law expressly leaves unprotected in order to stimulate further creativity (ie works which have fallen into the public domain). The TPM circumvention prohibition will prevent the circumvention for non-infringing usage, and interfere with the rights of consumers to deal with the goods that they have legitimately purchased. In addition, the scope of fair use online will be narrowed down, as the owners can require payment for any use or excerption of a digital work, regardless of the user's purpose. The use of the internet and digital works for educational or private non-commercial purposes, or the use by educational and library organisation will be increasingly hindered because of this prohibition.[40]

TRIPS-plus rules, while introducing a higher standard of copyright protection, will not harmonise aspects of US law that protect the public. The incorporation of TPMs into national copyright law will cut down the ability of the public to engage in fair dealing or fair use. While consumers in the US have a constitutional guarantee of free speech and are protected by broad fair use provisions, users of information in countries that sign an FTA with the US will have more restricted access to copyright material than users in the US due to the lack of the same aspects of consumer protection in those countries.

b) Temporary copying

The US FTAs provide greater protection than TRIPS for works in digital form. Temporary reproduction such as temporary storage in electronic form is considered copyright infringement under the bilateral trade deals between US and

[39] US–Singapore FTA, Art 16.4(7).

[40] JE Cohen, 'Lochner in Cyberspace: The New Economic Orthodoxy of "Right Management" ', 97 *Mich L Rev* 462 (1998).

its trading partners.[41] This provision clearly extends the author's right over their works on the internet.

Compared with the conventional copyright rules, the prohibition of temporary reproduction allows the copyright owner to control the use of the internet. This is because every use of an internet browser, which requires a few seconds of storage in RAM, will constitute copying. While the use of conventional copyrighted works, such as the reading a book, is not considered infringement, the browsing or using of the internet will be barred on the grounds of violation of copyright.

c) Internet service provider liability

The US FTAs have gone further than TRIPS by permitting right holders to take legal action against internet service providers (ISP) for the copying of works by subscribers.[42] Further, trading partner must ensure that the owners of copyright can track every use made of digital copies and trace where each copy resides on the network and what is being done with such copies at any time. These two requirements will greatly affect the public right of fair use with respect to digital works.

VI. CONCLUSION

In light of the considerable and long term efforts of developing countries to minimise the impact of the TRIPS Agreement, one might conclude that most developing countries do not favour the overall and high level IP protection as required by TRIPS. That conclusion, however, is contradicted by the widespread and enthusiastic support of many developing countries for entering into FTAs that demand higher commitments on IP protection. While the US has a clear motive for demanding such strong IP protection, as it exports a disproportionately high share of IP rights and products that contain IP rights, most countries that sign an FTA with the US are net importers of IP-related products and would lose more than gain by adopting TRIPS-plus standards.

FTAs are signed by countries in pursuit of their economic self-interest, but in the long term may undermine multilateral trade liberalisation. Such a bilateral and regional trade policy aimed at providing reciprocal benefits amounts to a clear contradiction of the multilateralism that many nations advocate. In order to sustain the spirit of international cooperation, it is necessary for WTO's Contracting Parties to eliminate this practice, which is a major and fundamental departure from the multilateral trade system. Instead of removing the last

[41] See US–Singapore FTA, Art 16.4(1).

[42] *Ibid*, Art 16.9(22). This provision is basically taken from the US Digital Millennium Copyright Act of 1998. There are three newly introduced copyright rules under the Act: the liability of ISPs, protection against anti-circumvention devices and protection against satellite signal theft.

remaining barriers to liberalise trade and investment, a better alternative would be to negotiate *fair* trade agreements that respect existing environmental, social and labour treaties in order to completely reform the undemocratic multilateral WTO system, and to put some genuine concern for development into the Doha Development Agenda.

Part II

Law and Policy of Multilateral v Bilateral Agreements

Chapter 3

The Changing Landscape of International Intellectual Property

DANIEL J GERVAIS*

I. INTRODUCTION

ANY NATIONAL OR regional economy is necessarily a complex 'system'.[1] This means that changes to one aspect or policy 'lever' will inevitably affect other areas. Therefore, an intellectual property regime must be viewed as forming part of a broader set of measures designed to optimize knowledge development and utilization. That optimization in turn should enhance economic growth, cultural prosperity and human development. The policy dilemma may be summarized as follows: while importing 'foreign' intellectual property rules wholesale into the legislative and industrial fabric of a developing economy is insufficient to succeed, it is fair to assume that a country's technology imports and foreign investment are unlikely to grow without adequate intellectual property rules. In other words, intellectual property rules are required. At the international level, those rules are now essentially enshrined in the TRIPS Agreement.[2]

This paper suggests that TRIPS norms should be integrated in a broader strategy designed to optimize innovation and access to knowledge. Viewed pragmatically, a part of any short or medium-term strategy should include working with TRIPS as a given, and perhaps even as a common reference point or even

* Financial assistance from the Social Sciences and Humanities Research Council of Canada (SSHRC) and research assistance from Ms. Shalisa Khan (LLB, Univ. of Ottawa) and Marina Pavlovic (LLD candidate, Univ of Ottawa) are most gratefully acknowledged.

[1] The definition proposed by the International Technology Education Association illustrates the point. It defines 'system' as '[a] group of interacting, interrelated, or interdependent elements or parts that function together as a whole to accomplish a goal' (as found via Google.com, 19 March 2005). On a more scholarly level, complex systems may be defined as 'systems with multiple elements [. . .] constantly evolve and unfold over time.' W Brian Arthur, 'Complexity and the Economy'. Science, Vol 284, (April 1999) at 107.

[2] World Trade Organization Agreement on Trade-Related Intellectual Property Rights, 15 April 1994, Marrakech Agreement Establishing the World Trade Organization, Annex 1C, Legal Instruments—Results of the Uruguay Round Vol. 31; 33 ILM 1197 [hereinafter referred to as 'TRIPS Agreement' or 'TRIPS'].

a 'defence' against TRIPS-plus demands in bilateral discussions. TRIPS is not perfect of course but there is some degree of built-in flexibility that developing economies can use. More importantly, however, by developing a comprehensive knowledge optimization strategy, a country can limit the negative impacts and welfare costs of transitioning to higher intellectual property protection and increase its chances of reaping the benefits thereof, including technology-related foreign direct investment (FDI) and growing domestic Internet, pharmaceutical or other technology based industries. To achieve this objective, it is essential not to limit the analysis to narratives about the history of TRIPS or to efforts to limit the impact of TRIPS, but focus instead on evidence-based policy choices and adopt a more systematic application of policy reform analysis.

That being said, it is not a contradiction to consider, in the longer term, that TRIPS is not static. TRIPS evolves with each panel and Appellate Body interpretation. That Body has indicated, for instance, that TRIPS should not be read in 'clinical isolation' from public international law.[3] Developing and other countries can coalesce to develop alternative sets of norms and the inclusion of TRIPS and WTO rules in the broader framework of public international law.

Against this backdrop, this Chapter examines, in Part I, the emergence of the World Trade Organization (WTO) Agreement on Trade-related Aspects of Intellectual Property Rights (TRIPS).[4] TRIPS was negotiated as part of the Uruguay Round of Multilateral Trade Negotiations. TRIPS was an effort both to increase (for most WTO members) the level of intellectual property protection, and reduce differences among relevant national rules. TRIPS also added a significant level of comfort for multinational corporations deciding when and where to export to new markets or expand research and development efforts[5] (other factors those corporations tend to consider include the tax structure and available subsidies, the availability of qualified workers and the labour relations environment, the protection of investments, a low level of corruption, the quality of the legal and judicial system and law enforcement, to name some of the most important ones). The Chapter then turns to the changing face of international intellectual property agenda, evidenced inter alia by the Doha Ministerial Declaration of November 2001 and follow-up work on access to medicines and the recent adoption of a 'development agenda' by the World Intellectual Property Organization (WIPO).

[3] See 'US—Standards for Reformulated and Conventional Gasoline', Report of he Appellate Body, WTO Doc. WT/DS2/AB/R, at para III. B.

[4] 15 April 1994, Marrakesh Agreement Establishing the World Trade Organization, Annex 1C, Legal Instruments—Results of the Uruguay Round Vol. 31; 33 ILM 1197.

[5] See E Mansfield, Intellectual Property Protection, Foreign Direct Investment, and Technology Transfer, Int'l Fin Corp Discussion Paper No 19 (1994). Not surprisingly, it is a group funded by US-based multinationals that first suggested linking trade and intellectual property in the GATT context, and which produced the first draft text. See A Koury Menescal. Those behind the TRIPS Agreement: The Influence of the ICC and the AIPPI on International Property Decisions, [2005] IPQ 155; and SK Sell. Private Power, Public Law: The Globalization of Intellectual Property Rights. Cambridge Univ Press, 2003, at 96–120.

In Part II, the Chapter discusses recent economic analyses of the impact of intellectual property protection on bilateral trade flows and FDI. Appropriate distinctions are made between trade and FDI. Wherever possible, lessons about the 'right' level of intellectual protection are drawn. Recent efforts in the World Intellectual Property Organization (WIPO) and World Trade Organization (WTO) are also discussed.

In the third and final Part, the paper looks at the current quest for a 'balanced' approach and suggests ways in which such a balanced intellectual property regime could be put in place, as part of a broad knowledge-oriented economic strategy.

II. TRIPS LESSONS

1. The Emergence of the TRIPS Agreement

The TRIPS Agreement was negotiated as part of the Uruguay Round of Multilateral Trade Negotiations. In fact, TRIPS is only Annex 1C of the Agreement Establishing the World Trade Organization.[6] As such, it was part of a package. Its negotiators came from a group of initially 20 countries, subsequently increased to approximately 30. Half of the negotiators came from industrialized nations, while others hailed from developing countries. The representatives of developing nations were often trade negotiators with little or no prior exposure to intellectual property. Few had advanced legal training. This knowledge asymmetry put them at a disadvantage when discussing detailed arcane drafting points, especially those linked to the specific history of existing treaties such as the Berne and Paris Conventions.[7] In addition, the disparity in bargaining knowledge may have been enhanced by the negotiating process itself.

Indeed, in the first few months of 1990, a number of industrialized countries tabled, with little advance notice,[8] draft legal texts of what they saw as the future TRIPS Agreement. Prior to the tabling of these texts, the discussions had focused on identifying existing norms and possible trade-related gaps therein, but the emerging outline of a possible TRIPS result had essentially been at the level of principles, not legal texts. The draft legal texts, which emanated from

[6] April 15, 1994, Final Act Embodying the Results of the Uruguay Round of Multilateral Trade Negotiations; Legal Instruments-Results of the Uruguay Round 6, 6–18, 33 ILM 1140, 1144–53 (1994).

For a detailed negotiating history, see Daniel Gervais, The TRIPS Agreement: Drafting History and Analysis, 2nd ed (London: Sweet & Maxwell, 2003).

[7] Berne Convention for the Protection of Literary and Artistic Works, Paris Act of 24 July 1971, as amended on 28 September 1979, 828 UNTS 222 [hereinafter Berne Convention]; Paris Convention for the Protection of Industrial Property, 20 March 1883, as last revised 14 July 1967, 21 UST 1583, 828 UNTS 305 [hereinafter Paris Convention].

[8] Formally, that is. A draft TRIPS text (though not as detailed) prepared by the private sector and a Washington, DC, lawyer, had been in circulation since the mid-1980s. See *supra* n 5.

the European Communities, the United States, Japan, Switzerland and Australia,[9] foreshadowed a detailed agreement covering all intellectual property rights then in existence, even the seldom used *sui generis* protection for computer chips. The proposals also included detailed provisions on the enforcement of those rights before national courts and customs authorities and a provision bringing future TRIPS disputes under the GATT/WTO dispute-settlement umbrella.[10] These proposals were far from obvious in light of the limited mandate of the TRIPS negotiating group.[11]

As a reaction, a group of 12 developing countries, which later grew to 14,[12] proposed another 'legal' text, much more limited in scope, with few specific normative aspects. They insisted on the need to maintain flexibility to implement economic and social development objectives. In retrospect, some developing countries may feel that the Uruguay Round secretariat did them a disservice by preparing a 'composite' text in July 1990 that melded all industrialized countries' proposals into one, with square brackets used to signal differences in the various legal texts and which became the 'A' proposal, while the developing countries' text became the 'B' text.[13] The final Agreement mostly mirrored the A text. As such, it essentially embodied norms that had been accepted[14] by industrialized countries. The concerns of developing countries were reflected mainly in two provisions—Articles 7 and 8.

In most cases, TRIPS negotiators incorporated existing international norms by reference. Those norms were altered only to the extent that there was a 'consensus' that they should be updated.[15] This is true of the Paris, Berne and Washington treaties, which deal with copyright, industrial property (patents,

[9] See Gervais, *supra* n 7, at paras 1.18–9. The US and EC text were suggested by private interest groups, funded mostly from the pharmaceutical and entertainment industries. See Sell, *supra* n 6 and J Bhagwati. In Defense of Globalization (Oxford Univ Press, 2004), at 182–5.

[10] The lack of a dispute resolution mechanism on the international level (state-state) was the main problem in enforcing the obligations under the Berne Convention and the Paris Convention. The WTO dispute-settlement mechanism applies only to the disputes between States.

[11] See the Punta del Este Declaration (launching the Uruguay Round). Document MIN.DEC of 20 September 1986, pp 7–8: 'In order to reduce the distortions and impediments to international trade, and taking into account the need to promote effective and adequate protection of intellectual property rights, and to ensure that measures and procedures to enforce intellectual property rights do not themselves become barriers to legitimate trade, the negotiations shall aim to clarify GATT provisions and elaborate as appropriate new rules and disciplines. Negotiations shall aim to develop a multilateral framework of principles, rules and disciplines dealing with international trade in counterfeit goods, taking into account work already undertaken in GATT. These negotiations shall be without prejudice to other complementary initiatives that may be taken in the World Intellectual Property Organization and elsewhere to deal with these matters'.

[12] Argentina, Brazil, Chile, China, Columbia, Cuba, Egypt, India, Nigeria, Peru, Tanzania and Uruguay. Pakistan and Zimbabwe joined later on.

[13] Then again, the Secretariat would perhaps respond that its mandate was to get to an agreement, which did in fact happen. Is it the secretariat's function somehow to 'compensate' for the respective clout of the countries involved and/or the degree of interest they took in various aspects of the Round?

[14] In some cases just a few years before, such as the Berne Convention only ratified by the United States in 1989.

[15] Gervais, *supra* n 7, at p 68.

designs and trademarks) and integrated circuits, respectively.[16] By and large, the so-called 'North' imposed its then most-advanced set of norms on the 'South'. In fact, there were relatively few concessions made by major industrialised countries, despite their disagreements on some issues,[17] except the need to submit themselves to binding dispute-settlement. By contrast, developing countries were forced to accept a package that a number of countries did not fully understand and which contained a complete set of intellectual property norms they now had to implement into their national law. The only true measures obtained by developing nations (in addition to Articles 7 and 8)[18] were transitional periods to implement the Agreement. For developing countries other than least-developed ones, such transitional periods expired in January 2000.[19]

Developing countries accepted the Agreement in many if not most cases because of significant political concessions[20] in other sectors of the Round, such as tariffs on tropical fruit or textiles.[21] At the time, there were very few people

[16] The Berne Convention, the Paris Convention and the Washington Treaty on Intellectual Property in Respect of Integrated Circuits (this last treaty which never entered into force but was nonetheless used as a foundation for TRIPS).

[17] The United States could not accept the Rome Convention for the Protection of Performers, Producers of Phonograms and Broadcasting Organizations, which protects neighbouring (or 'related') rights. Therefore, the wording of TRIPS only refers to Rome in respect of exceptions (Art 14). See Gervais, supra n 7, at p 99–100. Also on this list are moral rights, the protection of biotechnological inventions (which was not settled in Europe at the time), plant varieties and geographical indications. Given the comparable clout of the industrialised countries involved in discussions of these issues, they were solved either by introducing exceptions (as in Art 9 on moral rights or 27 for biotechnology) or by rather vague undertakings to negotiate further, as in Art 24 (concerning geographical indications).

[18] TRIPS Art 7: The protection and enforcement of intellectual property rights should contribute to the promotion of technological innovation and to the transfer and dissemination of technology, to the mutual advantage of producers and users of technological knowledge and in a manner conducive to social and economic welfare, and to a balance of rights and obligations.

Art 8: (1). Members may, in formulating or amending their laws and regulations, adopt measures necessary to protect public health and nutrition, and to promote the public interest in sectors of vital importance to their socio-economic and technological development, provided that such measures are consistent with the provisions of this Agreement. (2) Appropriate measures, provided that they are consistent with the provisions of this Agreement, may be needed to prevent the abuse of intellectual property rights by right holders or the resort to practices which unreasonably restrain trade or adversely affect the international transfer of technology.

[19] The transitional period for least developed countries has been extended to 2016 for pharmaceuticals (by the Doha Declaration) and to 2013 for most other provisions (by a decision of November 2005). This is in recognition that introducing high levels of IP protection is unlikely to generate positive economic growth in countries below certain developmental thresholds. See infra n 125.

[20] For an interesting empirical analysis of how and why developing countries adopt higher intellectual property norms (in many cases not because they believe they need or will benefit from them), see RL Ostergard Jr, The Development Dilemma: The Political Economy of Intellectual Property Rights in the International System. LFB Scholarly Publishing, 2002.

[21] A key difference between the WTO and organizations such as WIPO is that concessions are made in WTO negotiations across negotiating sectors. IP policy issues may be 'abandoned' for lower tariffs of cotton or coffee, for example. Interestingly, these issues are sometimes linked. The protection of intellectual property rights in agricultural products, such as seeds is becoming an increasingly important issue.) See U Lele *et al* Intellectual Property Rights in Agriculture: The World Bank's Possible Future Role in Assisting Borrower and Member Countries. (World Bank, Environmentally and Socially Sustainable Development Series: Rural Development, 1999).

arguing that TRIPS *qua* TRIPS was good in the short term for all developing countries. Developing countries accepted it as part of a package. There was, however, a two-prong belief in demander countries and certain lobbies that (a) TRIPS was necessary to maximize the rent that could be extracted from emerging foreign markets (and related beliefs that unpaid and unlicensed use of 'Western' intellectual property was comparable to theft or 'piracy' and that increased foreign revenues would lead to higher overall levels of research and development) and (b) that TRIPS was a difficult but essential measure to jump-start global economic development.[22] Intellectual property as policy castor oil, as it were: countries should overlook the distasteful aspects of introducing or increasing intellectual property protection and enforcement in exchange for longer term economic health.[23]

[22] This debate was present in China when it was first considering the adoption of a 'Western-style' patent law. As Prof Alford explains:

> Proponents of a patent law placed primarily emphasis on its likely salutary economic effects, arguing that China needed to smash the [. . .] mentality of the Cultural Revolution that rewarded all equally, irrespective of the quality of their work [. . .]. This could only be accomplished, they contended, by adopting a patent system that provided meaningful material incentives. By permitting those who had so contributed to reap the fruits of their labours, a patent law would also, it was suggested, allow China's most innovative organizations to accumulate additional capital and strengthen their management, which would spur further inventive activity [. . .]
>
> Opponents of a patent system [. . .] expressed concern about Western 'literary-industrial complex', which some believed might patent so broadly in China as to stifle the development of indigenous science and so leave the nation dependent on the outside world economically, scientifically, and militarily. It would be foolhardy, they argued, to risk draining China's limited foreign exchange reserves to pay royalties—especially when the same technology could be acquired at no cost, albeit without authorization.

WP Alford, To Steal a Book Is an Elegant Offense: Intellectual Property Law in Chinese Civilization. (Stanford Univ Press, 1995), at 67–8.

[23] A point articulated in a recent article in the *International Herald Tribune*:

> By protecting market exclusivity, the industry says, the trade agreement [in this CAFTA, the Central American Free Trade Agreement] would spur innovation and encourage pharmaceutical companies to register drugs in the smaller countries, ultimately helping to deliver drugs to the needy. It is a philosophical argument that the Office of the US Trade Representative has embraced. 'Trade rules that protect innovation foster a system that produces the type of medicines that American health consumers and health consumers around the world use and need to fight diseases', said Richard Mills, a spokesman for the trade office.

Stephanie Saul. 'US Drug makers win little-seen victory in trade pact', International Herald Tribune, July 2–3, 2005, at 10.

> One can readily infer that the higher level of protection ('TRIPS Plus') will allow international pharmaceutical companies to extract higher rents from those countries. The article does not explain how 'health consumers' in Central America would afford the new medicines and how the pact will help 'deliver drugs to the needy.

The article makes it plain, however, that Central American countries did not agree to the pact because they thought the intellectual property was beneficial *per se*, but rather because of concessions made by the United States in the textile and agricultural sectors. What several NGOs and so-called 'civil society' groups point out is that while such trade deals may globally help the respective balance sheets of the signatory countries, the new riches may not alleviate poverty or contribute to overall economic development at least not in the short term. This is one of the areas in need of substantially more empirical research, as is explained below.

As a result of this process, TRIPS adjusted the level of intellectual property protection to what was the highest common denominator among major industrialized countries as of 1991. It was implemented in almost all WTO member countries, often by incorporating with little change model laws provided by WIPO.

2. Post-TRIPS Developments in the WTO

We are now in the midst of the Doha Development Round, which started in Qatar in November 2001.[24] The language of the Declaration adopted in Doha is a measure of the changes since 1994. In the three paragraphs concerning TRIPS, there are few openings for demands to increase intellectual property protection.

The first paragraph (17) states that TRIPS should be implemented 'in a manner supportive of public health, by promoting both access to existing medicines and research and development into new medicines'.[25] In the following paragraph (18), the Declaration addresses a mostly North-North issue, the completion of the negotiations on geographical indications on wines & spirits.[26] The third and perhaps most famous paragraph (19) instructs the TRIPS Council to 'examine, inter alia, the relationship between the TRIPS Agreement and the Convention on Biological Diversity, the protection of traditional knowledge and folklore' and other new developments. In undertaking this work, the Declaration says, 'the TRIPS Council shall be guided by the objectives and principles set out in Articles 7 and 8 of the TRIPS Agreement[27] and shall take fully into account the development dimension'.[28] In other words, apart from the possible increase in protection of names of wines & spirits, the Doha Declaration essentially reflects concerns expressed by certain developing countries. Paragraph 17 also insists on the balance between the need for access to intellectual property and its protection, which some might be tempted to see as a philosophical underpinning for ongoing discussions.

3. TRIPS and Public Health

The separate *Declaration on the TRIPS Agreement and Public Health*[29] also adopted at Doha emphasizes what had already been said in the Declaration itself—that the TRIPS Agreement should not prevent WTO Members from taking measure to protect public health. Such an interpretation means that the

24 Ministerial declaration WT/MIN(01)/DEC/1 20 November 2001.
25 *Ibid* para 17.
26 *Ibid* para 18.
27 See *supra* n 19.
28 Ministerial declaration WT/MIN(01)/DEC/1 20 November 2001 at para 19.
29 Document WT/MIN(01)/DEC/2.

TRIPS Agreement should be interpreted in the light of its objective and purpose, as expressed in the Agreement itself: 'Each member has the right to grant compulsory licenses and the freedom to determine grounds upon which such licenses are granted'; each member has the right to determine what constitutes a national emergency or the other circumstances of extreme urgency (where public health crises may represent national emergency); 'the effect of the provision in the TRIPS Agreement that are relevant to the exhaustion of intellectual property rights is to leave each member free to establish its own regime for such exhaustion without challenge, subject to the MFN and national treatment provisions'.[30]

After intensive and difficult negotiations, the WTO General Council adopted the *Decision on Implementation the Doha Declaration on the TRIPS Agreement and Public Health* in 2003.[31] This Decision will allow, under certain conditions, WTO members to export generic versions of drugs used to treat diseases such as HIV/AIDS to countries that can neither afford nor manufacture these pharmaceuticals. The Decision is imperfect,[32] but the point here is not to criticize the result but to draw attention to the process which was in place to take account of the needs of developing countries. That being said, the importance of patents in preventing or reducing access to life-saving pharmaceuticals is the subject of debate among experts. While a compulsory license may reduce the patent (royalty) cost, it does not eliminate the production costs, nor the problems associated with distribution and timely administration of the medicines.[33] However, if patents are indeed more a part of the problem than of the solution for certain developing countries living with HIV/AIDS or other epidemics, then the Decision may help them overcome that obstacle.[34]

[30] Document WT/MIN(01)/DEC/2.

[31] Decision of the General Council of 30 August 2003, Document number WT/l/540. See also CM Correa, 'Supplying pharmaceuticals to countries without manufacturing capacity: Examining the solution agreed upon by the WTO on 30 August, 2003' (2004), 1 Journal of Generic Medicines 105–119.

[32] See, eg, BC Mercurio, TRIPS, Patents, and Access to Life-Saving Drugs in the Developing World (2004), 8 *Marq Intell Prop L Rev* 211, 237 ('Unfortunately, as drafted, several paragraphs of the Implementation Agreement lend themselves to the possibility of abuse or are otherwise unsatisfactory and potentially destabilizing to the entire system of compulsory licensing'). Interestingly, as of April 2005, no country had made the necessary notification to the WTO secretariat to be able to invoke the Decision.

See also D Matthews, WTO Decision on Implementation of Paragraph 6 of the Doha Declaration on the TRIPS Agreement and Public Health: A Solution to the Access to Essential Medicines Problem? (2004), 7 *J Int'l Econ L* 73; PJ Heald, Mowing the Playing Field: Addressing Information Distortion and Asymmetry in the TRIPS Game, (2003) 88 *Minn L Rev* 249; Th F Cotter, Market Fundamentalism and the TRIPS Agreement (2004), 22 Cardozo *Arts & Ent LJ* 307. For a view saying that the Declaration goes too far in favour of developing countries and act as a disincentive to research, see AO Sykes, TRIPS, Pharmaceuticals, Developing Countries, and the 'Doha 'Solution' (2002), 3 *Chi J Int'l L* 47.

[33] See, eg Attaran, Amir and L Gillespie-White. Do Patents for Antiretroviral Drugs Constrain Access to AIDS Treatment in Africa?, (2001) *J of the Amer Med Assoc* 286, 15: 1886–1906.

[34] See KM Gopakumar, The WTO Deal on Cheap Drugs—A Critique, (2004), 7 *J World Intell Prop* 99 (2004).

It has also been argued that recourse to compulsory licensing may be ill-advised when considered in a longer term perspective. The purpose of TRIPS, it is said, is to enhance *global* welfare, not welfare measured country by country or region by region. If multinational pharmaceutical firms can reap additional profits from developing nations, then new products will result due to higher investment in research & development. While this may benefit mostly consumers in richer countries, it still increases welfare measured globally.[35] Professor Sykes for instance suggests that introducing high levels of intellectual property protection in developing countries induces firms to invent things of particular interest to developing countries (eg, anti-malaria drugs) and to engage in technology transfer. In addition, without uniform rules, there may be a 'collective action' problem. The problem arises because an individual developing country may be better off if it chooses to have weak patent laws, while the other developing countries have strong patent laws; that way, an individual country can obtain the benefits of inducing the invention of things of particular interest to developing countries, without having to pay the costs. TRIPS solves the collective action problem by requiring all of the member nations to have strong intellectual property protection.[36]

In responding to Professor Sykes arguments, Professor Cotter suggests that 'even in the presence of strong patent rights, the developing nations' willingness to pay may be so constrained that little incentive will exist anyway for the pharmaceutical companies to engage in much of this type of research and development. Indeed, most observers who have considered this issue have concluded that it will take much more than strong patent rights to induce this type of research. Even in the United States, it took the *Orphan Drug Act* to make research into some drugs with relatively small demand profitable'[37] (under the *Orphan Drug Act*,[38] the United States government provides funding, tax benefits, and exclusive marketing rights to drug companies undertaking research into diseases affecting relatively small numbers of people).

If one takes the view that welfare-enhancing measures must produce positive effects in each country (which may make it easier to 'sell' intellectual property rules to domestic constituencies), then even a 'global' welfare increase may be insufficient to allay the concerns of developing nations.

[35] See, eg, Alan O Sykes, TRIPS, Pharmaceuticals, Developing Countries, and the Doha 'Solution' *loc cit*, at 62–6).

[36] *Ibid.*

[37] Th F Cotter, 'Market Fundamentalism and the Trips Agreement' *supra* n 33, at 335–6.

[38] 21 USC. § 360aa (2004).

4. TRIPS and Traditional Knowledge

The protection of traditional knowledge[39] has been discussed in international fora over last few years,[40] however, the Doha declaration has now put it at centre stage.[41] There are several reasons for the issue's sudden move to the forefront. First, a large number of countries believe that up to now they have not derived great benefits from 'traditional' forms of intellectual property, yet find themselves rich with traditional knowledge, especially genetic resources and folklore. They would like to exploit these resources, and several major companies share this interest. The second reason is the growing political importance of Aboriginal communities in several countries. While pharmaceutical and biotechnological companies are looking at ways to exploit indigenous medicinal knowledge, plants and other resources that are often found in developing countries, the Internet is progressively allowing creators of folklore or folklore-based copyrighted material to disseminate their material worldwide at very low cost.

In addition to the development of treaty or model provisions under the aegis of WIPO,[42] which could serve, at least initially, to produce norms on a regional basis, work in the Doha Round might lead to political recognition of the validity of some of the demands made by TK-rich developing countries.[43]

5. Factors Influencing Current Changes

The changing face of international intellectual property in respect of traditional knowledge is confirmed inter alia by the reference in the Doha Declaration to

[39] Traditional knowledge is a shorter form of 'traditional knowledge, innovations and practices'. See, eg, the Convention on Biological Diversity, 5 June 1992, Art 8(j). The Draft UN Declaration on the Rights of Indigenous Peoples, UN Document E/CN.4/1995/, uses the expression 'indigenous knowledge, cultures and traditional practices.' In its more recent documents, WIPO uses the expression 'traditional knowledge, innovations and creativity'. See Intellectual Property Needs and Expectations of Traditional Knowledge Holders, WIPO Report on Fact-finding Missions on Intellectual Property and Traditional Knowledge 21–2 (1998–1999) Traditional knowledge includes a broad range of subject matters, for example traditional agricultural, biodiversity-related and medicinal knowledge and folklore. See D Gervais, Traditional Knowledge and Intellectual Property: A TRIPS-Compatible Approach [2005] *Mich St L Rev* 137.

[40] For WIPO activities in this area see http://www.wipo.int/tk/en/. See also Ch Raghavan, ASEAN for Protecting Indigenous/Traditional Knowledge, Third World Network (May 5, 2000); J Mugabe, Intellectual Property Protection and Traditional Knowledge: An Exploration in International Policy Discourse, (Dec 1998); and A Cosbey, The Sustainable Development Effects of the WTO TRIPS Agreement: A Focus on Developing Countries (March 1999).

[41] Paragraph 19 reads in part as follows: '[Ministers] instruct the Council for TRIPS, in pursuing its work programme [. . .] to examine, inter alia, the relationship between the TRIPS Agreement and the Convention on Biological Diversity, the protection of traditional knowledge and folklore, and other relevant new developments raised by members pursuant to Article 71.1'.

[42] WIPO. Draft Provisions on the Protection of Traditional Knowledge (TK) and Draft Provisions on the Protection of Traditional Cultural Expressions/Expressions of Folklore (TCEs). Available at http://www.wipo.int/tk/en/consultations/draft_provisions/draft_provisions.html.

[43] See Gervais, *supra* note 40.

Articles 7 and 8 of TRIPS, ie the two provisions inserted originally to reflect the concerns of developing countries. Though they have been given little regard up to now in dispute-settlement proceedings in the WTO, these two provisions could be given a somewhat higher normative profile in future disputes because of what is a possible 'special status' in the Doha text.

Article 7 is cut from the same tree as paragraph 17 of the Doha Declaration embodying the idea of balance between protection and access.[44] This need for balance is voiced of course by many people in industrialized countries, which is another factor contributing to the fundamental change of the intellectual property landscape. There is increasingly recognition that, while intellectual property is necessary in certain areas to justify research and development expenditure, the optimal configuration of intellectual property norms cannot be readily ascertained on the basis of available empirical data, as s discussed below in Part II. Any ex ante analysis of the 'optimal system' is highly problematic and even ex post adjustments to the system are difficult to justify conclusively based on available data. Countries should ideally move towards evidence-based policy reforms, but that evidence is not always there. There is, in other words, an unavoidable element of (hopefully somewhat educated) guessing in making intellectual property policy.

The international intellectual property landscape was altered fairly radically over the last few years. This change was ostensibly driven by three main factors. First, many newcomers at the intellectual property table, those who may not have fully grasped the scope and depth of TRIPS obligations they signed up to in 1994, now possess much more sophisticated knowledge in the area of intellectual property norms. That knowledge is provided in part by movements in 'civil society' against intellectual property or at least against higher IP norms, which have led to a number of studies and alternative proposals.[45] Better knowledge about intellectual property has also prompted the development of research into the second factor, namely a more complete recognition that theoretically at least intellectual property has an optimal protection point. In other words, more intellectual property does not necessarily work better when measured in terms of the effectiveness of implementing the policy objective of incentivizing (ex ante) or rewarding (ex post) innovation. To quote the Supreme Court of Canada on this point: 'Excessive control by holders of copyrights and other forms of intellectual property may unduly limit the ability of the public domain

[44] See *supra* n 19.

[45] For a fairly comprehensive view, see the introductory chapter of this book by A Kamperman Sanders. One could mention the work done, mostly since 1995, by several well-known actors, including Lawrence Lessig, Frederick Abbott, Peter Drahos, Jerome Reichman, and Carlos Correa, to name but a few. Of course, scholarly work on the impact and optimal structure of intellectual property did not start with TRIPS, but the clash between copyright and privacy on the Internet (see D Gervais. Use of Copyright Content on the Internet: Considerations on Excludability and Collective Licensing, in M Geist (ed). Copyright Reform in Canada (Irwin Law, 2005) and the very public debacle over pharmaceutical patents on HIV and malarial drugs in Brazil and South Africa have taken the issue out of (only) specialized circles and into the public spotlight.

to incorporate and embellish creative innovation in the long-term interests of society as a whole, or create practical obstacles to proper utilization.'[46]

Falvey, Foster and Greenaway explain that balancing act as follows:

> A role for IPR protection arises because intellectual property displays many of the characteristics of a public good. It is typically non-rival and can be non-excludable. In the extreme these characteristics could remove the incentive to invest in R&D, and IPR protection can therefore restore that incentive. The importance of R&D and innovation has been emphasised by new growth theory [. . .]. In these models entrepreneurs invest in R&D in the expectation of profiting from their inventions. In addition to new products, innovation adds to a public stock of knowledge which lowers the cost of future innovation. Besides rewarding innovation, IPR protection stimulates the acquisition and dissemination of knowledge, since the information in patent claims is then available to other potential inventors. The rate of growth depends upon the rate of innovation and the stock of knowledge. Strong IPR protection need not always yield higher innovation and growth, however. Giving innovators too much protection may limit the spread of new ideas and lead to monopoly. Entry by rivals may be impeded, and successful innovators may have reduced incentives for developing and exploiting subsequent innovations.[47]

This allows us to posit that there must be an *intrinsic equilibrium* in intellectual property policies. Ideally, given the broader societal interests at play, one should not protect beyond what is necessary to achieve the policy objective(s) because the risk of a substantial negative general welfare impact is too high. However, as we will see below, it is extremely difficult to pinpoint that exact level, and governments thus have to make rules based on other criteria. One must also consider that many developing countries no longer accept the fact that TRIPS is a negative that must be accepted because of cross-sectoral concessions in the Uruguay Round. They want to learn how to benefit from intellectual property, maximizing the positives[48] while minimizing the negatives in terms of higher consumer prices, job losses and other welfare costs. They also have a better understanding of the trade-strategic game in which they are necessarily players.[49]

[46] *Théberge v Galerie d'Art du Petit Champlain inc*, 2002 SCC 34, <http://www.lexum.umontreal.ca/csc-scc/en/pub/2002/vol2/html/2002scr2_0336.html>, [2002] 2 SCR 336 at para 32.

[47] R Falvey, N Foster and D Greenaway, Intellectual Property Rights and Economic Growth (2004). Internationalisation of Economic Policy Research Paper No 2004/12. http://ssrn.com/abstract=715982, at 2.

[48] Prof Peter Yu explains that intellectual property may appeal to leaders in developing countries because it holds out the promise of new jobs, FDI, tax revenues, technology transfer and the development of local artists, inventors and indigenous industries. PK Yu, From Pirates to Partners: Protecting Intellectual Property in China in the Twenty-First Century (2000), 50 *Am U L Rev* 131, 192–3.

[49] See S Scotchmer. Innovation and Incentives (MIT Press, 2004), at 329:

> . . . intellectual property rights are no longer a way to encourage domestic innovation. They also become a strategic instrument to affect profit flows among nations. To affect profit flows favorably, each country wants the strongest possible protections in foreign countries, and the weakest possible protections for foreigners in its own domestic market.

The third and last factor influencing current changes is the increasingly visible intersection between intellectual property and other rights broadens the base of the search for balance. The search for an *extrinsic equilibrium* then becomes unavoidable. The interplay between the intrinsic and extrinsic equilibriums is apparent in a recent Canadian Supreme Court decision:

> Our Court has often spoken of 'the balance struck under the *Patent Act*' in which the public gives an inventor the right to prevent anybody else from using his or her invention for a period of 20 years in exchange for disclosure of what has been invented. As a general rule, if the patent holder obtains a monopoly for something which does not fulfil the statutory requirements of novelty, ingenuity and utility, then the public is short-changed. [. . .]
>
> In the present appeal, the Court is required to consider this 'balance' in the much-litigated field of patented medicines, where Parliament is concerned not only with the balance between inventors and potential users, but between the protection of intellectual property on the one hand and, on the other hand, the desire to reduce health care costs while being fair to those whose ingenuity brought the drugs into existence in the first place'.[50]

Indeed it seems difficult to contradict that intellectual property policy should be solidly based on economic grounds. It would seem almost absurd to limit the analysis of intellectual property to traditional natural right theories, such as the Lockean view of a right in one's labour, or as a Kantian/Hegelian view of (mostly copyright) creations being imbued with their author's personality (creating an inextinguishable link between the creator and the creation).[51] When the societal impacts of intellectual property are factored in, those philosophical views seem to provide insufficient justifications, at least when the debates focus not generally on whether intellectual property should exist[52] but on what it should protect, in what circumstances and for what period of time. That debate tends to be more productive when participants accept an instrumentalist version of utilitarianism as the proper starting point. That foundation recognizes that intellectual property is essential to avoid certain market failures, because ideas, creations and inventions are (without legal protection) non-exclusive and non-rivalrous, profits are not. In other words, while many people can share an idea, the same cannot be said in many cases of companies seeking to profit from the

[50] *Bristol-Myers Squibb Co v Canada* (Attorney General), 2005 SCC 26, at paras 1–2.

[51] 'Natural rights are those which always appertain to [human beings] in right of [their] existence. Of this kind are all the intellectual rights, rights of the mind, and also all those rights of acting as individuals of [their] own comfort and happiness, which are not injurious to the rights of others.' (Thomas Paine, The Rights of Man). For a general overview of the various theories, see T Fisher, Theories of Intellectual Property, in S Munzer, ed, New Essays in the Legal and Political Theory of Property (Cambridge University Press, 2001).

[52] A debate at that level is not altogether helpful. It often rests on a rejection of the dominant neo-liberal model and/or emphasizes the fact that corporations are only thinking on profits and those who manage them are only driven by greed and power. That said, the higher level critiques of the 'system' may lead to better 'corporate citizenship'. Cynics are quick to argue that those efforts are themselves usually marketing driven so as to allow the corporation to make more profit (and hence tends to demonstrate the fact that the two are not incompatible).

making and selling of creations or inventions embodying the idea. By the same token, however, intellectual property rules should aim to improve general welfare and be fair to social interests at play even if this cannot be or is not measured at the level of individuals. That is, in fact, the apparent paradox of intellectual property: the law grants a monopoly to allow society to gain access to new creations and inventions: to ensure that we can gain access, we limit access.

I suggest that the two results of the above analysis, namely the recognition of the two equilibria (intrinsic/extrinsic) and the adoption of an instrumentalist view of intellectual property are here to stay, at least for the predictable future. Future multilateral discussions will necessarily have to take that into account. That may explain why, as other Chapters of this book demonstrate, the best escape for those who do not want to explore this new policy terrain are quickly moving their ammunition to the bilateral field.[53]

III. ECONOMIC ANALYSIS

1. Recent Economic Surveys

This Part looks at a number of recent analyses of available empirical evidence about the impact of intellectual property protection. Clearly, the analysis is far from exhaustive. It only tries to identify trends based on the latest available data.

a) Impact of intellectual property protection on economic growth

As we embark on this analysis, it is worth noting that, in contrast to the very large number of studies dealing with the impact of intellectual property protection of one type or another in major industrialized nations, there is a relative dearth in empirical analyses of the nature and impact of intellectual property in developing economies.[54] Studies are starting to emerge, however and those[55]

[53] See RL Okediji, Back to Bilateralism? Pendulum Swings in International Intellectual Property Protection (2003-2004) 1 *Univ Ottawa L & Tech J* 125, available at http://www.uoltj.ca/articles/vol1.1-2/2003-2004.1.1-2.uoltj.Okediji.125-147.pdf

[54] Thus it is not surprising that in its proposal concerning WIPO's Development Agenda in June 2005 a group of Arab countries led by Bahrain proposed that WIPO should 'prepare studies on intellectual property, in cooperation with Member States, to demonstrate the economic, social and cultural impact of the use of intellectual property systems in Member States, with particular emphasis on the contribution of cultural industries to national economies.' Proposal by the Kingdom of Bahrain on the Importance of Intellectual Property in Social and Economic Development and National Development Programs, WIPO document IIM/2/2, June 14, 2005, Annex, at p 6.

In his interesting book on intellectual property in China (see *supra* note 22) Professor William Alford aptly notes:

> ". . . there are all too few attempts to portray [the] operation [of intellectual property] in any systematic fashion. Most such efforts are either anecdotal or uncritically dependent on data provided

consulted in the preparation of this paper offer a fairly blurred and complex picture of the advantages of higher intellectual property protection in developing economies. A simple equation cannot be drawn between an increase in trade following the introduction of TRIPS-compatible intellectual property protection, on the one hand, and economic development on the other, especially when measured in terms of welfare increases.[56] As Falvey, Foster and Greenaway stated in their 2004 study: 'the overall effects of stronger IPRs on technology acquisition and aggregate growth are in general ambiguous'.[57] Differences in the level of economic development of each country[58] matter greatly. One must also make appropriate distinctions between the various types of intellectual property protection (patents, trade marks, copyrights, plant variety, etc) or within a subsystem (patents for industrial machines compared to patents for pharmaceutical products, computer software or chemical agricultural inventions).

A study by Thompson and Rushing showed that IPRs were unlikely to generate positive effects below a certain minimum threshold of economic development. Thompson and Rushing had set that level at US$3,400 (in 1980 dollars)[59] or more than $8300 in 2005 dollars. An interesting 2004 study by Falvey, Foster and Greenaway,[60] which used a different regression model, demonstrated the non-linearity of the relationship between IPRs and economic

> by trade associations and other interested parties [. . .] Moreover, the intangible nature of intellectual property complicates the detection of its unlawful appropriation.

(*Ibid* at 6).

[55] Some of the recent most non-country-specific noteworthy efforts include: C Fink and KE Maskus (eds). Intellectual Property and Development (2004); W Martin and L Alan Winters. The Uruguay Round and Developing Countries (1996); Falvey *et al*, *supra* note 48; S Scotchmer, The Political Economy of Intellectual Property Treaties (2004), 20 *J of L Econ and Org* 415, 435–6: 'National treatment increases incentives to innovate, especially in an environment where local markets are not large enough to support invention. However, national treatment also creates problems. [. . .] it can lead to an asymmetry where, for a particular subject matter, one country protects all innovation that takes place in the member states, and consumers in the other member states free ride. But for subject matters that do not require extensive protection, there is a more natural and more equitable asymmetry, which national treatment does not permit. The more natural solution would be for each country to protect its own innovators, and for countries to exchange spill-over benefits.'

See also OECD Science, Technology and Industry Outlook 2004. (OECD, 2004); also by the OECD, Patents, Innovation and Economic Performance: Conference Proceedings (OECD, 2004); and the report of the UK IPR Commission, infra note 75 and accompanying text; and

[56] C Fink and CA Primo Braga, 'How Stronger Protection of Intellectual Property Rights Affects International trade Flows', in C Fink and KE Maskus, *supra* n 55, at 21 ('The implications of IPRs for economic welfare are complex. The simple fact that trade flows rise or fall in response to tighter IPRs is not sufficient for drawing conclusions regarding economic welfare. Both static and dynamic effects need to be considered'). Obviously, increase in overall economic development may not translate in a reduction of poverty. Other factors, such as wealth distribution and corruption are relevant. See, eg, Jagdish Bhagwati, *supra* n 10.

[57] Supra n 56, at 1.

[58] Something that TRIPS recognized at least indirectly by treating least-developing countries differently than developing ones. See TRPS Art 66. See Falvey *et al*, *supra* n 56.

[59] MA Thompson and FW Rushing. An Empirical Analysis of the Impact of Patent Protection on Economic Growth, [1996] *J of Econ Dev* 21, 61–79.

[60] *Supra* n 48.

growth and identified 'threshold effects'. Essentially, the level of the positive effect of IPRs depends on whether a developing country is capable of imitating and innovating. Otherwise, IPRs may merely reinforce the market power of exporters.

According to that study, IPR protection is growth enhancing in both low (beyond a strict minimum) and high income countries, but has only a small positive impact on growth in middle income countries. In fact for middle income countries, 'no significant relationship was found' between the level of intellectual property protection and growth. In other words, poorer developing countries (but probably not least-developed ones) are poised to benefit from IPR protection due to inward Foreign Direct Investment (FDI) and new imports, as a new source of technology transfer. The Falvey, Foster and Greenaway study did not find any evidence that introducing intellectual property protection had reduced growth in any country.

b) FDI vs trade

In parsing the results of available studies, in is clear that there are two main indicators that are helpful to analyse the precise impact of increasing intellectual property protection, namely (a) the increase of trade flows in goods that include a significant intellectual property component (as compared to the physical value of the material and components—two examples would be a music CD and a patented pharmaceutical molecule, areas which may be referred to as 'intellectual property sensitive'; and (b) the increase in inward FDI concerning goods or services that require a high level of intellectual property protection. It is essential to measure both because, to a certain extent at least, they cancel each other out: a company in country A (export) may send goods to country B but it may instead opt for local production (under license) in country B.

On the link between trade flows and intellectual property, Carsten Fink and Carlos Primo Braga conclude one recent analysis as follows:

> Economic analysis suggests that the effects of IPR protection on bilateral trade flows are theoretically ambiguous. Because of the complex static and dynamic considerations related to a policy of tighter protection, it is difficult to generate normative recommendations. When we estimate the effects of IPR protection in a gravity model of bilateral trade flows, our empirical results suggest that, on average, higher levels of protection have a significantly positive effect on nonfuel trade. However, this result is not confirmed when confining the estimation to high technology goods, for which we found IPRs to have no significant effect. These results are consistent with the literature.[61]

Their analysis is based on data available from 89 countries. If their conclusion is correct, then higher levels of protection are useful in areas other than fuel (and presumably raw resources pre-value added transformation) and, surprisingly

[61] *Supra*, n 56.

high technology.[62] They suggest five possible explanations as to why there is no measurable positive impact in the case of high technology goods:

— strong market power which may offset the positive market expansion effects of higher protection;
— higher foreign direct investment (FDI) may lower international trade (as discussed above);
— it is possible that the impact of intellectual property protection was not accurately measured;
— factors in the destination country (country of export) may matter more than intellectual property. These include first mover advantage;
— finally, tariff and non-tariff barriers may impede trade flows.[63]

These factors, they argue, could reduce the sensitivity to the level of intellectual property protection, seen as a mere adjuvant to protection stemming from market power or, at the other end of the axis, the absence of exports of FDI in a given country may be the result of factors other than the unavailability of enforceable adequate intellectual property rules. There may be softer issues at play, one could suggest, including cultural barriers or an imperfect dissemination of information about a country's situation. I will come back to this issue in Pat IV below.

In a recent analysis of the FDI component and its relation to intellectual property, Professor Maskus concluded as follows:

> . . . although there are indications that strengthening IPRs can be an effective means of including additional inward FDI, it is only one component of a far broader set of important influences. Emerging economies should recognize the strong complementarities among IPRs, market liberalization and deregulation, technology development policies, and competition regimes.[64]

While one may agree with the 'broader picture' painted by the author, unfortunately the conclusions of the study are based on IMF data showing increases in inward and outward FDI between the years 1987 and 1995. In many cases, IPR protection increased sharply after the entry into force of the TRIPS Agreement in developing countries, which, except for least-developed ones, had until January 2000 to comply.[65] In China's case, the date of TRIPS compliance coincided with its becoming a WTO member on 11 December 2001.[66] Pre-2000 data

[62] In fact those results seem at odds with Mansfield's 1994 study of US business executives, which found that IP protection influenced mostly executives in high tech industries. The study is referenced at note 6, *supra*. For a discussion, see PJ Heald, Misreading a Canonical Work: An Analysis of Mansfield's 1994 Study (2003), 10 *J of Int Prop L* 309.

[63] *Ibid*, at 28.

[64] KE Maskus, Intellectual Property Rights in Encouraging FDI and Technology Transfer, *in* C Fink and KE Maskus (eds), *supra* n 55, at 70–1.

[65] TRIPS Agreement, Art 65. For patents on pharmaceuticals in countries where patents were previously unavailable for inventions of that type, the transitional period ended on 1 January 2005 (TRIPS Art 65(4)).

[66] See www.wto.org (last accessed 2 July 2005). See also Yahong Li. Pushing For Greater Protection—The Trend Toward Greater Protection of Intellectual Property in the Chinese Software Industry and the Implications for the Rule of Law in China (2002), 23 *U Pa J Int'l Econ L* 637.

may thus not offer ideal parameters to do a full analysis of the current situation. Another study dealing with China tended to show that there was only a weak correlation between higher intellectual property and increased FDI in that market, perhaps as a reflection of the size of the Chinese market and the political clout of the 'new China'.

In another analysis of the situation in China, economists found that there had been a very significant increase in patent and trademark activity in China. Their data tended to show that:

> . . . IPRs are effective devices for handling particular market failures associated with cultural creation and invention and technology use. These market failures become more acute as economies grow, meaning that the need for effective patents, trademarks, trade secrets protection, and copyrights increases over time.[67]

However, they also concluded that

> . . . stronger IPRs alone are not sufficient to establish effective conditions for technology development and growth. Rather, they must be embedded in a broader set of complementary initiatives that maximize the potential of IPRs to be dynamically procompetitive.[68]

A different study concerning the situation of FDI in so-called 'transition economies'[69] is perhaps more illuminating because those countries were for the most part closed to FDI until 1990 or so. The study concludes confirmed intuitive conclusions, in particular that FDI in intellectual property sensitive areas is discouraged when intellectual property protection is weak; and that, across all sectors, low IPR protection encourages foreign firms to focus on distribution rather than local production.[70]

In the specific area of pharmaceuticals, available data analyzed in another study show that, at least for the large Indian market, the introduction of patent protection is likely to lead to both price increases (and related welfare effects) and increased research and development. However, the research also shows that only 10.9 per cent of the top 500 pharmaceuticals in that market are patented. Additionally, the government retained certain tools, including price controls and, in cases where this is allowed by Article 31 of TRIPS, compulsory licenses.[71]

[67] KE Maskus, SM Dougherty and A Mertha, Intellectual Property Rights and Economic Development in China, in *ibid*, at 327.

[68] *Ibid.*

[69] Essentially countries in Central and Eastern Europe that formed part of the former Soviet block. Art 65(3) of the TRIPS Agreement refers to them as 'Member[s] which [are] in the process of transformation from a centrally-planned into a market, free-enterprise economy and which [are] undertaking structural reform of [their] intellectual property system.'

[70] See B Smarzynska Javorcik, The Composition of Foreign Direct Investment and Protection of Intellectual Property Rights: Evidence from Transition Economies (2004), 48:1 *Eur Econ Rev* 39.

[71] See C Fink, Patent Protection, Transnational Corporations, and Market Structure: A Simulation Study of the Indian Pharmaceutical Industry in C Fink and KE Maskus (eds), *supra* n 55, at 250–1.

In an analysis in a much different and smaller market, namely Lebanon, a team of economists concluded that introducing TRIPS-compatible intellectual property protection would lead to:

> . . . additional technology transfer [to Lebanon] and further local product development. The average quality of products and services on the market should rise. Although the associated price effects would be problematic for low-income consumers, there should be dynamic gains from greater efficiency of inputs over time, while consumers will benefit from additional certainty about the signalling value of trademarks.[72]

The 2002 Report produced by the UK Commission on Intellectual Property Rights[73] presented a picture generally in agreement with the above findings but also stressed that it was important no to consider developing countries as a homogeneous group. As the Report noted:

> . . . it is important to remember the technological disparity between developed and developing countries as a group. Low and middle income developing countries account for about 21 per cent of world GDP, but for less than 10 per cent of worldwide research and development (R&D) expenditure. The OECD countries spend far more on R&D than India's total national income. Almost without exception, developing countries are net importers of technology.

It is essential to consider the diversity of developing countries in respect of their social and economic circumstances and technological capabilities. Altogether more than 60 per cent of the world's poor live in countries that have significant scientific and technological capabilities, and the great majority of them live in China and India. China and India, along with several other smaller developing countries, have world class capacity in a number of scientific and technological areas including, for instance, space, nuclear energy, computing, biotechnology, pharmaceuticals, software development and aviation. By contrast, 25 per cent of poor people live in Sub-Saharan Africa (excluding South Africa), mainly in countries with relatively weak technical capacity. It is estimated that in 1994 China, India and Latin America together accounted for nearly 9 per cent of worldwide research expenditure, but sub-Saharan Africa accounted for only 0.5 per cent and developing countries other than India and China only about 4 per cent.

Thus developing countries are far from homogeneous, a fact which is self-evident but often forgotten. Not only do their scientific and technical capacities vary, but also their social and economic structures, and their inequalities of income and wealth. The determinants of poverty, and therefore the appropriate policies to address it, will vary accordingly between countries. The same applies to policies on IPRs. Policies required in countries with a relatively advanced

[72] KE Maskus, Strengthening Intellectual Property Rights in Lebanon, in C Fink and KE Maskus (eds), *supra* n 55, at 289.

[73] Entitled Integrating Intellectual Property Rights and Development Policy (2002), available at http://www.iprcommission.org/graphic/documents/final_report.htm

technological capability where most poor people happen to live, for instance India or China, may well differ from those in other countries with a weak capability, such as many countries in sub-Saharan Africa. The impact of IP policies on poor people will also vary according to socio-economic circumstances. What works in India, will not necessarily work in Brazil or Botswana.[74]

In sum, economic analysis on the IP/FDI/Trade economic triangle tends to demonstrate that sufficient intellectual property protection is an essential component of increased inward FDI and trade flows (in intellectual property sensitive goods) for countries above a certain economic development threshold. The trade regime (especially tariffs and non-tariff barriers), tax and competition laws are also potent influences. This seems consistent with studies that tend to show that the propensity to patent (as opposed to, eg, protect as confidential information) is also directly dependent on such factors.[75] It also shows that not

[74] Entitled Integrating Intellectual Property Rights and Development Policy (2002) at pp 1–2 (footnotes omitted).

[75] See N Gallini, J Putnam and A Tepperman, Intellectual Property Rights and the Propensity to Patent, paper prepared for the OECD Conference on Intellectual Property and Innovation in the Knowledge-based Economy (May 2001). Available at http://strategis.ic.gc.ca/pics/ip/gallini.pdf (last accessed 2 July 2005); W Cohen, RR Nelson and J Walsh, 'Protecting their intellectual assets: Appropriability conditions and why US manufacturing firms patent (or not)', NBER Working Paper 7522 (2000); and JP Walsh, A Arora and WM Cohen, Effects of Research Tool Patents and Licensing on Biomedical Innovation, in WM Cohen and SA Merrill (eds). Patents In The Knowledge-Based Economy (Nat'l Academies Press, 2003), 285–6:

> Over the last two decades changes in technology and policy have altered the landscape of drug discovery. These changes have led to concerns that the patent system may be creating difficulties for those trying to do research in biomedical fields. [. . .] We find that there has in fact been an increase in patents on the inputs to drug discovery ('research tools'). However, we find that drug discovery has not been substantially impeded by these changes. We also find little evidence that university research has been impeded by concerns about patents on research tools. Restrictions on the use of patented genetic diagnostics, where we see some evidence of patents interfering with university research, are an important exception. There is, also, some evidence of delays associated with negotiating access to patented research tools, and there are areas in which patents over targets limit access and where access to foundational discoveries can be restricted. There are also cases in which research is redirected to areas with more intellectual property (IP) freedom.

And at 333–4:

> We have observed that holders of IP on nonrival research tools often charge prices that permit broad access, at least among firms. In some of these cases, the IP holders have also charged higher prices to commercial clients and lower prices to university and other researchers who intended to use the tool largely for noncommercial purposes. From a social welfare perspective, such price discrimination expands the use of the tool and is welfare enhancing. There are, however, cases in which the IP holder cannot or does not develop a pricing strategy that allows low-value and academic projects access to the tool [. . .]

The concern with regard to IP access tends to be the greatest when a research tool is rival-in-use and is potentially key to progress in one or more broad therapeutic areas. When a foundational research tool is rival-in-use, the IP holders often either attempt to develop the technology themselves or grant exclusive licenses. As suggested above, exclusive exploitation of a foundational discovery is unlikely to realize the full potential for building on that discovery because no one firm can even conceive of all the different ways that the discovery might be exploited, let alone actually do so. [. . .] The social welfare analysis of this situation is, however, not straightforward. Even though knowledge, once developed, can be shared at little additional cost and may be best exploited through broad access, it does not follow that social welfare is maximized by mandating low-cost

all developing or least-developed nations can be treated alike. It seems that whether a particular country has the capacity to make good use of an imported technology and eventually to compete with its own research and development efforts (including to adapt the technology to local demand, if need be) are determinative.

c) FDI v 'comfort levels'

Those conclusions are hardly surprising. It is well known that FDI decisions are based on the level of 'comfort' of global technology exporters. The impact is greater as the intellectual property sensitivity increases, though not necessarily for high technology goods, probably due to the factors identified by Fink and Primo Braga.[76] The difference in 'comfort level' can be measured by comparing the rise in research and development expenditures in various recipient countries. For example, in OECD countries, where intellectual property and a number of other normative aspects are harmonized, and where business and cultural ties may, in certain cases, be relevant, the picture which emerges is fairly clear:

> Recent analysis based on firm-level data indicates that MNEs make sizeable contributions to productivity growth in their home and host countries and are important conduits for technology transfer. MNEs accounted for more of the growth in labour productivity in Belgium, the United Kingdom and the United States than uni-national or unaffiliated domestic firms; they also contributed to technological spill-overs that improve innovative performance in both home and host countries[77]

And further:

> Foreign affiliates account for a growing share of business R&D. Although R&D remains less internationalised than production, total R&D expenditures of foreign affiliates increased between 1991 and 2001 by more than 50 per cent in the OECD area. In 2001, foreign affiliates accounted for 15 per cent to 20 per cent of total manufacturing R&D in France, Germany and the United States; between 30 per cent and 40 per cent in Canada, the Netherlands, Spain, Sweden and the United Kingdom; and more than 70 per cent in Hungary and Ireland. Not surprisingly, R&D investments by foreign affiliates are highly sector-specific, with the ICT, chemicals (including pharmaceuticals) and transport sectors accounting for the vast majority. While patterns of R&D investment by foreign affiliates correspond to patterns of manufacturing investment, the location of business R&D is influenced not only by the need to tailor products to local markets but also by a desire to tap into local sources of scientific and technical knowledge. Nevertheless, the R&D intensity (R&D as a share of turnover) of foreign affiliates is below that of firms indigenous to the host country in all countries except Hungary and Ireland, and by a wide margin in most cases.[78]

access if such access dampens the incentive to develop the research tool to begin with. Many of the same kinds of 'working solutions' that mitigate the prospect of an anticommons also apply to the issue of access for research. Our interviews suggest that a key 'working solution,' however, is likely infringement under the guise of a 'research exemption.'

[76] See *supra* n 64 and accompanying text.

[77] OECD Science, Technology and Industry Outlook 2004, *supra* n 55, at 17–18.

[78] *Ibid* at 170.

OECD statistics show that total net FDI (outflows minus inflows) for the years 1990, 1995, 1998, 1999, 2000 and 2001 stood at 1.02 trillion US dollars, 862 billion US dollars of which (85 per cent) came from the 15 pre-expansion member countries of he European Union.[79] The same statistics show that while the total penetration in manufacturing (defined as the percentage of imports in domestic demand) grew in OECD countries from 20 per cent to 26 per cent between 1992 and 1999, in the high-technology manufactures area,[80] that percentage grew from 31 per cent to 43 per cent and in pharmaceuticals specifically from 17 per cent to 27 per cent.[81] And it must be borne in mind in that respect that almost all patents and trademarks belong to enterprises based in Western Europe, North America and Japan:

> By 2001, R&D spending in [China, Israel and the Russian Federation] had risen to USD 85 billion, or 14.7 per cent of OECD R&D expenditures. When a fuller set of non-member economies, including Argentina, Romania, Singapore and Chinese Taipei, are added to the calculation, the share rises to 17 per cent. Hence, while R&D spending has grown rapidly in non-[OECD]member economies, it remains at about one-sixth the level of OECD countries. Relative shares of patent families show a similar pattern. The United States, the EU25 and Japan accounted for 94.4 per cent of all triadic patent families in 1991; by 2000, that share had declined modestly to 92.7 per cent, with most of the reduction in the shares of EU and Japanese patent holders. The share of all countries outside the United States, EU25 and Japan rose from 5.6 per cent to 7.3 per cent. It can be expected that this share will continue to rise as other countries become more fully integrated into global innovation structures.[82]

The same data confirm a significant growth in both exports and global research and development. Two important caveats are in order, however. First exports grew more quickly than 'delocalized' R&D. Second, the growth in exported R&D activity was far from uniform, with growth in OECD countries outpacing most non OECD member countries, with some exceptions, especially China, Israel and the Russian Federation.

More importantly perhaps for our purposes, there seems to be an important difference between increased trade flows (in this case in the form of imports) and inward FDI when economic development is taken into account. When higher intellectual property rules allow foreign firms to begin exporting intellectual property sensitive goods and services to a country, local consumers and industries gain (lawful) access to those products ands services. This may result in welfare gains, though it may also lead to price increases especially when goods whose status changes to 'pirate' or 'counterfeit' after the introduction of IPR protection are displaced by genuine goods sold at a higher price.[83] Increased

[79] OECD Science, Technology and Industry Outlook 2004, *supra* n 55, at 234.

[80] Pharmaceuticals, office and computing machinery; radio, television and communication equipment; medical, precision and optical instruments; and aircraft and spacecraft

[81] OECD Outlook, *supra* n 55, at 233.

[82] *Ibid*, at 39.

[83] See Falvey *et al*, *supra* n 48, at 2.

trade flows may lead to new jobs in distributorships and the retail sector, but those are likely to be low-skilled, low-paying positions. There may also be significant gains in terms of product quality and reliability, especially in the area of pharmaceuticals.

Inward FDI is a more powerful economic development lever. It transfers technology and usually creates jobs requiring a higher level of skills. This may be the case for manufacturing of technology-intensive goods, requiring engineering and quality control jobs, as well as management and other softer skill sets. In the best scenario, some research and development jobs are created, which may have spill-over effects in higher education, local laboratories, etc.

If one were to pinpoint sector-specific impacts, it would seem reasonable to conclude that in the copyright area music, films and books are unlikely to be distributed—and national cultural industries able to develop—in the absence of sufficient rights and enforcement options. In those areas, the gains generated by establishing sufficient protection are 'unambiguous'.[84] However, the introduction or beginning of enforcement of copyrights will lead to the closure of businesses that rely on copying, thus displacing (mostly unskilled) workers. Hopefully, some of them will be able to find work in the new, creative industry jobs made possible by the adequate protection of copyrights.[85] These new jobs are likely to pay higher wages and stimulate creativity, while reducing the need felt by local creators to live in higher protection countries, but as exiles. In high technology areas, such as computer chips or advanced electronic components, the level of protection is possibly less crucial due, at least in part, to the lack of ability to reverse engineer and produce pirated versions, and the market power of the main international players.[86]

Trade mark protection is an essential ingredient to generate higher inward FDI. The purpose of trade marks is two-fold: first, to protect the public by indicating the source of goods and services in order that purchasers can identify the level of quality they seek and receive a similar product or consistent service over time; and second, to protect the trade mark owner against commercial misappropriation of the mark and/or the goodwill associated with the mark. The value of a mark stems from the mental link that is created over time in the minds of prospective buyers between particular goods or services and a particular source. Many people buy a product or service because consciously or unconsciously they associate qualities such as value, excellence, or efficiency, with the trade mark. The capacity of a mark to raise these associations explains why a strong trade mark is invaluable—it directs a potential buyer towards a company's own product or service rather than those of a competitor. Trade marks are influenced both by seller's perceptions about buyer psychology and the public's marketing-influenced perceptions of goods and services and how they are differentiated. Trade marks also serve an informational purpose: The legal

[84] KE Maskus, Strengthening Intellectual Property Rights in Lebanon, *supra* n 74, at 286.
[85] See *ibid*, at 286–7.
[86] See *supra* n 64 and accompanying text.

protection of marks gives companies an incentive to invest in making their marks more easily recognized and more easily remembered by consumers so consumers can identify which particular good or service they want, and consumers save time searching for the appropriate product or service.

Trademark protection will, as in the case of copyrights, lead to the closure or businesses producing counterfeit goods, but that economic activity could be replaced by jobs in distribution, retail and franchises.[87] These are often low-level, low-skilled jobs, however. Trade mark protection will also benefit consumers who will benefit from 'genuine' goods, ie, goods that come with the assurance of quality associated with the mark through domestic or international advertising and reputation. Over time, the experience in product assembly, delivery and servicing, as well as management acquired in franchise and distributorship arrangements may be transferred to new, local businesses.

The area of patents is also critically important, but not because patent ensures that new products will be supplied in the short term. When patent protection is unavailable, products that would otherwise infringe a patent could be made available legally for the domestic market. In terms of FDI, however, the impact is exactly the reverse because global firms that rely on patent protection need assurances about the level of protection and enforcement before considering any significant technology transfer. Working a patent often requires know-how that is not fully disclosed in the published patent or patent application. Ongoing research and variants of the patented inventions may also exist. For this reason, firms also consider the level of protection of trade secrets (confidential information) for information that, for strategic or other reasons, is not disclosed in a patent. In fact, for certain process patents, even in the presence of a presumption that a product not previously available results from a new patented process,[88] many companies prefer not to disclose new processes in patent applications.[89] Direct patent-related inward FDI is often the best way to create high-paying, highly skilled jobs and it is therefore highly sought after by many governments, who sometimes bend over backwards to attract foreign firms.[90]

2. 'Balance'

> . . . our goal, which we hope is one that can be shared by all Member States, of ensuring that the international IP system functions for the good of all, with benefits out-

[87] See AH Khoury. The Effects of Trademarks on Arab Countries in the Middle East. Doctoral dissertation, University of Haifa (2005).

[88] Article 34(1) of the TRIPS Agreement reads in relevant part as follows:

> . . . if the subject matter of a patent is a process for obtaining a product, the judicial authorities shall have the authority to order the defendant to prove that the process to obtain an identical product is different from the patented process.

[89] See W Cohen, RR Nelson and J Walsh, *supra* n 77; and SA Merrill, RC Levin, and MB Myers. A Patent System for the 21st Century (Nat'l Academies Press, 2004), at 20–3.

[90] See B Smarzynska Javorcik, *supra* n 72, at 60.

weighing any costs and in a way which encourages, and does not hinder, sustainable economic, social and cultural development.[91]

Balance is ostensibly what everyone is striving towards.[92] But what is it? It is not, contrary to what often reads or hears in policy debates concerning intellectual property, a simple axis with rightholders at one end, and users of intellectual property on the other. For one thing, there is no uniform categorization that holds up to serious scrutiny. All rightholders have to get their 'inspiration' from somewhere or someone.

How can a government who wishes to do so adopt a 'balanced' innovation policy? Should that government err on the side of high protection or rather protect the 'public domain' and limit protection until a need for protection is shown? Should it take the policy gamble of increasing protection to see if it produces positive results without major or even overwhelming negative externalities? Clearly, it seems easier to make intellectual property policy ex post facto and adjust the framework, rather than wait for a perfect model to emerge from theoretical economic analysis. That analysis is complex inter alia because each sector of intellectual property (and sub-sectors: should industrial machines, business models, biotechnology, HIV drugs and chemical agricultural products be treated the same because they are protected by patents?). I suggest that not only should a government favour a 'balanced' approach, it must also decide where to intervene and when.

Balance, then, is far from being a simple game of 'pulling covers' and trying to please the often short-sighted demands of lobbies representing rightholders or various users or public interest groups. Balance means achieving an optimal

[91] Proposal by the United Kingdom to the Inter-Sessional Intergovernmental Meeting on a Development Agenda for WIPO (Annex), WIPO Document IIM/2/3, June 14, 2005.

[92] Examples include: Federal Trade Commission, To Promote Innovation: The Proper Balance of Competition and Patent Law and Policy Executive Summary, 19 Berkeley *Tech L J* 861 (2004); S Rodriguez Hurley, Failing to Balance Patent Rights and Antitrust Concerns: The Federal Circuit's Holding in *In Re Independent Service Organizations* Antitrust Litigation (2003–2004), 13 Fed Circuit BJ 475; PJ Gardner, US Intellectual Property Law and the Biotech Challenge: Searching for an Elusive Balance [2003] BJ 28; H Soehnge, The Drug Price Competition and Patent Term Restoration Act of 1984: Fine-Tuning the Balance Between the Interests of Pioneer and Generic Drug Manufacturers (2003), 58 Food & Drug LJ 51; KE Maskus, E Vivian Wong, Searching for Economic Balance in Business Method Patents (2002), 8 *Wash U JL & Pol'y* 289; A Lacayo, Seeking A Balance: International Pharmaceutical Patent Protection, Public Health Crises, and the Emerging Threat of Bio-Terrorism (2002), 33 *U Miami Inter-Am L Rev* 295 ; JS Golian, Without a Net: The Supreme Court Attempts to Balance Patent Protection and Public Notice in *Festo Corp. v Shoketsu Kinzoku Kogyo Kabushiki Co* (2003), 36 *Creighton L Rev* 541; J Langenfeld, Intellectual Property and Antitrust: Steps Toward Striking a Balance (2001), 52 Case *W Res L Rev* 91; JA Harrelson, TRIPS, Pharmaceutical Patents, and the HIV/AIDS Crisis: Finding the Proper Balance Between Intellectual Property Rights and Compassion (2001), 7 Widener L Symp J 175; T Klein, The Uncertain Balance Between Parody and Trademark Rights (2001), 12 J Contemp. Legal Issues 356; RG Frenkel, Intellectual Property in the Balance: Proposals for Improving Industrial Design Protection in the Post-TRIPS Era (1999), 32 *Loy LA L Rev* 531; AN Littman, Restoring the Balance of Our Patent System (1997), 37 IDEA 545; JC Yates MR Greenlee, Intellectual Property on the Internet: Balance of Interests Between the Cybernauts and the Bureaucrats (1996), 8:7 *J Proprietary Rights* 8.

degree of protection, which appropriately protects and rewards creativity and ingenuity, thus providing a good incentive to continue, while not deterring others' creativity and inventiveness. That optimal point is hard to define, and in fact will likely vary from country to country based on socio-economic, industrial and even cultural factors,[93] as will be more fully explained below.

Because TRIPS establishes a uniform normative 'common denominator', its implementation should be a combination of a careful analysis of the proper intellectual property policy of a country or region and use of flexibility left in TRIPS to achieve this policy objective. That determination of the most appropriate TRIPS-compatible legal framework must then be combined with corresponding policies in relevant sectors, use of systems such as compulsory licensing but only where appropriate etc, as well as training of government and private sector players. While this may seem self-evident, one of the most striking problems of many developing countries as a group is the absence of advanced research on determining an adequate intellectual property policy to maximize a country's growth, culturally and economically. There are, however, signs that this is changing, in countries like Brazil, China and India for instance.

This kind of analysis is necessary because the pre-TRIPS historical development of norms was a haphazard process and may not offer sufficient economic, social or philosophical justifications for continuing along the same path without further analysis.[94] In parallel, many countries argue that major industrialised countries only adopted high protection norms *after* they had developed economically. All this is now strongly reinforced by views emerging within industrialized countries not only about the possible negative impact of imposing too high protection norms on developing countries but also on the development of a vibrant technological and creative culture.[95] But, as will be seen below, those may not be valid reasons to pour scorn on TRIPS.

3. WIPO's Development Agenda

A more 'balanced' approach to intellectual property regulation was adopted by the World Intellectual Property Organization (WIPO). Argentina and Brazil put forward a proposal for the establishment of the development agenda for WIPO in August 2004.[96] The proposal was supported by a number of developing coun-

[93] See, eg, WP Alford, *supra* n 23.

[94] See D Gervais Spiritual But Not Intellectual? The Protection of Sacred Intangible Traditional Knowledge (2003), 11 Cardozo *J of Int'l & Comp Law* 467–95.

[95] See L Lessig. Free Culture: How Big Media Uses Technology and the Law to Lock Down Culture and Control Creativity (Penguin Books, 2004). Examples range from open source software to creative commons in the field of copyright to analyses of the sometimes poor social value of letting only the market dictate the path of innovation.

[96] Proposal by Argentina and Brazil for the Establishment of a Development Agenda for WIPO, 27 August 2004, WIPO document WO/GA/31/11, http://www.wipo.int/documents/en/document/govbody/wo_gb_ga/pdf/wo_ga_31_11.pdf .

tries, as well as civil society and non governmental organizations.[97] After intensive negotiations,[98] the WIPO General Assembly adopted Decision on a Development Agenda[99] based on the proposal by Argentina and Brazil. WIPO conducted inter-sessional intergovernmental meetings to examine this issue. A 'Civil Society Coalition,' which represents a number of non-governmental organizations, issued a much publicized statement about the Agenda.[100] The Coalition proposed a new Treaty on Access to Knowledge,[101] which should, inter alia, include the implementation of Articles 4, 5, 6 and 7 of the Doha Declaration on TRIPS and Public Health, and the implementation of Articles 7, 8 and 40 of the TRIPS Agreement. The proposals under consideration include several references to the TRIPS Agreement (Articles 7 & 8).

WIPO inter-sessional meetings were held in April, June and July of 2005, with a new proposal being tabled by the African Group of Countries[102] and followed by another Statement of the civil society groups.[103] Then a Provisional Committee for the Development Agenda (PCDA) was established. The first session held in February 2006 resulted in the 'clustering' of proposals.[104] At the second meeting of the PCDA in June 2006, the Chairman circulated a draft proposal including an annex of items around which 'emerging consensus' was discerned. The second PCDA meeting essentially ended with the delegates from Argentina and Brazil (two of the co-sponsors of the original Development Agenda proposal) insisting that each item be discussed on its merits and all

[97] See Geneva Declaration on the future of WIPO, http://www.cptech.org/ip/wipo/futureofwipodeclaration.html. The development agenda has been supported by 'Five hundred scientists, academics, legal experts and consumer advocates, including two Nobel laureates'. Frances Williams Development needs 'override intellectual property protection' Financial Times, 30 September 2004, 2004 WL 93033069. See also J Boyle, A Manifesto on WIPO and the Future of Intellectual Property, (2004) *Duke L & Tech Rev* 0009, online http://www.law.duke.edu/journals/dltr/articles/2004 dltr0009.html.

[98] 'Clash likely on intellectual property rights' Financial Times, Tuesday, 14 September 2004, 2004 WL 93029614; Frances Williams Development needs 'override intellectual property protection'. BRIDGES Weekly Trade News Digest—Vol 8, Number 33, 6 October 2004.

[99] General Assembly Decision on a Development Agenda, 4 October 2004.

[100] Civil Society Coalition Statement on WIPO General Assembly Decision on a Development Agenda, 4 October 2004, http://www.civilsocietycoalition.org/wipo/csc10042004.html. See also J Boyle, *A Manifesto on WIPO and the Future of Intellectual Property*, 2004 *Duke L & Tech Rev* 9.

[101] http://www.cptech.org/a2k/consolidatedtext-may9.pdf

[102] Proposal by Morocco on Behalf of the African Group Entitled 'The African Proposal for the Establishment of a Development Agenda for WIPO', WIPO document IIM/3/2, http://www.wipo.int/edocs/mdocs/mdocs/en/iim_3/iim_3_2.pdf.

[103] WIPO: Development Agenda—IIM/3 NGO Statement, http://www.ipjustice.org/WIPO/IIM3/IIM3_NGO_stmt_DA.shtml

[104] The six clusters are:

(A) Technical Assistance and Capacity Building;
(B) Norm-setting, Flexibilities, Public Policy and Public Domain;
(C) Technology Transfer, Information and Communication Technology (ICT) and Access to Knowledge;
(D) Assessments, Evaluation and Impact Studies;
(E) Institutional Matters Including Mandate and Governance; and
(F) Other Issues.

proposals to be discussed as a package. They refused to proceed according to the Chair's proposed consensus approach. The PCDA process resulted in no consensus. Nonetheless, at the fall 2006 WIPO General Assembly meeting, member states decided to renew the PCDA's mandate for another year.

The third session of the PCDA was held from 19 to 23 February, 2007. The meeting reached consensus as to forty 'recommendations for action'—of the original one hundred eleven proposals—, but participants recognized that the development debate initiated by member states in the global South was finally moving forward. The fourth session is scheduled to be held in June 2007 as this book is going to press.

4. Bilateral Trade Agreements and Intellectual Property

Post-TRIPS development has been going into two (arguably diverging) ways—TRIPS related development within WTO, as well as the recent developments in WIPO, have tried to be more responsive to the perceived needs of developing countries and the interests of users in securing access to protected content and material on terms they consider reasonable, including broad exceptions to obligations to obtain permissions and licenses. On the other hand, intellectual property developments in recent bilateral and regional trade agreements mirror the so-called maximalist approach.[105] The latter trend to regulate intellectual property rights through bilateral regimes may not be immediately threatening to the approach of WTO and WIPO, but these bilateral initiatives likely will have a significant impact in the long run.[106]

IV. TOWARDS A COMPREHENSIVE KNOWLEDGE STRATEGY

Many of the studies mentioned in Part III insist on the fact that sufficient and adequate intellectual property protection is but one ingredient in a complex recipe to achieve innovation-based economic development. Put differently, IPR

105 For example, recent US Trade Agreements export the Digital Millennium Copyright Act, Pub L No 105–304, 112 Stat 2860 (1998), a specific piece of legislation concerning the protection and circumvention of Technological protection measures (TPMs) that fits into the whole of the US Copyright Act, with its various safeguards, including constitutional protections stemming from the Bill of Rights. DMCA-like provisions are or will soon be part of national legislations in Central America and Asia as something of a stand-alone legislative instrument. See United States Bilateral Trade Agreements with Morocco, Chile, Bahrain, Australia and Central American Free Trade Agreement (http://www.ustr.gov/Trade_Agreements). These provisions are also being negotiation in a number of other agreements as well as within the Free Trade Area of Americas. See Susan Sell, *supra* n 6, at 121–62.

106 Professor Peter K Yu from Michigan State University labels this approach as the double backdoors in international intellectual property lawmaking'. If a number of countries import higher level of intellectual property protection, it is likely that that high level will be codified as the existing norm in is any revision of TRIPS. See Gervais, *supra* n 7, at p 68.

protection is essential, but in itself insufficient to ensure growth. In fact, by themselves, intellectual property rules arguably benefit mostly major owners of intellectual property, who are largely concentrated in a few highly industrialised countries.[107] To successfully exploit intellectual property to maximize its economic growth in areas that are information and intellectual property-intensive and be able to produce goods and services with a higher ideational content (which is what intellectual property rules tends to protect), each country needs a comprehensive knowledge optimization strategy. The adequate protection of commercially or industrially relevant knowledge necessarily forms part of such a strategy.

If the above seems a fair conclusion in light of economic studies discussed in Part III, those studies are also illuminating by what they do not and perhaps cannot show. It is extremely difficult to isolate the importance of the intellectual property factor in the growth of bilateral trade flows and foreign direct investment (FDI). It is even more difficult to determine ex ante what the optimal level of protection is. This is partly due to the fact that the TRIPS Agreement imposes global minimum standards, and there remain very few statistically significant options to compare various levels of protection below that floor. Ex post analysis is not a policy panacea either due to the uneven quality of econometric studies, in turn due to the quality of available (vs ideal) field of empirical data. However, I suggest that what is a problem in theory actually forms part of the solution once we shift to policy-setting.

The TRIPS Agreement is the strongest normative vector in setting intellectual property policy. In other words, because WTO members cannot legislate below the TRIPS levels without incurring the risk of dispute-settlement proceedings under the Dispute-Settlement Understanding,[108] and because it is unlikely that TRIPS norms will be diluted in the Doha Round,[109] one it would seem to be pragmatically justified to take TRIPS as a given quantity in the policy equation. The remaining parts of the equation are to determine how the reasonably available flexibility in implementing the Agreement should be used, which should only be done, I would submit, as part of a comprehensive domestic strategy. I will argue below that, integrating TRIPS norms into such a strategy is tactically sound and that by and large TRIPS strikes an adequate balance if properly implemented.

[107] According to UNIDO, 94% of all privately-funded research and development was located in those countries during the 1990s. See UNIDO, *Industrial Development Report 2002/03* (Vienna, 2002).

[108] WTO Agreement, Annex 2, Understanding on Rules and Procedures Governing the Settlement of Disputes, *in* Results of the Uruguay Round, *supra* n 7 [hereinafter 'DSU'].

See also Gervais, *supra* n 7, at pp 340–4. One should note that not all countries are equal when it comes to the DSU. The EU and US have resisted applying decisions of the DSU that found their legislation incompatible with their WTO obligations. The long-standing dispute between the EU and the so-called 'dollar banana' countries (*see* Conditions for the Granting of Tariff Preferences to Developing Countries, document WT/DS246/AB/R) is an example, while in the United States a panel decision concerning the incompatibility of exceptions contained in s 110(5)(b) of the Copyright Act rendered in 2000 remains unimplemented as of this writing.

[109] See Gervais, *supra* n 7, at pp 43–51.

What emerges below as a strategy is certainly not a series of measures designed to nominally implement TRIPS rules and find loopholes that essentially shrink the protection away. Certain proposed interpretations of Articles 27 and 30 of TRIPS,[110] or the fact that the Agreement in many cases imposes no clear rules as to the ownership of IPRs may mean that a country can formally implement TRIPS while systematically de-implementing parts of it through legal 'gimmickry' while 'getting away with it' as far as the WTO dispute-settlement system is concerned. The objective of this chapter is not to suggest ways to avoid being found 'guilty' by a WTO panel. Rather, it is to optimize knowledge and economic development using TRIPS rules as an ingredient. This may involve some flexibility in the TRIPS implementation process but as part of a comprehensive strategy.

1. TRIPS Viewed as Part of the 'Right Balance'

As mentioned previously,[111] it is difficult and probably impossible on the basis of available empirical data to determine the optimal level of intellectual property protection. Is the best term of protection of a patent 20 years, 18 or 22? Or is it 5 or 35? One would probably be led to conclude that, for certain forms of invention—indeed for specific inventions—, a certain term is optimal, while a different one is more adequate in a different context.[112] This analysis could depend, for example, on the added value of the invention, which depends in turn on the size of its inventive step[113] and the degree to which this step overlaps the predictable industrial or commercial applicability of the invention. One could

[110] For example, UNCTAD recently suggested that:

> The exclusions in Art 27:3 are framed more narrowly, yet again leave substantial room for interpretation. For example, Art 27:3(a) permits the exclusion of 'therapeutic methods' for the treatment of humans. The use of pharmaceuticals is a method of therapy for treating human health conditions, and so arguably . . . a Member could exclude the use of drugs for medical treatment from patent protection.

UNCTAD. Course on Dispute Settlement: WTO: Module 3.14 TRIPS, UNCTAD/EDM/Misc. 232/Add.18, http://www.unctad.org/en/docs/edmmisc232add18_en.pdf (2003), at 20.

I do not believe that a WTO DS panel would agree with this interpretation.

On Art 30, the same report indicates that '[t]he ordinary meaning of the terms in Article 30 would appear to allow considerable flexibility to Members in adopting exceptions to the rights of patent holders,' (*ibid* at 22) which may create a sense of 'flexibility' that a panel may or may not agree with.

[111] See Part II.

[112] One ex post sign would be whether the invention is still actively being worked at the expiration of the patent. But then again, if only inventions whose value had lapsed fell into the public domain, the societal value of granting a 20-year monopoly would come into question. Then again, in the United States, there is a long history of extending the term of specific patents by private bills. See CL Stanley, A Dangerous Step toward the Over Protection of Intellectual Property: Rethinking *Eldred v Ashcroft* (2003), 26 *Hamline L Rev* 679, 694–5. Historically, the term of a patent was set by private bill until a standard term was introduced into federal law. See TB Nachbar, Intellectual Property and Constitutional Norms (2004), 104 *Colum L Rev* 272, 338–9.

[113] In the area of pharmaceuticals, a difference is often made between pioneer drugs and so-called 'me-too' drugs. The latter are variations on a molecule developed by another laboratory which tends to have the same physiological/therapeutic effect, but without infringing the 'pioneer's' patent.

add to the equation the degree of true competition in the industrial or economic sector impacted by the invention and, correlatively, whether there are dominant players by market share. This interesting theoretical discussion led a Canadian economist to suggest a protection term based on the social value of 'non-lifestyle' (ie curative) pharmaceutical inventions.[114] However, even if such a proposal could pass the test of transaction costs, experts could only guess the future utility of the invention. In terms of predictability, time, and transition/protection costs, a single term may thus be a better, if theoretically less refined solution. It is certainly simpler.

TRIPS, one could argue, is a valid instrument also because it harmonizes national laws only to a degree.[115] This is not the place for a summary of the content of TRIPS.[116] Evidently, it contains more than simple wishes, in contrast to many provisions of the Paris Convention.[117] On the whole, however, while a country must provide protection of copyrights, certain related rights, trade marks, industrial designs, certain geographical indications, patents on most classes of inventions, certain forms of confidential information and, last—and in this case least—, topographies of integrated circuits, in each case for a specified period of time, there is considerable flexibility in how the rights and protected subject matter are defined,[118] owned,[119] managed,[120] or indeed subject to exceptions.[121] In the area of enforcement, the Agreement recognizes that the implementation in a given WTO member may be impacted by the availability of resources.[122] Another

[114] See A Hollis, An Efficient Reward System for Pharmaceutical Innovation (2004), available at http://econ.ucalgary.ca/fac-files/ah/drugprizes.pdf (last accessed 28 March 2005).

[115] See J Reichman, The TRIPS Agreement Comes of Age: Conflicts or Cooperation with the Developing Countries? (2000), 32 *Case Western Reserve J of Int'l L* 441.

[116] See generally Gervais, *supra* n 7.

[117] To take two trade mark-related examples, one could think of the wording of Art 6(1):

> The conditions for the filing and registration of trade marks shall be determined in each country of the Union by its domestic legislation.

Or of Article 7*bis*:

> The countries of the Union undertake to accept for filing and to protect *collective marks* [. . .]
>
> (2) Each country shall be the judge of the particular conditions under which a collective mark shall be protected.

Article 9 and especially 9(6) could also be mentioned.

[118] For example, while Article 27 states that WTO Members must protect 'inventions, whether products or processes, in all fields of technology, provided that they are new, involve an inventive step and are capable of industrial application,' the terms 'new,' 'inventive step,' and 'capable of industrial application' are not defined.

[119] As was recognized by the Appellate Body in 'United States—Section 211 Appropriation Act of 1998', document WT/DS176/AB/R, at paras 215–21.

[120] For instance, rules as to the ownership of collective marks (see the previous Note) or whether and how copyright and related rights are to be managed (collectively or otherwise) are not explicitly mentioned in the Agreement.

[121] Many exceptions are only limited by the 'three-step test' contained in TRIPS Articles 13, 26(2) and 30. See, D Gervais, Towards a New Core International Copyright Norm: The Reverse Three-Step Test (2005) 9:1 Marquette *Intell Prop L Rev* 1–35.

[122] TRIPS Article 41(5). In addition, with respect to least-developed countries, the Preamble adds the following: *cont./*

example is the delay in protecting pharmaceuticals by patents granted least-developed countries, ie, until 2016.[123]

2. Intellectual Property as Part of an Economic Development Strategy

It is often said that developing economies need a different set of rules. As UNCTAD puts it:

> . . . experience shows that there is a need for policy instruments specifically designed with the aim of helping countries at lower stages of development to converge on the levels of efficiency and affluence achieved by the more advanced economies, and to improve the welfare of all groups of the population. Making this the principle for policy design at both the domestic and the international level requires recognition of the fact that successful development and integration of the developing countries is in the mutual interest of all countries, as longer-term growth and trading opportunities of the more advanced economies also depend on the expansion of industrial capacity and markets in the poorer economies.[124]

Yet, as far as intellectual property is concerned, there is sufficient policy-related 'room to move' within TRIPS, even though the major 'concession' to developing countries other than least-developed ones was a set of transitional periods, which ended in January 2000 for the most part and in January 2005 for pharmaceutical patents.[125] What I am suggesting, therefore, is that countries should not spend most of their energies to 'fight' TRIPS. They can and should use its built-in normative elasticity to reconcile the new norms to the extent possible with their industrial, cultural, legal and economic parameters, based on their determination of priorities. However, the purpose should not be to try to cir-

> Recognizing also the special needs of the least-developed country Members in respect of maximum flexibility in the domestic implementation of laws and regulations in order to enable them to create a sound and viable technological base.

UNCTAD published a detailed document on the flexibility of TRIPS. See *supra* n 112.

[123] Extension of the transition period under Article 66.1 of the TRIPS Agreement for least-developed country Members for certain obligations with respect to pharmaceutical products. Decision of the Council for TRIPS of 27 June 2002.

[124] UNCTAD, United Nations Conference on Trade and Development. Trade and Development Report, 2004, UNCTAD/TDR/2004 at 96. (Geneva: UNCTAD, 2004) at 96.

[125] TRIPS, Articles 65(2) and (4). In the case of pharmaceutical patents, least-developed countries now have until 2016. See *supra* n 125. See also Reichman, *supra* n 117.

[126] By which I mean copyright (and the bundle of rights it contains, together with exceptions and a long term of protection) for literary and artistic works; a twenty-year patent for new, useful and non-obvious inventions (to use North American terminology, reflected in the footnote to Art 27 in TRIPS), etc.

One could in theory devise a different system from scratch but the internationalization of any such new system would not be without very significant transition costs, and there is no guarantee that one could do better on the basis of available 'performance indicators' for the various types of ip protection. The temptation to build *sui generis* systems thus far has not been met with complete success, as the database and computer chip examples demonstrate. That being said, the existing traditional structures of protection are far from perfect and can be improved upon, but most likely only in an incremental fashion. See D Gervais, The Internationalization of Intellectual Property: New Challenges from the Very Old and the Very New (2002), 12:4 *Fordham Intel Prop, Media & Entertainment L J* 929–90.

cumvent TRIPS, because by and large it incorporates a rather well-honed set of norms establishing structures of protection[126] the impact, use and misuse of which have been extensively analyzed and commented upon in industrialized nations. Developing countries should assist in generating comparative research to identify ways in which those known intellectual property norms affect them differently and whether a different implementation method is required. Of course, developing countries are all different, which complicates the task, but perhaps parallels can be drawn based on, eg, geography or comparative levels of economic development. As has begun to emerge in countries such as China, local research and development efforts after years of FDI have transformed China as a major holder of domestically-developed intellectual property.

Developing countries should gain more by integrating TRIPS norms in a broader innovation and knowledge optimization strategy. As with market openness, intellectual property rules *per se* are at best a catalyst. While part of that suggested strategy includes accepting TRIPS as a given and perhaps even as some argue as a common reference/defence point against TRIPS-plus demands made in bilateral discussions, it is also important to note that[127] TRIPS is not a static bundle of norms. It evolves with each panel and Appellate Body interpretation. It is also not to be read in 'clinical isolation' from public international law,[128] which may support efforts to develop alternatives sets of public international law norms and/or to shift fora.[129] Developing and other countries can thus coalesce to develop alternative sets of norms[130] and the inclusion of TRIPS and WTO rules in the broader framework of public international law.

The suggested approach is not incompatible with the views of, eg, UNCTAD, which wrote in its 2004 Trade & Development Report:[131]

> . . . most of the evidence suggests that the impact of trade openness has been highly uneven, and contingent on a variety of institutional factors, and that there is room for discretionary policy measures at the micro and macro level.
>
> A more balanced perspective, also taking its cue from Adam Smith, links a process of successful integration back to productivity gains from specialization, gains that are

[127] See generally Part IV of this book and PK Yu, 'Currents and Crosscurrents in the International Intellectual Property Regime', (2004) 38 *Loy LAL Rev* 323; and D Vivas-Eugui, Regional and Bilateral Agreements and a TRIPS-Plus World: The Free Trade Agreement of the Americas, (Geneva: Quaker United Nations Office, 2003), available at http://www.geneva.quno.info/pdf/FTAA%20(A4).pdf.

[128] See 'US—Standards for Reformulated and Conventional Gasoline', Report of he Appellate Body, WTO Doc. WT/DS2/AB/R, at para III. B.

[129] See GB Dinwoodie and RC Dreyfuss, TRIPS and the Dynamics of Intellectual Property Lawmaking (2004), 36:1 Case *W Res J of Int'l L* 95, 120–1: '. . . developing countries have recently seen regime-shifting as a bulwark against the established power balance in international lawmaking, and over time user groups might likewise view the ability to shift forum as a valuable defense technique'.

[130] The recent example of the Brasilia summit between Arab and Latin American Nations comes to mind. The UNESCO draft Towards a Convention on the Protection of the Diversity of Cultural Contents and Artistic Expressions is also relevant, as would the Convention on Biological Diversity. See also R. Okediji, The Institutions of Intellectual Property: New Trends in an Old Debate (2004), 98 *Am Soc'y Int'l L Proc* 219.

[131] UNCTAD, *supra* n 126.

> amplified through innovation, the use of better equipment, scale economies at the firm level and by 'externalities' such as learning and improvements in human capital. This ties economic success to a heightened degree of economic interdependence through the mutually reinforcing interactions between expanding markets and an increasingly complex division of labour). Extending and deepening such interactions depends on new investments under conditions of objective uncertainty. To improve and expand existing capacity as well as to introduce new products and processes, a 'profit-investment nexus' is needed that requires supporting financial arrangements, including accommodative monetary policy and relatively stable legal institutions.[132]

And further:

> . . . the openness agenda has perpetuated a lopsided view of the forces driving economic integration. It stresses the potential gains from participation in international markets while downplaying adjustment costs, and it stresses convergence tendencies while ignoring potential sources of cumulative divergence. As the previous sections have suggested, this approach has its limitations. Trade is just one among several interrelated factors shaping integration. Its impact is largely contingent on thepresence of dynamic forces—specialization, learning and innovation, scale economies and capital formation—that do not respond in a simple or predictable way to the incentives generated from rapid opening up. Strengthening these forces requires a series of complementary institutional reforms and discretionary macroeconomic, industrial and social policy measures. This implies considerable diversity in the pattern of integration, even among countries at similar levels of economic development.[133]

True, importing intellectual property rules wholesale into the legislative and industrial fabric of a developing economy is insufficient for that country to succeed.[134] However, it is fair to assume that a country's technology imports and inward FDI are unlikely to grow without intellectual property rules. We can conclude that (a) intellectual property rules are required but insufficient; (b) it is more pragmatic to accept TRIPS (which does not mean that efforts to develop alternative sets of norms are ill-founded); and (c) intellectual property rules must be properly calibrated as part of a broader domestic innovation and knowledge optimization strategy.

Except perhaps in specific areas such as traditional knowledge protection, it would be counterproductive to focus all efforts to the development of new and independent rules for at least two reasons. First, there is little if any evidence that a new form of intellectual property or even variations on known themes would work better. Second, there would be huge transition costs and friction in

[132] UNCTAD, *supra* n 126, at 79.

[133] *Ibid*, at 95.

[134] That point was well articulated in the Report of the UK Commission on Intellectual Property Rights, *supra* n 75:

> . . . it may be unwise to focus on TRIPS as a principal means of facilitating technology transfer. A wider agenda needs to be pursued, as is currently being done in the WTO. Developed countries need to give serious consideration to their policies for encouraging technology transfer. In addition, they should promote more effective research and cooperation with and among developing countries to strengthen their scientific and technological capabilities. (Exec Summary, at p 5).

convincing foreign partners of the validity of such new or customized rules. For multinational corporate investors, there is value in predictability and dealing with a known set of regulatory parameters.

The policy flexibility needed by developing economies is partly there in TRIPS. More importantly, by developing a comprehensive strategy, a country can limit the negative impact of transitioning to higher intellectual property protection and increase its chances of reaping the benefits thereof, including technology-related FDI and growing domestic Internet, pharmaceutical or other technology based industries.

3. Towards a National Strategy

The realization that intellectual property rules *per se* do not automatically lead to an increase in inward FDI, and that much more than a set of IP rules is required to develop domestic innovation and creativity is what has prompted many developing countries to insist on the technology transfer part of the TRIPS bargain, which is enshrined in Article 66.2,[135] as well as capacity-building under Article 67. This is linked to the quest for an intrinsic equilibrium, measured country-by-country (even in the face of uniform multilateral rules), in the way intellectual property protection is implemented.[136]

Granted, the task at hand is not a simple one. Yet, instead of trying to turn back the clock of extant liberalization and intellectual property rules, I suggest that they can be put to good use. There is no room in this Article to cover all aspects of a comprehensive knowledge optimization strategy the primary purpose of which would be to strengthen a country's economy and its growth. However, the following paths are probably some of those that could be followed:

a) Priority setting

Based on existing industrial infrastructures, successes, education programs, available natural and human resources, and potential domestic and regional markets, what are the realistic areas that a country should prioritize? The

[135] Which reads as follows:

> Developed country Members shall provide incentives to enterprises and institutions in their territories for the purpose of promoting and encouraging technology transfer to least-developed country Members in order to enable them to create a sound and viable technological base.

The Council for TRIPS is actively following the implementation of this provision, notably by requiring reports on technology transfer initiatives taken by developed countries. See the WTO Annual Report 2005, at 13 (available at http://www.wto.org/english/res_e/booksp_e/anrep_e/anrep05_e.pdf). See also WTO document IP/C/W/431 and addenda for a summary of the information provided.

[136] See *supra* n 49 and accompanying text.

primary target of a Strategy[137] should not be to obtain new imports, though they may be useful, but rather to build domestic intellectual property generating activities, in part through FDI (which almost always includes a knowledge and technology transfer component) and technology transfer and acquisition.

b) Education and Institutional Capacity Building

This is probably the most important aspect once priorities have been set. Education, both in the country and abroad, is the cornerstone of a viable, long-term knowledge strategy and economic growth in the information society. For example, a country should pay to send some of the best students to the top foreign universities, especially in field where the knowledge brought back can directly contribute to the Strategy in light of priorities set. This could include engineering, biology, chemistry, physics and all other sciences but also in almost all cases management & law (including intellectual property law!).

Because both art and science designs now rely on computers and computer code, all students finishing high school should be fully computer literate. This does not require huge investments (especially when compared to hard science or engineering labs) and the returns are likely to be many times the cost of that investment Financial mechanisms may be used to ensure that trained graduates will return to their country of origin—if a country does not have patent protection, it will have a hard time attracting technology oriented employers and will have a hard time retaining nationals that have studied in this area.[138]

Training for policy makers, judges, high officials and other persons involved in economic development projects should similarly be organized. It cannot be stressed enough that successful education program outcomes will depend on selecting the best candidates for each program, and not base decisions solely or mainly on other factors.

Developing educational institutions and services is naturally very costly. Developing intellectual property institutions such as patent and trademark offices perhaps even more. Yet, developing countries can either delegate these roles to foreign institutions, a majority of which are located in the 'First World', thereby losing the some of their ability to customize the services, or take the policy bull by the horns and pay the price. Ideally, more industrialized nations should fund training and establishment of local patent and trademark offices, also because of their educational role with local businesses and research facili-

[137] The Arab countries' proposal to WIPO on its Development Agenda (*supra* n 55, p 6 of Annex) contained the following:

> As a first step, Member States should be encouraged to and assisted in setting up national strategies on intellectual property, which identify areas of strength and weakness in dealing with intellectual property systems. Remedies should be found for weak areas and areas of strength should be further enhanced with a view to attaining a successful and efficient functioning of the intellectual property system.

[138] See EW Kitch, The Patent Policy of Developing Countries (1994), 13 *UCLA Pac Basin L J* 166.

ties. Absent this kind of funding, another option, used in some parts of Africa for example,[139] is to build regional offices.

c) Subsidies

Within WTO and other applicable rules, there is room for subsidies in the form of tax breaks or otherwise. These may also be used to attract FDI. By granting merit-based research subsidies or grants to local creators, an incentive to local innovators and creators is given. By rewarding significant achievements at, *eg*, an annual ward ceremony successful innovators and creators are recompensed but a strong social signal is sent about the value of creation and innovation, which then functions as an additional incentive for others.

d) FDI 'marketing'

FDI is not an economic panacea, but in the game of economic growth and development. It seems a better than solution than a simple increase in imports. FDI generally comes with formal or informal knowledge and technology transfer and creates more and better local jobs than simple distributorships. Each country (and may are doing it aggressively already) should thus market its advantages bilaterally, at international fairs, through graduate students, etc. It could survey multinational companies operating in its priority areas to determiner their perception of the country's strengths and weaknesses, address shortcomings identified in the survey and provide information on positive aspects that are simply not known in interested circles.

e) Non IP- Regulatory Adaptation

Based on WTO and other rules and surveys, regulatory shortcomings should be addressed. Usually, an efficient legal system, investment protections rules, a competitive tax system and access to a qualified workforce will rate fairly high in the list of FDI preconditions.

f) Patent mining

Patent databases are publicly available. By mining recent patents and published applications[140] and providing copies to local companies with product development abilities, a number of upward technological steps may be taken fairly rapidly. Of course the obligation to comply with TRIPS means that if the patent is granted in the developing country in question, the technology cannot be used

[139] See, eg, the African Regional Industrial Property Organization, http://www.aripo.wipo.net/index.html.

[140] Which typically implies an 18-month delay after the initial filing. Unfortunately, in certain industries, much can happen in 18 months.

directly, but even a reasonable license cannot be obtained, the knowledge could be used, eg, for non-commercial research. As was noted by the UK Commission on Intellectual Property Rights,[141] TRIPS allows (Articles 8 and 40) a WTO Member to determine an appropriate interface between intellectual property and competition law. However, many countries that implemented TRIPS recently did not and still do not have competition legislation.

These are of course only examples of the components of a full strategy.

V. CONCLUSION

Without adequate intellectual property protection, economic development will not happen, at least from a certain level—it is unclear whether intellectual property rules have any positive effect on the development of the truly poorer nations. In addition, we now know that while intellectual property is an essential ingredient, it does not an economic plan make. Many more elements are needed. This Article has argued that both for practical reasons and on the basis of available empirical data, TRIPS should be seen, indeed fully accepted as a given. It may also be defended as an appropriate reference point for developing nations in the context of TRIPS plus bilateral trade discussions.[142]

TRIPS does contain a number of rules that WTO Members must implement, but it also affords a fair margin of 'policy flexibility.' Implementing TRIPS should be viewed as part of a broader Knowledge Strategy resting on priority-setting, a strong focus on technical and advanced education and institutional capacity-building, regulatory adaptation, FDI 'marketing' and patent mining.

[141] See *supra* n 75.

[142] See *supra* n 129.

Chapter 4

TRIPS and FTAs: A World of Preferential or Detrimental Relations?

ROGER KAMPF*

I. INTRODUCTION

THE NUMBER OF bilateral and regional free trade agreements (FTAs) negotiated and concluded is steadily increasing, adding to those already in force. The same goes for the discussions and assessments of such agreements and their potential impact on the multilateral system—they are equally numerous. It is therefore by no means exaggerated to characterise the subject-matter of this chapter, eg the relationship between the TRIPS Agreement (Agreement on Trade-Related Aspects of Intellectual Property Rights) and FTAs, as being among the topical issues these days.

The TRIPS Agreement only sets minimum standards for the protection of intellectual property. Article 1.1 TRIPS expressly provides for the implementation by WTO Members of more extensive protection than under the TRIPS Agreement. This is an option, but by no means an obligation under multilateral rules. The so-called 'TRIPS plus' approach, which can be found in many of the FTAs with more extensive IPR (intellectual property rights) protection, has nevertheless raised a number of questions which will be looked at in this contribution.

The article starts from a broader perspective, looking at the World Trade Organization (WTO) and FTAs in general, the possible role such agreements could play in and for the multilateral trading system, as well as the institutional framework covering them at the WTO. The following section more specifically analyses the TRIPS Agreement and how it deals with FTAs. Particular attention is given to the application of the basic principles of national treatment and most-favoured-nation treatment and their consequences for provisions on intellectual property protection contained in bilateral or regional agreements.

Based on this analysis, the widespread phenomenon of 'TRIPS plus' provisions is closely examined. To do so, the 'four Ws' are looked at first, eg *where*

* This article has been prepared in a personal capacity. The views expressed are the author's and must not be attributed to the WTO, its Secretariat or its Members.

can such provisions typically be found, *what* do they cover, *why* are they inserted in bilateral or regional agreements and *who* is calling for 'TRIPS plus' provisions. This allows some conclusions as regards the impact of such provisions on the intellectual property regime and beyond and also discusses the frequently raised question of what the WTO is specifically doing to address this issue.

A short overview of the role and impact of bilateral investment treaties follows to complete the picture, providing some typical examples of coverage of intellectual property rights and the principles affecting their protection. At the same time, some insights into present objectives and tools in the context of the provision of technical assistance are given.

As the WTO is a Member-driven organisation and therefore bound to be neutral, the aim of this contribution is not and should not be to judge the phenomenon of the rising number of bilateral and regional agreements which include 'TRIPS plus' provisions. Its sole purpose is to offer an overview of the current situation, to provide examples of typical 'TRIPS plus' provisions and to summarize the implications of this trend for participants in such agreements, as well as for the multilateral trading system.[1]

II. GENERAL OVERVIEW: THE WTO AND FTAS

1. Current Situation

The negotiation and conclusion of comprehensive bilateral and regional trade agreements is no longer limited to specific regions, subject-matters or players. On the contrary, such agreements can nowadays be found in all regions of the world, often even in the form of cross-regional agreements, and involve both developed and developing countries. This tendency has repeatedly been attributed to the lack of results and the slow process of multilateral negotiations, but other factors, such as economic or domestic policy considerations, may be equally important in this context.[2] A recent Annual Report by the Director-

[1] Criticism with respect to the 'TRIPS plus' approach has been, inter alia, voiced by: Frederick M Abbott, The Doha Declaration on the TRIPS Agreement and Public Health and the Contradictory Trend in Bilateral and Regional Trade Agreements, Quaker United Nations Office, Occasional Paper 14, Geneva 2004; Frederick M Abbott, The WTO Medicines Decision: World Pharmaceutical Trade and the Protection of Public Health, The American Journal of International Law, Vol 99 2005, pp 317, 349 and following; Frederick M Abbott, Intellectual Property Provisions of Bilateral and Regional Trade Agreements in Light of US Federal Law, UNCTAD-ICTSD Issue Paper No 12, Geneva 2006; Pedro Roffe, Intellectual Property Provisions in Bilateral and Regional Trade Agreements: The Challenges of Iimplementation, CIEL, 2006; Germán Velásquez, Bilateral Trade Agreements and Access to Essential Drugs, in: Bermudez/Oliviera (ed), Intellectual Property in the Context of the WTO TRIPS Agreement, Rio de Janeiro 2004, p 63; Jean-Frédéric Morin, Les accords bilatéraux et régionaux de propriété intellectuelle dans la francophonie, Centre international Unisfera, Canada, June 2003.

[2] Jo-Ann Crawford/Roberto V Fiorentino, The Changing Landscape of Regional Trade Agreements, WTO Discussion Paper No 8, Geneva 2005, p 16.

General to the WTO Trade Policy Review Body provides some interesting statistics that support the assumption of an ever-growing number of regional trade agreements. According to this report, a total of 206 preferential agreements in force have been notified to the WTO. To this figure should be added another 30 regional agreements signed, but not yet entered into force, and some 60 agreements under negotiation.[3]

2. The Role of FTAs Next to Multilateral Agreements

Two WTO agreements explicitly permit Members to provide preferences under regional trade agreements: GATT Article XXIV for agreements in the area of trade in goods, and GATS Article V, for agreements covering trade in services. In addition, the so-called Enabling Clause, or more formally the 1979 Decision of the GATT Council on Differential and More Favourable Treatment, Reciprocity and Fuller Participation of Developing Countries,[4] allows developed Members to accord differential and more favourable treatment to developing countries insofar as trade in goods is concerned and developing countries to provide preferential treatment to each other.

The Doha Declaration recognises the important role that regional trade agreements can play in promoting the liberalisation and expansion of trade and in fostering development, while emphasising the commitment of Members to the WTO as the unique forum for global trade rule-making and liberalization.[5]

Because of their preferential and thus discriminatory nature, FTAs depart from one of the cornerstones of the multilateral trading system, ie the principle of MFN treatment. This may result in a distortion of resource allocation, as well as trade and investment diversion. In addition, the coexistence of different trade regimes in a country as a result of its membership to multilateral, regional and bilateral agreements implies the risk of regulatory confusion and implementation problems because of conflicting obligations and inconsistencies.[6] It is therefore not surprising that the proliferation of such agreements is received with a certain concern. In his intervention at the meeting of the Trade Policy Review Body in December 2004, the Director-General of the WTO highlighted the fundamental change brought about by regional trade agreements to the world trade landscape, considering that this would constitute a challenge to the multilateral trading system.[7] According to his assessment, the consequences could be posi-

[3] Overview of Developments in the International Trading Environment, Annual Report by the Director-General, WT/TPR/OV/10 of 15 November 2004, para 83. See also the factual information contained in the note by the Secretariat: 'Mapping of Regional Trade Agreements', WT/REG/W/41, prepared for the Committee on Regional Trade Agreements; the World Bank Report 'Global Economic Prospects—Trade, Regionalism, and Development', Washington 2005.

[4] Decision L/4903 of 28 November 1979.

[5] WT/MIN(01)/DEC/1, para 4.

[6] For more details see the analysis of the interaction between trade policy disciplines enforced through RTAs and multilateral rules, WT/REG/W/37, paras 7–9.

[7] Minutes of the meeting of 16 December 2004, WT/TPR/OV/M/5, para 7.

tive or negative: Such regional trade agreements could complement efforts to achieve further trade liberalisation at a multilateral level, but they could also produce systemic risks to the global trading system through discrimination and diversion of trade and investment, undermining at the same time the transparency and predictability of trade relations.[8] Other voices have recently more openly criticized the erosion of the non-discrimination principle because of the current spread of preferential trade agreements, calling upon governments to show restraint and suggesting making such agreements subject to a meaningful review and effective disciplines in the WTO.[9] To contain the potentially negative impact of FTAs on the multilateral trading system, GATT Article XXIV and GATS Article V establish, at least, minimum criteria for FTAs to qualify for the MFN exemption, ie the reduction or removal of barriers in substantially all sectors of trade without raising the overall level of trade barriers for non-participating Members.

3. Institutional Framework

a) Committee on Regional Trade Agreements

The WTO Committee on Regional Trade Agreements (CRTA)[10] has two main functions: to examine individual agreements notified by Members, and to examine their systemic implications for the multilateral trading system[11] and the interaction between the two. The examination of an agreement ensures transparency and a check of its consistency with WTO rules. After conclusion of the examination,[12] the WTO Secretariat drafts a report, which needs to be agreed by the Committee, and subsequently adopted by the General Council. Notwithstanding those clear procedural rules, no report has been completed since the establishment of the WTO due to the absence of consensus among Members. This is, inter alia, due to the potential impact on dispute settlement cases, which such reports could have.[13] In addition, the interpretation of relevant WTO rules against which such FTAs are checked is not without controversy.

Virtually all major regional trade agreements have been referred to the CRTA for examination following their prior notification to the Council for Trade in

[8] International Trade Reporter, Vol 21, No 51 (23 December 2004), p 2063. See also the interesting, but inconclusive analysis of preferential trade agreements, their objectives, costs and benefits, submitted by Crescenzo dell'Aquila / Marijke Kuiper, Which Road to Liberalisation?, ENARPRI Working Paper No 2, Brussels 2003, available at http://www.ceps.be.

[9] The Future of the WTO, Report by the Consultative Board to the WTO Director-General, Geneva 2005, para 58.

[10] Established by a Decision of the General Council, WT/L/127 of 7 February 1996.

[11] For details see background note prepared by the WTO Secretariat: 'Synopsis of Systemic Issues', WT/REG/W/37.

[12] Current RTA examination procedures are summarised in TN/RL/W/8/Rev 1, p 32.

[13] See Jo-Ann Crawford/Roberto V Fiorentino (fn 2), p 19.

Goods, the Council for Trade in Services and the Committee on Trade and Development pursuant to GATT Article XXIV, GATS Article V and the Enabling Clause.[14] However, the examination of trade agreements by the Committee is not primarily meant to cover intellectual property, since notifications are made on the basis of provisions stemming from the GATT and GATS Agreements and the Enabling Clause. Consequently, the mandate of the Committee is limited to an examination of agreements in accordance with the procedures and terms of reference adopted by the Council for Trade in Goods, the Council for Trade in Services or the Committee on Trade and Development, whereas no reference is made to the Council for TRIPS.[15] This has been confirmed by the above mentioned new transparency mechanism.

b) Negotiating Group on Rules

Persisting divergences of views among Members and the rather slow process of examination of regional trade agreements by the competent WTO Committee may, inter alia, explain the adoption of the negotiating mandate at the Fourth Ministerial Conference in 2001 to clarify and improve the disciplines and procedures under existing WTO provisions applying to regional trade agreements.[16] Since then, negotiations have been taking place within the so-called Negotiating Group on Rules, reporting to the Trade Negotiations Committee. The work of this body is focusing on two areas, ie the identification of issues for negotiation[17] and procedural issues in relation to an increased transparency of RTAs.[18] As regards the latter, the General Council recently adopted a new transparency mechanism negotiated in the Negotiating Group on Rules.[19] It provides for the early announcement of any regional trade agreement and notification to the WTO. Under this mechanism, Members agreed to consider the notified regional trade agreements on the basis of a factual presentation by the WTO Secretariat. For reasons similar to those outlined in the previous section, the TRIPS Agreement will hardly be affected by this work, as an examination of IP rules in RTAs is not mandated.

c) Trade Policy Review Body

Annex 3 to the Marrakesh Agreement contains the Trade Policy Review Mechanism which aims at the surveillance of national trade policy. All

[14] Regional trade agreements notified comprise, inter alia, ASEAN, CARICOM, COMESA, EC, EEA, EFTA, GCC, the General System of Trade Preferences among Developing Countries, MERCOSUR, NAFTA and SADC.

[15] See General Council Decision establishing the CRTA, WT/L/127, para 1(a).

[16] WT/MIN(01)/DEC/1, para 29.

[17] See, for example, background note prepared by the Secretariat: 'Compendium of Issues Related to Regional Trade Agreements', TN/RL/W/8/Rev 1.

[18] See, for example the informal note by the Chairman of the Negotiating Group on Rules: 'Elements for an RTAs' Transparency Process', JOB(05)/63 of 29 April 2005.

[19] TN/RL/18 of 13 July 2006.

Members are subject to periodic reviews which are carried out by the Trade Policy Review Body.[20] Country reports extend to all aspects of trade policies covered by the Multilateral Trade Agreements in Annex 1, thus also including the TRIPS Agreement. On the other hand, as regional and bilateral agreements form part of a country's trade environment, they may also form an integral part of the examination. This mechanism therefore offers another opportunity to report on FTAs and IPRs, and for other WTO Members to comment on the relationship in individual cases. However, the functioning of the Trade Policy Review Mechanism is clearly defined and shall allow 'for the regular collective appreciation and evaluation of the full range of individual Members' trade policies and practices and their impact on the multilateral trading system'. However, it is not 'intended to serve as a basis for the enforcement of specific obligations under the Agreements or for dispute settlement procedures, or to impose new policy commitments on Members'.[21] Its primary importance with respect to the relationship between the TRIPS Agreement and FTAs can therefore be summed up as the achievement of transparency and a forum for views to be aired.

d) TRIPS Council

It goes almost without saying that issues related to bilateral or regional FTAs can also be raised in the TRIPS Council. Access to or detailed information on bilateral agreements could, for example, be requested under Article 63.3 TRIPS. This provision explicitly obliges Members to respond to written requests submitted by another Member having reason to believe that a specific judicial decision or administrative ruling or bilateral agreement in the area of IPRs affects its rights under the TRIPS Agreement. Members have occasionally made use of Article 63.3 TRIPS to collect information of another Member's national laws, regulations, judicial decisions and administrative rulings.[22]

III. THE TRIPS AGREEMENT AND FTAS

1. Absence of General Exemption Clause for FTAs

As mentioned above, GATT Article XXIV and GATS Article V contain explicit clauses allowing Members to provide preferences under FTAs covering goods and services. Provided that certain conditions are met, such as, in the case of

[20] For more details see Report of the Trade Policy Review Body for 2005, WT/TPR/173 of 8 November 2005.

[21] Section A (i) of the Trade Policy Review Mechanism; confirmed recently by the Second Appraisal of the Operation of the TPR Mechanism, Report to Ministers, WT/MIN(05)/1 of 21 September 2005, para 4.

[22] See, for example, the most recent communications from the US (IP/C/W/461), Switzerland (IP/C/W/462) and Japan (IP/C/W463) concerning IPR enforcement in specific cases in China.

GATS, substantial sectoral coverage and the absence or elimination of substantially all discrimination, the benefits of the agreements do not have to be automatically extended to the entire WTO membership. This constitutes an exemption to the otherwise applicable principle of MFN treatment. However, the TRIPS Agreement does not incorporate a comparable provision which would allow extending a higher level of intellectual property protection negotiated under a free trade agreement only to partners of such an agreement. Although Article 24.1 TRIPS could be read as an explicit invitation to enter into bilateral (or multilateral) negotiations aimed at increasing the level of protection of geographical indications for wines and spirits,[23] it does, for example, not incorporate a specific derogation from the principle of MFN treatment.

2. Application of Basic Principles: National Treatment and MFN Treatment

As with the other multilateral agreements concluded under the auspices of the WTO, the basic principles of national treatment and most-favoured-nation (MFN) treatment are enshrined in the TRIPS Agreement, in its Articles 3 and 4.[24] Thus, non-discrimination between nationals of WTO Members should be the normal case, which implies, inter alia, that reciprocity provisions are, as a general rule, no longer admissible.

a) National Treatment

Pursuant to Article 3 TRIPS, Members are obliged to extend the treatment accorded to their own nationals with regard to the protection of intellectual property to the nationals of other Members,[25] even where specific measures, such as those resulting from FTAs, provide a higher level of protection. Consequently, where a Member implements the obligations resulting from a bilateral or regional agreement covering intellectual property rights into its domestic legislation without discriminating against its own nationals, any 'TRIPS plus' elements would have to be automatically granted to nationals of

[23] See the interpretation given by David Vivas/Christoph Spennemann, The Treatment of Geographical Indications in Recent Regional and Bilateral Free Trade Agreements, in: The Intellectual Property Debate: Perspectives from Law, Economics and Political Economy, Edward Elgar Publishing Ltd, 2006, Chapter 17.

[24] For more details on drafting history and possible interpretations see UNCTAD/ICTSD Resource Book on TRIPS and Development, Cambridge 2005, Ch 4, § 2; see also Background Note by the Secretariat, The Fundamental Principals of National Treatment, MFN Treatment and Transparency, WT/WGTCP/W/114 of 14 April 1999.

[25] The Appellate Body decision on *United States—Section 211 Omnibus Appropriations Act of 1998* (WT/DS 176/AB/R), paras 242 and following, provides a detailed analysis of the scope of Art 3 TRIPS. See also *European Communities—Protection of Trademarks and Geographical Indications for Agricultural Products and Foodstuffs* (WT/DS 174/R and WT/DS 290/R), paras 7.123–7.213; GATT panel report *United States—Section 337 of the Tariff Act of 1930* (BISD 36S/345), para 5.11.

all WTO Members on the basis of the national treatment obligation of the TRIPS Agreement. In such cases, reliance by nationals of non-parties on the obligation to grant MFN treatment, as exposed in the following section, in order to ensure non-discriminatory treatment would not be necessary. This could be of particular interest where a Member makes use of the grandfathering clause in Article 4(d), which exempts earlier agreements from the MFN obligation, but not from the requirement to grant national treatment. The co-existence of the two non-discrimination principles is thus likely to, de facto, significantly diminish the importance of the MFN principle and the otherwise available exception from it. This somewhat higher significance of the national treatment principle in the area of intellectual property is different from the GATT. As the latter essentially aims at controlling and liberalising border measures applying to products in international trade in the first place, it is not surprising that the principle of MFN treatment has been referred to as the cornerstone of the GATT. Under the GATT, the MFN treatment principle has thus its own place next to the principle of national treatment, which only ensures that 'internal' measures, as opposed to border measures, are applied in a non-discriminatory manner.

b) MFN Treatment

Subject to certain exemptions discussed in the following sections, Article 4 TRIPS provides that 'with regard to the protection of intellectual property, any advantage, favour, privilege or immunity granted by a Member to the nationals of any other country shall be accorded immediately and unconditionally to the nationals of all Members'. This represents the standard MFN clause used in other WTO Agreements, except the exclusive reference to nationals, and not to products, as under GATT, or to services and service suppliers, as under GATS. Interestingly, it is the first time that the MFN principle has been made applicable in a multilateral agreement on intellectual property rights, since earlier WIPO Conventions and Treaties only enshrined national treatment obligations. This was mainly based on the assumption that national treatment would in any event require the best treatment available to be offered in normal circumstances, which would make MFN guarantees redundant.[26] The introduction of the MFN principle in the TRIPS Agreement was motivated by the desire to address exceptional cases in which countries had accorded more favourable treatment to the nationals of another country than to its own nationals and thus had not been obliged by national treatment obligations to extend this better treatment to the nationals of third countries.

The interpretation of Article 4 TRIPS has been addressed substantively in only one TRIPS dispute settlement case so far. In the *United States-Section 211*

[26] UNCTAD/ICTSD (fn 23), Ch 4, p 63; WIPO, Implications of the TRIPS Agreement on Treaties Administered by WIPO, Geneva 1997, p 8.

Omnibus Appropriations Act of 1998, the Appellate Body recognised the fundamental importance of the MFN principle for the TRIPS Agreement and the world trading system and came to the conclusion that it was violated because of the possibility of different procedures applying to foreign right holders.[27] It is also worthwhile noting that, in response to questions raised in the context of the current examination of the US-Singapore FTA in the Committee on Regional Trade Agreements, the US and Singapore confirmed that the FTA does not affect their obligations *vis-à-vis* other WTO Members, including the MFN obligation under Article 4 TRIPS.[28]

The application of the MFN principle, together with the absence of a provision relating to preferential trade agreements, thus leads to the conclusion that every advantage, favour, privilege or immunity in regard to the protection of intellectual property, negotiated under a free trade agreement between two or more countries needs to be automatically extended to all nationals of WTO Members. Benefits are to be granted on an MFN basis to nationals of WTO Members also in cases where agreements are concluded between WTO Members and non-WTO Members, as Article 4 TRIPS refers to nationals of 'any other country'. In sum, WTO Members are required to extend the results of FTAs which incorporate a section on intellectual property rights, offering higher protection than the minimum standards set by the TRIPS Agreement, to other WTO Members, independently of whether the latter are parties to the FTAs. This basic rule can only be deviated from where the exemption clauses in Article 4 (a) to (d), which are examined below, apply.

3. Exceptions to MFN treatment

a) Article 4(a) TRIPS

WTO Members are not obliged to grant MFN treatment where benefits of higher protection of intellectual property rights are derived from international agreements on judicial assistance or law enforcement of a general nature. Traditionally, such agreements would foresee certain reciprocal commitments in relation to evidence, extradition, investigation and enforcement of judgments across borders, without addressing specifically the area of intellectual property. The exception of such agreements from the MFN principle appears to be commonsense, given that it is certainly not within the ambit of the TRIPS Agreement to ensure non-discriminatory treatment at such a general level. As it can be assumed that higher protection standards for IPRs in FTAs normally focus on

[27] WT/DS176/AB/R, para 297. In *European Communities—Protection of Trademarks and Geographical Indications for Agricultural Products and Foodstuffs* (WT/DS 174/R and WT/DS 290/R), paras 7.54–7.55, claims in relation to MFN treatment obligations have not been further considered by the Panel.

[28] WT/REG161/5 of 28 April 2005.

other matters and not on judicial or law enforcement of a general nature, it would appear that Article 4(a) TRIPS was not meant to provide a means to exempt the standard FTAs from the general principle of MFN treatment under the TRIPS Agreement.

b) Article 4(b) and 4(c)-Type Exceptions

When it comes to the question of whether an exception can be provided to the otherwise quasi-automatic extension of rights and obligations emanating from FTAs to all WTO Members, Article 4(b) and 4(c) TRIPS address particular situations in the field of copyright and neighbouring rights.[29] Article 4(b) essentially preserves the possibility under the Berne and Rome Conventions to apply in this respect differential treatment between foreigners on the basis of reciprocity, by relying on the treatment accorded in another country. Article 4(c) excludes rights of performers, producers of phonograms and broadcasting organizations going beyond Article 14 TRIPS from the obligation to provide MFN treatment. Thus, higher standards of protection granted under national law in those fields, for example following the implementation of the WIPO Performances and Phonograms Treaty, are not necessarily available immediately to nationals of all WTO Members. Therefore, where such higher standards are agreed as part of an FTA, those standards would not be subject to the principle of MFN treatment, as long as they are within the scope of what is covered by Article 4(c). Contrary to Article 4(d) TRIPS, which is analysed below, no notification requirement applies to this specific exception. It is therefore somewhat more difficult to keep track of privileges granted by a WTO Member only to nationals of a selective range of other WTO Members. In addition, no time-limit is foreseen, implying that bilateral or regional agreements providing more advantageous rights to performers, producers of phonograms and broadcasting organizations could also qualify for this MFN exemption even if such agreements are concluded after the entry into force of the TRIPS Agreement. This is again broader than Article 4(d) TRIPS.

c) Article 4(d) TRIPS Exceptions

According to the 'grandfathering' provision in Article 4(d) TRIPS, benefits arising under international agreements related to the protection of intellectual property rights do not need to be extended on an MFN basis to nationals of other WTO Members, provided that such agreements entered into force prior to the entry into force of the WTO Agreement, eg 1 January 1995. This limited application in time of the grandfathering clause constitutes an important restriction of the available exceptions to the MFN treatment. The granting of new

[29] See the detailed comments by Daniel Gervais, The TRIPS Agreement, Drafting History and Analysis, 2nd edn, London 2003, Art 4, para 2.50.

preferential treatment to selected trading partners will thus be increasingly difficult, if not excluded.

(i) Conditions

To make use of this possibility, agreements must meet two other conditions in addition to their entry into force before January 1995: they must be notified to the Council for TRIPS[30] and must not constitute an arbitrary or unjustifiable discrimination against nationals of other Members. Although used in a different context, the latter condition tracks similar language in the general exception clause in GATT Article XX, by which WTO Members are entitled to apply, inter alia, measures to protect patents, trademarks and copyrights, subject to certain conditions, such as the absence of any 'arbitrary or unjustifiable discrimination between the countries where the same conditions prevail'.

(ii) Users

Fairly widespread use has been made of this exemption by various countries in the past. To date, 25 Members, including both developed and developing countries, have notified agreements under Article 4(d) TRIPS. Such notifications include bilateral agreements, as well as regional agreements, such as the EC Treaty, the Agreement on the European Economic Area (EEA), the North American Free Trade Agreement (NAFTA), Mercosur and the Andean Community.

(iii) Coverage

Notifications cover all sorts of treaties and agreements. In many cases, a comprehensive list of pre-existing WIPO Treaties, to which a WTO Member had adhered, was submitted. Other notifications contain sector-specific agreements, namely in the area of geographical indications, copyrights and the registration of trademarks and patents. Finally, a number of FTAs which include intellectual property provisions, were also submitted to the TRIPS Council in this context. The question has been raised whether all of those agreements are 'related to the protection of intellectual property', as stipulated by Article 4(d) TRIPS, or whether this term should be interpreted as referring only to agreements covering exclusively intellectual property rights.[31] However, such an interpretation would unnecessarily limit the scope of the exception clause, already quite narrow as a result of the mandatory guarantee of national treatment under Article 3 TRIPS. None of the notifications relating to FTAs has been questioned in the TRIPS Council on this ground.

(iv) Later Acts

Notifications made under Article 4(d) TRIPS raise the specific question of whether later acts under a covered agreement can also qualify for the exemption

[30] Notifications made under Article 4(d) TRIPS can be found in WTO document series 'IP/N/4/country code'.

[31] UNCTAD/ICTSD (fn 23), Ch 4, p 79.

from the MFN principle. For example, the EC and their member States notified the Treaty establishing the European Community and the Agreement establishing the European Economic Area.[32] The notification goes on to state that not only the provisions of those agreements, as interpreted by the relevant jurisprudence, are considered to be covered, but also 'existing or future acts adopted by the Community as such and/or by the member States which conform with these agreements following the process of regional integration'. Similar language referring to future acts can be found in the notifications made on behalf of Mercosur States Parties[33] and the Members of the Andean Community.[34] Interestingly, two of the three NAFTA States which notified have not (US) or not explicitly (Mexico) made reference to future acts under the NAFTA.

When the notifications made under Article 4(d) TRIPS were examined by the TRIPS Council, the view was expressed that such notifications needed to be precise and clear as to the scope of the MFN exceptions, and that many of the notifications made did not meet this qualification.[35] It could be argued that an interpretation by which the scope of exemptions under Article 4(d) TRIPS would extend to any later piece of legislation or jurisprudence under notified agreements, could be based on the drafting of Article 4(d) TRIPS which refers to benefits '*deriving* from international agreements'. However, this would raise certain questions in relation to legal security: in theory, a mere reference to intellectual property rights under a notified agreement would then suffice to exempt any future benefits subsequently accorded from the MFN principle, and, in cases of expanding regional agreements, the group of countries covered by the MFN exemption could vary too.

If future acts under a notified agreement were covered, as advocated by some WTO Members, this raises an interesting question that could be posed in relation to a recent case brought against the EC under the WTO dispute settlement mechanism. The US and Australia requested the Dispute Settlement Body to establish a panel to examine the consistency of EC Regulation 2081/92 of 14 July 1992[36] on the protection of geographical indications and designations of origin for agricultural products and foodstuffs.[37] Among others, both countries claimed that the MFN principle enshrined in Article 4 TRIPS was violated, arguing that the Regulation would impose conditions of reciprocity and equivalence on the availability of protection. Following its notification pursuant to Article 4(d) TRIPS, the EC could have argued that EC Regulation 2081/92 constitutes a legislative act adopted by the Community under the Rome Treaty as part of its regional integration efforts and would thus be exempted from the obligation in Article 4 TRIPS to grant MFN treatment. This argument was,

[32] IP/N/4/EEC/1 of 29 January 1996.
[33] IP/N/4/ARG/BRA/PRY/URY/1 of 14 July 1998.
[34] IP/N/4/BOL/COL/ECU/PER/1 and IP/N/4/VEN/2 of 19 August 1997.
[35] See, for example, the minutes of the TRIPS Council in IP/C/M/14 of 15 August 1997.
[36] OJEC L 208 of 24 July 1992, p 1.
[37] WT/DS174/20 and WT/DS/290/18.

however, not advanced by the EC. In any event, even if this could have been done to address the question of compatibility with the obligation to provide MFN treatment, it would not have helped to argue against claims regarding the alleged violation of national treatment obligations, as no 'Article 4(d)-type' exception to this principle applies under the TRIPS Agreement.[38]

IV. OVERLAP OF NON-DISCRIMINATION PROVISIONS IN TRIPS, GATT AND GATS

Another set of interesting and complex questions arises at the crossroad of obligations to grant non-discriminatory treatment resulting from the GATT and the GATS on the one hand and the TRIPS Agreement on the other hand. Those questions cannot be examined in detail here (but see also Chapter 5 of this book for a broader coverage of this subject matter), but a few points deserve mention.

The relationship between WTO Agreements in general has repeatedly been the subject of WTO jurisprudence. For example, the panel in 'European Communities—Protection of Trademarks and Geographical Indications for Agricultural Products and Foodstuffs' found that 'there is no hierarchy between the TRIPS Agreement and GATT 1994'. Obligations under both agreements could thus coexist. According to the theory of 'harmonious interpretation', 'covered agreements apply cumulatively and consistency with one does not necessarily imply consistency with them all'.[39]

Moreover, it should be recalled that the requirement of non-discriminatory treatment applies to different subjects: In the case of GATT, the objective consists of guaranteeing equal conditions of competition between *products*, whereas under the TRIPS Agreement, the aim is to ensure equal opportunities for *nationals* of all WTO Members.[40] The exercise is, however, less distinct as regards the potential overlap between the GATS and the TRIPS Agreement, as the GATS aims at ensuring equal treatment both of *services* and *services suppliers* from other WTO Members and therefore covers nationals in a manner comparable to the TRIPS Agreement.

Since the GATS and the TRIPS Agreement both seek to ensure non-discriminatory treatment of nationals from other WTO Members, questions linked to the co-existence of obligations are most likely to arise when there is a potential of interference between the MFN obligations under those agreements. For example, audiovisual services form an integral part of the GATS and cover motion picture and video tape production and distribution services, motion

[38] See Section III.2.(a).

[39] *European Communities—Protection of Trademarks and Geographical Indications for Agricultural Products and Foodstuffs* (WT/DS 174/R and WT/DS 290/R), para 7.208, with further references to other relevant Panel and Appellate Body Reports.

[40] *European Communities—Protection of Trademarks and Geographical Indications for Agricultural Products and Foodstuffs* (WT/DS 174/R and WT/DS 290/R), para 7.206.

picture projection services, radio and television services, radio and television transmission services and sound recording.[41] Because of their social and cultural implications, audiovisual services are considered as politically sensitive in some Members which explains why MFN exemptions have been scheduled in this sector in the Annex on Article II Exemptions. Therefore, the treatment granted by one WTO Member to service suppliers from another WTO Member may not necessarily have to be extended on a non-discriminatory basis to service suppliers from all WTO Members. On the other hand, there could be an obligation to grant, for example, certain rights under Article 14 TRIPS to performers, producers of sound recordings and broadcasters from all WTO Members as regards the fixation, the reproduction of fixations and broadcasting by wireless means on an MFN-basis pursuant to Articles 3 and 4 of the TRIPS Agreement, where none of the exceptions apply. However, this potentially more extensive requirement to grant MFN treatment pursuant to the TRIPS Agreement is unlikely to impact on the co-existence of obligations under the GATS and the TRIPS Agreement, since TRIPS protection standards are limited in scope: They provide for negative rights to prevent certain acts without authorisation and do not extend, for example, to the right of non-discriminatory treatment with respect to the act of performance itself.

V. THE PHENOMENON OF 'TRIPS PLUS' PROVISIONS

1. Where: Sources of 'TRIPS plus' Provisions

a) National Law

Virtually all national laws contained 'TRIPS plus' elements, even before the entry into force of the TRIPS Agreement in 1995. This is due to the fact that, in many cases, the TRIPS Agreement required lower standards, as compromises had to be made to reach agreement. In addition, the TRIPS Agreement did not cover all aspects of IPR protection. The phenomenon of 'TRIPS plus' provisions is therefore not just related to international agreements, but finds its source also in domestic legislation.[42]

b) WIPO Conventions and Treaties

The TRIPS Agreement only incorporates certain major WIPO Conventions, whereas the majority of WIPO instruments are not covered, such as, for example, the 1996 treaties in the field of copyright and related rights (WIPO

[41] For more details see WTO Secretariat Background Note on Audiovisual Services, S/C/W/40 of 15 June 1998.

[42] See John R Thomas, Intellectual Property and the Free Trade Agreements, Innovation Policy Issues, Congressional Research Service Report for Congress, December 2005, p 13.

Performances and Phonograms Treaty and WIPO Copyright Treaty). They could therefore be considered as producing 'TRIPS plus' obligations, if and when they are accepted and implemented by countries. In addition, current efforts to harmonise patent law as part of the work in relation to the Substantive Patent Law Treaty (SPLT),[43] as well as the discussion in the Intergovernmental Committee on the disclosure of origin requirement, and the protection of traditional knowledge and folklore, can be referred to as possible 'TRIPS plus' elements under discussion in WIPO.

c) IPR Agreements

As for other categories, agreements exclusively dealing with intellectual property rights, or certain categories of IPRs, and providing for a higher level of protection than the TRIPS Agreement, can be found both at the bilateral and regional level.[44] The EU, for example, has made use of specific bilateral agreements to achieve stronger protection for geographical indications.

d) FTAs

Many of the recently concluded FTAs cover a broad range of areas, and include specific provisions or detailed chapters on the protection of intellectual property.[45] Some examples are given and examined in more detail in Section V.4. below.

e) Investment Treaties

Bilateral investment treaties do not normally include a detailed chapter in relation to the protection of IPRs. However, given their open-ended coverage and the regular inclusion of IPRs in the definition of protected assets, they merit a mention here as provisions with a potential 'TRIPS plus' nature. A brief overview of the potential impact of bilateral investment rules on IPRs is provided in Section VI. below.

f) WTO Accessions

The WTO accession process has occasionally served to clarify and further develop obligations of acceding countries in the field of the TRIPS Agreement in response to requests made by Members. The accession of Tonga represents the

[43] Sisule F Musungu / Graham Dutfield, Multilateral Agreements and a TRIPS-plus World: the World Intellectual Property Organisation, Quaker United Nations Office, Geneva 2003, p 12.

[44] See, for example, the agreement concluded between the US and Nicaragua; David Vivas, Regional and Bilateral Agreements and a TRIPS-plus World: the Free Trade Area of the Americas, Quaker United Nations Office, Geneva 2003, p 9.

[45] The World Bank Report (fn 3), p 99, contains a useful comparative table of intellectual property coverage in FTAs concluded by the US, the EU and others.

most recent example. While the country was granted a transitional period to 30 June 2008, it undertook, inter alia, not to permit the reliance on test data submitted in support of applications for marketing approval of pharmaceutical or of agricultural chemical products which utilise new chemical entities for a period of at least five years to implement Article 39.3 TRIPS.[46] Tonga also accepted to establish a so-called 'patent linkage', requiring its relevant Ministries to determine the existence of a patent covering a generic product for which an application for marketing approval had been filed and not to approve such an application until the patent expires. The TRIPS Agreement does not specify that a five period of data exclusivity or the establishment of a 'patent linkage' is required. Cambodia has made similar commitments during its accession process.[47] However, formal commitments of other newly acceded WTO Members are limited to the immediate application of the TRIPS Agreement from the date of WTO accession, whereas issues such as five years data exclusivity are merely reflected in the descriptive part of the Report of the Working Party.[48]

2. What: Common 'TRIPS plus' Elements

Typical ways to extend the scope and coverage of rights and obligations in bilateral and regional agreements are the inclusion of new areas and longer terms of protection, the implementation of higher protection and enforcement standards, as well as the restriction or elimination of flexibilities available under the TRIPS Agreement. Mainly affected by this are the areas of patent and copyright protection, as well as provisions in relation to enforcement of IPRs. But it could also serve to extend coverage to new areas of interest to developing countries, such as the protection of traditional knowledge and folklore which has been proposed in the context of negotiations on the Free Trade Area of the Americas (FTAA) and is currently discussed in WIPO.

3. Why: Motivations to Include 'TRIPS plus' Provisions in FTAs

a) Trade-Offs

Where countries enter into negotiations on agreements covering several areas at the same time, there are usually opportunities to engage in trade-offs and obtain

[46] Report of the Working Party on the Accession of Tonga to the WTO, WT/ACC/TON/17, para 167, 169.

[47] Report of the Working Party on the Accession of Cambodia to the WTO, WT/ACC/KHM/21, para 205, 206.

[48] Report of the Working Party on the Accession of Saudi Arabia to the WTO, WT/ACC/SAU/61, para 261, 272; Report of the Working Party on the Accession of Viet Nam to the WTO, WT/ACC/VNM/48, para 437, 471.

certain advantages in one area in exchange for concessions in another area. Thus, it is frequently the case that developing countries agree to provide for higher protection of intellectual property, because the counterpart, usually an industrialised country which relies heavily on technology-based industry, undertakes an obligation to grant improved market access or tariff preferences for goods originating from the developing country in question.

b) Securing Investment and Technology Transfer

It has been argued that stronger rules on IPR protection help to attract foreign investment and provide an incentive for enhanced technology transfer, and this in all sectors ranging from high-tech to agricultural products. Some have referred to the case of Jordan, considering that foreign investment in the pharmaceutical sector, for example, has considerably increased since the conclusion of the FTA with the US, which included a fully-fledged IPR chapter, thus generating employment, building capacity, securing transfer of technology, etc.[49] Others have concluded from their empirical studies that the introduction of higher standards of IPR protection does not necessarily increase trade flows or foreign direct investment in all cases,[50] as many other factors, such as infrastructure, the political situation in general, the presence of skilled labour forces, etc. are equally important for major investment decisions of multinational companies. Given the complexity of the issue, it seems, indeed, difficult to exactly assess the impact of stronger IPR protection on foreign investment, as well as on technology transfer.[51] But it can certainly be assumed that the perspective of attracting foreign investment and to benefit from increased transfer of technology has in many cases been one, amongst many other, reasons for countries to sign up to higher levels of IPR protection in bilateral agreements.

c) Higher Level of IP Protection and Lack of Results at Multilateral Level

At the multilateral level, discussions underway on enhanced protection, such as in the field of patent law or on the extension of additional protection, currently available under Article 23 TRIPS for wines and spirits, to geographical indications of all products are not yielding much by way of results, and some attempts are being made to cut down the existing level of protection provided by the TRIPS Agreement. It is against this background that a certain degree of frustra-

[49] See the former US Secretary of Commerce Micky Kantor, US Free Trade Agreements and the Public Health, p 10, available at http://www.who.int/intellectualproperty/submissions

[50] Carsten Fink / Carlos A Primo Braga, How Stronger Protection of Intellectual Property Rights Affects International Trade Flows, in: Carsten Fink / Keith E Maskus (ed), Intellectual Property and Development, The World Bank, Washington 2005, p 19; Beata Smarzynska Javorcik, The Composition of Foreign Direct Investment and Protection of Intellectual Property Rights: Evidence from Transition Economies, in: Carsten Fink / Keith E Maskus (ed), Intellectual Property and Development, The World Bank, Washington 2005, p 133.

[51] The World Bank Report (fn 3), p 109 and following.

tion on the part of some countries is often taken as a reason for increased pressure to engage in 'TRIPS plus' obligations at bilateral or regional level.

FTAs may thus offer an alternative, allowing progress within a group of like-minded countries to develop and harmonise IP protection standards that are higher than what is achievable at the multilateral level at this moment in time. This may serve to extend the existing level of protection or to cover new areas of protection. FTAs could also promote certain WIPO instruments, for example by ensuring adherence to a selected range of WIPO Treaties by trading partners or by increasing the legal status of otherwise soft law-type instruments, such as the Joint Recommendations concerning the protection of well-known marks and the protection of marks, and other industrial property rights in signs, on the Internet.

d) Interpretation of TRIPS Provisions

The TRIPS Agreement leaves in many places considerable room for interpretation of its provisions. FTAs could therefore be used to push certain ways of interpreting TRIPS provisions. For example, according to Article 27.1 TRIPS, patents shall be available for inventions that are new, involve an inventive step and are capable of industrial application. Almost all FTAs[52] concluded by the US specify that the terms 'inventive step' and 'capable of industrial application' may be treated as being synonymous with the terms 'non-obvious' and 'useful', which reflects the approach chosen in US legislation. Constituting a critical mass of countries that have subscribed to the same interpretation as part of a network of bilateral or regional agreements may serve to support the acceptance of such an interpretation at multilateral level in the long run. But it also bears the risk of being at the heart of future disputes, at least where countries have subscribed to different interpretations and obligations as a result of bilateral agreements concluded with various trading partners.[53]

e) Domestic Policy Considerations

In certain cases, concessions made in bilateral or regional agreements also serve domestic purposes. For example, the reform of the national regime may sometimes be controversial and could therefore be easier to achieve if presented as a necessary step to implement international obligations. This consideration may play an important role in facilitating the introduction of new legislation, but also in securing a more stable legislative environment for the future, which would not be easily overtaken by political changes at domestic level.[54]

[52] Art 7.1 US–Viet Nam FTA; Art 16.7.1 US–Singapore FTA; Art 17.9.1 US–Chile FTA; Art 15.9.11 US–Morocco FTA; Art 17.9.1 US–Australia FTA; Art 15.9.1 US-CAFTA FTA.

[53] David Vivas/Christoph Spennemann (fn 22) refer to Chile as a potential example for the risk of opposing obligations in the case of conflicting EU geographical indications and US trademarks as a result of the bilateral FTAs concluded with the US and the EU.

[54] On the other hand, obligations subscribed to in FTAs may have an impact on future reform efforts at the national level. This may, for example, concern potential attempts in the US to alter

4. Who: Selected Examples of 'TRIPS plus' Provisions

a) General Remarks

It is suggested here to focus on the far-reaching network of bilateral and regional FTAs concluded by two major trading powers, ie the US and the EU, as they represent interesting IPR features for the purposes of this analysis. This does by no means imply that other regions or countries have been inactive as regards the negotiation or conclusion of FTAs covering IPRs.[55] Chile and EFTA, for example, have also negotiated a considerable number of such FTAs. An increase in the Asian region has been observed more recently[56] and many countries in that region, including Japan, for a long time remarkably absent from FTA negotiations, have started to negotiate FTAs. In addition, many FTAs concluded between countries in the Southern hemisphere do not include any specific provisions in relation to IPRs.[57]

The promoters of 'TRIPS plus' provisions in FTAs have been increasingly facing criticism for an allegedly over-ambitious negotiating agenda. In some cases, this has even led to calls for exclusion altogether of IPRs from bilateral agreements.[58] Without wanting to judge the appropriateness of such criticism, it has to be borne in mind that the inclusion of 'TRIPS plus' does not always mean a significant legislative change at domestic level. In some cases, the 'TRIPS plus' elements may have already formed part of a country's existing national legislation and the implementation of a bilateral agreement would thus cause no difficulties. Concern has nevertheless been expressed that such 'TRIPS plus' provisions in already concluded FTAs may serve as a precedent for future negotiations with other countries.

current legislation in relation to parallel imports, given the obligation in the FTAs with Singapore, Australia and Morocco not to limit the exclusive right of the patent owner by the sale or distribution of the product outside a Party's territory, see John R Thomas (fn 41), p 18.

[55] See the complete list of regional trade agreements notified to the GATT/WTO and in force as of February 2005 in Jo-Ann Crawford/Roberto V Fiorentino (fn 2), p 26.

[56] An analysis of this new trend is provided by Ramkishen S Rajan / Rahul Sen, The New Wave of FTAs in Asia: With Particular Reference to ASEAN, China and India, 2004, http://www.economics.adelaide.edu.au/staff/rrajan/pubs/RAJAN-SENFTATEXT.pdf. The launch of negotiations on an FTA between Australia, New Zealand and the 10 ASEAN countries in early 2005 constitutes a recent example.

[57] The World Bank Report (fn 3), p 99.

[58] For example, negotiations between SACU (Southern African Customs Union, including South Africa, Botswana, Lesotho, Namibia and Swaziland) and the US, as well as between SACU and EFTA have been stalled over differences on IPRs, with developing countries rejecting the inclusion of higher standards, in particular in the field of public health and agriculture; see various press reports released by the Berne Declaration, http://www.evb.ch; see also Testimony of Doctors without Borders on IP provisions in the CAFTA plus Dominican Republic FTA and consequences for access to essential medicines, submitted to the Committee on Ways & Means of the House of Representatives, April 2005. In a similar vein, bilateral FTA negotiations between the US and Thailand have been heavily criticised for the potential inclusion of an IPR chapter and activist groups have called for the deletion of intellectual property from the negotiating agenda.

b) Agreements Concluded by the United States

For a long time, the US trade policy mainly relied on the multilateral trading system and the conclusion of major regional trade agreements like NAFTA constituted the exception rather than the rule. However, there has recently been a remarkable focus on bilateral agreements. The figures since 2001 are impressive: bilateral FTAs have been concluded with Viet Nam, Jordan, Singapore, Chile,[59] Morocco, Australia, Bahrein and Oman. A regional FTA has been negotiated with Central American Countries (CAFTA—Costa Rica, El Salvador, Guatemala, Honduras, Nicaragua) and the Dominican Republic.[60] Trade Promotion Agreements, including a full chapter on intellectual property rights, have been signed with Peru[61] and Colombia. Furthermore, negotiations on a number of other bilateral and regional FTAs are underway (Free Trade Agreement of the Americas—FTAA,[62] Republic of Korea, Thailand, Malaysia, Ecuador, Panama, United Arab Emirates and the Southern African Customs Union (Botswana, Lesotho, Namibia, South Africa, Swaziland)). The scope and content of those agreements have considerably evolved over time, are generally tailored to the particular economic conditions of each trading partners and respond to the US objective of promoting stronger IPR protection. Virtually all of those agreements comprise a variable range of 'TRIPS plus' provisions.[63] Future FTA talks could include Algeria, Egypt, Tunisia, Saudi Arabia and Qatar.

This tendency finds it origins, at least in part, already in the Uruguay Round Agreements Act and the related Statement of Administrative Action, which made significant amendments to US legislation to comply with the TRIPS Agreement, and, in particular, in the Trade Promotion Authority of 2002[64] which fixed, inter alia, as a principal negotiating objective regarding intellectual property the promotion of adequate and effective protection reflecting a standard similar to that found in US law. Interestingly, the same TPA states that the Doha Declaration on the TRIPS Agreement and Public Health shall be respected, thus requiring the flexibilities inherent in that Declaration to be preserved by US negotiators. The promotion of strong IPR protection is generally driven by US private sector interests and is frequently presented as a compensation for US market access commitments in sectors of interest to the trading partners concerned. The 2005 Special 301 Report[65] emphasises once more the US

[59] See the analysis by Pedro Roffe, Bilateral Agreements and a TRIPS-plus world: the Chile-US Free Trade Agreement, Quaker United Nations Office, Geneva 2004.

[60] See the earlier report by William New, Clash Continues on US–Central America Trade Deal, Intellectual Property Watch, 1 March 2005, available at http://www.ip-watch.org.

[61] See the report by Martin Vaughan, Peru's Acceptance of IP Terms Led to Trade Pact With US, Intellectual Property Watch, 9 December 2005, available at http://www.ip-watch.org.

[62] See analysis by David Vivas (fn 45), p 10.

[63] For details and historical background, see the critical analysis by Peter Drahos, Expanding Intellectual Property's Empire: the Role of FTAs, November 2003, available at www.grain.org.

[64] Part of the Trade Act of 2002, adopted on 6 August 2002, available at http://www.tpa.gov.

[65] Available at http://www.ustr.gov/assets/Documents_Library/Reports_Publications/2005/2005 Special301/asset_upload_file95_7636.pdf.

commitment to a 'policy of promoting increased IP protection', including through the negotiation of FTAs. See Table 1 below.

Table 1. US FTAs: Incorporation of Pre-existing Treaties and Soft Law

	Pre-existing Treaties	*Pre-existing Soft Law*
Vietnam (2001)	***Give effect to and make effort to accede to:*** — Geneva Convention for the Protection of Producers of Phonograms Against Unauthorized Duplication of their Phonograms (1971) — Berne Convention(1971) — Paris Convention (1967) — UPOV 1978 or 1991 — Convention Relating to the Distribution of Programme- Carrying Signals Transmitted by Satellite (1974)	
Jordan (2001)	***Give effect to:*** — UPOV 1991 — WIPO Copyright Treaty (1996) — WIPO Performances and Phonograms Provisions on the ***Make best efforts to accede to:*** — PCT (1984) — Madrid Protocol (1989)	***Give effect to:*** — Joint Recommendation Concerning Treaty (1996) Protection of Well-Known Marks (1999)
Singapore (2003)	***Accede to:*** — Convention Relating to the Distribution of Programme-Carrying Signals Transmitted by Satellite (1974) — UPOV 1991 — WIPO Copyright Treaty (1996) — WIPO Performances and Phonograms Treaty (1996) — PCT (1984) ***Give effect to:*** — Trademark Law Treaty (1994) ***Make best efforts to accede to:*** — Hague Agreement Concerning the International Registration of Industrial Designs (1999) — Madrid Protocol (1989)	***Give effect to:*** — Joint Recommendation Concerning Provisions on the Protection of Well-Known Marks (1999)
Chile (2003)	***Accede to:*** — PCT (1984)—before January 2007 — UPOV 1991—before January 2009	

Table 1. *cont.*

	Pre-existing Treaties	*Pre-existing Soft Law*
	— Trademark Law Treaty (1994)—before January 2009 — Convention Relating to the Distribution of Programme-Carrying Signals Transmitted by Satellite (1974)—before January 2009 ***Make reasonable efforts to accede to:*** — Patent Law Treaty (2000) — Hague Agreement Concerning the International Registration of Industrial Designs (1999) — Madrid Protocol (1989)	
Morocco (2004)	***Accede to:*** — PCT (1970) as amended in 1979 — Convention Relating to the Distribution of Programme-Carrying Signals Transmitted by Satellite (1974) — Madrid Protocol (1989) — Budapest Treaty on the International Recognition of the Deposit of Microorganisms for the Purposes of Patent Procedure (1977), as amended in 1980 — UPOV 1991 — Trademark Law Treaty (1994) — WIPO Copyright Treaty (1996) — WIPO Performances and Phonograms Treaty (1996) ***Make all reasonable efforts to accede to:*** — Patent Law Treaty (2000) — Hague Agreement Concerning the International Registration of Industrial Designs (1999)	
Australia (2004)	***Affirm accession to:*** — PCT (1970) — Convention Relating to the Distribution of Programme-Carrying Signals Transmitted by Satellite (1974) — Madrid Protocol (1989) — Budapest Treaty on the International Recognition of the Deposit of Microorganisms for the Purposes of Patent Procedure (1977), as amended in 1980 — UPOV 1991 — Trademark Law Treaty (1994) — Berne Convention(1971)	

	Pre-existing Treaties	*Pre-existing Soft Law*
	— Paris Convention (1967) ***Affirm rights and obligations under the TRIPS Agreement*** *Accede to:* — WIPO Copyright Treaty (1996) — WIPO Performances and Phonograms Treaty (1996) ***Make best efforts to comply with:*** — Geneva Act of Hague Agreement Concerning the International Registration of Industrial Designs (1999) — Patent Law Treaty (2000)	
CAFTA+ Dominican Republic (2004)	*Accede to:* — WIPO Copyright Treaty (1996)—by date of entry into force of FTA — WIPO Performances and Phonograms Treaty (1996)—by date of entry into force of FTA — PCT (1970)—by January 2006 — Budapest Treaty on the International Recognition of the Deposit of Microorganisms for the Purposes of Patent Procedure (1980)—by January 2006 — Convention Relating to the Distribution of Programme-Carrying Signals Transmitted by Satellite (1974)—by January 2008 — Trademark Law Treaty (1994)—by January 2008 — UPOV 1991 (varying deadlines; not applying to Parties providing effective patent protection for plants by date of entry into force of FTA) ***Make all reasonable efforts to accede to:*** — Patent Law Treaty (2000) — Hague Agreement Concerning the International Registration of Industrial Designs (1999) — Madrid Protocol (1989) ***Affirm rights and obligations under the TRIPS Agreement and IP Agreements concluded or administered under the auspices of WIPO to which FTA members are a Party***	
Bahrein (2004)	*Accede to:* — PCT (1970) as amended in 1979 — Convention Relating to the Distribution of Programme-Carrying Signals Transmitted by Satellite (1974)	

Table 1. *cont.*

	Pre-existing Treaties	*Pre-existing Soft Law*
	— Madrid Protocol (1989) — Budapest Treaty on the International Recognition of the Deposit of Microorganisms for the Purposes of Patent Procedure (1977), as amended in 1980 — UPOV 1991 — Trademark Law Treaty (1994) — WIPO Copyright Treaty (1996) — WIPO Performances and Phonograms Treaty (1996) ***Make best efforts to accede to:*** — Patent Law Treaty (2000) — Hague Agreement Concerning the International Registration of Industrial Designs (1999)	
Peru (2006)	***Accede to:*** — PCT (1970) as amended in 1979 — Convention Relating to the Distribution of Programme- Carrying Signals Transmitted by Satellite (1974) — Budapest Treaty on the International Recognition of the Deposit of Microorganisms for the Purposes of Patent Procedure (1977), as amended in 1980 — UPOV 1991 — Trademark Law Treaty (1994) — WIPO Copyright Treaty (1996) — WIPO Performances and Phonograms Treaty (1996) ***Make best efforts to accede to:*** — Patent Law Treaty (2000) — Hague Agreement Concerning the International Registration of Industrial Designs (1999) — Madrid Protocol (1989)	
Colombia (2006)	***Accede to:*** — PCT (1970) as amended in 1979 — Convention Relating to the Distribution of Programme- Carrying Signals Transmitted by Satellite (1974) — Budapest Treaty on the International Recognition of the Deposit of Microorganisms for the Purposes of Patent Procedure (1977), as amended in 1980	

	Pre-existing Treaties	*Pre-existing Soft Law*
	— UPOV 1991 — Trademark Law Treaty (1994) — WIPO Copyright Treaty (1996) — WIPO Performances and Phonograms Treaty (1996) ***Make best efforts to accede to:*** — Patent Law Treaty (2000) — Hague Agreement Concerning the International Registration of Industrial Designs (1999) — Madrid Protocol (1989)	

The IPR chapters of FTAs recently concluded by the US are generally quite detailed and address the protection and enforcement of rights in all TRIPS sectors, based on the principles of national treatment and MFN treatment to be granted to the nationals of the other Party. While there is no unique approach or text for the IPR chapters, certain commonalities regarding 'TRIPS plus' provisions can nevertheless be retrieved and are briefly presented below.[66]

All FTAs in place require adherence or best efforts to adhere to a comprehensive list of WIPO Treaties and Conventions,[67] as well as, in the case of Jordan and Singapore, certain WIPO soft law instruments.[68] In most cases, this list incorporates at least the Patent Cooperation Treaty, UPOV 1991, the Madrid Protocol, the 1996 WIPO Copyright Treaties and the Convention relating to the distribution of programme-carrying signals transmitted by satellite. The Berne and Paris Conventions are explicitly referred to only in the FTAs concluded with Viet Nam and Australia. Rights and obligations under the TRIPS Agreement are specifically reaffirmed only in two US FTAs (Australia, CAFTA and the Dominican Republic).

As regards individual intellectual property rights, some sector-specific observations can be made. In the area of patents and undisclosed information and test data, for example, the level of protection available under the TRIPS Agreement has been clarified and increased in various ways. This is politically sensitive and has been closely scrutinised by interested circles because of the potential impact on public health and access to medicines.[69] For example, while the normal term

[66] For a more detailed analysis see Carsten Fink/Patrick Reichenmiller, Tightening TRIPS: The Intellectual Property Provisions of Recent US FTAs, Trade Note 20, The World Bank, Washington, February 2005; John R Thomas (fn 41), p 14.

[67] See Table 1 for more details.

[68] Joint Recommendation Concerning Provisions on the Protection of Well-Known Marks (1999).

[69] Frederick Abbott (fn 1), with comprehensive references to further reading material; Oxfam Briefing Note, Undermining Access to Medicines: Comparison of Five US FTAs, June 2004, available at http://www.oxfam.org.uk/what_we_do/issues/health/undermining_access_ftas.htm; Isabelle Scherer, The Domino Effect of US FTAs: Public Health Groups, Members of Congress

of protection for patents is 20 years and thus the same as under the TRIPS Agreement, in all seven recently concluded FTAs, an extension of the term of patents for pharmaceutical products must be made available to compensate the patent owner for any unreasonable curtailment of the patent term as a result of the marketing approval process. Certain agreements[70] also provide for a patent term extension in case of processing delays at a national patent office. The picture is more varying with respect to compulsory licensing: some agreements are satisfied with the application of the standards established by the TRIPS Agreement and further clarified by the Doha Declaration on the TRIPS Agreement and Public Health, whereas those concluded with Viet Nam, Jordan, Singapore and Australia explicitly limit the issuance of compulsory licences to the grounds of anti-trust remedies, national emergency or other circumstances of extreme urgency and public non-commercial use. In the case of Jordan, non-working of the invention is also included. Furthermore, most agreements[71] and draft agreements establish a direct link between the patent and the marketing approval of medicines. The relevant 'patent linkage' provision prohibits the grant of marketing approval for generics during the lifetime of a patent, unless the right holder authorizes it. Finally, the agreements concluded with Singapore, Morocco and Australia may also have an impact on the flexibility of WTO Members in relation to the exhaustion of rights, as addressed by Article 6 TRIPS.[72] They require the possibility for granting to the patent owner the right to limit parallel imports through licensing contracts.[73]

The approach to the patenting of life forms is not coherent across the FTAs. Some agreements preserve the possibility to exclude certain inventions from patentability pursuant to Articles 27.2 and 27.3 TRIPS but request reasonable efforts to be undertaken to provide patent protection for plants.[74] Others do not incorporate the possibility of excluding patents for certain life forms as contained in Article 27.3(b) TRIPS.[75] Article 15.9.2 of the US-Morocco FTA contains the clearest obligation in this regard since it explicitly requires each Party to make patents available for inventions regarding plants and animals.

claim CAFTA will choke Access to Medicines, Intellectual Property Watch, 4 November 2005, available at http://www.ip-watch.org/weblog/index.php?p=8&res=1024&print=0; 3D Trade, Human Rights, Equitable Economy, International Trade, Health and Children's Rights—Thailand, December 2005, available at www.3dthree.org; see also Congressmen letter to USTR Portman of 10 November 2005, expressing serious concerns that the IP standards for pharmaceuticals under the draft US–Andean FTA, as well as other FTAs, could severely undermine the balance between innovation and affordable health care in the US and abroad. The Generic Pharmaceutical Association takes a similar line in its letter to USTR Portman, also dated 10 November 2005.

[70] See US FTAs with Australia, Morocco, Singapore, Chile, CAFTA and the Dominican Republic.

[71] The only exception are the FTAs concluded with Viet Nam and Jordan.

[72] See also para 5(d) of the Doha Declaration on the TRIPS Agreement and Public Health, WT/MIN(01)/DEC/2 of 20 November 2001.

[73] Art 16.7.2 US–Singapore FTA; Article 15.9.4 US-Morocco FTA; Article 17.9.4 US–Australia FTA.

[74] See Art 15.9.2 of the US–CAFTA and Dominican Republic FTA; Article 17.9.2 US–Chile FTA.

[75] This concerns the following FTAs: US–Jordan, US–Singapore and US–Australia.

As regards the protection of undisclosed information and test data submitted for marketing approval of pharmaceutical or agricultural chemical products utilizing new chemical entities, Article 39.3 TRIPS does not prescribe how exactly protection has to be implemented.[76] The US-Viet Nam FTA does not address this issue at all, and the US-Jordan FTA merely incorporates the text of Article 39.3 TRIPS. However, obligations in the more recent FTAs[77] regularly seem to specify this protection as they require exclusivity of such data to be granted for a minimum period of five years for pharmaceuticals and ten years for agricultural chemical products,[78] following the model implemented by the US and also the EU. It is argued that this is justified because of the long and costly process to produce test data. In concrete terms, where the submission of information concerning the safety and efficacy of a regulated product is required for marketing approval, generic competitors are not permitted during the five or ten year period to market the same or a similar product on the basis of the approval granted to the manufacturer generating the test data, unless the latter authorities such reliance. But generic suppliers could still apply for approval using their own data. In the FTAs concluded with Singapore, Australia and CAFTA and the Dominican Republic, this so-called 'data exclusivity' is also extended to cases where a FTA member permits the granting of a marketing approval of regulated products on the basis of a marketing approval of the same or similar product in a third country.

In some cases, the US has signed or has proposed the signing of side letters on public health.[79] Those are apparently meant to alleviate fears that obligations under the bilateral agreements could limit the flexibilities available under the TRIPS Agreement to take measures to protect public health,[80] as confirmed by the Doha Declaration and further developed by the General Council Decision of 30 August 2003 on the Implementation of Paragraph of the Doha Declaration on the TRIPS Agreement and Public Health.[81] At a recent formal meeting of the TRIPS Council,[82] the US reiterated its position according to which none of the bilateral agreements concluded constitutes an obstacle for countries to take

[76] See John R Thomas (fn 41), p 10.

[77] Art 16.8 US–Singapore FTA; Art 17.10 US–Chile FTA; Art 15.10.1 US–Morocco FTA; Art 17.10.1 US–Australia FTA; Art 15.10.1 US–CAFTA and Dominican Republic FTA, Art 16.10 US–Peru TPA; Art 16.10 US–Colombia TPA.

[78] See the most recent example of Guatemala, where such protection was made a prerequisite for the conclusion of the FTA with CAFTA and the Dominican Republic. See also the analysis prepared by Lorna Brazell, A World United? The US Approach to the Protection of Regulatory Data, Patent World No 168, December 2004/January 2005, p 23; Pedro Roffe (fn 57), p 24.

[79] FTAs concerned: US–Morocco, US–CAFTA plus Dominican Republic, US–Bahrain, US–Peru, US–Colombia. The text of the side letter with Morocco is quoted by Frederick M Abbott (fn 1), p 10.

[80] The Testimony of Doctors without Borders (fn 56) provides some specific examples of alleged limitations to flexibilities available under the TRIPS Agreement in the case of the CAFTA plus Dominican Republic FTA, in particular as regards data exclusivity, the role for national drug regulatory authorities, and the extension of patent terms.

[81] WT/L/540.

[82] Minutes of the TRIPS Council, IP/C/M/47 of 3 June 2005, para 156.

measures to address public health problems.[83] This is also in line with an earlier policy brief on CAFTA issued by the Office of the USTR, explicitly stating that the proposed FTA will not affect Guatemala's ability to take measures necessary to protect public health or to use the mechanism established under the WTO's August 2003 Decision.[84]

Next to patents, copyright protection is the second most important area in which certain 'TRIPS plus'-type provisions can be found. For example, the term of protection is 70 years after the death of the author, except as regards the FTAs with Viet Nam and Jordan, instead of the 50 years foreseen in Article 9.1 TRIPS and Article 7(1) of the Berne Convention. The more recent FTAs also require adequate measures to be put in place to prohibit acts of circumvention of technological measures to protect works, including manufacturing, importation or distribution of devices to do so. In a similar vein, some FTAs mandate the liability of Internet Service Providers who distribute copyright-infringing content through their servers and networks. Those obligations are inspired by Article 18 of the WIPO Performances and Phonograms Treaty and Article 11 of the WIPO Copyright Treaty, as well as the US Digital Millenium Copyright Act of 1998.

In addition, most FTAs concluded by the US address issues on which the TRIPS Agreement remains silent. This is the case with respect to the protection of encrypted programme-carrying satellite signals, as well as the inclusion of specific provisions in relation to domain names, such as mandatory participation in the Governmental Advisory Committee of the Internet Corporation for Assigned Names and Numbers (ICANN), the promotion of responsible code Top Level Domain administration and the availability of appropriate dispute resolution procedures.[85]

Finally, certain FTAs appear to incorporate stronger rules in the field of enforcement. Article 51 TRIPS obliges WTO Members to have border measures in place in relation to the importation of counterfeit trademarks or pirated copyright goods only. Extension to goods which involve infringements of other intellectual property rights, as well as the inclusion of procedures applying to goods destined for exportation or transit is optional. The agreement between the US and Viet Nam makes border measures mandatory for imported and exported goods, and the agreements with Singapore, Chile and Morocco cover in addition border measures applying to transiting goods. Furthermore, enforcement provisions have generally been strengthened by making the imposition of fines mandatory irrespective of the injury suffered by the right holder, and, in some FTAs, by extending the scope of criminal procedures.[86]

[83] See also USTR Special 301 Report 2005 (fn 63).

[84] See USTR Policy Brief of 6 February 2005, available at http://www.ustr.gov/assets/Trade_Agreements/Bilateral /CAFTA-DR/Briefing_Book/asset_upload_file433_7198.pdf.

[85] See, for example, Art 15.4 of the US–CAFTA and Dominican Republic FTA.

[86] Details regarding the enforcement sections in the US–Singapore and US–Jordan FTAs are set out by UNCTAD/ICTSD (fn.23), p 631; see also Sheena Jacob, Singapore Gets the US Treatment, Managing IP, Issue 145, December 2004/January 2005, p 48.

c) Agreements Concluded by the EU

As with the US, the EU has put a network of bilateral and also regional trade agreements in place that contain a more or less developed chapter on intellectual property rights, and is in the process of negotiating an additional number of such agreements with several countries and regions in the world. The relevant IPR chapters typically include some or all of the following substantive elements: a definition of the intellectual property rights protected, an obligation to join certain WIPO Conventions and Treaties, and an undertaking to protect and enforce IPRs according to certain standards which are defined differently in the existing agreements. In addition, IPR chapters regularly emphasise the importance of technical cooperation and include the possibility of providing technical assistance by the EU upon mutually agreed terms and conditions.

However, it is difficult to give a summary picture here since the level of commitments undertaken varies considerably. The following section can therefore only provide an overview of the current situation in the most important bilateral or regional agreements recently concluded by the EU. Those agreements can be typically divided into at least three different categories of standards applying to countries from Eastern Europe and Central Asia, developing countries, and ACP countries.

Agreements with countries from Eastern Europe and Central Asia, including agreements with EU accession candidate countries[87] and the partnership and cooperation agreements with the former Soviet republics, probably set the most ambitious agenda for IPR protection. They generally aim at achieving a level of protection and enforcement comparable to that existing in the EU. In addition, those countries are required to accede to all multilateral conventions on IPRs to which EU member States are Parties, or which are, de facto, applied by them. The application of EU standards can be explained by the objective to pave the way either to future accession to the EU or to a privileged partnership.

The majority of agreements with developing countries take a slightly different approach. They generally seek to refer to the highest international standards as the guideline for the protection of intellectual property rights, and, in certain cases, list the relevant WIPO instruments to which parties agreed to adhere. For example, the Euro-Mediterranean Agreements establishing an association between the EU and individual countries located in that region[88] contain a specific provision requiring the parties to the agreement to provide 'suitable and effective protection of intellectual, industrial and commercial property rights in line with highest international standards', including effective means of enforcing such rights. This is complemented by a regular assessment of the

[87] See, for example, Art 67 of the Europe Agreements concluded with Bulgaria (OJEC L 358 of 31 December 1994) and Romania (OJEC L 357 of 31 December 1994).

[88] See, for example, Art 39 of the EU–Israel Agreement, OJEC L 147/10 of 21 June 2000; EU–Morocco Agreement, OJEC L 70/11 of 18 March 2000; EU–Tunisia Agreement OJEC L 97/11 of 30 March 1998.

implementation of this section, and a consultation mechanism to find mutually satisfactory solutions in case of difficulties.

In a similar vein, the FTAs with Chile, Mexico and South Africa equally contain specific sections relating to IPRs. The Economic Partnership, Political Coordination and Cooperation Agreement with Mexico, for example, also envisages protection in accordance with highest international standards. A decision of the Joint Council on detailed measures to achieve this objective, taking into account the relevant multilateral conventions,[89] is still outstanding. But the Joint Council has already established a Special Committee on Intellectual Property Matters providing for a rather detailed consultation mechanism.[90] Article 46 of the Trade, Development and Cooperation Agreement concluded between the EU and South Africa again refers to protection in conformity with the highest international standards.[91] In addition, both sides agreed to apply the TRIPS Agreement from January 1996 and undertook to improve the protection available, where appropriate. South Africa accepted to consider accession to certain WIPO Treaties and Conventions listed in the agreement, and both sides confirmed the importance of another series of WIPO instruments. The Association Agreement with Chile[92] seems to be the only one in this category with less stringent and more open-ended terms. Article 32 merely provides for the cooperation, according to each party's capabilities, in matters relating to the protection and enforcement of IPRs, including the establishment and strengthening of national organisations for the control and protection of such rights and a rather comprehensive list of activities under technical cooperation. No specific reference to the level of protection standards is made, nor is there a requirement to adhere to certain WIPO Treaties and Conventions. Finally, one particularity deserves to be highlighted in relation to the agreements with Chile and South Africa: Both contain or envisage specific provisions on the protection of geographical indications for wines and spirits in separate agreements attached to the FTA.[93] In the case of the agreement concluded with Chile, for example, the use of the names listed in the agreement has been exclusively reserved for the products originating in the Party to which they apply and only under the conditions laid down in the laws and regulations of that Party. Chile also undertook to cancel certain trademarks listed in appendix VI to the agreement. This seems to go beyond the TRIPS Agreement, as certain exceptions otherwise available in Article 24.4 to 24.6 TRIPS, eg the provisions relating to the grandfathering of a

[89] OJEC L 276/47 of 28 October 2000.

[90] Art 24 of Decision 2/2000, OJEC 157/24 of 30 June 2000.

[91] OJEC L 311/17 of 4 December 1999.

[92] OJEC L 352/11 of 30 December 2002.

[93] Furthermore, the EU has concluded agreements with Hungary, Bulgaria, Romania, Australia, Mexico and Switzerland which cover, in some cases exclusively, the protection of certain wine and/or spirit names. A complete list of those agreements with further references is available at http://europa.eu.int/comm/agriculture/markets/wine/third/index_en.htm. The most recent example is the EU–US Agreement on Trade in Wine, initialled in September 2005, see http://www.ustr.gov/assets/Document_Library/Fact_Sheets/2005/asset_upload_file917_8030.pdf.

continued and similar use of a geographical indication, or to the good faith acquisition of a trademark and generic names, are eliminated with respect to the geographical indications listed in the agreement.

The Cotonou Agreement,[94] successor to the Lomé Convention, currently governs the relationship between the EU and ACP countries. The need for adequate and effective IPR protection in line with international standards is recognised, and the importance of adherence to the TRIPS Agreement and the Convention on Biological Diversity (CBD) underlined. In addition, both sides agreed on the need to accede to those WIPO Conventions referred to in the TRIPS Agreement, in line with the level of their development. The possibility of concluding specific agreements for the protection of trademarks and geographical indications for products of particular interest to either party is also explicitly envisaged. In sum, the Cotonou Agreement does not require adherence to the highest international standards of IPR protection, nor does it seek to ensure accession to a long list of WIPO Conventions and Treaties. It is thus somewhat less ambitious with respect to the protection of IPRs to take account of the level of development and of the capacities of ACP countries. On the other hand, it is probably the only agreement so far which has emphasized the importance of adhering to the CBD.

Finally, the EU is currently negotiating a series of agreements, including an FTA with Mercosur (Argentina, Brazil, Paraguay and Uruguay), a Cooperation and Free Trade Agreement with the Gulf Cooperation Council (Bahrain, Kuwait, Oman, Qatar, Saudia Arabia and UAE), a Euro-Mediterranean Association Agreement with Syria, and Economic Partnership Agreements to establish FTAs with various ACP regions (Western Africa, Central Africa, Eastern and Southern Africa, SADC, Carribean countries, Pacific countries).

In sum, the IPR chapters of bilateral and regional trade agreements concluded or negotiated by the EU have so far been less specific and ambitious than those put in place by the US, establishing only a few reference points for the protection and enforcement of IPRs, without making an attempt to regulate details. There is no standard model for the protection of intellectual property rights. Obligations in the IPR chapters are in most cases adapted to the level of development of the trading partners. This also explains, at least in part, the variety of clauses in agreements concluded or negotiated by the EU. The agreements recently concluded by the EU with developing countries do not generally appear to attempt to curtail existing flexibilities or to extract 'TRIPS plus' concessions from its trading partners,[95] except where the list of WIPO instruments to which parties agreed to adhere goes beyond the protection standards available under the TRIPS Agreement. Nor does the EC appear to push for certain interpretations of the TRIPS Agreement through its bilateral agreements. An exception is the protection of geographical indications, such as in the EU-Chile Association

[94] OJEC L 317/24 of 15 December 2000.
[95] The World Bank Report (fn 3), p 102.

Agreement. However, the rather vague concept of protection according to highest international standards or simply international standards is not further defined. This has led to questions concerning the interpretation of the actual obligation resulting from such a provision.

As part of the current work in the WTO under the Doha Round, the EU has an offensive interest in the area of geographical indications, and more recently also expressed a desire to strengthen the fight against piracy and counterfeiting with a view to ensuring an adequate and effective enforcement of the TRIPS Agreement.[96] It can therefore be assumed that those priorities will be increasingly reflected in bilateral and regional agreements, in particular as long as perspectives of progress in the TRIPS Council remain rather limited. This is likely to favour a tendency towards the inclusion of more 'TRIPS plus' provisions in the future. According to recent statements by European Commission officials, the EU is thus planning to include more detailed chapters on IPR protection in its FTAs, adopting the US model and focusing on industrial designs, geographical indications, test data exclusivity and enforcement.[97]

Finally, it seems worthwhile noting in this context that the EU's Generalized System of Preferences[98] incorporates special incentive arrangements only for the protection of labour rights and the environment, but not for the protection of intellectual property rights. This is different from the situation in the US.[99] It may put the EU in a somewhat weaker position in ensuring the respect by its trading partners of 'TRIPS plus' obligations resulting from bilateral agreements.

5. Some Potential Implications of 'TRIPS plus' Provisions

a) Enhanced Protection 'For All'

In general, the higher level of IPR protection resulting from a bilateral or regional FTA should be automatically available to all WTO Members. As the exceptions listed in Articles 3 and 4 TRIPS are unlikely to apply in most cases, the mandatory principles of national treatment and MFN treatment oblige all WTO Members, including developing and least-developed countries, to guarantee non-discriminatory treatment to IPR owners from all WTO Members in relation to rights granted to its own nationals or those from any other country, whether it is a WTO Member or not. This applies where the scope of rights and

[96] See Enforcement of Intellectual Property Rights, Communication from the European Communities to the Council for TRIPS, IP/C/W/448 of 9 June 2005.

[97] See Tove Gerhardsen, Japan Resurfaces Global Enforcement Framework—EU Refers To FTAs, Report on the Third Global Congress on Combating Counterfeiting and Piracy, Geneva, 30–31 January 2007, available at http://www.ip-watch.org/weblog/index.php?p=520&res=1024&print=0.

[98] Council Regulation (EC) 2501/2001, OJEC L 346/1 of 31 December 2001.

[99] See USTR Special 301 Report 2005 (fn 63)

obligations is, for example, extended through the inclusion of higher protection and enforcement standards or the coverage of new areas, as long as those fall under 'intellectual property' as defined in Article 1.2 TRIPS. It equally applies where the flexibilities available under the TRIPS Agreement are restricted or eliminated. Next to the predominant factor of national laws adopting higher standards for domestic reasons, FTAs may therefore also be considered as having contributed to the fact that the level of IPR protection available to nationals from all WTO Members is in many countries higher today than the level of protection provided by the TRIPS Agreement. However, there is one significant difference between obligations under the TRIPS Agreement as compared to 'TRIPS plus' commitments under an FTA: The latter are not binding under multilateral rules. The implementation and application of such higher standards can therefore not be enforced through the WTO dispute settlement mechanism, although the national treatment and MFN treatment rules of the TRIPS Agreement are, of course, enforceable where a WTO Member applies those standards.

b) Future Inclusion of 'TRIPS plus' Provisions in the TRIPS Agreement?

The adoption of 'TRIPS plus'-type provisions outside the WTO may be perceived in certain quarters as paving the way towards their future inclusion in the TRIPS Agreement. However, albeit bearing a certain logic, there are no signs of such a move in the foreseeable future now that IPRs have become the subject of a highly politicised debate of interest to a wide public, as compared to being the playing field of technical experts and lawyers as was the case in the past. The 1996 WIPO Treaties[100] seem to support this point of view: Their incorporation in the TRIPS Agreement has not been the subject of a substantive debate in the TRIPS Council, nor does there appear to be any likelihood that this will happen soon.

c) Legal Issues

Whereas 'TRIPS plus' provisions in FTAs are likely to raise a certain number of questions of a legal nature, it seems worthwhile taking up two particular issues in this context, as they may, inter alia, either lead to dispute settlement cases in the future or have repercussions on the active use of certain flexibilities in the TRIPS Agreement.

First, some WTO Members may find themselves in a difficult situation as a result of different obligations subscribed to in two or more FTAs concluded with various trading partners. The protection of geographical indications either under the trademark system or a *sui generis* regime, as well as the relationship between prior trademarks and later geographical indications may serve as a

[100] WIPO Copyright Treaty and WIPO Performances and Phonograms Treaty.

good example, as those issues have been differently approached by the US and the EC in their respective bilateral FTAs.

Second, it cannot be excluded that some FTA provisions introduce a certain degree of uncertainty in relation to rights available and obligations to be respected. For example, the exact meaning of compliance with highest international standards of IP protection, as required under some of the FTAs negotiated by the EC, may lead to uncertainty in the trading partners concerned about the exact scope of commitments they are required to respect. In a similar vein, the trend in FTAs negotiated by the US to include provisions which set a higher level of protection in the area of pharmaceutical patents has led to uncertainty in some quarters about the residual right of countries to take measures to protect public health, including under the flexibilities available under the TRIPS Agreement and the Doha Declaration on the TRIPS Agreement and Public Health, notwithstanding US assurances on this point.[101]

6. The WTO and 'TRIPS plus' Provisions

Given the political and economic importance of 'TRIPS plus' provisions in bilateral and regional agreements, as well as their potential impact on the multilateral system, the question as to the role of the WTO in all this is not surprising. Frequently, there is the impression, or even expectation, that the WTO could, and maybe should, intervene so as to limit the phenomenon of such obligations which lead countries to subscribe to standards of protection which go well beyond the level of the TRIPS Agreement. The following section illustrates, however, that the WTO can only play a limited role here.

To start with, it is important to recall that the TRIPS Agreement only sets minimum standards and preserves each Member's freedom to adopt higher standards of protection, including eventually to forego the flexibilities enshrined in the TRIPS Agreement, which are permissive, not mandatory in nature. Therefore, whenever Members decide to make use of those prerogatives as a result of negotiations in the context of bilateral or regional agreements, they do not act in breach of the TRIPS Agreement. On the other hand, Article 1.1 TRIPS makes it also clear that Members are not obliged to implement in their national law more extensive protection than is required by the TRIPS Agreement.

The aim of the TRIPS Agreement is, inter alia, to ensure that disputes are settled through the multilateral process and not through unilateral sanctions. Members are committed to use the DSU procedures for this purpose to the exclusion of any other system of unilateral measures or sanctions.[102] Other Members, which are not parties to the FTA, would thus be free to initiate consultations under the DSU in case of an alleged infringement of TRIPS provisions

[101] See Frederick Abbott (fn 1), p 10.

[102] See Art 23.1 DSU and the Panel Report *United States—Sections 301–10 of the Trade Act of 1974*, WT/DS152/R, para 7.43.

through the provisions of an FTA.[103] However, only WTO Members can invoke the dispute settlement mechanism, but not the WTO or a body, such as the Council for TRIPS or the Dispute Settlement Body, or the Secretariat.

The WTO nevertheless has certain useful tools for monitoring and awareness raising. First, in most cases, FTAs are notified to the CRTA and thus subject to a thorough examination. This, at the same time, allows the tracking of 'TRIPS plus' provisions in such agreements and the monitoring of the evolution more generally. Second, the regular review of national trade policies under the Trade Policy Review Mechanism offers another forum for the monitoring of IPR provisions in FTAs and the discussion of specific issues and concerns in this respect. Third, based on Article 63.3 TRIPS, each WTO Member can seek access to or information on bilateral agreements from another Member. Fourth, as part of its technical cooperation and capacity building activities, the WTO can raise awareness about the rights and obligations, as well as the flexibilities available under the TRIPS Agreement. This can be a valuable contribution to ensure that countries take at least an informed decision in the future when they accept 'TRIPS plus' standards at bilateral or regional level.

VI. THE ROLE AND POTENTIAL IMPACT OF INVESTMENT RULES

In the absence of any substantive multilateral set of rules on investment,[104] bilateral investment treaties and rules on investment in FTAs play an important role and have been concluded in large numbers.[105] Coverage of IPRs is normally not the main driving force for the conclusion of such agreements, and they do not contain any detailed rules in relation to the protection of intellectual property. However, the close relationship between effective IPR protection and foreign direct investment in research and development is generally recognised,[106] including by the TRIPS Agreement, which sees IPR protection as a contribution to the promotion of technological innovation and to the transfer and dissemination of technology, Article 7 TRIPS. The 2005 Special 301 Report of the USTR lists Trade and Investment Framework Agreement negotiations as another tool to strengthen the protection and enforcement of IPRs. The latter are regularly included as a form of investment covered by the rules where an assets-based definition of investment exists, sometimes by explicitly listing the

[103] Frederick Abbott (fn 1), p 357.

[104] Other than the rules contained in the Agreement on Trade-Related Investment Measures (TRIMS) which only applies to trade in goods and prohibits measures, such as local content requirements, that are inconsistent with basic GATT provisions, and rights and obligations under the GATS which relate to investment.

[105] See the comprehensive collection of bilateral investment treaties assembled by UNCTAD at www.unctadxi.org/templates/DocSearch_779.aspx; see also UNCTAD, World Investment Report 2005, New York, Geneva 2005, and the table prepared by Carsten Fink (fn 64), p 7.

[106] See OECD Working Party of the Trade Committee, The Impact of Trade-Related Intellectual Property Rights on Trade and Foreign Direct Investment in Developing Countries, TD/TC/WP (2002)42/Final, 28 May 2003.

sub-sectors covered. Consequently, broad obligations under many investment treaties appear to extend to most, if not all, IPRs, making their protection subject to the application of some major principles, such as fair and equitable treatment and the prohibition of expropriation or nationalisation. In the case of expropriation, there is in some instances also an obligation to accord nationals or companies of the parties to the agreement the right of prompt judicial or administrative review (investor-state disputes). In addition, the basic rules of national treatment and MFN treatment also seem to apply to IPRs, although some bilateral treaties explicitly exempt procedures provided for in multilateral agreements concluded under the auspices of the WIPO.[107] Thus, certain procedural preferences granted, for example, under the PCT would fall outside the scope of the investment treaty concerned. Finally, it is also important for the overall context to note that investment treaties often include a non-derogation clause according to which the treaties shall not derogate from international legal obligations, which can be assumed to include the TRIPS Agreement.

The inclusion of IPRs in bilateral investment treaties and FTA investment chapters has given rise to a number of rather complex questions, in particular as regards the potential impact on the protection currently available under the TRIPS Agreement and in WIPO administered treaties and conventions.[108] Deliberately or not, bilateral investment rules covering IPRs may alter the set of obligations resulting from the TRIPS Agreement and may also lead to certain types of 'TRIPS plus' provisions. Without being exhaustive, a few examples may serve to illustrate this assumption. First, the definition of IPRs may in some cases be broader than the scope of the TRIPS Agreement. It has, for example, been asked whether IPR applications would already qualify as an asset under an investment treaty.[109] Second, Articles 3 and 4 TRIPS foresee a certain number of well-defined exceptions to the obligations of national treatment and MFN treatment. Those exceptions are not regularly reflected in investment treaties, which often contain a more generally drafted clause on national treatment and MFN treatment without any similar exceptions. Third, the question has been raised whether a compulsory licence is to be considered as a form of expropriation or measure of equivalent effect prohibited under investment treaties.[110] If so, the right holder could engage in legal action against the host country and ask for compensation for alleged economic losses caused by the granting of a compulsory licence. The issue is not finally settled and depends on the specifics of the case. Although some agreements explicitly provide that the provisions on expropriation and compensation do not apply to compulsory licences granted in

[107] See Art II para 2(b) of the Treaty between the US and the Hashemite Kingdom of Jordan concerning the encouragement and reciprocal protection of investment, concluded in July 1997.

[108] See the extensive analysis by Carlos M Correa, Bilateral Investment Agreements: Agents of New Global Standards for the Protection of Intellectual Property Rights?, August 2004, available at www.grain.org; David Vivas (fn 45), p 7.

[109] Carlos M Correa (fn 105), p 9.

[110] Carlos M Correa (fn 105), p 15.

relation to IPRs,[111] others remain silent in this respect. Finally, the availability of different legal avenues may also raise certain issues of a more general nature, in particular in relation to the possibility of 'forum shopping'. Bilateral investment treaties normally allow investors, including IPR owners, to directly sue the host country in case of alleged illegal expropriation and to claim compensation. This is different from and more far-reaching than the resolution of disputes under FTAs, as well as under the WTO dispute settlement mechanism. The latter is only available for settlement of disputes among states, and does not provide for damages to be awarded to private parties.

VII. TECHNICAL ASSISTANCE AND CAPACITY BUILDING

The WTO is a significant provider of technical assistance and capacity-building activities for developing countries and economies in transition. This is reflected in its Technical Assistance and Training Plan,[112] which includes a series of regional and national workshops, as well as Geneva-based events, in the field of intellectual property.[113] The objective is to assist Members and Observers to be fully aware of their rights and obligations under the TRIPS Agreement, including the available options and flexibilities resulting from that agreement and other relevant decisions of WTO bodies. The regional workshops, for example, focus on certain topical issues under discussion or negotiations in the TRIPS Council, in particular as regards public health, issues related to biotechnology, biodiversity, traditional knowledge and folklore, as well as geographical indications. Participants from the trade and health ministries, and intellectual property offices are made aware of the issues at stake. This should help countries concerned to effectively implement TRIPS provisions, including the available flexibilities, and to facilitate their effective participation in ongoing work in the TRIPS Council. In delivering its technical assistance programmes, the WTO is cooperating closely with other intergovernmental organizations, such as the WIPO and WHO. A Cooperation Agreement was concluded between the WTO and the WIPO as early as 1995 to ensure accessibility of laws and regulations in the field of intellectual property, but first and foremost also to enhance cooperation in both organizations' legal-technical assistance and technical cooperation activities. Two Joint Initiatives were launched to help developing countries meet the deadline for the implementation of the TRIPS Agreement at the end of

[111] Article 10.9.5 of the US–Chile Free Trade Agreement, concluded in 2003, clarifies that the provisions on expropriation and compensation do not apply 'to the issuance of compulsory licenses granted in relation to intellectual property rights in accordance with the TRIPS Agreement, or to the revocation, limitation or creation of intellectual property rights, to the extent that such revocation, limitation or creation is consistent with Chapter Seventeen (Intellectual Property Rights)'.

[112] WT/COMTD/W/133/Rev 2 of 16 December 2004, WT/COMTD/W/142 of 16 September 2005 and WT/COMTD/W/151 of 17 October 2006.

[113] The Annual Report on the Training and Technical Cooperation 2005 provides an analysis of the activities carried out in 2005, WT/COMTD/W/146 of 14 February 2006.

the transition period in 2000, and the second to assist least-developed countries to meet the implementation deadline of 2006, recently extended to July 2013.[114]

Those activities are intended to raise awareness and build capacities in the area of intellectual property in developing countries. They could thus constitute an important element in ensuring that developing countries are fully informed about their rights and obligations pursuant to the TRIPS Agreement. This should put them in a position to take informed decisions on any concessions that may be considered or pressed for in the course of negotiations on bilateral or regional trade agreements. Thus, it can be expected that an agreement on certain 'TRIPS plus'-type provisions would, at least, be taken in full recognition of the consequences in terms of signing up to obligations going beyond multilateral standards or curtailing flexibilities available under the TRIPS Agreement.

VIII. CONCLUSIONS

There seems to be no straightforward answer to the question posed at the beginning of this article. The impact of 'TRIPS plus' standards on the multilateral trading system, in particular the TRIPS Agreement, can be complementary, for example by preparing the insertion of new forms of IPR protection. But FTAs also risk being exposed to criticism, namely when they are perceived as an attempt to achieve an overly ambitious agenda of protection.

This article has shown that the setting of 'TRIPS plus' standards through bilateral and regional trade and investment agreements involves a number of complex questions in relation to the principles of non-discriminatory treatment enshrined in the TRIPS Agreement. The analysis of those principles leads to the conclusion that, as a rule, the benefits of 'TRIPS plus' provisions in FTAs are to be extended to all WTO Members.

There are several sources of 'TRIPS plus' standards, including domestic legislation and multilateral treaties concluded outside the WTO, which countries may rely upon in their efforts to achieve higher levels of IPR protection. FTAs represent therefore only one out of many instruments, but an increase of the already dense network of FTAs, often including 'TRIPS plus' standards, has been observed more recently. Various reasons may explain this tendency, the lack of results in multilateral fora being most frequently referred to. Major trading powers, such as the US and the EU, have regularly negotiated the inclusion of more or less developed sections on IPR protection in FTAs and future agreements are likely to follow this policy.

Under its present rules and procedures, the WTO assumes no more than a limited role in regard to 'TRIPS plus' standards in FTAs. It can monitor the developments, and this contribution has listed various fora within the organization to do so. But it has no influence on the substance of such agreements.

[114] TRIPS Council Decision of 29 November 2005, IP/C/40.

Pursuant to Article 1.1 TRIPS, the TRIPS Agreement only sets minimum standards and Members are free, but not obliged, to agree on higher standards of protection either at the multilateral level, for example in the WIPO, or at the bilateral or regional level.

Chapter 5

The Most-Favoured Nation Treatment and Intellectual Property Rights

CHRISTOPHER HEATH

I. INTRODUCTION

INTERNATIONAL TREATIES ON intellectual property (IP) have long been governed by the principle of **national treatment** first enshrined in the Paris Convention. Arguably due to this approach, the most favoured nation treatment (**MFN**) never fared prominently in IP treaties. TRIPS, on the other hand, lists both national treatment and MFN as its pillars. This article with thus start with an outline of the principle of national treatment of the Paris Convention (subsequently referred to as the Paris Convention as far as the Convention itself is concerned, and to the Paris Union for the underlying system of protection) and subsequent IP treaties, its limits and principles of application, prior to a discussion of the MFN principle as set out in trade agreements, particularly GATT. Both provisions will then by analysed against the background of regional free trade agreements.

II. THE PRINCIPLE OF NATIONAL TREATMENT

1. Treatment of foreigners or foreign goods

IP rights being fundamentally territorial in nature, international, regional or bilateral agreements on IP could approach protection of foreigners in various ways: The point of reference could be either the **nationality/residence of the person seeking protection**. This is the starting point for the principle of national treatment (typically: 'The subjects of each of the contracting states shall enjoy in the other state/states the same protection as nationals'), reciprocal treatment ('A national of one of the contracting states shall enjoy in the other state/states such protection as a national of such state/states does enjoy in the state of the national seeking protection'), or MFN ('All favours granted to nationals of one of the contracting states shall be granted to the nationals of all other contracting states').

One could of course also think of tailor-made privileges in bilateral treaties ('Nationals of country X shall enjoy the following privileges in country Y). The other point of reference could be **the IP rights as obtained.** This would be the case for a reciprocal acknowledgement of rights (typically: 'Patent rights validly registered in country X shall be given unconditional recognition also in country Y /in all countries of the Union').

Most IP treaties prior to the Paris Union were reciprocal treaties granting nationals (or citizens) of the other country the privilege of national treatment.[1] Also the bilateral treaties involving non-members of the Union (until this day Taiwan and Thailand as major countries)[2] were based on the principle of national treatment, although on a bilateral basis only. Some systems such as the European Patent Convention do not require an explicit bilateral treaty to grant foreigners national treatment, but rather a declaration from another country that reciprocity will be accorded.[3]

2. The Paris Union 1883

The Paris Union adopted the principle of national treatment as to the person seeking protection in Art 2 (1) (current text as adopted in 1925):

> Nationals of any country of the Union shall, as regards the protection of industrial property, enjoy in all the other countries of the Union the advantages that their respective law now grant, or may hereafter grant, to nationals, without prejudice to the rights specifically provided by the present Convention. Consequently, they shall have the same protection as the latter, and the same legal remedy against any infringement of their rights, provided they observe the conditions and formalities imposed upon nationals.

The principle is supplemented by Art 2 (2) whereby no requirement of domicile may be imposed, and Art 3 that puts nationals and residents of a country on the same footing. While the adoption of the principle of national treatment in the Paris Union was but a logical consequence of the various bilateral treaties that had adopted this principle, two issues deserve mention. First, that the Union also included certain minimum standards of protection, eg in Arts 9 and 10 on the suppression of counterfeit goods, that foreign applications were granted a right of priority (absent in previous treaties) and that no reciprocity was required even for those countries that did not provide for certain forms of protection, thereby granting their nationals better protection at home than abroad.

[1] A list of such treaties with further explanations can be found in Ladas, Patents, Trademarks and Related Rights, Cambridge Mass 1975, vol I, pp 43–55.

[2] A list of members to the Paris Union can be found on the WIPO website http://www.wipo.int/treaties/en/ShowResults.jsp?lang=en&treaty_id=2

[3] Art 87 (5) EPC the question arose for priority rights of applications coming from a WTO/TRIPS Member State that was not member to the Paris Convention (India). The EPO decision 2/94 of 26 April 2004 denied automatic reciprocity.

The latter was the case for the citizens of Switzerland and the Netherlands in respect of patents, as these two countries at that time had no patent law. Another solution could have been a uniform IP law, as was indeed favoured by the preparatory conference of 1880 and that could have led to the automatic validation of IP rights in different countries. This avenue, however, was not pursued and until this day is still elusive. Therefore, the principle of national treatment could remedy any case of discrimination between foreigners and nationals, but not guarantee foreigners a uniform treatment throughout the Union.

The principle of national treatment applies to the protection of **'industrial property'** as defined in Art 1 (2)–1 (4). The definition is broader than the catalogue of rights listed in the TRIPS Agreement and includes utility models, trade names and unfair competition. **'Protection'** refers to the acquisition, the scope, duration and enforcement of rights. Art 2 (3) allows countries to make an exception regarding the requirement of an agent for non-residents, and the imposition of certain requirements in connection with judicial actions, eg the posting of a financial security.

Apart from the Paris Union, also the Bern Convention of 1886 enshrines the principle of national treatment in respect of copyrights. Different from the Paris Union, the Bern Convention provides for the principle of reciprocity (ie protection according to the country of origin) for works of applied art (Art 2(7) Bern Convention) and for the duration of protection (Art 7(8)). As otherwise there is no difference between agreements on industrial property and copyright, the subsequent remarks only refer to industrial property and the Paris Union.

3. Suggested amendments to the Paris Union

In the course of the subsequent Hague Revision Conference 1925, the principle of national treatment was questioned by a US proposal to add to Art 2 the following amendment:

> In any case, it is understood that each of the contracting countries reserves the right to impose in any matters of industrial property to nationals of any other contracting country, the compliance with some or all of the conditions imposed in such matters to its own nationals in such other country.

This amendment, motivated by the different duration of patents in different countries, would have replaced the principle of national treatment by the principle of reciprocity and was consequently rejected by the other members of the Union.[4]

[4] Actes de la Conférence de la Haye (1926), pp 333, 413, 573. A Osterrieth, Die Haager Revisionskonferenz 1925.

4. Additional advantages by the Unionist Treatment under the Paris Union

In addition to the privilege of national treatment, the Paris Union has accorded a number of other advantages to nationals of Member States that is referred to as **'Unionist Treatment'**: The right of priority (Art 4), the independence of patents (Art 4bis) and trade marks (Art 6(3)), the global protection of trade names (Art 8), the registration of trade marks *telle quelle* (Art $6^{\text{quinquies}}$), the protection of process patents (Art 5^{quater}), service marks (Art 6ter) and the protection against unfair competition (Art 10bis). To the extent that minimum protection standards are involved, these need not follow the principle of national treatment to the extent that nationals may be treated less favourable than foreigners (reverse discrimination). An example are trade names that under domestic laws may require registration, while such requirement may not be imposed on foreign trade names under Art 8 Paris Convention.

5. The relationship between the Paris Union and prior bilateral agreements

De facto, the bilateral agreements entered into between countries that subsequently became Member States to the Paris Union were no longer necessary, as the Paris Union provided either the same or more rights to nationals of Member States than they had been previously granted under such bilateral agreements. Still, the question to what extent such bilateral agreements remain in force is of relevance in case a member state withdraws from the convention, or the Convention cannot be invoked for other reasons. In the past, some academic writers took the view that the Union had to be regarded as an agglomeration of bilateral agreements that remained in force only for those parts that gave rights beyond what the Union provided for.[5] However, the prevailing view these days is that a bilateral agreement is not implicitly abrogated by an international agreement stipulating the same or more favourable provisions, but rather remains in force.[6] The question became of importance in a dispute between Anheuser Busch and Budweiser Budvar in Portugal. Here, the Lisbon District Court in default judgement had revoked certain Czech appellations of origin registered under the Lisbon Agreement. Still, the Supreme Court ruled that Budweiser Budvar could still rely on the same indications protected under a bilateral agreement on the protection of geographical indications between the Czech Republic and Portugal.[7] Some support to this view is also given by Art 19 Paris Union[8] that will be discussed under 6. below.

[5] A Osterrieth/O Axster, Die Pariser Konvention (1903), p 240.

[6] Already Swiss Federal Court, Journal des Tribunaux 1888, 705; Neuberg, Der internationale gewerbliche Rechtsschutz, 2nd edn 1923, p 49; S Ladas (above n 1), 192.

[7] Portuguese Supreme Court, 23 January 2001, 34 IIC 682 (2003)—'Budweiser III'.

[8] Actes de la Conférence de Paris 1880 (Paris 1880), p 121.

6. The relationship between the Paris Union and subsequent agreements

Not least due to the fact that the Paris Union in some cases only provided for a level of protection that reflected only the minimum consensus of its member states, Art 19 (previously Art 15) Paris Convention provided as follows:

> It is understood that the countries of the Union reserve the right to make separately, between themselves, special arrangements for the protection of industrial property, insofar as these arrangements do not contravene the provisions of the present Convention.

Art 19 only concerns agreements between member states, and not between member states and third countries. For neither category does the Paris Union specify any notification requirements. On a bilateral level, a good number of agreements on the protection of geographical indications have been entered into between member states.[9] The more important agreements between member states are those on a multilateral level, however. These are:

(1) The Patent Cooperation Treaty of 1970 as of 1979 (PCT) with a total membership of 124 states as of 24 September 2004.[10]

In the absence of a world patent, the PCT facilitates the filing of patents in several countries by delaying the actual filing procedures in other countries, providing for a search report and a preliminary examination. A search report is prepared by a number of designated national patent offices within eight months after the 12-month priority period, and provides the applicant with a preliminary examination within an additional ten months. Thereby, patent applications only enter the domestic phase 30 months after the initial filing.

(2) The Patent Law Treaty 2000 with 54 signatories and 8 ratifications as of 24 September 2004 (not yet in force).

The Patent Law Treaty that was signed in Geneva on 2 June 2000 streamlines certain formalities of the application procedure, does away with the requirement of representation of foreigners for the mere purpose of paying a fee, and requires reinstatement where certain deadlines were missed.

(3) The Budapest Treaty on the International Recognition of the Deposit of Micro-organisms for the Purposes of Patent Procedure 1977, as of 1980 with a membership of 59 states as of 24 September 2004.

The Budapest Treaty facilitates the international filing of patents for micro-organisms. Since micro-organisms cannot be properly described,

[9] S Ladas (above note 1), vol I, p 195; vol III, p 1573. C Heath, Geographical Indications: International, Bilateral and Regional Agreements, in: C Heath & A Kamperman Sanders (eds), New Frontiers of Intellectual Property Law, 25 IIC Studies, Oxford 2005, pp 97–123.

[10] A very interesting analysis of the Patent Cooperation Treaty and its possible further development is provided by M Nolff, TRIPs, PCT and Global Patent Procurement, London 2001.

they have to be submitted by way of sample. This is not done at the individual patent offices, but may be done at one of the recognised international depository authorities, currently 33.

(4) The International Convention for the Protection of New Varieties of Plants (UPOV) of 1961 as of 1991 with a membership of 55 States as of 24 September 2004.[11]

As many domestic patent systems exclude plant varieties from the subject matter of patent protection, the UPOV Convention provides for a system of *sui generis* protection for plant varieties that are new, distinct and stable. The so-called breeders' exemption shall allow further research and development into new varieties, and the so-called farmers' exemption permits a re-sowing of the protected varieties for purposes of personal consumption.

(5a) The Madrid Agreement Concerning the International Registration of Marks of 1891 as of 1967 with a membership of 56 states as of 24 September 2004.

(5b) The Madrid Protocol of 1989 relating to the Madrid Agreement with a membership of 66 states as of 24 September 2004.

The Madrid Agreement provides for the registration of marks in all member states with one single application and initially upon the payment of one single fee. Since the agreement granted rights in all other member states based upon a registration rather than an application, those countries which conducted a substantive examination were at a disadvantage, thus delaying the actual registration. Automatic registration in all countries was abolished in 1957 and replaced by an explicit request for each country. Also the fee structure changed. The working language of the Madrid Agreement is French. The Madrid Protocol coexists with the Agreement and allows for an international filing already on the basis of an application rather than a registration. The working languages are French and English.

(6) The Trade Mark Law Treaty of 1994 with a membership of 32 states as of 24 September 2004.

The Trade Mark Law Treaty contains some substantive provisions, eg, the obligation for service and three-dimensional marks to be registrable, to adopt the Nice Agreement on the International Classification of Goods, and to allow filing of one application for several classes. Further, it streamlines application procedures.

(7) Nice Agreement Concerning the International Classification of Goods and Services for the Purposes of the Registration of Marks of 1957 as of 1977 with a membership of 72 states as of 24 September 2004.

The Nice Agreement is one of the so-called classification treaties and relates to trade marks. There are other classification agreements that relate

[11] Greengrass, UPOV and the Protection of Plant Breeders—Past Developments, Future Perspectives, 20 IIC 622 [1989].

to designs (Locarno Agreement) and patents (Strasbourg Agreement). The Nice Agreement of 1957 is of particular importance when it comes to filing trade marks abroad. If every country had adopted its own classification system, the applicant (or his attorney) would need to reclassify the goods or services for which the trade mark was meant to be used. This is unnecessary in countries that are members or adhere to the Nice Agreement which lists 38 classes for goods and four for services. Although membership to the treaty is not as widespread as one might expect, a good number of countries follow the Nice Classification without being members.

(8) The Lisbon Agreement for the Protection of Appellations of Origin and Their International Registration 1958 as of 1967 with a membership of 21 states as of 24 September 2004.

The Lisbon Agreement provides for a system of international registration of appellations of origin defined in Art 2 as 'the geographical name of a country, region, or locality, which serves to designate a product originating therein, the quality and characteristics of which are due exclusively or essentially to the geographical environment, including natural and human factors.' International registration may only be requested by states rather than individuals of undertakings. Once registered, the other member states have one year to reject the appellation for their territory, otherwise protection is afforded on an absolute basis. Membership is mostly confined to wine-growing countries.

(9) The Madrid Arrangement for the Repression of False and Deceptive Indications of Source on Goods of 1891 as of 1958 with a membership of 34 states as of 24 September 2004.

As some countries deemed the Paris Convention insufficient to protect geographical indications, an arrangement was concluded in 1891 to prevent the use of false or misleading indications of source. The definition of 'false' or 'misleading' indications is within the jurisdiction of the national courts. The courts may also determine to what extent an indication has become generic with the exception of indications for wines.

(10a) The Hague Agreement Concerning the International Deposit of Industrial Designs of 1925 as of 1961 with a membership of 39 states as of 24 September 2004.

(10b) The Geneva Act of the Hague Agreement, adopted 2 July 1999, signed by 39 states and ratified by 15 (as of 24 September 2004, not yet in force).

The Hague Agreement on the International Deposit of Designs is similar in structure to the Madrid Agreement in that one single deposit would grant automatic protection in several countries. Efforts to make membership more interesting for countries with a substantive examination system were undertaken by the revisions of 1960 and 1999 (neither of them in force). Official languages of the agreement are French and English.

(11) The European Patent Convention of 1973 with a membership of 32 states as of 2007.

With this Convention, the member states have delegated some of their powers to grant patents to a central granting authority, the European Patent Office with its seat in Munich. The Convention provides for a uniform system of patent grant, while after grant and (if necessary) translation into the national languages, the patent becomes a bundle of national patents.

With respect to patent law, there are other regional agreements for the grant of patents for some ex-Soviet Union countries (Eurasian Patent Office), for African countries (ARIPO), and for Latin America (ANDEAN).

Agreements between members and non-members are frequent and relate to a variety of issues, eg patents and priorities (particularly agreements entered into between Taiwan and member states), geographical indications (between the EC as a non-member and Australia, South Africa, Hungary etc), or in general as the Pan-American conventions on industrial property.[12] Often, trade agreements or friendship treaties also contained IP issues.

Art 19 Paris Convention thus encouraged member states to enter into bilateral or multilateral agreements in order to increase the level of protection in certain areas, eg the repression of unfair competition (Madrid Arrangement 1890), the protection of appellations of origin (Lisbon Agreement 1957), the international filing of marks (Madrid Agreement 1891 and Madrid Protocol 1989) or of patents (PCT 1970). Most of the above-mentioned agreements are open to accession for all members of the Paris Union, yet provide for national treatment only vis-a-vis its members rather than all members of the Paris Union. In other words, only nationals (or residents) of a member to the Madrid Agreement may make an international filing of a trade mark in accordance with the provisions of this agreement. Nationals of members to the Paris Union, yet not the Madrid Agreement, do not enjoy these privileges. In effect, and this has become very clear in the Madrid Revision Conference 1890 and the negotiations on the Madrid Arrangement 1890, *Art 19 is a recognition that different levels of IP protection may best serve the needs of countries at a different level of industrial development, or with different natural and human resources*. The point is important to note because neither the TRIPS Agreement nor other trade conventions including a most-favoured nation clause seem to have taken this issue into account.

7. Shortcomings of the Paris Union

Not in all cases does the above-mentioned system of the Paris Union make sense. It is most suitable for industrial or intellectual property rights such as patents, utility models, designs and copyrights. It is less suitable for trade marks and the

[12] See Ladas (above n 1), vol III, p 1770.

protection against unfair competition. To the extent that confusion is caused in trade, consumers are likewise affected by the misleading use of indications associated with industrial or geographical origins from member states, or those from non-member states. While, for example, the first Japanese Unfair Competition Prevention Act of 1934 only protected well-known indications owned by nationals of Union Members (due to the obligation to do so under Art 10bis Paris Convention), confusion could equally arise by the use of indications from non-member nationals, to the detriment of honest trade in general. Thus, for indications to be used in commerce (in other words, truly *trade-related rights*), the MFN principle looks more suitable, as honest practices in commerce are not only in the interest of competing right owners, but the public at large. An equal playing field for all market participants is thus better served by a principle that makes all equal (MFN), while the acquisition and enforcement of rights (that are per se unequal) is better served by a principle that combines membership with equal treatment. Apart from this, the MFN is also more appropriate where the origin of goods or services are concerned (the main issue in matters of trade marks or unfair competition), while the national treatment looks more suitable for dealing with persons (applicants, right owners). And this is already the starting point for looking at the MFN principle in more detail under III. below.

8. National Treatment under GATT

Also the 1947 GATT Agreement in Art III contains a requirement of national treatment in respect of internal taxation and regulation. In respect of intellectual property rules, Art III.4 is of particular interest:

> The products of the territory of any contracting party imported into the territory of any other contracting party shall be accorded treatment no less favourable than that accorded to like products of national origin in respect of all laws, regulations and requirements affecting their internal sale, offering for sale, purchase, transportation, distribution or use. The provisions of this paragraph shall not prevent the application of differential internal transportation charges which are based exclusively on the economic operation of the means of transport and not on the nationality of the product.

As is clear from the text, the provision concerns the national treatment of goods rather than persons, a feature that also applies to the MFN enshrined in GATT. It is clear that the principle when applied to goods has a completely different scope of application, as the most important issue for foreigners in the IP field is the registration or ownership of IP rights abroad. And while the enforcement of IP rights for imported goods may well affect their internal sale and concern issues of distribution or use, such enforcement would also depend on the prior acquisition of such rights. It is thus clear that Art III GATT is of very limited use in connection with IP rights, and has only been discussed in connection with issues of exhaustion. This issue will be dealt with below after analysing to what extent GATT 1947 is still applicable alongside TRIPS.

III. THE MFN PRINCIPLES IN GATT AND TRIPS

1. History of the MFN in the GATT Agreement

Historically, the MFN principle has been used in connection with bilateral trade agreements such as the one between England and the Duke of Burgundy in 1417, whereby English vessels were granted the right to use the harbours of Flanders 'in the same way as French, Dutch, Sealanders and Scots'. Some later treaties did no longer mention specific countries for the equal treatment, but simply any third state, eg the treaty between the Hanseatic League (Hanse) and Denmark in 1692, or the Cobden Treaty between England and France in 1860. In the 20th century, the MFN clause was adopted by the League of Nations in a model treaty on tariffs, and subsequently by the GATT 1947, Art I (1):

> 1. With respect to customs duties and charges of any kind imposed on or in connection with importation or exportation or imposed on the international transfer of payments for imports or exports, and with respect to the method of levying such duties and charges, and with respect to all rules and formalities in connection with importation and exportation, and with respect to all matters referred to in paragraphs 2 and 4 of Article III, any advantage, favour, privilege or immunity granted by any contracting party to any product originating in or destined for any other country shall be accorded immediately and unconditionally to the like product originating in or destined for the territories of all other contracting parties.

The MFN has thereby become a standard feature of trade agreements, be it bilateral or multilateral. As mentioned above in connection with the national treatment, the MFN clause refers to *goods*, not to *persons*. To the extent that it refers to customs duties or charges of any kind, it does apply to imported goods only and thereby allows a discrimination between *foreign and domestic goods, but not amongst foreign goods*. In order to achieve an equal footing between foreign and domestic goods as well, Art III.4 provides for national treatment in this respect (see above).

2. The GATT Treatment

In addition to Art I, GATT accords a number of other advantages to the goods originating from member states: Limits on the imposition of duties (Art II), national treatment on internal taxation and regulations (Art III), freedom of transit (Art V), general elimination of quantitative restrictions (Art XI).

3. Exceptions, regional or bilateral free trade agreements

Exceptions to the above rules relate to 'the protection of patents, trade marks and copyrights, and the prevention of deceptive practices' (Art XX (d) unless such exception amounts to an 'arbitrary or unjustifiable discrimination between countries where the same conditions prevail, or a disguised restriction on international trade.

In similar fashion to Art 19 Paris Union, also GATT does not discourage further agreements between its members, Arts XXIV (4) and (5):

> 4. The contracting parties recognize the desirability of increasing freedom of trade by the development, through voluntary agreements, of closer integration between the economies of the countries parties to such agreements. They also recognize that the purpose of a customs union or of a free-trade area should be to facilitate trade between the constituent territories and not to raise barriers to the trade of other contracting parties with such territories.
>
> 5. Accordingly, the provisions of this Agreement shall not prevent, as between the territories of contracting parties, the formation of a customs union or of a free-trade area or the adoption of an interim agreement necessary for the formation of a customs union or of a free-trade area.

For Member States in order to avail themselves of the above exceptions, three requirements must be met: First, notification, second the liberalisation of substantially all trade amongst members of the preferential trade agreement, and third, no further disadvantages to non-members. At least under the aegis of GATT, control mechanisms in this respect have not been effective, particularly in respect of the MFN principle: 'The seeming collapse of the MFN rules is probably the single most important cause of the present day pessimism about the GATT substantive rules'.[13] This certainly has to do with procedure: Notification of an agreement to the Committee on Regional Trade Agreements (CTRA) is mostly done ex post rather than ex ante, and a challenge by other members via a Dispute Settlement Understanding has not produced any unanimous result yet: 'The record under the current proceedings is not encouraging. During the past three decades about 50 working parties have been established to examine RIAs [Regional Integration Agreements]. None of them was able to reach a unanimous conclusion on the GATT-consistency of the agreement examined . . .'.[14] Of the fifty cases mentioned, three have dealt with the EC in particular.[15] But different from many decisions reached by WTO panels, 'the

[13] R Hudec, GATT or GABB? The future design of the General Agreement on Tariffs and Trade, 80 Yale Law Journal 1299, 1362 (1972).

[14] F Roessler, The relationship between regional integration agreements and multilateral trade order, in: Anderson/Blackhurst (eds), Regional integration and global trading system, Exeter 1993, 321.

[15] The first at the request of Canada after the accession of the UK, Ireland and Denmark to the European Community (Gatt Doc C/W/250). Here, an agreement was reached. The second on the preferential import of certain citrus products by the EC (GATT Doc L/5776, 7 February 1985) and

CTRA did not manage to contribute much in terms of clarifying the GATT contract. In fact, a survey of CRTA practice demonstrates the impossibility of WTO Members to reach workable understandings of the three requirements that could, in principle, be applied across the board'.[16] Difficulties of interpretation already concern the general requirement in Art III (4) GATT to treat imported goods 'like' domestic products.[17] In the specific case of agreements under Art XXIV, the term 'substantially all trade' has been subject to wider disagreements.[18]

4. The MFN Principle under TRIPS

The TRIPS Agreement in Art 4 stipulates an MFN treatment that is different from the one in GATT:

> Article 4
>
> Most-Favoured-Nation Treatment
>
> With regard to the protection of intellectual property, any advantage, favour, privilege or immunity granted by a Member to the nationals of any other country shall be accorded immediately and unconditionally to the nationals of all other Members. Exempted from this obligation are any advantage, favour, privilege or immunity accorded by a Member:
>
> (a) deriving from international agreements on judicial assistance or law enforcement of a general nature and not particularly confined to the protection of intellectual property;
>
> (b) granted in accordance with the provisions of the Berne Convention (1971) or the Rome Convention authorizing that the treatment accorded be a function not of national treatment but of the treatment accorded in another country;
>
> (c) in respect of the rights of performers, producers of phonograms and broadcasting organizations not provided under this Agreement;
>
> (d) deriving from international agreements related to the protection of intellectual property which entered into force prior to the entry into force of the WTO Agreement, provided that such agreements are notified to the Council for TRIPS

the third on the EC banana import regime under the Lomé Convention (GATT Doc. DS 38/R, 11 February 1994) remain unadopted.

[16] P Mavroidis, If I Don't Do It, Somebody Else Will—Testing the Compliance of Preferential Trade Agreements with the Multilateral Rules, 40 Journal of World Trade 187, 198 (2006).

[17] L Ehring, De facto Discrimination in WTO Law: National and Most-Favored-Nation Treatment—or Equal Treatment?, Jean Monnet Working Paper 12/01, http://www.jeanmonnetprogram.org/papers/01/013201.html (accessed 15 September 2006); J Goco, Non-Discrimination, 'Likeness', and Market Definition in World Trade Organization Jurisprudence, 40 Journal of World Trade 315–40 (2006).

[18] GATT Analytical Index—Guide to GATT Law and Practice, Updated 6th Edition (1995) vol 2, 824 with references to panel decisions.

and do not constitute an arbitrary or unjustifiable discrimination against nationals of other Members.

The differences between this MFN clause and the one under GATT are the following:

a) As mentioned above, GATT relates to the treatment of *goods*, TRIPS to the treatment of *nationals of member states*. The difference is a fundamental one, as the MFN treatment of persons in TRIPS is of little relevancy when combined with a national treatment obligation (TRIPS Art 3). Where a Member State is already obliged to treat foreign nationals as its own, there is little room for an MFN clause unless in cases of reverse discrimination, ie where foreigners due to certain minimum requirements of protection are treated better than nationals. In these rare cases (see above), there would indeed be the possibility of distinguishing between nationals of different nations. However, this is rather academic due to the fact that minimum protection requirements, even if only for foreigners, already establish a level playing field at least amongst this group. The 2005 Macao mock trial case (see the Annex) also concerned the issue to what extent a bilateral exhaustion agreement on trade marks could mean a discrimination vis-a-vis nationals of other countries. This, however, is a difficult case to argue, as even a bilateral exhaustion agreement does not refer to *nationals* of country A or B, but rather to goods bearing *trade marks of certain countries*, and thus refers to the origin of goods and to trade mark owners of certain countries. That is: There might be a *discrimination as to the origin of goods* (Goods being imported from country C may be subject to a trade mark infringement suit, as there is no exhaustion, while goods being imported from country B are not), *but not to certain nationals* (all trade mark owners in country A will be deprived of arguing trade mark infringement vis-a-vis trade marked goods that have been marketed in country B, and vice versa, while this may not be the case for trade marked goods from other countries).

b) *Nationals* as referred to in Arts 3 (national treatment) and 4 TRIPS in Art 1.3 TRIPS are defined by reference to the Paris and Berne Conventions. As the Paris Convention in Art 3 gives equal rights to those who are domiciled in a member state, or have a commercial establishment there, the same would apply for TRIPS to the extent that IP rights regulated in the Paris Convention are concerned. For copyrights, the TRIPS reference relates to the Berne Convention. Thus, a Thai national resident in Malaysia can enjoy the benefits of the Paris Convention if not via Art 2 (because Thailand is not a member to the Paris Convention), but via Art 3 (because Malaysia is a member, and foreign residents in Malaysia enjoy the same rights as Malaysian nationals). The same would be true under TRIPS for a Russian resident of Germany. Although Russia is not a member of the WTO, residence in a WTO country would be sufficient under TRIPS to enjoy the benefits of this agreement.

c) *Exceptions* to Art 4 TRIPS are provided in Art 4 (second part) and Art 5. The first of these exceptions in **Art 4(a)** refers to favours and advantages granted in *agreements on judicial assistance of a general nature*, in particular regarding enforcement matters. In the field of enforcement, a number of multilateral and bilateral agreements refer to the service of documents abroad,[19] the recognition of foreign judicial[20] and arbitration[21] awards. A similar exception can already be found in Art 2 (3) Paris Convention regarding the principle of national treatment. It thereby seems that civil procedures are unsuitable for the application of both national treatment and most favoured nation principles. The counterpart to Art 4 (a) is **Art 5**: Hard-core IP agreement are also exempt where they have been negotiated under the auspices of the WIPO. Examples could be future treaties on the mutual recognition of patents, certainly a favour granted so nationals of members to such a future agreement, but not to others. Art 5 TRIPS thereby corresponds to Art 19 Paris Convention. By explicitly mentioning acquisition and maintenance, Art 5 TRIPS covers both treaties of a substantive and procedural nature. The gap between the exceptions provided by Art 4 (a) TRIPS and Art 5 TRIPS are thus specific IP treaties not negotiated under the auspices of WIPO. Given the highly biased nature of this organisation,[22] one may doubt the wisdom of giving WIPO such a monopoly. It is interesting to note in this context that not even an agreement such as GATT/WTO would benefit from the exemption provisions of Arts 4(a), 5, as it is neither concerned with procedure nor negotiated under the auspices of WIPO.[23] **Art 4 (b)** refers to those exceptions from the national treatment principle as stipulated in existing IP treaties, namely the Berne Convention with its above-mentioned rules on copyright duration and works of applied art that follow the rules of reciprocity.[24] **Art 4 (c)** concerns certain neighbouring rights not covered by Art 4 (b) (Rome Convention) or by Art 4 (d) (Neighbouring rights treaties entered into force prior to WTO/TRIPS). The provision tries to remedy the discrepancy between the broad term 'intellectual property' referred to in Art 4 that comprises 'all categories of intellectual property that are subject of Sections 1 through 7 of part II' (Art 1.2 TRIPS) and the fact that within these categories, there are conceivable rights the TRIPS Agreement does not address. However, of these TRIPS-plus rights, only those concerning neighbouring rights are excluded from the

[19] Hague Agreement on Civil Procedure of 1 March 1954 with 44 member states as of 13 July 2006 (www.hcch.net).

[20] Mostly on a bilateral basis where reciprocity is guaranteed. For Europe, see the Brussels Convention of 17 September 1968 on jurisdiction and the enforcement of judgements in civil and commercial matters, and the Lugano Convention of 16 September 1988 on the same subject matter. For most EU Member States, the Brussels Convention has now been superseded by the Brussels Regulation No 44/2001 of 22 December 2000.

[21] UN Agreement on the Recognition and Enforcement of Foreign Arbitral Awards of 10 June 1958 with currently 135 member states (www.uncitral.org).

[22] See, eg A Koury Menescal, Changing WIPO's Ways?, The Development Agenda in Historical Perspective, 8-6 The Journal of World Intellectual Property 761 (2005).

[23] Thus, an agreement on protecting geographical indications under the auspices of the WTO might not profit from the exception provided for in Art 5.

[24] It may be, though, that such reciprocal treatment is not permissible under other agreements. The ECJ held so in the case of the Treaty of Rome: ECJ, Joined Cases C-92/92 and C-326/92 *Phil Collins and Others* [1993] ECR I-5145.

MFN obligation (unless, of course, they fall under another exemption, eg Art 5). Finally **Art 4(d)** concerns an exemption for agreements entered into prior to the TRIPS Agreement. 'Entry into force of the WTO Agreement' is 1 January 1995 across the board irrespective of the transitional arrangements in Arts 65, 66. First, because save an entry into force, also the transitional arrangements could not be effective, either. And second, because Art 4 is explicitly excluded from any transitional arrangements for developing or least developed countries, Arts 65.1, 66.1. The application of Art 4(d) seems to require the following conditions: An (1) international agreement entered into prior to 1 January 1995, (2) that has been notified, and (3) does not discriminate arbitrarily. **'International Agreements'** is a general term that comprises both bilateral and multilateral agreements. Not the number of participants, but the fact that at least two different contracting parties are involved makes it an international agreement. National rules do not qualify for this exception, as the different treatment between domestic nationals and foreigners is not ruled under the MFN, but rather the obligation of national treatment. In the Dispute Settlement DS 290 (geographical indications), the US and Australia claimed that EC Regulation 2081/92 violated both Arts 3 and Art 4. As the Regulation was not an international agreement, but a law by the EC as a WTO member, the case in fact could only be argued as a violation of the principle of national treatment.[25] Yet the latter is not subject to the exception under Art 4(d), as this only applies to the MFN requirement. As mentioned above, a good number of bilateral agreements exist in the field of geographical indications that qualify as international agreements under the definition of Art 4(d). And, of course, all agreements concluded under Art 19 Paris Convention, eg the 1958 Lisbon Arrangement on Appellations of Origin, qualify under this provision. If GATT's past practice on **notification** is anything to go by,[26] it is sufficient to notify once a dispute is imminent. In addition, Art 4 of course cannot stipulate an ex ante notification requirement as is contained in Art XXIV:7(a) GATT, since the agreements in question were necessarily concluded in the past. Neither does Art 4 TRIPS stipulate any deadline for notification.

d) Particularly in view of rule a) above, the MFN treatment under TRIPS as such does not give advantages to foreigners that would go beyond those conferred under the principle of national treatment at least where nationals or enterprises of Paris member states are concerned. Only in the case of states that are not

[25] In fact, the claims under Art 4 TRIPS were not further pursued. In the Regulation 2081/92, registration of non-EC geographical indications was only allowed on the basis of reciprocity (ie the possibility of registering EC geographical indications in that other country). The Panel Report (DS 290 of 15 March 2005, www.wto.org) (correctly) held that this amounted to a discrimination between domestic (EC) nationals and others and thus a contravention of Art 3 TRIPS. Art 4 TRIPS could only have been invoked had the EC indeed registered (at least one) non-EC geographical indication, as this would have allowed a comparison of treatment between foreigners of different countries. But at the time the complaints were raised, no favours to foreigners had actually been granted that could have been extended to others as well.

[26] P Mavroidis (above note), 203.

members to the Paris Union, a discrimination of treatment is conceivable. This could apply to bilateral treaties regarding the acknowledgement of the right of priority with countries not members to the Paris Union, but to TRIPS, eg Taiwan and Thailand. This issue has become moot, though, due to the national treatment obligation under Art 3 TRIPS that specifically makes reference to the advantages conferred by the Paris Convention. *As a result, the most-favoured nation principle would be of interest in the IP context only if apart from Art 4 TRIPS, also the GATT rules were to apply.* On the other hand, cases where the MFN principle could be invoked are mostly those that do not relate to intellectual property rights. The bilateral EC-US Wine Agreement of 14 September 2005, for example, allows the importation of wine grown in the US if in conformity with US standards (rather than European ones that, eg, did not allow for the importation of wine polluted by wood chips).[27] This is a de facto benefit to US citizens (as these would overwhelmingly own the vineyards in question) that could give rise to claims for equal treatment.[28] However, since the relevant criterion for granting such favour is the origin of goods, the case on behalf of wine from other countries would better be argued under the MFN principle of GATT.

5. Applicability of GATT alongside TRIPS?

a) In principle. The question if GATT 1994 could be applied alongside TRIPS has led to an interesting academic discussion. Proponents have argued that particularly issues concerning the origin of goods (rather than the nationality of right owners) should more appropriately dealt with in the GATT context,[29] and

[27] Council Decision of 20 December 2005 on the conclusion of the Agreement between the European Community and the United States of America on trade in wine, OJL 87/2006, 2. According to Art 4 of this Agreement,

1. Each Party recognises that the laws, regulations and requirements of the other Party relating to wine making fulfil the objectives of its own laws, regulations and requirements, in that they authorise wine-making practices that do not change the character of wine arising from its origin in the grapes in a manner inconsistent with good wine-making practices. These practices include such practices that address the reasonable technological or practical need to enhance the keeping or other qualities or stability of the wine and that achieve the winemaker's desired effect, including with respect to not creating an erroneous impression about the product's character and composition.
2. Within the scope of this Agreement as defined in Art 3, neither Party shall restrict, on the basis of either wine-making practices or product specifications, the importation, marketing or sale of wine originating in the territory of the other Party that is produced using wine-making practices that are authorised under laws, regulations and requirements of the other Party listed in Annex I and published or communicated to it by that other Party.

[28] The Panel decision in DS 290 (as above) applied the de facto rule with respect to national treatment in the case of geographical indications that would overwhelmingly be claimed by nationals or residents of the country in question.

[29] Th Cottier, Implications of WTO Law for the Exhaustion Issue and Parallel Imports, presentation, at: Dispute Resolution in the World Trade Organisation, Brussels, 12 June 1998; *ibid*, The WTO System and Exhaustion of Rights, presentation at: Committee on International Trade Law, Conference on the Exhaustion of Intellectual Property Rights and Parallel Importation in World

that the MFN clauses in GATT and TRIPS concerned different issues, thereby not precluding the applicability of GATT by TRIPS.[30] The opposite view essentially argues that conflicts between IP rights and the principles of free trade had been conclusively dealt with by the framework of TRIPS.[31] After a WTO panel had already established that the GATT rules should be applicable alongside GATS,[32] DS 290 has held that the principles established in GATT 1994 and TRIPS apply cumulatively:

> 7.246 The Panel notes that there is no hierarchy between the TRIPS Agreement and GATT 1994, which appear in separate annexes to the WTO Agreement. The ordinary meaning of the texts of the TRIPS Agreement and GATT 1994, as well as Article II:2 of the WTO Agreement, taken together, indicates that obligations under the TRIPS Agreement and GATT 1994 can co-exist and that one does not override the other. This is analogous to the finding of the Panel in *Canada—Periodicals*, with which the Appellate Body agreed, concerning the respective scopes of GATS and GATT 1994.[33] Further, a 'harmonious interpretation' does not require an interpretation of one that shadows the contours of the other. It is well established that the covered agreements apply cumulatively and that consistency with one does not necessarily imply consistency with them all.[34]
>
> More specifically, the Panel notes that Article 8 of the TRIPS Agreement sets out the principles of that agreement. Article 8.1 provides as follows:
>
> > 1. Members may, in formulating or amending their laws and regulations, adopt measures necessary to protect public health and nutrition, and to promote the public interest in sectors of vital importance to their socio-economic and technological development, provided that such measures are consistent with the provisions of this Agreement.
>
> These principles reflect the fact that the agreement does not generally provide for the grant of positive rights to exploit or use certain subject matter, but rather provides for the grant of negative rights to prevent certain acts. This fundamental feature of intellectual property protection inherently grants Members freedom to pursue legitimate public policy objectives since many measures to attain those public policy objectives lie outside the scope of intellectual property rights and do not require an exception under the TRIPS Agreement.

Trade, Geneva 6–7 November 1997; Cottier/Stucki, Parallelimporte im Patent-, Urheber- und und Muster- und Modellbereich aus europarechtlicher und völkerrechtlicher Sicht, in: Conflit entre importations parallèles et propriété intellectuelle?, Actes du Colloque de Lausanne, Comparativa No 60, Geneva 1996.29, 54.

[30] Ch Freytag, Parallelimporte nach EG—und WTO Recht, Berlin 2001, 239; D Kraus, Les importations parallèles de produits brevetés, Zurich 2004, 173.

[31] M Bronckers, The Exhaustion of Patent Rights under World Trade Organization Law, 32 Journal of World Trade, Issue 5, 1 (1998); K Mager, Parallel Imports in Patented Goods, Working Paper, AIPPI Meeting Rio de Janeiro, 28 Mai 1998, 2.

[32] DS 31 of 16 March 1996 (Canada-Periodicals).

[33] Panel report on *Canada—Periodicals*, at para. 5.17; Appellate Body report on *Canada—Periodicals*, DSR 1997:I, 449, at 465.

[34] See, for example, the Appellate Body report on *Argentina—Footwear (EC)*, para 81; and the Appellate Body report on *Korea—Dairy*, para 74; and the Panel reports on *EC—Bananas III*, para 7.160.

> The scope of the national treatment obligation in Article 3.1 of the TRIPS Agreement also differs from that of the national treatment obligation in Article III:4 of GATT 1994, as it is subject to certain exceptions in Articles 3.1, 3.2 and 5, one of which is inspired by the language of Article XX of GATT 1994.[35] There is also a series of specific exceptions in the provisions relating to the minimum standards in Part II of the TRIPS Agreement and Part VII contains a provision on security exceptions analogous to Article XXI of GATT 1994, but none on general exceptions.
>
> For all these reasons, in the Panel's view, the fact that a general exceptions provision analogous to Article XX of GATT 1994 was not included in the TRIPS Agreement has no impact on its analysis of Article 3.1.[36]

In other words, the provisions of GATT 1994 and TRIPS apply cumulatively, and exceptions to certain principles provided in one of these agreements apply only in the context of this agreement.

b) The issue of exhaustion in particular. A specific problem relates to Art 6 TRIPS, according to which 'for the purposes of dispute settlement . . ., nothing in this agreement shall be used to address the issue of exhaustion of intellectual property rights.' Regardless if viewed as a procedural or substantive provision,[37] making the GATT rules applicable to agreements over exhaustion in the view of some academics would run counter to Art 6 TRIPS or to Arts 64, 65 TRIPS that temporarily exempt certain GATT rules from dispute settlements concerning intellectual property.[38] On the other hand, the fact that *certain* provisions of GATT should not apply in the TRIPS context is rather an argument in favour of applying all remaining ones, as otherwise, it would make little sense to exempt only some. Art 6 TRIPS makes reference to *this agreement* only, thereby referring to TRIPS rather than to the whole WTO Agreement, and in addition does not refer to the TRIPS' national treatment and MFN provisions. Against this background, it would be rather doubtful why certain agreements even relating to exhaustion could be reviewed by a GATT panel in light of the TRIPS MFN provision, but not the GATT one. Thus, the better arguments favour an interpretation whereby the GATT provisions (at least those that concern MFN issues that are discussed in the context of this paper) can be invoked by a GATT panel even when judging compliance of an exhaustion rule therewith.[39] Within the course of the mock trial case, it was also argued to what

[35] Art 24.9 of the TRIPS Agreement also provides that there shall be no obligation under the TRIPS Agreement to protect geographical indications which are not or cease to be protected in their country of origin, or which have fallen into disuse in that country.

[36] Panel Decision DS 290, as above.

[37] For a discussion on this matter, see C. Heath, Parallel Imports and International Trade, 28 IIC 623, 629 [1997]; H Ullrich, Technology Protection according to TRIPS, in: Beier/Schricker (eds), From GATT to TRIPS, IIC Studies 18, Weinheim 1996, 357.

[38] This view is taken by M Bronckers, as above n 31, 11.

[39] Also Ch Freytag (above n 30), 239, M. Döbler, Die Einführung des WTO-weiten Erschöpfungsgrundsatzes in das Markenrecht der EU und der USA, Frankfurt 2002, 111; D Kraus (above n 31) does not even mention the issue as a problem, but assumes that once GATT is applicable alongside TRIPS, this would unrestrictedly apply to issues of exhaustion as well.

extent other *TRIPS provisions* could be applied despite Art 6, yet this is a topic that cannot be further elaborated here.[40]

IV. INTERPRETING COMPLIANCE—IP AND POSSIBLE DISCRIMINATION SCENARIOS UNDER GATT AND TRIPS

Once it has been established that the GATT principles are indeed applicable to IP disputes under TRIPS, rules or agreements may also be scrutinised for compliance with the MFN provisions under GATT or TRIPS. Of particular relevance both for the conference mock trial and for practical purposes are exhaustion rules.

1. Favour or Advantage

Starting point for both a contravention against the principle of national treatment and MFN must be a comparison between, either, nationals and foreigners / domestic or foreign goods, or foreigners / foreign goods of different origin. As mentioned above, in the case of TRIPS, the comparison refers to *nationality*, in the case of GATT to the *origin of goods*. The treatment in question must be *less favourable*, referring to a *favour, advantage, privilege or immunity* granted to some, but not to others. Neither GATT nor TRIPS concern any definition thereof, although these terms are used in Art I.1 GATT and Art 4 TRIPS. The national treatment provisions of Art III.4 GATT and Art 3 TRIPS make reference to a treatment 'no less favourable' and thus also require a definition of what can be considered a 'favour'.

a) TRIPS. The objectives of TRIPS are laid down in the preamble and in Arts 7 and 8. These provisions show that the equation 'more rights = more favours' is not necessarily correct. The agreement (at least on paper) does not equal the highest level of protection with the most ideal one. Rather, the proper balance of rights and obligations should be achieved so that IP rights are 'conducive to social and economic welfare' and 'do not themselves become barriers of legitimate trade'. To the extent that TRIPS concerns the possibility of obtaining rights, the panel in DS 290 has defined the term 'favour' as follows:

> The Panel recalls that the standard of examination is based on 'effective equality of opportunities'. It follows that the nationals that are relevant to an examination under

[40] The argument centres around the applicability of Art 16 TRIPS for cases of parallel importation of trade marked goods. One could argue that a trade mark law compliant with Art 16 can only find infringement for cases of *confusion*. Such confusion may well be absent, however, in the case of importation of original goods. For such cases, Art 16 2nd sentence would either have to be interpreted in that the presumption of confusion is rebuttable, or in that for cases of parallel importation, the provision would not be applicable at all. Even if so interpreted, one would than have to argue that the conflict was none of exhaustion (in which case Art 6 would apply), but about the proper interpretation of the scope of trade mark rights. The issue is further elaborated by M Döbler (above n 39), 99–110.

> Article 3.1 of the TRIPS Agreement should be those who seek opportunities with respect to the same type of intellectual property in comparable situations.[41] On the one hand, this excludes a comparison of opportunities for nationals with respect to different categories of intellectual property, such as GIs and copyright. On the other hand, no reason has been advanced as to why the equality of opportunities should be limited a priori to rights with a territorial link to a particular Member.[42]

Apart from the case at issue that concerned the registration of geographical indications open to foreigners only upon the basis of reciprocity, an obvious case of discrimination are the so-called *Hilmer* rules in the US whereby a foreign filing could not count as prior art reference (while a US filing could),[43] and that under the first-to-invent system, proof of prior conception could only be furnished for inventions made in the US, while for inventions made abroad, the filing date would count rather than abroad.[44,45] Regarding scope and enforcement of rights, it has been mentioned above that hardly any scenarios might be conceivable under the current international framework of IP whereby foreigners face a disadvantage.

b) GATT—National treatment. The point of reference in this case are goods, not persons. Of particular relevance in this context is the requirement of national treatment in Art III.4 (quoted above).

It is relatively easy to understand that all intellectual property rights act as import barriers. They are barriers to trade. Yet, this as such does not allow the conclusion that such barrier also amounts to discriminatory treatment. To the extent that a right owner can pursue infringing goods in the domestic context, the same should be possible vis-a-vis imported goods. For a contravention of Art III.4, it is thus necessary to indicate a difference between the scope of an IP right vis-a-vis domestic and foreign goods. Once could think of the 'right of importation' conceded by TRIPS, eg Art 28.1(a) for patents. Yet the right of importation can also be invoked against goods first marketed domestically and subsequently re-imported to the extent that such goods are infringing. To this extent, there is no difference between domestic and foreign-made goods. The issue is slightly different in cases of national or regional exhaustion regimes. As a general rule, the seller of goods covered by an intellectual property right, be it a patent, trade mark or copyright, 'exhausts' such IP right for those goods marketed with his consent. Bar any subsequent rights (in the case of copyrights, rental or lending, in the case of trade marks, tampering with the goods so that the function of ori-

[41] The Appellate Body in *EC—Asbestos* adopted an analogous approach to the term 'like' products in Article III:4 of GATT 1994, which it interpreted in terms of the competitive relationship between products: see its report at para 99.

[42] See the European Communities' responses to Panel questions Nos 25, 101 and 103.

[43] *In re Hilmer I*, CCPA, 359 F.2d 859 (1966).

[44] *In re Hilmer II*, CCPA, 424 F.2d 1108 (1970).

[45] The view that these rules discriminate and are thus contrary to the national treatment principle is taken by T Takenaka, Rethinking the United States First-to-Invent Principle, Houston Law Review 621, 659 (2002).

gin is corrupted), no further claims can be made in respect of the subsequent use of such goods.[46] Depending on the exhaustion regime, the same might not necessarily true for goods marketed abroad with the IP owner's consent. Such goods cannot be considered counterfeits or pirated goods, yet their importation may be deemed infringing under those regimes that allow the IP owner to prevent importation[47] based on the respective right in question. The IP owner may thus invoke his right against imported goods although goods marketed domestically under the same conditions would be outside the IP owner's rights. Can this be considered a discrimination? Some have argued that it is,[48] as it amounts to an additional possibility of enforcing the IP right in the case of imported goods[49] (once upon the first marketing, and once upon importation), while this is not possible for domestically marketed goods. Others have argued against a discrimination, as the exhaustion regime would be applied regardless of the origin of goods,[50] an argument that fails to convince: For one, a regime of national exhaustion can only affect goods that are imported,[51] and furthermore, there is indeed a discrimination in the case of re-imports of goods previously put on the domestic market and subsequently exported. For these goods, there are no importation barriers (as they fall under the domestic exhaustion regime), while for those first marketed abroad, there may be if the country adopts a national or regional exhaustion regime.[52] TRIPS is no justification in this respect (if it could be one in the first place), as it does not impose a certain exhaustion regime: At least for trade marks, there are good arguments that Art 16 TRIPS de facto requires a regime of international exhaustion. Rules of national and regional exhaustion could thus only be justified under Art XX (d) if they are not considered arbitrary or unjustifiable. See below 2.

c) GATT—MFN. A regime of national or regional exhaustion is prima facie not compliant with Art III.4 GATT, as it discriminates certain imported goods over

[46] The issues involving exhaustion are relatively complex and cannot be dealt here in more detail. An overview is provided by C Heath, Legal Concepts or Exhaustion and Parallel Imports, in: Heath(ed.) Parallel Imports in Asia, Max Planck Series on Asian Intellectual Property Law vol 9, Kluwer Law International London 2004, 13–23.

[47] It is clear that the right of importation as such does not determine the issue of exhaustion. The importation right is part of a bundle of rights of use that exhaust upon first marketing. If a distinction is made between domestic marketing and marketing abroad, the importation right as well as other rights can be invoked against imported goods, if the law makes no such distinction, the right of importation as well as all other rights of use are exhausted. In other words, the right of importation follows the exhaustion rule and not vice versa.

[48] Yusuf/Moncayo von Hase, Intellectual Property Protection and International Trade—Exhaustion of Rights Revisited, 16 World Competition 115, 128 [1992]; S Verma, Exhaustion of Intellectual Property Rights and Free Trade—Art 6 of the TRIPS Agreement, 29 IIC 534, 553 [1998].

[49] Preventing importation as such is equivalent to a quantitative restriction under Art XI GATT.

[50] H Bale, Exhaustion in the Field of Patents: Public Policy and the Pharmaceutical Industry, Paper presented at the Geneva ILTC Conference on Intellectual Property Rights and Parallel Importation in World Trade, 6–7 November 1998.

[51] C Freytag (above note 30), 246.

[52] The difference became clear in the US cases *Quality King v Lanza*, US Supreme Court, 9 March 1998 (for copyrights), and *Jazz Photo Corp v US International Trade Commission*, Fed Cir 264 F.3d 1094 (2001) (for patents).

those domestically marketed, although the relevant marketing conditions are the same (consent by the IP owner). Leaving this aside for the moment, a regime envisaged by the mock trial case would amount to a *preferential* exhaustion—goods from some countries are treated different from those originating from others—the classical case of Art I.1 GATT if such exhaustion (and thereby facilitation of trade) were to be regarded as a *favour or advantage*. While some have argued in respect of TRIPS that any increase in protection of rights amounts to a favour (and consequently an agreement of mutual exhaustion could not amount to a favour, but rather the contrary),[53] this is doubtful in view of the preamble and Art 8 TRIPS (as above). In the case of GATT, any lowering of customs duties[54] or facilitating conditions of sale[55] is considered an advantage. The right of the IP owner to block importation is thus a disadvantage (in the sense of GATT, and with respect to the goods) whose abolition can thus be considered a favour in respect of goods originating from a certain country (or, in the mock trial case at issue), having been put on a certain market with the IP owner's consent.[56] Such favour according to GATT has to be granted to other imported goods as well, unless one of the exceptions under Art XX or Art XXIV applies. Outside the field of exhaustion, it is difficult to conceive scenarios that might give rise to GATT MFN complaints (for the case of the EU–US Wine Agreement, see above). One could think of agreements that for goods originating from certain countries, the act of transit of infringing goods is not considered reason to detain such goods, while from others, it is. Also this would be amount to a different scope of IP rights depending on where the goods come from.[57]

2. Exceptions under Art XX

Intellectual property rights in Art XX (d) are recognised as a legitimate barrier to free trade. The GATT provisions thus do not apply to the exercise of IP rights unless this would amount to an arbitrary and unjustifiable discrimination. In addition, the adoption of measures formally compliant with one of the exceptions under XX might fall foul under the general non-discrimination rule in the preamble of Art XX if in fact adopted for other, eg protectionist, purposes.[58] Some authors thus have concluded that under GATT, import-limiting IP rules have to be measured by the same standard as is applied under Art 30, 36 EC

[53] Straus/Katzenberger, Erschöpfung des Patentrechts, Bern 2003, 50.

[54] *Indonesia—Certain Measures affecting the Automobile Industry*, WTO DS 54, 55, 59 and 64 of 2 July 1998, at 357.

[55] *European Communities—Regime for the Importation, Sale and Distribution of Bananas*, WTO DS 27 of 9 September 1997, at 206.

[56] Also argued by D Kraus (above note 30), 185.

[57] On condition that an interpretation of IP rights that applies the act of 'importation' is consistent with Art V.6 GATT in the first place (unlikely), or that the exception of Art XX GATT could be invoked as being neither arbitrary nor unjustifiable.

[58] *United States—Standards for Reformulated and Conventional Gasoline*, WTO DS2 of 20 May 1996.

Treaty.[59] According to this standard, limiting exhaustion in view of the different price levels in different countries (arbitrage) is difficult to justify, as it has nothing to do with the specific subject matter of the right as such. Different price levels, however, are one of the main reasons to justify the prohibition of parallel imports. The issue of exhaustion may be different in cases where goods have been marketed in the exporting country without a corresponding IP right yet with the right owner's consent (the right owner chose not to request a patent in this specific country), as in such case, no reward under monopolistic conditions could have been reaped.[60] For trade marks, limiting exhaustion by reasons other than the danger of confusion is similarly questionable. A better case can be made for countries that regard the transit of goods as an actionable IP infringement in cases where the goods would indeed infringe when brought on the domestic market, and where there is a real danger that transit becomes importation.[61]

3. Exceptions under Art XXIV

The exception under Art XXIV refers to Customs Unions and Free Trade Area. The provision is rather complicated not least in view of an Additional Memorandum of Understanding (1994) and of the complexity of customs unions in general. Subsections 5 and 6 of Art XXIV read as follows:

> (5) Accordingly, the provisions of this Agreement shall not prevent, as between the territories of contracting parties, the formation of a customs union or of a free-trade area or the adoption of an interim agreement necessary for the formation of a customs union or of a free-trade area; *Provided* that:
>
> (*a*) with respect to a customs union, or an interim agreement leading to a formation of a customs union, the duties and other regulations of commerce imposed at the institution of any such union or interim agreement in respect of trade with contracting parties not parties to such union or agreement shall not on the whole be higher or more restrictive than the general incidence of the duties and regulations of commerce applicable in the constituent territories prior to the formation of such union or the adoption of such interim agreement, as the case may be;

[59] H Ullrich (above n 37), 376; S Verma (above n 48), 534, 555; C Freytag (above n 30), 244.

[60] The ECJ did not even find an objective obstacle of patenting (no patents were available for pharmaceuticals) a reason to deny exhaustion in the Common Market: ECJ, *Merck v Primecrown*, 13 July 1995, which is highly questionable, as it goes against the very subject matter of patent rights: P Demaret, Industrial Property Rights, Compulsory Licences and the Free Movement of Goods, 18 IIC 161, 177 (1981).

[61] It is not possible to deal with the finer points of customs rules at this stage (But see: Vrins/Schneider, Enforcement of Intellectual Property Rights through border measures: Law and Practice in the EU, Oxford 2006). In Europe, Council Regulation (EC) 1383/2003 of 22 July 2003 concerning customs action against goods suspected of infringing certain intellectual property rights and the measures to be taken against goods found to have infringed such rights, OJ L 196 of 2 August 2003, 7, includes the transit as an actionable infringement, yet it seems that the ECJ makes this dependent upon the possibility that such goods reach the domestic market: ECJ, 28 October 2005, *Class International v Unilever*.

(*b*) with respect to a free-trade area, or an interim agreement leading to the formation of a free-trade area, the duties and other regulations of commerce maintained in each of the constituent territories and applicable at the formation of such freetrade area or the adoption of such interim agreement to the trade of contracting parties not included in such area or not parties to such agreement shall not be higher or more restrictive than the corresponding duties and other regulations of commerce existing in the same constituent territories prior to the formation of the free-trade area, or interim agreement as the case may be; and

(*c*) any interim agreement referred to in subparagraphs (*a*) and (*b*) shall include a plan and schedule for the formation of such a customs union or of such a free-trade area within a reasonable length of time.

(6) If, in fulfilling the requirements of subparagraph 5 (*a*), a contracting party proposes to increase any rate of duty inconsistently with the provisions of Article II, the procedure set forth in Article XXVIII shall apply. In providing for compensatory adjustment, due account shall be taken of the compensation already afforded by the reduction brought about in the corresponding duty of the other constituents of the union.

If by way of a Customs Union, or, as in the mock trial case, a Free Trade Area, intellectual property rights are selectively strengthened so that this leads to a trade discrimination regarding certain goods, this is not in conformity with GATT. If, on the other hand, national exhaustion regimes in the course of such an agreement are converted into regional exhaustion regimes, this is discriminatory (regarding goods from third countries), yet a lessening of trade barriers when compared to the previous situation. Thus, for the mock trial case at issue, a legitimate complaint against FUFTA could only be raised against Futura on condition that FUFTA required Futura to switch from a system of international trade mark exhaustion to one of regional exhaustion. According to the facts, both is uncertain: The current exhaustion regime for trade marks in Futura, and the interpretation of Art 1204 as a maximum provision that also concerns exhaustion regarding trade marked goods from third countries. The same provision has been interpreted differently by the ECJ[62] (for the EU) and the EFTA court (for EFTA).[63]

V. CONCLUDING SUMMARY

The above analysis has shown that the MFN principle, while new to the arena of intellectual property rights, has a very limited scope of application when referring to persons rather than goods. In fact, there is hardly any conceivable scenario of a contravention of Art 4 TRIPS that would not also contravene the principle of national treatment. Things are different for the MFN as enshrined in GATT 1947. Here, a particularly difficult issue concerns exhaustion rules and agreements on mutual exhaustion.

[62] ECJ, Silhouette *International v Haslauer*, 16 July 1998.
[63] EFTA Court, *Mag Instruments v California Trading Company*, 3 December 1997.

APPENDIX

2005 Mock Trial*

Rules of Engagement

1) **Applicable law**: WTO/TRIPS, but plaintiff and defendant may rely on (ie present to the court in writing) case law from any jurisdiction

2) **Rules of procedure**: WTO, but the panellists must seek an opinion from the jury (ie the audience) before rendering judgment.

3) Both parties, plaintiff and defendant are to prepare their oral arguments.

4) In the oral hearing, both sides shall present their case in opening statements very briefly within 10 minutes. Thereupon, the witnesses shall be heard. Thereafter, both parties shall present their reasoned arguments for about 20 minutes each as a summing up, whereupon both sides shall have another 10 minutes to rebut arguments by the other side.

5) Finally, the panellists shall consider his verdict during the recess and pronounce judgement after having sought an opinion from the jury.

6) A verdict on the substantive legal questions should be provided even if the court considers it has no jurisdiction.

Mock Trial—'The Free Trade Agreement between Futura and Utopia'

This case involves a dispute over the free trade agreement between 'Futura' and 'Utopia' of 5 September 2000. The Futura-Utopia Free Trade Agreement (FUFTA) contains a chapter (12) on intellectual property. In Article 1204 Futura and Utopia agree to the free circulation of trade marked goods. The wording of the provision can be found in the appendix.

Utopia is a developed nation and WTO member that has agreed to such bilateral exhaustion in order to stimulate development in neighbouring Futura, a former communist state. Futura has recently taken significant steps to move towards a free market economy and is a recent WTO member, but it must still be considered a least developed nation.

The above Article 1204 became necessary because Utopia otherwise follows a rule of national trade mark exhaustion, as was clarified by a ruling of the Utopian House of Gimmicks (the Supreme Court of Utopia) of 16 July 2003 (Chief Justice Thomas Morus presiding):

* The following mock trial was drafted by Gonçalo Cabral together with the editors of this book and argued during the conference by Anselm Kamperman Sanders and Gonçalo Cabral (for the defence), Jared Margolis and Christopher Heath (for the plaintiff), and presided by His Honour Judge Michael Fysh.

An exhaustion of trade mark rights in respect of products put on the market outside Utopia under that mark by the proprietor or with his consent is contrary to s 7(1) Utopian Trade Mark Act.

The case at issue concerned the parallel importation of so-called 'Giggling Goggles' (a futuristic kind of sunglasses with inbuilt communication skills) that were first marketed by the Utopian trade mark owner in neighbouring Blogdonistan. The goods were of identical quality to those marketed by the same trade mark owner in Utopia.

Trade mark exhaustion rules in Futura are not as clear-cut. There are no decisions to rely upon, and the relevant section of the Trade Mark Act reads as follows:

'The trade mark shall not entitle the proprietor to prohibit its use in relation to goods which have been put on the market under that trade mark by the proprietor or with his consent.' (Sec 2)

'Morgana' is a neighbouring country to both Futura and Utopia. It exports 40 per cent of its goods to Utopia, but increasingly exports (15 per cent and growing) to the recently opened market in Futura. The goods exported are sold in each respective market at a price that corresponds to the level of development of each respective country.

Imports and sales of Morganan goods in Utopia are typically handled by subsidiaries or licensees of Morganan companies.

In Futura, the situation is rather different. Under former communist rule, all imports and legitimate sales into Futura had to be undertaken by Futuran licensees, or joint ventures consisting of a foreign (Morganan) and a Futuran partner. These joint ventures have been partly state-owned, but are now being privatized.

Morgana feels locked-out by the FUFTA Agreement, but is also worried about its significant economic interests in Utopia and Futura. It is particularly worried about the fact that a significant amount of cheap Futuran imports — Morganan or other goods—end up in its prime Utopian market.

Morgana brings a complaint against Futura and Utopia before the WTO, of which it is a member, raising the following points:

1. Article 1204 of the FUFTA is not in compliance with the TRIPS agreement.
2. Should the above provision of the FUFTA comply with TRIPS, the most-favoured nation principle under Art 4 TRIPS would require that the same treatment be given to Morganan (parallel) importers of trade marked goods first marketed in Morgana and subsequently exported to Utopia or Futura.

Futura and Utopia petition for the complaint to be dismissed. Reciprocal exhaustion requirements could not be interpreted as a 'favour'. Futura further relies on its status as a least developed nation and counter-petitions that should the panel recommend that Morgana's request be granted, Morgana should also be obliged to acknowledge exhaustion for goods first marketed in Futura or Utopia under the above conditions.

The WTO has established a panel and is willing to hear oral arguments from all parties.

Futura-Utopia Free Trade Agreement (FUFTA)

Chapter 12—Intellectual Property

Article 1201

Objective

1. The objective of this Chapter is to increase the benefits from trade and investment through the protection and enforcement of intellectual property rights.
2. 'Intellectual property rights' refers to copyright and related rights, rights in trade marks, geographical indications, industrial designs, patents, and layout designs (topographies) of integrated circuits, rights in plant varieties, and rights in undisclosed information, as defined and described in the WTO *Agreement on Trade-Related Aspects of Intellectual Property Rights*.

Article 1202

Observance of International Obligations

The Parties shall fully respect the provisions of the WTO *Agreement on Trade-Related Aspects of Intellectual Property Rights* and any other multilateral agreement relating to intellectual property to which both are parties.

Article 1203

Measures to Prevent the Export of Goods that Infringe Copyright or Trade Marks

Each Party, on receipt of information or complaints, shall take measures to prevent the export of goods that infringe copyright or trade marks, in accordance with its laws, regulations, or policies.

Article 1204

Exhaustion of Trade Mark Rights

In respect of intra-parties trade, the Parties shall ensure the free movement of trade marked goods that have been put on the market in the territory of one of the Parties with the consent of the right owner or licensee that is entitled to the use of a trade mark in that territory on the basis of:

a. a registration in the local bureau of industrial property rights; or
b. a valid licensing agreement; or
c. international obligations.

Article 1205

Cooperation on Enforcement

The Parties shall cooperate with a view to eliminating trade in goods infringing intellectual property rights, subject to their respective laws, regulations, or policies. Such cooperation may include:

a. the notification of contact points for the enforcement of intellectual property rights;
b. the exchange, between respective agencies responsible for the enforcement of intellectual property rights, of information concerning the infringement of intellectual property rights;
c. policy dialogue on initiatives for the enforcement of intellectual property rights in multilateral and regional fora; and
d. such other activities and initiatives for the enforcement of intellectual property rights as may be mutually determined by the Parties.

Article 1206

Other Cooperation

The Parties, through their competent agencies, shall:

a. exchange information and material on programs pertaining to education in and awareness of intellectual property rights, and to commercialisation of intellectual property, to the extent permissible under their respective laws, regulations and policies; and
b. encourage and facilitate the development of contacts and cooperation between their respective government agencies, educational institutions, organisations and other entities concerning the protection and development of intellectual property rights with a view to:

   i. improving and strengthening the intellectual property administrative systems in areas such as patents examination and trademarks registration;
   ii. stimulating the creation and development of intellectual property by persons of each Party, particularly individual inventors and creators as well as small to medium-sized enterprises (SMEs); and
   iii. enhancing the capacity of and opportunity for the owners of intellectual property rights to obtain the maximum utilisation and commercial benefits from those rights.

Part III

FTAs and Patents

Chapter 6

Parallel Imports of Pharmaceuticals: Doha versus Free Trade Agreements

NG-LOY WEE LOON

I. INTRODUCTION

THE PURPOSE OF this paper is to examine how bilateralism has been used to restrict parallel importation of on-patent pharmaceutical drugs in a manner which challenges—or, as one critic has put it, undermines[1]—the international consensus reached at the Doha WTO Ministerial Conference. The bilateral agreements which have this effect are the US–Singapore, US–Australia and US-Morocco free trade agreements.

To explain the various issues involved in the debate surrounding parallel importation of medicines, it is convenient to start with the litigation between the Pharmaceutical Manufacturers' Association (PMA) and the South African Government when the latter proposed a law in 1997 aimed at, inter alia, legitimising parallel importation of drugs.[2] PMA opposed the enactment of this new law on various grounds, claiming that it conflicted, for example, with the principles in the TRIPs Agreement. This action turned out to be a public relations nightmare for the drug companies, and it was withdrawn by PMA in April 2001.[3] The 'amicable settlement' was recorded in a Joint Statement of Understanding issued by the parties, together with these points:[4]

[1] Drahos, 'The free trade agreement between Australia and the United States' (2004) BMJ 1271.

[2] *Pharmaceutical Manufacturers Association of South Africa & Ors v President of the Republic of South Africa & Ors* (Case 4183/98).

[3] Many have written on the background to this litigation, the specific nature of PMA's complaints and the events that led to the settlement of the case: see, for example, Woolridge, 'Analysis: Affordable Medicines—TRIPs and the United States Policies' [2000] IPQ 103; Hoen, 'TRIPS, Pharmaceutical Patents, and Access to Essential Medicines: A Long Way From Seattle to Doha' (2002) 3 Chi J Intl L 27; Van der Merwe, 'Use of Pharmaceutical Patents Without Authorisation: Some Thoughts From South Africa' [2004] IPQ 198. In fact, it was this South African case that first brought the world's attention to the role that 'parallel importation'—an obscure term for many a lay person—can play in a country's public health care programme.

[4] This Statement of Joint Understanding is available at the following webpage of the South African Government Information: http://www.info.gov.za/speeches/2001/010426345p1003.htm.

— The new law was to meet the 'the challenges of accelerating access to care and treatment for the diseases that affect the health of the South African population'.
— PMA's opposition to this new law was driven by its concern 'to continue its investment in the search for new medicines and vaccines'.
— PMA specifically recognised and reaffirmed that 'the Republic of South Africa may enact national laws or regulations, . . ., or adopt measures necessary to protect public health and broaden access to medicines in accordance with the South African Constitution and TRIPS'.

Using this South African litigation as a backdrop, the following issues will be examined: What are the arguments for and against parallel importation of medicines? What is the multilateral consensus on the permissible scope of parallel importation of medicines, ie under the Doha Declaration on the TRIPs Agreement and Public Health, and the WTO decision of 30 August 2003? Then, this paper will assess the impact of the provisions in the three bilateral free trade agreements which restrict parallel importation.

II. THE CASE FOR AND AGAINST PARALLEL IMPORTATION OF MEDICINES

The objective of the South African Government in enacting a law to allow parallel importation of medicines was to meet 'the challenges of accelerating access to care and treatment for the diseases that affect the health of the South African population'. This was also made clear in the provision in question itself, which empowers the Minister of Health to 'prescribe conditions for the supply of more affordable medicines in certain circumstances so as to protect the health of the public'.

The case for allowing parallel importation of medicines is therefore very simple: it makes available cheaper medicine to the public in the country of importation. There exist different price structures for the same drug in different markets/countries; and the public in the country where the drug is more expensive should benefit from the lower prices charged for the same drug in another country. Proponents of parallel importation would also point out that parallel importation concerns the importation of medicines which are manufactured by the drug company/patent holder[5] or with its consent, and put on the market in another country. Parallel importation concerns, in truth, importation of *genuine* goods, and the drug company should not be allowed to control the re-distribution of its own goods after their first sale.

[5] Note that the other intellectual property right which is also very important to pharmaceutical drugs is trade marks. In many cases involving parallel importation of pharmaceuticals, especially in the EEA, the drug companies exercised the trade-marked drug name to stop parallel importation: see, for example, *Glaxo Group v Dowelhurst* [2004] CMLR 4 (UK Court of Appeal, which has referred questions to the ECJ) and the Advocate-General's Opinion in C-348/04 (6 April 2006).

Ironically, prices of medicines are often higher in developing countries than in developed countries.[6] Various reasons have been given for this.[7] Economists, for example, explain that the drug companies engage in 'niche pricing', that is, they supply a small volume of the medicine with high mark-ups to the price insensitive (wealthy) consumers in the developing countries, in order to maximise profits.[8] The situation in South Africa has been explained on this basis: because it is a country where 'income is unusually unequally distributed' and where 'the affluent minority tends also to have comprehensive health insurance that covers prescription drug purchases', drug companies find it more profitable to sell only to the affluent minority.[9]

Drug companies, on the other hand, point the fingers at governmental drug price control regulation in many developed countries, such as Canada and Australia;[10] this is why drug prices in Canada are lower than in South Africa.[11] Related to this is the fact that some developed countries' price control regulation use 'external reference pricing' which peg the domestic prices of drugs to the prices in poorer (developing) countries. For this reason, the drug companies are reluctant to sell cheaper to developing countries.[12]

Therefore, the drug companies' case against parallel importation of medicine is equally simple: often price disparity in different markets has little to do with their pricing strategies, and parallel importation allows a leakage of their drugs from the lower-priced markets into its higher-priced markets. This adversely affects their global profits, making it difficult for them to recoup their R&D costs. This, as explained by PMA in the Joint Statement of Understanding issued in the South African litigation, reduces the incentive for them 'to continue its investment in the search for new medicines and vaccines'. To this threat, Prof

[6] See Markus, 'Parallel Imports in Pharmaceuticals: Implications for Competition and Prices in Developing Countries' (2001), a report to the WIPO, in s 5.1 and Table 1 (presenting a comparison of per-dosage prices in 1998 for 20 brand-name drugs in the US, Canada, Mexico, Brazil, UK, Sweden, Italy, Spain, Czech Republic, Japan, Korea, Thailand, India and South Africa). See also the conclusion made in the Background paper for the WHO-WTO Secretariat Workshop in Høsbjør, Norway, 8–11 April 2001 on Differential Pricing and Financing of Essential Drugs, at p 3 (recording the finding that 'drugs prices for newer medicines in low income countries are sometimes equal to or higher than those in developed countries').

[7] See Markus, *ibid*, at pp 33–34; Hammer, 'Differential Pricing of Essential AIDS Drugs: Markets, Politics and Public Health' (2002) 5 *J Int'l Econ L* 883, at 888 (linking the higher drug prices in developing countries to the fact that, unlike in developed countries where private health insurance is usually available, pharmaceutical purchases in many developing countries are privately financed, and therefore these sales do not benefit from economies of scale or negotiated group discounts).

[8] See Markus, *supra*, n 6, at Section 5.2.

[9] Scherer & Watal, *Post-TRIPs Options for Access to Patented Medicines in Developing Countries* (2001, Commission on Macroeconomics and Health).

[10] See Markus, *supra*, n 6, at p 34; Scherer & Watal, *ibid*, at p 49; Bartfield & Groombridge, 'Parallel Trade in the Pharmaceutical Industry: Implications for Innovation, Consumer Welfare, and Health Policy' (1999) 10 *Fordham IP Media & Ent LR* 189, at 246.

[11] See Markus, *supra*, n 6, at 29. In a survey of the existence of price control regulation in various developing and developed countries, Canada is indicated as a country with 'severe' price control whereas South Africa only has 'limited' price control: see Djolov, 'Patents, Price Controls, and Pharmaceuticals: Considerations from Political Economy' (2003) 6 JWIP 611, at 615–16 (Table 1).

[12] Markus, *supra*, n 6, at 34.

Abbott has this retort: '[w]ith regard to immediate disease crisis like HIV/AIDs, long-term R&D is not useful if the patients have already died'.[13] He is also sceptical about the drug companies' warning about 'killing the goose that lays the golden egg', pointing out, for example, that funding for R&D in American drug companies come not so much from their own sales but from very generous public funding.[14]

The case for and against parallel importation of medicines may be simple to state, but the resolution is by no means easy or clear. So contentious is this issue that all that has been achieved at the international level is this: each WTO country to decide for itself (except, perhaps, where the medicine is made under compulsory licence).

III. MULTILATERAL CONSENSUS ON PARALLEL IMPORTATION OF MEDICINE

1. The TRIPs Agreement

PMA's eventual acknowledgement that 'the Republic of South Africa may enact national laws or regulations, . . ., or adopt measures necessary to protect public health and broaden access to medicines in accordance with the South African Constitution and TRIPS' accords with the view, long held by many, that a law favouring parallel importation does not conflict with international obligations owed under the TRIPs Agreement.[15] More specifically, the patentee's exclusive right of importation guaranteed to the patentee by Art 28 is subject to Art 6 which provides that 'nothing in this Agreement shall be used to address the issue of the exhaustion of intellectual property rights': it is clear that each WTO country is free to adopt either a doctrine of an *international* exhaustion of rights (where the IP rights in the product are exhausted upon its first sale in any other country) or a doctrine of *national* exhaustion (where the IP rights in the product are exhausted upon first sale in that country).[16]

[13] Abbott, 'The Doha Declaration On The TRIPs Agreement And Public Health: Lighting A Dark Corner At The WTO' (2002) 5 *J Int'l Econ L* 469, at 473.

[14] Abbott, 'Toward A New Era of Objective Assessment in the Field of TRIPs and Variable Geometry for the Preservation of Multilateralism' (2005) 8 *J Int'l Econ L* 77, at 92. Prof Abbott's scepticism about the link between healthy revenue streams and innovation is not shared by other academics: see, for example, Rey & Venit, 'Parallel Trade and Pharmaceuticals: A Policy in Search of Itself' (2004) 29 E L Rev 153, at 165–6 (under heading 'Parallel Trade adversely affects R&D efforts').

[15] See Sun, 'The Road to Doha and Beyond: Some Reflections on the TRIPs Agreement Public Health' (2004) 15 EJIL 123, at 132 (noting that 'even though no decision was made [in the South African case], the case has given rise to a wealth of expert opinions on the TRIPs Agreement. Encouragingly, the bulk of expert opinion is that the [South African proposed law] is consistent with the TRIPs Agreement'). Heath, Parallel Imports and International Trade, 28 IIC 623 [1997].

[16] A sub-species of the concept of national exhaustion of rights is the *regional* exhaustion of rights, typified by the situation in the EEA (subject to Art 22 and Annex IV.2 of the 2004 Accession Treaty, concerning pharmaceuticals manufactured in the 10 new member states). See also Art 10 of the EU Directive (98/44/EC) on the Legal Protection of Biotechnological Inventions.

Often, it is said that a country which recognises international exhaustion of patent rights allows parallel importation. It should be noted that, within this category, there are countries whose international exhaustion of rights is premised on the existence of *consent* of the patentee to the further movement of his products after first sale in a foreign territory—consent which may be express or implied.[17] Such countries would disallow the parallel imports where the patentee explicitly *negates* such consent, for example by imposing restrictions on the re-distribution of the goods outside the territory of first sale.[18] Examples of countries with such a qualified international exhaustion of patent rights include Japan,[19] Taiwan,[20] Hong Kong[21] and Thailand.[22]

South Africa's proposed law was not so qualified. The provision in question is to be found in the South African Medicines and Related Substances Control Act,[23] which empowered the Minister of Health to:

> prescribe the conditions on which any medicine which is identical in composition, meets the same quality standard and is intended to have the same proprietary name as that of another medicine already registered in the Republic, but which is imported by a person other than the person who is the holder of the registration certificate of the medicine already registered and which originates from any site of manufacture of

[17] There may be insurmountable difficulties involved in showing that there is implied consent: see the ECJ decision in *Zino-Davidoff v A&G Imports Ltd* [2002] RPC 20, where the ECJ, while accepting that trade mark rights in non-EEA goods can be exhausted when there is implied consent from the trade mark proprietor, was not prepared to hold that implied consent could be inferred from the fact that the goods carried no warning prohibiting their sale in a market within the EEA etc. This decision has been interpreted by the UK court in *Levi Strauss v Tesco Stores* [2003] RPC 18 to mean that only express consent from the trade mark proprietor to resale of non-EEA goods within the EEA would exhaust trade mark rights.

[18] Note that there can be difficult issues raised on whether the means used by the patentee to restrict re-distribution is effective in the sense that it binds the defendant-importer.

[19] See *BBS Wheels III* case (Supreme Court, 1997), as explained by C Heath, 'Exhaustion and Parallel Importation in Japan', in: C Heath (ed), Parallel Imports in Asia, Max Planck Series on Asian Intellectual Property vol 9, Kluwer Law International, London 2004, pp 55–8.

[20] See Art 57(6) of Taiwan's Patent Law which, at first glance, appears to provide for an international exhaustion of rights. However, this provision is subject to a troublesome proviso, which has caused Prof Liu Kung Chung from Taiwan to conclude that that the exhaustion of patent rights in Taiwan is subject to contractual arrangements between the patent owner and purchaser of the goods: see Liu, 'Exhaustion and Parallel Importation in Taiwan', in: C Heath (ed), Parallel Imports in Asia, Max Planck Series on Asian Intellectual Property vol 9, Kluwer Law International, London 2004, at p 42.

[21] See Kennedy, 'Exhaustion and Parallel Imports in Hong Kong', chapter in C Heath (ed), Parallel Imports in Asia, Max Planck Series on Asian Intellectual Property vol 9, Kluwer Law International, London 2004, at pp 149–150 (explaining that the situation in Hong Kong 'comes close to that of international exhaustion', but that this is subject to restrictive conditions placed on the goods).

[22] See s 36(7) of Patents Act BE 2522 allowing 'the use, sale, having in possession for sale, offering for sale or importation of a patented product when it has been produced or sold with the authorization or consent of the patentee'. See Ariyanuntaka, 'Exhaustion and Parallel Importation in Thailand', in: C Heath (ed), Parallel Imports in Asia, Max Planck Series on Asian Intellectual Property vol 9, Kluwer Law International, London 2004, at 98 (noting that the impact of contractual arrangements made by patent holders to prevent importation on the question of consent, is unclear).

[23] See s 15C(b).

the original manufacturer as approved by the Council in the prescribed manner, may be imported.

Three other countries' laws merit special mention: Singapore, Malaysia and India.

When Singapore enacted its own patent law, the Patents Act 1994, it provided for an international exhaustion of rights in very clear terms: importation of a patented product is allowed if it was 'produced by or with the consent (conditional or otherwise) of the proprietor of the patent or any person licensed by him'.[24] This means that a term or condition imposed by the patentee restricting the resale of the patented product outside the territory of first sale would be disregarded for the purposes of determining if the product was produced by or with his consent. In other words, the patentee is *deemed* to have consented to the making of the product in spite of such a condition. PMA has never challenged Singapore on the legality of this parallel importation provision in her patent law; at least, not on the basis that it was inconsistent with the TRIPs Agreement. However, during the FTA negotiations with the US, Singapore was persuaded to change her position.[25]

Like Singapore, Malaysia also has a provision in her patent law that allows importation of a patented invention which 'is produced by, or with the consent, conditional or otherwise, of the owner of the patent or his licensee'.[26] This provision was enacted in 2000,[27] as part of Malaysia's efforts to bring down the high drug prices in Malaysia, in particular, drugs for HIV/AIDS-infected patients.[28] Not only was the legality of this provision not challenged by PMA, its enactment brought the drug companies to the negotiating table resulting in a significant drop in the price of retroviral drugs. Where the monthly cost of treating one HIV/AIDS patient used to be RM1200, it fell to a range of RM200–RM250.[29]

In India's case, parallel importation of medicines has never been an issue in the past; after all, she is one of the world's leading generic drug manufacturers. However, as the deadline for her to introduce product patent for drugs—1 January 2005[30]—drew closer, she had to look seriously at her stance on parallel importation. In 2005, she amended a provision in her patent law to permit 'importation of patented products by any person from a person *who is duly*

[24] See s 66(2)(g) of Singapore's Patents Act 1994. For the purpose of this section, 'patent' includes a patent granted in any country outside Singapore in respect of the same or substantially the same invention as that for which a patent is granted in Singapore.

[25] See discussion in Part (4), *infra*.

[26] See s 58A of Malaysia' Patents Act 1983. For the purpose of this section, 'patent' includes a patent granted in any country outside Malaysia in respect of the same or essentially the same invention as that for which a patent is granted in Malaysia.

[27] It came into force on 1 August 2001.

[28] See Chong, 'Exhaustion and Parallel Imports in Malaysia', chapter in C Heath (ed), Parallel Imports in Asia, Max Planck Series on Asian Intellectual Property vol 9, Kluwer Law International, London 2004, at pp 126–7 and 133–5.

[29] This was announced by the Malaysian Minister for Health, Dato' Mr Dr Chua Soi Lek, *The Star* 7 June 2004.

[30] This extension of time is provided for in Art 65(4) of the TRIPs Agreement.

authorized under the law to produce and to sell or distribute the product'[31] (emphasis added). The legitimacy of parallel importation in India, by this 2005 amendment, has been de-linked from the patentee's consent.

2. The Doha Declaration on the TRIPs Agreement and Public Health

If at all it could be said that the TRIPs Agreement was ambiguous on parallel importation, this claim could no longer be sustained after the Doha 14th WTO Ministerial Conference adopted the Declaration on the TRIPs Agreement and Public Health ('Doha Declaration') on 14 November 2001. According to one commentator on the Doha Declaration, paragraph 5(d) therein contains an 'unequivocal recognition of the right of each [WTO] Member to permit parallel importation of medicines'.[32] This provides as follows:

> The effect of the provisions in the TRIPS Agreement that are relevant to the exhaustion of intellectual property rights is to leave each member free to establish its own regime for such exhaustion without challenge, subject to the MFN and national treatment provisions of Articles 3 and 4.

There is, though, one question on which there remains some uncertainty: does TRIPs/Doha Declaration allow for a doctrine of exhaustion of rights that extends to drugs made or sold under compulsory licence in the country of first sale? Even amongst those countries with very generous pro-parallel importation laws, the approach varies.

South Africa permits importation of medicines 'which originate from any site of manufacture of the original manufacturer'. This has been interpreted to exclude importation of medicine manufactured under a compulsory licence.[33]

On the other hand, India's patent law authorises 'importation of patented products by any person from a person *who is duly authorized under the law* to produce and to sell or distribute the product'. This appears to allow importation of products made under compulsory licence.

Where Singapore and Malaysia are concerned, the situation is not entirely clear. These two countries allow importation if the product is produced by the patentee or with his consent, 'conditional or otherwise'. Where goods are made under a compulsory licence, it may be argued that the goods are made with the consent of the patentee—because the patentee cannot sue for infringement—although such consent was 'conditional' in the sense that it was subject to the compulsory licence imposed on him. Such 'conditional' consent is, according to the Singapore/Malaysian provision, ineffective; as mentioned above, the patentee is deemed to have given consent, in spite of any condition attached to the consent. In the case of Singapore, a comparison with the situation in her

31 See s 107A(b) of India's Patents Act 1999.

32 See Abbott, *supra*, n 13, at 494.

33 Van de Merwe, *supra*, n 3, at 202–3.

copyright law lends support to this argument. Singapore's Copyright Act also allows importation of articles (embodying a copyright work) which are made with the consent of the copyright owner, and it is expressly provided that: the 'making of the article shall be deemed to have been carried out with the consent of the [copyright] owner . . . if, after disregarding all conditions as to the sale, distribution or other dealings in the article after its making, the article was made with his licence (*other than a compulsory licence*)'[34] (emphasis added). When the parallel importation provision in copyright law explicitly excludes compulsory-licensed goods from its ambit, the absence of a corresponding exclusion in the parallel importation provision in patent law is glaring.

On the other hand, it is also possible that the 'deemed consent' concept in Singapore/Malaysia's patent law applies only when the conditions are imposed by the patentee himself, and not where the conditions are imposed by third parties—the government, in the case of a compulsory licence—on the patentee. In such a scenario, it may be said that the consent of the patentee was involuntary, and therefore there was no consent at all.

The different approaches in these countries reflect the divergent views on whether TRIPs sanctions an exhaustion of rights doctrine which extends to compulsory-licensed goods. Prof Abbott offered the view that paragraph 5(d) of the Doha Declaration left each WTO member with a sufficiently wide discretion, and he encouraged developing countries to exercise this discretion to allow parallel importation of compulsory-licensed drugs.[35] It is very tempting to agree with Prof Abbott, and further advance his case by arguing that drug price control regulation is really a subtle form of compulsory licensing scheme: if parallel importation of drugs sold under price control regulation in another country is not forbidden under the TRIPs Agreement, neither is parallel importation of compulsory-licensed drugs. However tempting this argument may be, the two cannot be equated.[36] The situation on compulsory licence is specifically provided for in the TRIPs Agreement: compulsory licences are allowed under the TRIPs Agreement under Art 31 therein, but they are subject to stringent conditions. In particular, Art 31(f) restricts the grant of compulsory licence 'predominantly for the supply of the domestic market' of the WTO member issuing the compulsory licence.[37] Art 31(f) records the agreement of WTO countries

[34] See s 25(4) of Singapore's Copyright Act 1987.

[35] *Supra*, n 13, at 494–7.

[36] Note that the principle of regional exhaustion of rights in the EEA, *supra*, n 16, makes a distinction between the two situations: the doctrine of regional exhaustion still applies where the drugs are sold under price control regulation in one member state (*Centrafarm BV v Sterling Drug Inc* [1974] ECR 1147), but it does not apply where the drugs are made in one member state under compulsory licence (*Pharmon BV v Hoechst AG* [1985] ECR 2281). See also Art 76(3) of Community Patent Convention, providing for an exception to the Community exhaustion principle 'in the case of a product put on the market under compulsory licence').

[37] There is one exception to Art 31(f), namely, where the compulsory licence granted is to remedy anti-competitive practices: see Art 31(k). Where Art 31(k) applies, a view has been offered that the compulsory licence should prevail over the patentee's rights, not just in the country which issued the compulsory licence, but also in the country where the product is exported to: Rott, 'The Doha Declaration—Good News for Public Health' (2003) IPQ 3 284, at 305.

that the compulsory-licensed goods are meant for the country issuing the compulsory license only. It is submitted that Art 31(f), given its specificity, should prevail over the generality of Art 6. In fact, so fundamental is Art 31(f) that it required another decision from the WTO to lift the injunction contained therein.

3. WTO Decision of 30 August 2003[38]

The WTO decision sheds some light on how parallel importation of compulsory-licensed drugs should be treated. This decision is the implementation of the 'Paragraph 6 issue' in the Doha Declaration concerning the predicament of poor countries, particularly the least developed countries (LDCs), who are unable to produce pharmaceuticals domestically. The significance of the decision lies in the waiver from the obligation in Art 31(f) of the TRIPs Agreement, thereby allowing countries with drug manufacturing capacities to issue a compulsory licence for the manufacture of drugs for export to 'eligible importing Members' such as the LDCs. But this waiver is subject to many conditions,[39] two of which are relevant for the purpose of this discussion. Paragraphs 4 and 5 of the decision provide as follows:

> 4. In order to ensure that the products imported under the system set out in this Decision are used for the public health purposes underlying their importation, eligible importing Members shall take reasonable measures within their means, proportionate to their administrative capacities and to the risk of trade diversion to prevent re-exportation of the products that have actually been imported into their territories under the system. In the event that an eligible importing Member that is a developing country Member or a least-developed country Member experiences difficulty in implementing this provision, developed country Members shall provide, on request and on mutually agreed terms and conditions, technical and financial cooperation in order to facilitate its implementation.
>
> 5. Members shall ensure the availability of effective legal means to prevent the importation into, and sale in, their territories of products produced under the system set out in this Decision and diverted to their markets inconsistently with its provisions, using the means already required to be available under the TRIPS Agreement. If any Member considers that such measures are proving insufficient for this purpose, the matter may be reviewed in the Council for TRIPS at the request of that Member.

[38] For the details on the post-Doha negotiations leading to this decision, and its scope: see, for example, Sun, *supra*, n 15, at 144–7; Matthews, 'WTO Decision on Implementation of Paragraph 6 of the Doha Declaration on the TRIPs Agreement and Public Health: A Solution to the Access to Essential Medicines Problem? (2004) 7 *J Int'l Econ L* 73; Gopakumar, 'The WTO Deal on Cheap Drugs—A Critique' (2004) 7 JWIP 99.

[39] Countries which have taken steps to implement this waiver in their patent law: Canada, Norway, India. See also the proposed EC Regulation to implement the WTO decision, discussed in Vandoren *et al*, 'A New EC Initiative to Allow Export of Medicines under Compulsory Licences to Poor Countries' (2005) 8 JWIP 103.

In particular, paragraph 5 contains an injunction to be observed by other WTO members to prevent entry of the compulsory-licensed drugs into their territories. This injunction is limited to the compulsory-licensed drugs made in accordance with the terms of the WTO decision. However, it is submitted that it is also indicative of the attitude of the international community vis-à-vis parallel importation of compulsory-licensed drugs in general.

IV. BILATERAL CONSENSUS ON PARALLEL IMPORTATION OF MEDICINE

The bilateral FTAs signed between the US and Singapore, Australia and Morocco each contains a specific provision on parallel importation. The table below sets out the relevant provisions.

US–Singapore FTA (signed in May 2003)	US–Australia FTA (signed in May 2004)	US–Morocco FTA (signed in June 2004)
Art 16.7.2: Each Party shall provide a cause of action to prevent or redress the procurement of a patented pharmaceutical product, without the authorization of the patent owner, by a party who knows or has reason to know that such product is or has been distributed in breach of a contract between the right holder and a licensee, regardless of whether such breach occurs in or outside its territory. (footnote) Each Party shall provide that in such a cause of action, notice shall constitute constructive knowledge. Footnote: A Party may limit such cause of action to cases where the product has been sold or distributed only outside the Party's territory before its procurement inside the Party's territory.	Art 17.9.4: Each Party shall provide that the exclusive right of the patent owner to prevent importation of a patented product, or a product that results from a patented process, without the consent of the patent owner shall not be limited by the sale or distribution of that product outside its territory, at least where the patentee has placed restrictions on importation by contract or other means.	Art 15.9.4: Each Party shall provide that the exclusive right of the patent owner to prevent importation of a patented product, or a product that results from patented process, without the consent of the patent owner shall not be limited by the sale or distribution of that product outside its territory. (footnote) Footnote: A Party may limit application of this paragraph to cases where the patent owner has placed restrictions on importation by contract or other means.

Based on an assessment of these three provisions *per se*, there is a progressive increase in the strength of the prohibition against parallel importation from one FTA to the next, the strongest being the US-Morocco provision. Although the US-Australia provision and US-Morocco provision are the same in substance, the formulation in the latter is slightly different: the qualification to the prohibition, namely, that patentee must have placed restrictions on importation, appears in a footnote to the main text of the US–Morocco provision.[40]

The real differences are found between the US–Singapore provision on the one hand, and the US–Australia and US–Morocco on the other. Firstly, the US–Singapore provision applies to a 'pharmaceutical product' only, whereas the other two are not so limited. Secondly, the US-Singapore provision prohibits importation to the situation where the patentee has imposed restrictions on importation in his contract with his licensee/distributor, whereas the other two FTAs prohibit importation where the patentee has imposed restrictions by contract *or by other means* (for example, by a label 'Not for Sale Outside Country X' placed on the goods). Thirdly, the US-Singapore provision requires knowledge on the part of the importer that importation and distribution would result in a breach of the contract, but the other two FTAs prohibit importation regardless of such knowledge.

Fourthly—and this is a critical difference—the US–Singapore provision has a footnote which cuts back the obligation to prevent importation: Singapore need only prevent importation 'where the product has been sold or distributed only outside [Singapore's] territory before its procurement inside [Singapore's] territory'. What does this footnote really mean? The answer is to be found in Singapore's implementation of this obligation: she has amended her patent law to prohibit importation of a patented pharmaceutical product where:[41]

(a) the product has not previously been sold or distributed in Singapore by or with the consent (conditional or otherwise) of the proprietor of the patent or any person licensed by the proprietor of the patent to sell or distribute the product in Singapore;
(b) the import of the product by the importer would result in the product being distributed in breach of a contract between the patentee and any person licensed by the proprietor of the patent to distribute the product outside Singapore; and

[40] See further, *infra*, n 51, and the accompanying main text.

[41] See the new s 66(2A) inserted into Singapore's Patents Act 1994 (as of 1 July 2004). Note that the term 'pharmaceutical product' is given specific meaning: in particular, it excludes any substance used solely for diagnosis or testing, or as a device or mechanism, or an instrument, apparatus or appliance (*cf* definition of 'pharmaceutical product' in the WTO decision of 30 August 2003 which includes diagnostic kits). Besides the amendments to her patent law, there were also amendments to the Medicines Act, which governs the issuance of licences to sell medicinal products in Singapore. These amendments require an applicant for such licences (who is not the patentee) to prove that the patentee has given his consent to or has acquiesced in the grant of the licence to the applicant, or that the patent is invalid or will not be infringed by the doing of the act for which the licence is sought.

(c) the importer has actual or constructive knowledge of the matters referred to in paragraph (b).

The impact of the condition in paragraph (a)—which implements the footnote in the US-Singapore provision—is explained to Parliament thus:[42]

> Under this new Section, a patent owner will have a right to bring an action to stop a parallel importer from importing the patent owner's patented pharmaceutical product, if the product has not previously been sold or distributed in Singapore. However, once the owner brings in the patented product, the right to bring action ceases, and he will be subject to the same competitive pressures from parallel imports. This is a delicate balance we have sought to preserve between the interests of the patent owner and the interests of users of pharmaceutical products. Essentially, the patent owner has a 'first mover advantage' in the Singapore market, but once he is in, will have to compete with the parallel importers.

In other words, the new right to stop importation is limited to the situation where the pharmaceutical product is not available in the Singapore market yet; once the drug company brings its product in, others can do the same.

The comparison between the three FTAs reveals that the US–Singapore provision provides an extremely limited right to stop parallel importation of medicine, compared to the other two FTAs. However, it has the greatest immediate impact in the sense that it resulted in a real, *albeit* limited, change in Singapore's law on parallel importation. On the other hand, Australia and Morocco, even before their FTA with the US, have had a *national* exhaustion of rights doctrine.[43] In other words, the provision in their FTA restricting parallel importation merely declares their domestic policy on parallel importation—or at least their policy as it existed at the date of their FTA. Agreeing to this provision means that Australia and Morocco have committed themselves to not *ever* changing their current prohibition against parallel importation,[44] even if the public health situation in the country should one day change such that they would, but for their FTA with the US, make use of the flexibilities provided for in the TRIPs Agreement and as confirmed by paragraph 5(d) of the Doha Declaration. In this sense, their FTA with the US does have a significant impact.

[42] See the speech of the Senior Minister of State for Law on 15 June 2004, at the Second Reading of the Patents (Amendment) Bill 2004.

[43] In the case of Morocco, the national exhaustion of rights is provided for in Art 55(d) of its Patent Law 2000. See also the Fact Sheet on Access to Medicine dated 19 July 2004 (available on the website of the US Trade Representative Office) declared that that the US-Morocco FTA 'simply reflects current law in the US and Morocco' as 'Morocco decided in 2000, well before the FTA negotiations, not to permit parallel imports of patented products'. In the case of Australia, see Richardson, 'Intellectual property rights and the Australia—US Free Trade Agreement' (Research Paper No 14 2003-04, dated 31 May 2004) available at the webpage of the Parliament of Australia at http://www.aph.gov.au/library/pubs/rp/2003-04/04rp14.htm.

[44] Richardson, *ibid*, cautioned against the 'entrenchment of the [FTA] prohibition against parallel importation' in Australian patent law, as 'the trend in Australia over the last decade and a half has been towards relaxing restrictions on parallel importation'. See Australia's amendments to her copyright law in 1998 and 2003 to allow parallel importation of sound recordings, computer programs and electronic literary and musical items.

Ironically, in the case of the US–Morocco FTA, there also exists a Side Letter on Public Health[45] which reserves each party's rights to 'take necessary measures to protect public health by promoting access to medicines for all', and recognized that the IP Chapter in the FTA 'does not prevent the effective utilization of the TRIPS/health solution' in the Doha Declaration and the WTO decision of 30 August 2003!

V. CONCLUSION

Much has already been said about the use of bilateral agreements to foist TRIPs-plus obligations on WTO countries. When millions are dying from diseases which can be combated with medicine, and parallel importation of medicine is seen as one possible solution to this problem, emotions are particularly raw when the drug companies seek, through FTAs, TRIPs-plus rights to prevent parallel importation. The truth of the matter is that the FTAs concluded so far have not managed to make as much inroad as feared on this issue. This paper's assessment of the provision limiting parallel importation in the three FTAs—US–Singapore, US–Australia and US–Morocco—reveals that the provision cost nothing to Australia and Morocco in the immediate future, and very little to Singapore.

Restricting parallel importation of medicines is not necessarily the antithesis of access to more affordable medicines. In fact, one solution to the public health problem pushed by WHO,[46] and more recently by the UK Government,[47] namely, 'differential pricing' or 'tiered pricing' where drug companies charge lower prices in markets which have less purchasing power, is not acceptable to drug companies unless laws are in place which prevent importation of the differentially-priced drugs meant for lower-income markets into the higher-income markets.[48] If market segmentation will indeed persuade drug companies to adopt a 'differential pricing' model,[49] the use of bilateralism to limit parallel

[45] A similar Side Letter exists in the US's FTAs with Bahrain,Central America , Colombia, Oman and Peru. There is, however, no provision on parallel importation in the main text of these FTAs.

[46] See the WHO-WTO Background Paper on Differential Pricing and Financing of Essential Drugs, *supra*, n 6.

[47] See the Department for International Development (DFID) Policy Paper on Increasing People's Access to Essential Medicines in Developing Countries: A Framework for Good Practice in the Pharmaceutical Industry (March 2005).

[48] See the EU council regulation (EC) No. 953/2003 offering manufacturers and exporters of tiered priced medicines reinforced prevention at border level against imports into the EU market where higher prices prevail.

[49] Note there are other problems associated with the 'differential pricing' solution which makes it unattractive to drug companies, even if market segmentation can be achieved through laws prohibiting parallel importation. For example, drug companies fear that consumers in the higher-income countries will see the huge difference in prices and lobby for lower prices: Matthews, *supra*, n 38, at 100; Hammer, *supra*, n 7, at 885. Another concern of the drug companies is that these 'tiered prices' would be taken into account by countries in fixing prices of drugs under their price control regulations: Scherer & Watal, *supra*, n 9.

importation is less objectionable—but only if high-income countries, and not the others, should be the targets. The US policy in this regard does not appear to have been very consistent. Its FTA with Australia and Singapore, but not its FTAs with Chile and Bahrain, has the parallel importation provision, when all these countries are classified by World Bank as 'high income' economies. Within the group of countries in the 'middle income' group which have a FTA with the US, Morocco ('lower middle') is imposed with the restriction, but not Central America ('upper middle'), Colombia ('lower middle'), Jordan ('lower middle'), Oman ('upper middle') nor Peru ('lower middle').[50]

Each of the US-negotiated FTAs, once concluded, is used as a template in the next FTA negotiations with another country. The current 'model' is the US-Morocco provision which provides for national exhaustion of patent rights subject to a footnote allowing Morocco to limit national exhaustion to the situation where the patentee has placed restrictions on the importation of the goods.[51] It remains to be seen whether the next US-negotiated FTA negotiations with countries whose patent laws favour an international exhaustion of rights, such as Thailand (lower middle income) and Malaysia (upper middle income), will contain the US-Morocco 'model' provision. Or worse, will the footnote be dropped, so as to impose on these countries an absolute national exhaustion of patent rights?

[50] If the reason lies in the fact that the laws in Chile, Bahrain, Central America, Colombia, Jordan, Oman or Peru existing as at the date of the FTA did not allow parallel importation, the same could be said of Australia and of Morocco.

[51] See, *supra*, n 40, and the accompanying main text.

Chapter 7

Free Trade Agreements, UPOV and Plant Varieties

MARISTELA BASSO AND EDSON BEAS RODRIGUES JR

I. INTRODUCTORY REMARKS

ONE OF THE main and preoccupying innovations brought about by the TRIPS/WTO agreement was the expansion of the Intellectual Property Rights (IPR) regimes to all areas of technology, with no exemption, encompassing subject matters that have been traditionally excluded, eg genetic resources. From the establishment of the WTO in 1995, all Member States took on the obligation to protect biotechnological inventions, microbiological processes, and plant varieties through IPR. The inclusion of this subject matter within the TRIPS agreement is criticised by a handful of civil society organizations and the 'traditional paradigm that genetic resources formed part of a global commons was also adversely affected by the increased assertion and expansion of other forms of intellectual property rights over plants, known as plant breeders' rights'.[1] It has been argued that 'by reducing plant and other biological material, to the status of private property capable of being the subject matter of a private property right greater harm will result than benefit. The form of this harm ranges from moral harm resulting from treating genetic material as private property through to potential environmental harm resulting form pressure to market before the full environmental impact of the engineered material has been assessed. This latter harm potentially taking many different forms including loss of biological diversity, adverse impacts on the farming community, and harm resulting from modified genetic material moving from one plant variety/species to another when released into the environment'.[2]

Despite all criticism generated by the TRIPS agreement, as far as the biotechnology clause[3] is concerned, it is offers the WTO Member States some leeway

[1] S Safrin, Hyperownership in a time of biotechnological promises: the international conflict to control the building blocks of life, American Journal of International Law. October, 2004, p 3.

[2] M. Llewelyn, Which Rules in World Trade Law—Patents or Plant Variety Protection?, Intellectual Property: The World Trade Forum, Vol 3. Cottier, Mavroidis, Panizzon and Lacey. University of Michigan Press, Ann Arbor, p 307.

[3] Art 27.3.b.

that can and should be utilised in order to reflect local peculiarities and development policies. There are, of course, some obligations that are absolute, with no room for manoeuvre left, such as the obligation of granting patents over micro-organisms, microbiological, biochemical and non-biological processes. Nevertheless, in the specific case of plant variety protection, Member States still can choose amongst the following options: (i) the traditional patent system, (ii) an effective *sui generis* system, or (iii) any combination thereof.

During the GATT Uruguay Round, the idea sponsored by the industrialised countries was that the UPOV Convention[4] would be the most satisfactory instrument for complying with the obligations enshrined in article 27.3.b TRIPS regarding the protection of plant varieties, specially because simultaneously to the Uruguay Round, a revision of the UPOV 1978 Act with the aim of rising the standards of protection was under way. In particular, more rights should be given to breeders over the propagating materials of varieties. It must be stressed, however, that TRIPS does not make any reference to the UPOV Convention that could be compared to the explicit mentioning of the Bern, Paris and Rome Conventions and to the Treaty on Intellectual Property in Respect of Integrated Circuits, Art 3 TRIPS. Hence, all Member States have the discretion to choose their own legal regime for the protection of plant varieties, and one of the options available—but not the only one—is the UPOV model.

It is well known that IPR are not an end in itself, but a very powerful tool to promote development, research and investment, and distribute social welfare.[5] In the field of protection of plant varieties, on account of its social and strategic importance, the legislature must be very cautious in order to avoid undue monopolies that restrict the access to agricultural goods, further investments in R&D, jeopardize food security, restrict the free flow of germ plasm, erode the local genetic diversity. While IPRs, when adopted to economic, industrial and social policies, may be an efficient tool for the achievement of higher standards of human and economic welfare, they may also set hurdles to such achievements. Everything depends on how the local needs and peculiarities are dealt with. Such singularities may and should be taken fully into account when drafting local legislation. Developing countries should fully use the flexibilities left by TRIPS[6] especially where agriculture plays an important economic and social role or where relevant genetic and agricultural heritage is present. Legislation in this field should be used as a strategic tool whose positive potentialities should not be taken for granted.

Yet, the current trend is the rising of standards of protection beyond TRIPS obligations through Free Trade Agreements (FTAs), imposing restrictions to the flexibilities and safeguards available in TRIPS. This new trend in agriculture

[4] Union for the Protection of New Plant Varieties (website: www.UPOV.int).

[5] Art 7 of TRIPS.

[6] According to Art 8.1 of TRIPS, Member States may adopt measures necessary to protect public health and nutrition, and to promote the public interest in sectors of vital importance to their socio-economic and technological development.

jeopardises the maintenance of the vegetal and agricultural diversity, the free flow of germ plasm and, last but not least, the self-determination of developing countries.

This paper deals with the pervasive tendency of reaching bilateral and regional free trade agreements which present TRIPS-plus provisions, devoting special attention to the main and most common features of Intellectual Property obligations under these agreements, and the major role played by the UPOV model in the suppression of the flexibilities available under Art 27.3.b TRIPS.

II. FROM MYTH TO REALITY—THE EFFECT OF FTAS

1. The resistance and persistence of developing countries in the TRIPS Council

The increasing number and proliferation of FTAs over the last couple of years is a direct result of the resistance of developing countries against proposals of industrialised countries submitted to TRIPS Council of the WTO aiming at strengthening the protection of IPRs. A good example of this resistance are the participation and lobbying efforts of civil society and non-governmental organisations in negotiations involving developing countries and least-developed countries.[7] In a considerable way, such players have been engaged in studies, technical advice and promoting global initiatives favourable to the position of developing countries within the multilateral trade negotiations, especially those concerning the subject matter of TRIPS/WTO.

In its attempt to deal with problems and needs of developing countries and LDCs,[8] the TRIPS Council approach has been another reason for developed countries to promote FTAs and thereby shift the forum.[9] By means of such FTAs, developed countries impose new obligations to developing and least-developed countries regardless of domestic institutional and socioeconomic issues and the level of local development. As mentioned above, the US has been using FTAs to impose US-oriented IP policies and standards of protection to their counterparts in such Agreements. This is not surprising, especially

[7] See R Maybe, The global campaign on patents and access to medicines: An Oxfam Perspective, in Global intellectual property rights: Knowledge access and development (edited by Peter Drahos and Ruth Mayne), Palgrave, Macmillan, 2002, p 244.

[8] There is a wide range array of initiatives, such as those related to the review of IP legislations, implementation of technical cooperation (Art 67 of TRIPS) and the unending debate on public health access and IPR emphasized after the Doha Declaration on TRIPS and Public Health and the Decision on the Implementation of Paragraph 6 of the Doha Declaration on the TRIPS Agreement and Public Health, adopted by the General Council on 30 August 2003.

[9] According to P Drahos, Expanding Intellectual Property's Empire: the Role of FTAs, Australian National University, November 2003, the expression forum shifting defines a strategy or process in which the US and EU countries shift the standard-setting agenda from forums in which they are encountering difficulties to those where they are likely to succeed (vg first from WIPO to WTO, then from WTO to bilateral and regional negotiations).

considering the analysis of the provisions of the *Trade Promotion Authority Act of 2002*, which states that: The Congress has stated that one overall negotiating objective for the US is to obtain in bilateral and multilateral agreements provisions that 'reflect a standard of protection similar to that found in the United States law'.[10]

It is worth noting that those developing and least developed countries that negotiate bilateral and regional agreements with the US, besides putting aside the flexibilities under TRIPS/WTO, have been implementing standards of IP protection that are not even foreseen in the US domestic legal framework. A clear example of this refers to compulsory licensing. While the *US Patent Act* has no provisions related to compulsory licensing, such instrument is foreseen by a handful of different legislative instruments,[11] as well as is deemed an important antitrust remedy in field of patent litigation by American courts. Thus, it is not hard to conclude that those countries adopting more restrictive rules regarding the use of compulsory licensing—'TRIPS-Plus' and 'TRIPS-Extra'—are indeed establishing a 'patent holder protection-oriented system' in their domestic IP legal framework which goes beyond the US legal standards and in disregard of the economic function of IPR and their effective social utility. This could be identified as a 'US-Law-plus' standard of protection.

In fact, there are a number of examples that clearly confirm the attempt of the US in bringing developing countries into compliance with US domestic legal standards, or even to higher levels of IP protection. This refers to the US-Singapore Free Trade Agreement, whose Article 16.8 states that: 'If a Party requires the submission of information concerning the safety and efficacy of a pharmaceutical or agricultural chemical product prior to permitting the marketing of such product, the Party shall not permit third parties not having the consent of the party providing the information to market the same or a similar product on the basis of the approval granted to the party submitting such information for a period of at least five years from the date of approval for pharmaceutical product and ten years from the date of approval for an agricultural chemical product'.[12] Article 39.3 of TRIPS contains a similar provision, clearly requiring data protection against 'unfair commercial use'. This brief comparison can show that the Article 16.8 of US-Singapore Agreement is a 'TRIPS-Plus' provision, bringing Singapore's domestic legal framework into compliance with US rules.[13]

[10] Section 2102(b)(4)(A)(i)(II), 19 USC 3802.

[11] See, for instance, the Clean Air Act, 42 USC Sec 7608, referring to compulsory licensing of inventions related to air pollution prevention (Title 42 'The Public Health and Welfare'), the provisions of Bay-Dole Act, 35 USC 203, regarding march-in rights, and the Atomic Energy Act, 42 USC, Sec 2183, related to the protection of the public interest in the energy production area (if the invention or discovery covered by the patent is of primary importance to the production or utilization of a special nuclear material or atomic energy; or if the licensing of such invention or discovery is of primary importance to effectuate the purposes of the Act).

[12] The full version of the Agreement is available online at: http://www.ustr.gov/assets/Trade_Agreements/Bilateral/Singapore_FTA/Final_Texts/asset_upload_file708_4036.pdf.

[13] J Watal, Intellectual property rights in the WTO and developing countries, OUP, New Delhi, 2001, p 200–1.

III. THE CASE OF LATIN AMERICA—A COMPARISON BETWEEN TRIPS AND THE FTAA

1. Past and Current Negotiations

The ongoing negotiations for the establishment of the Free Trade Area of the Americas (FTAA)[14]—were initiated at the 1994 Miami Summit of Americas. The FTAA is intended to be formed by thirty four members that agreed to complete negotiations towards this agreement by the year 2005. The agreement aims at the elimination of trade and investment barriers. The current existing regional free trade and bilateral agreements set up amongst FTAA Members are regarded as an important factor promoting a hemisphere-based economic integration. From the standpoint of the negotiators, several regional and sub-regional agreements were to be merged and result in only one comprehensive agreement, the FTAA.

The ongoing negotiations comprise several aspects related to trade in a common set of rights and obligations, which include provisions on the following matters: market access; agriculture; services; investment; government procurement; IPR; competition policy; subsidies, antidumping, countervailing duties; and dispute settlement.[15]

In 1999, the countries engaged in the FTAA negotiations established nine Negotiating Groups, among others the Negotiating Group on Intellectual Property Rights (NGIP). Those groups are assisted by a Tripartite Committee, which consists of the Inter-American Development Bank (IDB), the Organization of American States (OAS) and the United Nations Economic Commission for Latin America and the Caribbean (ECLAC).[16]

The goals of NGIP are akin to those agreed under the *Declaration of Punta del Este* of 1986 at the beginning of the GATT Uruguay Round.[17] The rationale underlying that Declaration was the establishment of a direct link between market access and protection of IPRs, as well as the elimination of trade distortions.[18] Almost all countries negotiating the chapter related to IP in the FTAA are also WTO Members and would theoretically speaking be up to the standards of protection provided by TRIPS as a guideline to the current negotiations.

[14] The present paper is based on the third draft of the FTAA, available at the website: http://www.ftaa-FTAA.org/FTAADraft03/ChapterXX_p.asp.

[15] See the Third Draft (2003) of the FTAA agreement at: http://www.ftaa-FTAA.org/FTAA Draft03. (herein defined as 'Draft')

[16] The Committee provides analytical, technical and financial support to the current negotiations process. Al the tripartite institutions also provide technical assistance concerning FTAA issues, particularly for smaller economies amongst the negotiating countries.

[17] The full version of Declaration is available at: http://www.sice.oas.org/trade/Punta_e.asp.

[18] Trade distortions are the overall negative effects caused by the measures affecting and altering the normal conditions of competition within international trade, at regional and multilateral level.

Different approaches underlie the existing regional trade agreements. The Member States of NAFTA[19] do not submit their opinions representing that free trade area. Indeed the US submits isolated proposals reflecting their standards of IPR protection. The US also attempts to enforce higher levels of IPR protection as provided by the TRIPS Agreement, eg a harmonisation of the patentability requirements, elimination of general exception clauses, and the strengthening of enforcement mechanisms. On the other hand, Canada argues that the IPR chapter in the FTAA should merely contain the NAFTA standards, and possibly some exceptions. Mexico, in turn, defends the insertion of an agreement similar to NAFTA, but with general exceptions that may be adequate to the regional peculiarities.

Countries of the Andean Community[20] state that the negotiations should not go beyond those standards established by TRIPS. Those countries defend that issues related to genetic resources and traditional knowledge are fundamental to the region, as well those related to *ordre public* and public health. The Caribbean Community—CARICOM[21]—advocates a strengthening of copyright protection for the phonogram industry.

The Member States of MERCOSUR[22] planned not to negotiate IPRs in the FTAA framework. These countries take the view that this topic should be limited to the scope of TRIPS/WTO and WIPO Treaties, thus should be kept in multilateral forums. In case of maintenance of that chapter in the FTAA negotiations, those countries will not accept proposals restricting or eliminating TRIPS safeguards and flexibilities. Chile has adopted an intermediate position between the US Agenda for strengthening the harmonisation of IP protection standards among FTAA negotiating parties and an effective implementation of TRIPS flexibilities.[23]

Although negotiations started in 1994, the First Draft was made public only in 2001, a few weeks before the Summit of Americas held in Québec. The Second Draft was issued at the Ministerial Conference in Quito in 2002. At that time, it was clear to most that FTAA negotiations were limited to uncontroversial topics such as democratic deficit and lack of transparency.

In fact, both democracy deficit and lack of transparency have undermined the potential and real extension of FTAA negotiations. Another important example is the 2003 Free Trade Agreement between Chile and the USA, which was made

19 http://www.nafta-sec-alena.org.

20 http://www.comunidadandina.org. See also the Andean Normative related to IPR at: http://comunidadandina.org.normativa/res/res_propint.htm.

21 http://www.caricom.org.

22 See http://www.mercosul.org.uy. or www.mercosur.org.uy. Within Mercosur, the following regulations concerning IPR were concluded and came into force: (a) Protocolo de Harmonização de Normas Sobre Propriedade Intelectual no Mercosul em Matéria de Marcas, Indicações de Procedência e Denominação de Origem (CMC/DEC. No 8/95); (b) Protocolo de Harmonização de Normas em Matéria de Desenhos Industriais (CMC/DEC. No 16/98); (c) Acordo de Cooperação e Facilitação Sobre a Proteção das Obtenções Vegetais nos Estados Partes do Mercosul (CMC/DEC. No 1/99).

23 See http://www.ftaa-FTAA.org/busfac/ctyindex/chl_s.asp.

public just weeks before its conclusion.[24] For these reasons, civil society organizations have already expressed their concerns related to the real possibilities of participating in the negotiations and contributing to the debates.[25]

2. Intellectual Property Rights in FTAA

A number of provisions of the Chapter XX of the FTAA Draft, dealing with IPR has been left in brackets and shall be subject to forthcoming negotiations.[26] Issues such as differential treatment and technology transfer have not been approached so far, at least not in the developing countries perspective. The Chapter in caption contains some provisions that go beyond TRIPS standards, expressing 'TRIPS-Plus', 'TRIPS-Extra' and other 'US Law-plus' standards.

No difficulty remains to understand how and to what extent the Chapter XX of Agreement exposes and highlights the institutional disparities between the Members, especially because the conclusion of the Agreement would radically change the domestic IP framework of the Member States by enhancing protection, eliminating the flexibilities and safeguards provided by WTO/TRIPS; raising the costs related to enforcement of IPR and creating new mechanisms aiming only at strengthening the protection standards regardless of different economic and social peculiarities of the Member States. In the following sections, those aspects will be further examined.

a) Expanding the Protection of Intellectual Property Rights in the FTAA

New areas of protection of IPRs were set during the negotiations for the establishment of the FTAA. The existing forms of protection are to be expanded by the Agreement. The following topics illustrate the areas in which feature both approaches adopted by Chapter XX (new forms/expansive IP protection):

— trademarks and well-known marks;
— domain names on the Internet;
— geographical indications;
— rights of management of information related to copyrights and related rights;
— protection of satellite signs transmission and related programs;

[24] See http://www.ustr.gov/fta/chile/text/index.htm.

[25] For an overview regarding the concerns of civil society organisations, see Let's harness trade for development–Why Oxfam opposes the FTA,, available at: http://www2.oxfam.ca/news/Peoples_Summit/opposes_FTAA.htm; CPTech comments on the Second Draft of the Free Trade Area of the Americas, available online at the website: http://www.cptech.org/ip/ftaa/cptech02282003.html; Essential action comments on proposal text of the Free Trade Area of the Americas, available online at the website: http://www.cptech.org/ip/ftaa/essential02282003.html and Access to affordable medicines under attack in the Americas, available online at: http://msf.org/content/page.cfm?articleid=27B539FD-5434-4FAF-B9F4DDC2F.

[26] This takes into account that the present article was delivered between the end of 2004 and early 2005.

— obligations related to technological measures;
— obligations related to management information;
— governmental use of computer programs;
— protection of industrial designs and utility models;
— protection of undisclosed information;
— protection of expressions of folklore;
— unfair competition;
— control of anticompetitive practices in contractual licenses;
— protection of New Varieties of Plants through the UPOV Convention of 1991

Once the FTAA introduces new fields of protection of IPRs, some concern remains regarding the suppression of creativity and regional innovation platforms. This brings some difficulties related to the appropriate use of knowledge and information, as well as impoverishment of the public domain. The IPR Chapter of the FTAA seems to expand the mechanisms of appropriation of common goods.

Except for TRIPS, many other treaties and conventions concluded under the auspices of WIPO and further international documents agreed at multilateral level are also to be directly incorporated by Chapter XX, in particular:

— WIPO Performances and Phonograms Treaty of 1996;
— WIPO Copyright Treaty of 1996;
— WIPO Patent Law Treaty;
— WIPO Joint Recommendation Concerning Provisions on the Protection of Well-Known Marks of 1999;
— WIPO Protocol on Trademark Licenses (to be defined);
— WIPO Joint Recommendation Concerning Provisions on the Protection of Marks, and Other Industrial Property Rights in Signs, on the Internet (to be defined);
— Instrument for the Protection of Audio-Visual Performers' Rights (to be defined)
— UPOV Convention of 1991;
— Convention Relating to the Distribution of Programme-Carrying Signals Transmitted by Satellite (1974) (Brussels Convention).

Once agreed upon on its current terms, the FTAA should present several difficulties and challenges to Latin-American and Caribbean countries, as the Agreement will suppress important domestic legislative freedom (currently intertwined with WTO/TRIPS flexibilities), as well as restrict the capacity of national policies to address challenges related to innovation, technology transfer and access to health.

Indeed some perplexity remains with regard to the Third Draft of the FTAA due to the fact that the negotiations made no reference to relevant international documents such as the Doha Declaration on TRIPS and Public Health,[27] the

[27] WT/MIN(01)/DEC/2, Declaration on the TRIPS Agreement and Public Health, adopted on 14 November 2001.

FAO International Treaty on Plant Genetic Resources for Food and Agriculture of 2001[28] and the Bonn Guidelines.[29] These documents—representing considerable advantages to developing countries—are able to recommend and encourage a positive review of the countries' agendas for development, as well as highlight the access to the necessary resources and tools for sustainable growth.

b) Limitations to the flexibilities and safeguards of TRIPS/WTO

The current negotiations for the establishment of the FTAA, summarised in its Third Draft, encompass many restrictions and suppressions affecting the flexibilities and safeguards established by TRIPS. Particular attention should be devoted to the following issues:

— *Extension of the subject-matter related to patent protection*: the Chapter XX of the FTAA, according to the current Draft, clearly removes the flexibilities provided by Articles 27.2 and 27.3 of TRIPS. It foresees that 'microorganisms shall be patentable as long as different measures are adopted as a result of the review established in Article 27.3 (b) of the TRIPS Agreement. For this purpose, account shall be taken of the commitments assumed by the Parties under the Convention on Biological Diversity'.[30]

— *Extension of the patent protection term*: 'The term of protection available shall not end before the expiration of a non-renewable period of twenty (20) years, counted from the filing date. (. . .) Each Party, at the request of the patent owner, shall extend the term of a patent to compensate for unreasonable delays that occur in granting the patent. For the purposes of this paragraph, an unreasonable delay shall at least include a delay in the issuance of the patent of more than four (4) years from the date of filing of the application in the Party, or two (2) years after a request for examination of the application has been made, whichever is later, provided that periods of time attributable to actions of the patent applicant need not be included in the determination of such delays'.[31]

— *Extension of the term of protection related to copyrights*: 'each Party shall provide that (a) where the term of protection of a work (including a photographic work), performance or phonogram is to be calculated on the basis of the life of a natural person, the term shall be not less than the life of the author and seventy (70) years after the author's death; (b) where the term of protection of a work (including a photographic work), performance or phonogram is to be calculated on a basis other than the life of a natural person, the term shall be not less than ninety-five (95) years from the end of the calendar year of the first authorized publication of the work, performance or

[28] See ftp://ext-ftp.fao.org/ag/cgrfa/it/ITPGRe.pdf.
[29] See htpp://www.biodiv.org/decisions/default.aspx?m=cop-06&d=24.
[30] Ss B.2.e, Art 1.4 of FTAA Draft.
[31] Ss B.2.e, Art 9.2 of FTAA Draft.

phonogram or, failing such authorized publication within twenty-five (25) years from the creation of the work, performance or phonogram, not less than one hundred twenty (120) years from the end of the calendar year of the creation of the work, performance or phonogram'.[32]

— *Limitation of the freedom of national governments to adopt measures related to public health protection*: A restrictive interpretation of FTAA provisions could lead to a 'Doha-minus' standard, despite the following reading of Chapter XX dealing with IP: 'No provision of this Chapter prevents, and should not prevent, any Party from adopting measures to promote and protect public health, and it should be interpreted and implemented in a manner that takes into account each Party's right to protect public health and, in particular, to promote access to [existing] medicines and to the research and development of new medicines'[33] In comparison with the Doha Declaration, it is possible to conclude that FTAA provisions are far removed from the real essence and concern related to health access issues. It is important to remark that §4 of the Declaration establishes that 'TRIPS does not and should not prevent members from taking measures to protect public health' and 'should be interpreted and implemented in a manner supportive of WTO members' right to protect public health and, in particular, to promote access to medicines for all', without making any distinctions between 'existing' or 'new' drugs.

— *Exclusive rights and undisclosed information*: clinical information is frequently required by governments to approve the commercialisation of new drugs. According to TRIPS, Member States shall protect the results of tests and further undisclosed information against 'unfair commercial use', 'subject to reasonable steps under the circumstances, by the person lawfully in control of the information', as a requirement for the approval of commercialisation of pharmaceutical and agricultural chemical products involving the use of new chemical entities. Members should also adopt measures to protect such information against disclosure by third parties, 'except where necessary to protect the public'.[34] Within the FTAA negotiations, the US insists on requiring exclusive marketing rights over such undisclosed information for a period of at least five years.[35] Such requirement would result in artificial barriers to potential competitors in the market for generic drugs.

[32] Ss B.2.c, Art 9.1 of FTAA Draft.

[33] Section A, General Aspects, Art 1.4.

[34] Art 39.3 of TRIPS.

[35] Ss B.2.j, Art 1.2: 'If a Party requires the submission of information concerning the safety and efficacy of a pharmaceutical or agricultural chemical product prior to permitting the marketing of such product, such Party shall not permit third parties not having the consent of the party providing the information to market the same or a similar product on the basis of the approval granted to the party submitting such information for a period of at least five (5) years from the date of approval.'

— *Regional Exhaustion*: 'This Chapter shall not affect the authority of each Party to determine the conditions under which the exhaustion of rights related to products legitimately introduced in the market by, or with the authorization of, the right holder shall apply. However, each Party undertakes to review its domestic legislation within a period not exceeding five (5) years after the entry into force of this Agreement, in order to adopt, at a minimum, the principle of regional exhaustion in regard to all Parties.[36]

— *Compulsory Licensing*. The Draft dramatically suppresses the flexibilities provided by TRIPS/WTO with regard to 'other uses of the patent without authorization of the right holder': '(a) the authorization shall be granted only for public non-commercial purposes or in situations of a declared national emergency or other situations of extreme urgency; (b) The authorization shall be limited to the making, using or importing of the patented invention solely to satisfy the requirements of the Government use, and shall not entitle a private party acting on behalf of the Government to sell products produced pursuant to such authorization to a party other than the Government, or to export the product outside the territory of the Party; (c) The patent owner shall be provided with reasonable and entire compensation for such use and manufacture; (d) No Party shall require the patent owner to transfer undisclosed information or technical 'know how' related to a patented invention that has been subjected to involuntary use authorization.[37] Such provisions are also 'Doha minus' and ' WT/Decision 2003 minus'.[38]

— *Expansion of protection related to plant varieties*. The Draft incorporates the standards of protection reflected in the UPOV conventions: 'Each Party shall grant protection to all plant varieties through patents, through an effective sui generis system or through a combination thereof. An effective sui generis system is understood to be the breeder's rights system established in the International Convention for the Protection of New Varieties of Plants (UPOV), 1978 or 1991 Acts, in accordance with the national legislation of each Party.' The scope of protection shall cover 'all botanical genera and species, provided that their cultivation, possession or use are not prohibited for reasons of human, animal or plant health, and shall apply, in general, to entire plants, including any type of flower, fruit or seed, and any other part of plants that can be used as material for reproduction or multiplication'.[39] The hidden costs of this provision often enshrined in FTAs will be further analysed below.

— *Implications for the conservation and sustainable use of biological diversity, and traditional knowledge*. The Draft also establishes connections between Traditional Knowledge and Genetic Resources: 'the relationship between

[36] Ss B.2.e, Art 7.1.

[37] Ss B.2e., Art 6.

[38] Decision of the General Council of 30 August 2003 on the Implementation of paragraph 6 of the Doha Declaration on the TRIPS Agreement and Public Health (document WT/L/540).

[39] Ss B.2.i, Art 1 and 2.

the protection of traditional knowledge of indigenous communities and local communities and intellectual property as well as the relationship between access to genetic resources and intellectual property shall comply with the provisions of the Convention on Biological Diversity, the commitments undertaken by each Party in the different international agreements addressing this subject matter and the national legislation of the country of origin of such knowledge or resources'.[40] It is well settled that there is a dichotomy between developing countries standpoint related to protecting traditional knowledge through a *sui generis* intellectual property regime and among those countries and their indigenous/traditional communities, which, in general, are reluctant to accept traditional knowledge as a mere category subject to appropriation and protection through IPRs. Negotiations relating to this matter without the active participation of those stakeholders would be anti-democratic and may have the negative impact of dismantling the sustainable use of genetic resources and associated traditional knowledge.[41]

— *General obligation of protecting expressions of folklore.* The Draft states that 'the Parties shall ensure effective protection of all expressions of folklore and artistic expressions, of the traditional and folk culture' and 'effective protection of those forms that are the product of the traditional and folk culture of indigenous people and communities, Afro-American and local communities'.[42] As mentioned above, there are several concerns related to the protection of folklore through IPRs. Some FTAA members have not reached a consensus regarding this issue, so that it would be not desirable or appropriate to establish a premature protection at a regional level.

— *Protection of digital and information technology.* The Draft provides a range of alternatives concerning the protection of IPRs in the field of digital and information technologies. The US has made a firm proposal to reproduce and spread their domestic protection standards throughout the Americas. The FTAA draft, in its third version, requires Member States to adhere to the *Government Advisory Committee of the Internet Corporation for Assigned Names and Numbers* (ICANN). This body is in charge of the management of domain names on Internet and is based on a particular dispute settlement system, the *ICANN Uniform Dispute Resolution Procedure* (UDRP) addressing issues related to cyber-piracy of trademarks.[43]

— *Competition policy.* Whereas IPRs may function, in some circumstances, as a pro-competition incentive, the strengthening of such rights could cause adverse effects on domestic markets. Abusive practices related to the use of

[40] S B.2.f, Art 1.2.

[41] Sophisticated and burdensome regimes of protection of traditional knowledge will lead to a bias towards stronger parties; if traditional communities will have to describe and pursue protection on their own, those communities will definitely not profit for the system. The more a *sui generis* system for protection of traditional knowledge resembles the traditional IPR regimes, the more the communities will lose power over their intellectual assets.

[42] Ss B.2.d, Art 1.1 of the Draft.

[43] See, for instance, Subs B.2.a, Art 13.1 of the Draft.

IPR are not excluded from the regional marketplaces and may comprise cartels, price fixing, market division and abusive prices. FTAA provisions are 'TRIPS-Plus' as they shift some standards related to antitrust enforcement on the IP field and go beyond Article 8.2 of TRIPS:[44] 'Any act of competition contrary to the honest practices in industrial or commercial matters constitutes an act of unfair competition'. The Draft moreover defines the scope of the protection related to unfair competition issues, enumerating the practices[45] and requiring Member States to establish administrative, judicial, criminal and civil remedies to prevent and punish acts considered commercially unfair.

— *Technology Transfer*: Although the Draft has chosen 'technological and socioeconomic development' at the regional level as one of FTAA objectives,[46] the extensive and detailed Section dealing with transfer of technology primarily favours the Unites States and Canada. Developing countries will have to wait for a long time to enjoy the potential benefits resulting from the Agreement. It is also recommended that FTAA Member States wait for the first reports and outcomes of the WTO *Working Group on Trade and Transfer of Technology*[47] before defining the goals and priorities intended to be pursued. In the same way, it is also preferable that developing countries engage in a joint work to review the UNCTAD Code of Conduct on the Transfer of Technology of 1995 (TOT).[48]

[44] Art 8.2 TRIPS: Appropriate measures, provided that they are consistent with the provisions of this Agreement, may be needed to prevent the abuse of intellectual property rights by right holders or the resort to practices which unreasonably restrain trade or adversely affect the international transfer of technology.

[45] See ss B.2.K:1.2: '[The following acts, inter alia, shall be considered contrary to honest commercial practices: deliberate breach of contract, fraud, breach of confidence, and inducement to infringe. The following in particular shall be prohibited:]

> [Any act in relation to industrial property carried out in the business domain that is contrary to honest practices and usage shall be considered as an act of unfair competition. The following acts, inter alia, constitute acts of unfair competition in relation to industrial property:]
>
> a) all acts of such a nature as to create confusion, by any means whatever, with the establishment, the goods, services or the industrial or commercial activities of a competitor;
> b) false allegations in the course of trade, of such a nature as to discredit the establishment, goods, or industrial or commercial activities of a competitor;
> c) indications or allegations the use of which in the course of trade, could mislead the public as to the nature, the manufacturing process, the characteristics, the suitability for their purpose, or the quantity of the goods;]

[46] Section A: General Aspects, Art 1°.

[47] See http://www.wto.org/english/tratop_e/devel_e/dev_wkgp_trade_transfer_technology_e.htm. The Group was established during the Doha Ministerial Conference with specific tasks, such as examining the relationship between trade and the transfer of technology from developed to developing countries, and strategies to increase the flow of technology to developing countries. For the last outcome, reference shall be made to the Report 2004 of the Working Group on Trade and Transfer of Technology to the General Council, dated as of December 01, 2004 (Document WT/WGTTT/6).

[48] The TOT Draft is available online at: http://www.unctad.org. For a comprehensive approach of the issue, see Wolfgang FIKENTSCHER, The Draft International Code of Conduct on the Transfer of Technology: A Study in Third World Development, International Review of Intellectual Property and Competition Law (IIC)—Study Series, Munich 1996.

— *Absence of specific provisions on differential treatment vis-a-vis certain developing countries.* With regard to the issue of differential treatment, the Draft is clearly 'TRIPS-minus'. Whereas Articles 65 and 66 of TRIPS/WTO establish a number of transitional arrangements for developing and least developed countries, Chapter XX of the FTAA does not confer special transitional periods related to the implementation of those expansive standards of IPR protection to developing and least-developed countries in Latin America. There is no special provision even to Haiti, the only country in the region regarded as least-developed.

c) Increasing costs and mechanisms related to the enforcement of Intellectual Property Rights within the FTAA

In the field of enforcement, the negotiations sought to establish 'TRIPS-plus' and 'TRIPS-extra' provisions, far beyond those obligations provided by Articles 41 *et seq.* of TRIPS. The FTAA Draft foresees that the each Party 'shall provide that decisions on the merits of a case in judicial and administrative enforcement proceedings shall: (a) preferably be in writing and state the reasons on which the decisions are based; (b) be made available at least to the parties in a proceeding without undue delay; and (c) be based only on evidence in respect of which parties were offered the opportunity to be heard presented in conformity with the rules of due process'.[49]

One of the most relevant obligations in this Section encompasses a duty of notification. The Members shall provide notification of laws, regulations and provisions regarding the subject matters of the Chapter XX to the *FTAA's Committee on Intellectual Property.*[50] This notification includes 'final judicial decisions, administrative rulings of general application that shall be published or made available to the public in a manner that allows governments and rights holders to have prima facie knowledge thereof'.

Furthermore, according to the Draft, the Parties shall provide that: 'defendants have the right to written notice that is timely and contains sufficient detail, including the basis of the claims; parties in a proceeding are allowed to be represented by independent legal counsel; the procedures do not include imposition of overly burdensome requirements concerning mandatory personal appearances; all parties in a proceeding are duly entitled to substantiate their claims and to present relevant evidence; and the procedures include a means to identify and protect confidential information'.[51] In fact, if we take into account that FTAA Members are countries both of *civil law* and *common law* legal tradition,

[49] Subs B.3 dealing with General Obligations and Enforcement.

[50] Section C ('Procedures and Institutions'), Art 5: The Committee on Intellectual Property shall be comprised, in an equitable manner, of representatives of each Party. The primary function of the Committee shall be to find the most appropriate means of applying and coordinating the provisions set forth in this Chapter.'

[51] Subs B.2, Art 2.1.

there would be no difficulty to predict that the provisions of the Agreement shall be contentious in the near future.

Finally, as regards *border measures* and *criminal procedures*, FTAA provisions establish 'TRIPS-plus' and 'TRIPS-extra' standards, expanding the subject matter of Articles 51–61 of TRIPS/WTO, thereby imposing new commitments and costs to the countries in the region.

3. The Dispute Settlement System of FTAA

The draft of the FTAA agreement has a chapter dedicated to dispute settlement, which appears to be considerably complex in many aspects.[52] Besides the classical methods of dispute settlement, such as those established by International Law: good offices, mediation, conciliation and arbitration,[53] the Draft foresees WTO like methods of dispute resolution, such as consultations, arbitration and appeal mechanisms (so-called 'neutral panel' and the appellate body).[54] In its general provisions, the dispute settlement mechanisms clearly state that 'non-governmental participation in the dispute settlement system shall not be permitted',[55] and that once a Party has initiated dispute settlement proceedings under FTAA provisions, any other jurisdiction shall be excluded.[56]

4. Implications of Bilateral Investment and Regional Free Trade Agreements for Developing Countries

The analysis provided above demonstrates that developing countries only in the long run might reap some benefits arising from BITs and FTAs to the trade

[52] Draft 03, Chapter XXIII, available at: http://www.ftaa-FTAA.org/FTAADraft03/ChapterXXIII_p.asp. (20 February 2005).

[53] Chapter XXIII, Art 44 et seq.

[54] Chapter XXIII, Art 44 et seq.

[55] Article 40—Public Access to Documents:
40.1. All documents and actions related to the procedure established in this chapter, including the hearings before the neutral panel, deliberations, and all written submissions and communications made to the group, as well as meetings of the neutral panel [and of the Appellate Body], shall be confidential, [except for the final reports.
40.2. Non-governmental participation in the dispute settlement system in this Chapter shall not be permitted. In no case may an organization, individual or groups of individuals, on its/their own initiative, make during any stage of the proceeding a presentation or written submission, or attend the hearings of the neutral panel.

[56] Article 8—Choice of Forum
8.1. Disputes within the scope of application of this Chapter that are also eligible for submission to the dispute settlement system of the World Trade Organization [or that of a regional agreement to which the Parties to the dispute are Party,] may be submitted to any of these fora, at the discretion of the complaining Party.
8.2. Once a Party has initiated dispute settlement proceedings under this Agreement or the Understanding [or a regional agreement], that Party shall not initiate dispute settlement proceedings in any other fora with respect to the same claim on actual or proposed measure or matter.

sectors in which those countries have substantial interests. In addition, in order to achieve such benefits, developing countries shall be required to accept special conditions and bet their future on uncertain negotiations. On the other hand, from the standpoint of developed countries, instant results emerging from the agreements will be available.

It is also clear that most developing countries appear not to notice the real extent of the imbalance of benefits (in short, medium and long term) resulting from the negotiated agreements. The following scheme looks typical for FTAs:

Developing countries + unrestricted concessions =
more and efficient benefits to developed countries

Developed countries + restricted concessions regarding time and object =
no (zero) immediate benefits to developing countries

There is no doubt that the proposal of extending the term of protection for patents, limitations to compulsory licensing, granting of data protection for pharmaceutical products for a minimum period of 5 (five) years, extension of the term of protection of copyrights and plant varieties, the general obligation related to protection of folklore, and the protection of undisclosed information will negatively impact the access to health, knowledge, culture, the sustainable use and conservation traditional cultural forms and lifestyles, as well as it may considerably reduce the levels of competition, innovation, research and technology transfers in the developing countries.[57]

BITs and FTAs also impair the unity of the multilateral trade system by reducing the scope of flexibilities and exceptions established under TRIPS/WTO and the Doha Declaration in detriment to the interests and needs of developing countries, and interfere with the general and substantial obligations originally taken on by WTO Member States, due to the fact that any condition or differential treatment agreed at bilateral and regional level shall according to the Most Favoured Nation clause (MFN) be accorded to all WTO Members automatically, with no exclusions.[58]

The implications of regionalism and bilateralism for the multilateral trade system is also subject to WTO concerns. The WTO Committee on Regional Trade Agreements (CRTA)[59] was established in 1996 with the mandate to analyse individual regional agreements and assess the systemic implications of

[57] See the opinion of P Drahos, Negotiating Intellectual Property Rights: Between Coercion and Dialogue, In Global Intellectual Property Rights—Knowledge, Access and Development' (edited by Peter Drahos and Ruth Mayne). Palgrave: Macmillan, 2002, p 161 *et seq*, *cit* p 174, highlighting that 'the economic price for this will be less competitive markets with no real corresponding gains in innovation, as well as new and more sophisticated global knowledge cartels.

[58] For a extensive and critical study on the Most Favoured Nation clause, see the document 'Most-Favoured-Nations Treatment'—In UNCTAD Series on Issues in International Investment Agreements, 1999, available online at: http://www.unctad.org/en/docs//psiteiitd10v3.en.pdf.

[59] WTO Committee on Regional Trade Agreements (CRTA), established in February 1996. For an overview of the tasks of the Committee see: http://www.wto.org/english/tratop_e/region_e/regcom_e.htm. Recently a Report concerning the Committee's activities was issued and submitted to WTO General Council (see document WT/REG/14, Report (2004), as of 29 November 2004).

those agreements for the multilateral trading system. The *Singapore Ministerial Declaration*[60] recognised the importance of the relationship between WTO and Regional Agreements: 'The expansion and extent of regional trade agreements make it important to analyze whether the system of WTO rights and obligations as it relates to regional trade agreements needs to be further clarified. We reaffirm the primacy of the multilateral trading system, which includes a framework for the development of regional trade agreements, and we renew our commitment to ensure that regional trade agreements are complementary to it and consistent with its rules. In this regard, we welcome the establishment and endorse the work of the new Committee on Regional Trade Agreements. We shall continue to work through progressive liberalization in the WTO as we are committed in the WTO Agreement and Decisions adopted at Marrakesh, and in so doing facilitate mutually supportive processes of global and regional trade liberalization.'

Recently, the CRTA presented its action plan, emphasising the necessity of a detailed legal analysis of the relevant WTO provisions at stake, a comparison between regional agreements and the encouragement of the debate on economical aspects underlying regional trade agreements. As previously observed by Peter Gallagher, 'concerns have been expressed that Regional Trade Agreements divert trade in inefficient directions and undermine the multilateral trading system'.[61]

FTAs and BITs are partially a result from the absence of more comprehensive goals related to the promotion of international development, effective poverty alleviation, access to health and protection of human dignity. In this scenario, the asymmetries amongst developed and developing countries are substantial. Consistent goals for progress of the countries are taken for granted in the policy-making process related to the negotiation of new IPR standards at an international level.

According to the World Bank, the Gross Domestic Product (GDP) *per capita* in Latin America and Caribbean is less than 10 per cent of the US one. Economic growth in those countries rose slightly through the 1990s, and poverty fell marginally.[62] Most of the population in the region affected by the externalities of the FTAA can be deemed poor by US standards. The perspectives for recovery of the world economy are more obscure and uncertain than those in the early 1990s. The international context is still shaped by several factors: the increasing disparities between rich and poor, the new and permanent pressures related to protectionist measures.[63] The increasing monetary instability and the

[60] See Singapore Ministerial Declaration, adopted on 13 December 1996, available online at: http://www.wto.org/english/thewto_e/minist_e/min96_e/wtodec_e.htm.

[61] P Gallagher, Guide to the WTO and Developing Countries. London. The Hague. Boston: Kluwer Law International—WTO. 2000, p 108.

[62] See information and further prognostics at http://www.worldbank.org/data/wdi2004/worldview.htm.

[63] See UNCTAD, Trade and Development Report, 2004—Overview, (Unctad/TDR/2004), available online at: http://www.unctad.org.

turbulences in the financial market have adverse implications for developing countries as well. The dependence of the global economy on the US economy is not a recent phenomenon, and the US trade deficit appears to be much more intense nowadays than in late 1990's. Besides the geopolitical conflicts, the pillars for the sustainable growth of most developing countries are still weak.

Thus, developing and least developed countries prior to the acceptance of any stricter standard of protection of IPRs beyond the WTO level should assess if the potential benefits are commensurate to the losses to be incurred by locally important sectors. The Ronald H. Coase's lessons which urge policy-makers to evaluate and compare the total social costs that may derive from policy decisions should be observed more frequently by developing and least developed countries.

> The problem which we face in dealing with actions which have harmful effects[64] is not simply one of restraining those responsible for them. What has to be decided is whether the gain from preventing the harm is greater than the loss which would be suffered elsewhere as a result of stopping the action which produces the harm.
> (. . .)
>
> Analysis in terms of divergences between private and social products concentrates attention on particular deficiencies in the system and tends to nourish the belief that any measure which will remove the deficiency is necessarily desirable. It diverts attention from those other changes in the system which are inevitably associated with the corrective measure, changes which may well produce more harm than the original deficiency.
> (. . .)
> It would clearly be desirable if the only actions performed were those in which what was gained was worth more than what was lost. But in choosing between social arrangements within the context of which individual decisions are made, we have to bear in mind that a change in the existing system which will lead to an improvement in some decisions may well lead to a worsening of others. Furthermore we have to take into account the costs involved in operating the various social arrangements (whether it be the working of a market or of a government department), as well as the costs involved in moving to a new system. In devising and choosing between social arrangements we should have regard for the total effect.[65]

For the aforementioned reasons and concerns, it is strongly suggested that developed countries shape their IP policies in a manner conducive to the effective promotion of the development of developing and least developed countries.

[64] No contexto do presente artigo, 'harmful effects' seriam as barreiras tributárias e não tributárias fixadas por países industrializados, que inviabilizam a entrada de produtos manufaturados pelos países em desenvolvimento. Com apoio nos ensinamentos de Coase, consideramos essencial que países em desenvolvimento e com menor desenvolvimento relativo conduzam estudos de impacto econômico e social, que avaliem os benefícios e malefícios econômicos e sociais decorrentes da adoção de determinados standards de proteção inseridos nos acordos de livre comércio. Apenas a partir de estudo que identifique os benefícios e malefícios será possível negociar, com um mínimo de segurança, acordos de livre comércio.

[65] Ronald H Coase, The Problem of Social Cost. Journal of Law and Economics (October 1960).

Developing countries should not to be required to accept and implement higher standards of protection of IPR as a trade-off for having access to foreign investment. The Commission on Intellectual Property Rights of the United Kingdom (CIPR), in line with this view, stated that 'IP policy must integrate development considerations and that should be done as much by developed countries as by developing. Developing countries should not have to accept IP rights imposed by the developed world, outside their existing commitments to international agreements. Negotiators for developed countries need to take account of the costs to developing countries of higher IP standards, as well as the benefits to their own industries. The imperative, then, is for developed countries to ensure that their policy objectives for IP standards in regional/bilateral trade agreements are demonstrably consistent with their broader objectives for promoting international development and poverty reduction. To that end we would encourage developed countries, rather like developing countries, to incorporate a wider range of stakeholders, within government and without, in their policy-making on IP. (. . .) In our view, most developed countries take insufficient account of development objectives when formulating their policies on IP internationally. More specifically, we believe that developed countries should discontinue the practice of using regional/bilateral agreements as a means of creating TRIPS-plus IP regimes in developing countries as a matter of course. Developing countries should be free to choose, within the confines of TRIPS, where to pitch their IP regimes'.[66]

IV. THE CASE OF PLANT BIOTECHNOLOGY: UPOV IN FTAS AND THE STRENGTHENING OF INTELLECTUAL MONOPOLIES OVER AGRICULTURE

1. Options for protection of plant varieties: patents or *efficient sui* generis system?

a) Protection through patents

Even though the patent system has already reached a certain level of international harmonisation, it cannot be denied that the lack of clear definitions of the patentability conditions by TRIPS gives a useful tool to restrict the granting of patents over plant varieties. Member States may adopt higher patentability standards, making the process of getting a patent over plant varieties harder, thereby protecting only genuine inventions and not those that entail trivial and cosmetic innovation.

Member States still can adopt mechanisms that forbid or difficult the granting of patents over plant varieties against the *ordre public* (Art 27.2 TRIPS). The

[66] Chapter 8 of CIPR Report, Integrating Intellectual Property Rights and Development Policy, London, September 2002, available online at: http://www.iprcommission.org.

unresolved issue is how to implement this flexibility. Generally speaking, patent offices are administrative bodies whose main role is assessing if the patent applications meet the patentability conditions and general formal requirements. Without the further local implementation of this flexibility that provides the patent offices with clear and express legitimacy to negate the granting of patents contrary to the *ordre public*, the flexibility turns out to be inexistent. There is thus the need of setting up special procedures to be followed by the patent offices examiners; pointing out data, factual evidence and documents necessary for denying the grant of patents; the establishment of a system that entitles third parties to submit documents that may support the patent offices decisions, among other measures.

The rule enshrined in article 8 of TRIPS that states that 'Members may, in formulating or amending their laws and regulations, adopt measures necessary to protect public health and nutrition, and to promote the public interest in sectors of vital importance to their socio-economic and technological development' completes and clarifies the contents of article 27.2. Public health, nutrition and protection of the general public interests are part of the wide concept of *ordre public*.

Patents are deemed the most efficient means of protecting biotechnological inventions and for stimulating massive investments in R&D. Nevertheless, a developing country or LDC, before the election of the patent system as the most suitable regime according to their development needs, must consider if other sectors of pivotal importance for their local development will not be impaired due to the expansion of the patent regime over plant varieties. It must be further analysed if the granting of patents over plant varieties will not pose imbalances rather than incentives and social and entrepreneurial benefits to the locals. It is also important to bear in mind that the practice of patent offices of taking for granted the associated traditional knowledge when examining the patent applications involving biotechnological inventions may stimulate bio-piracy; patents prevent the free use of the patented materials; in the absence of a multilaterally agreed consensus, it is much harder and trickier to integrate obligations arising from other relevant international conventions into patent legislation. Even in developed countries, there is still no homogeneous position regarding the grant of patents over plant varieties.[67] The 20 year minimum period of protection is very long especially because of the vital importance of plant varieties to the sustainability of human life.

Only when the above queries are answered and the further implications from the set up of a patent regime applicable over patent varieties analysed, will there be enough information to make a coherent and thoughtful decision about the suitability of widening the scope of patent protection. Finally, it is important to recall that, historically, the regimes of protection of intellectual property in developed countries only gradually grew stronger. The legal strengthening

[67] M Llewelyn, above fn 2, pp 312–13.

process was progressive and took place in parallel to the strengthening of the local economy.[68]

b) An efficient sui generis *regime?*

While the patent system already possesses a body of rules that can be deemed internationally homogenous, despite the differences that still persist from country to country, when it comes to moulding an effective *sui generis* regime for the protection of plant varieties, Member States can profit from the ambiguity of the wording of TRIPS, and draft a piece of law that protects the national interests related directly or indirectly to agriculture and breeding industry, as long as the international principles of IPR are taken full consideration. The only condition required is the efficiency of the regime. Nonetheless, this is actually a requirement of any legal entitlement in anywhere, regardless of the differences in terms of economic and social development and culture. The States are thus free to create a brand new system of protection of plant varieties, being allowed to choose the form of protection, the conditions required for protection, the period of protection, the scope, genera and species that may be protected, exemptions to the exclusive rights, compulsory licensing provisions, protecting, therefore, market from unfair competition practices. It is even possible—and, in our perspective, mandatory—to integrate other concerns that arise from important international binding instruments—specially the United Nations Convention on Biological Diversity (CDB) and the FAO International Treaty on Plant Genetic Resources for Food and Agriculture—into the framework that regulates the protection of plant varieties (ITPGRFA).

Due to the controversies involving the grating of intellectual monopolies over plant varieties, especially over crop varieties, developing and least developed countries succeeded, during the GATT Uruguay Round, in including in the wording of the article 27.3.b the possibility of Member States not having to adopt a pre-determined legal regime for the protection of plant varieties.

It was left to the discretion of the Members to adopt either the traditional patent regime, a *sui generis* regime, or dual protection.[69] For the second and perhaps most appropriate option, the UPOV model is only one regime sufficient to meet the obligation of providing protection for plant varieties. If UPOV is

[68] B Zorina Khan, in: Study commissioned by the United Kingdom Intellectual Property Rights Commission about the historical development of Intellectual Property Regimes in Europe and USA and their relationship with economic development concludes that 'the major lesson that one derives from this aspect of the economic history of Europe and America is that intellectual property rights best promoted the progress of science and arts when they evolved in tandem with other institutions and in accordance with the needs and interests of social and economic development in each nation. In short, the historical record suggests that appropriate policies towards intellectual property are not independent of the level of development nor of the overall institutional environment.' BZ Kahn, Intellectual Property and Economic Development: Lessons From American and European History. Study Paper 1a. Available at: http://www.iprcommission.org/papers/pdfs/study_papers/sp1a_khan_study.pdf, p 59.

[69] M Llewelyn, above n 2, p 317–18.

considered unsuitable, the Member States of WTO are entitled to develop a genuinely new regime, with no pre-determined criteria or conditions for protection. The only requirement is the efficiency of the regime.[70] However, this would not be the most convenient solution for industrialised countries.[71] All in all, TRIPS only sets minimum standards of protection pursued by industrialised countries. After all, UPOV 1991 is a regime more 'closely aligned to a patent with the result that the differences in the scope of the monopoly provided by a patent and that by a UPOV right would be marginal.[72]

As the UPOV 1991 model by the developing countries and LDCs was deemed very burdensome, the non-members of UPOV were allowed to adhere to the UPOV 1978 Act until April 1998, when the UPOV 1991 Act came into force. The implicit idea is that in the near future, all members to the UPOV 1978 will be required to adhere to the UPOV 1991. Many developing countries have not become members of UPOV 1978 and are still seeking alternative models to cope with the obligations taken on under TRIPS. These countries nevertheless are being pressured, through bilateral and regional free trade agreements, to adhere to UPOV 1991 and to give up their entitlement of developing their own *sui generis* regime for protection of plant varieties.

As already mentioned, one of the main reasons for developing and least developed countries having accepted the inclusion of IPRs in the mandate of the GATT Uruguay Round was the possibility of not being subject to unilateral retaliation imposed by developed countries or to pressure for bilateral or regional trade agreements stricter than that one agreed in multilateral forums.[73]

[70] There are different interpretations on what an 'efficient sui generis' regime means: i) the first refers to the availability of enforcement legal tools; ii) the second refers to the adoption of the UPOV model as the only efficient regime of protection of plant varieties; iii) the third refers to the mere availability of a legal system of protection of plant varieties. Para B Dhar, 'Accordingly, the legal framework that can provide protection to the largest range of new varieties developed can alone be considered an 'effective' system. This criterion can only be met if protection is extended to include all the stakeholders involved in plant breeding in various countries, ie, formal plant breeders—the focus of UPOV—and traditional farmers who continue to play a significant role in the development of agriculture across countries'. (*Sui Generis* Systems for Plant Variety Protection: options under TRIPS. Quaker United Nations Office, Geneva, 2002, p 8). iv) the regime has to set a clear definition of: the protectable subject matter; the conditions for granting protection; the nature of the rights conferred; exceptions to rights; national and most favoured treatment; transparency; a sufficient period of protection to allow breeders to recover costs; enforcement instruments.

[71] In determining the form a sui generis right would take, Members States are not bound by any existing substantive requirements as they would be if they were to provide patent protection (novelty, inventive step and industrial applicability). This means that when formulating the right it is possible to seek guidance and/or inspiration from other international agreements including those not wholly concerned with intellectual property protection. (. . .) In formulating non-traditional protection a common justification given is that the accepted norms of protection, patents and plant variety rights according to UPOV, do not enable a country to meet other commitments relating to genetic resources undertaken through membership of the CBD'. (M Llewelyn, above fn 1, p 308)

[72] M Llewelyn, above fn 2, p 318.

[73] P Drahos, above fn 9, pp 6–7.

2. FTAs, TRIPS-plus rules and UPOV

In recent bilateral and regional free trade agreements,[74] the following obligations are often inserted with respect to plant variety protection:

i) The State shall to adhere to UPOV;[75] or
ii) The State shall comply with the 'highest international standards' of protection of IPR. 'Highest international standards' mean either the adhesion to UPOV 1991 or the granting of patents over plant varieties, with no exemptions, or, finally can mean the granting of dual protection simultaneously, which is also allowed by article 27.3.b in fine and by UPOV 1991.

a) Africa and Middle East

— EFTA–Jordan FTA[76] (2001): Jordan must join UPOV by 2006.
— EFTA–Morocco FTA[77] (2000): Morocco must join UPOV by 2000.
— EFTA–Palestinian Authority FTA[78] (1998): Palestinian Authority must implement the 'highest international standards' of IPR protection.
— EU–Algeria FTA[79] (2002) (agreed, but not in force): Algeria shall accede to and implement UPOV (1991 Act) within 5 years of entry into force, although accession can be replaced by implementation of an effective sui generis system if both parties agree.
— EU–Egypt FTA[80] (2001) (agreed, but not in force): Egypt must join UPOV within 5 years of entry into force.
— EU–Jordan FTA[81] (1997): Jordan must join UPOV by 2007.
— EU–Lebanon FTA[82] (2002) (interim agreement in force as of March 2003): Lebanon must join UPOV (1991 Act) by 2008.

[74] GRAIN. Bilateral Agreements Imposing TRIPS-PLUS Intellectual Property Rights on Biodiversity in Developing Countries. October, 2004. Available at: http://www.grain.org/rights/tripsplus.cfm?id=68

[75] The only UPOV Convention open to adhesion is the 1991 Act. Even if the FTA states that the Contracting Party is allowed to adhere either to UPOV 1978 Act or to the UPOV 1991 Act, the Party will be obliged to adhere to the 1991 Act.

[76] EFTA–Jordan Free Trade Agreement.

[77] EFTA–Morocco Free Trade Agreement.

[78] Interim Agreement between the EFTA States and the PLO for the Benefit of the Palestinian Authority.

[79] Euro-Mediterranean Agreement establishing an Association between the European Community and its Member States, and the People's Democratic Republic of Algeria.

[80] Proposal for a Council and Commission Decision on the conclusion of a Euro-Mediterranean Association Agreement between the European Communities and their Member States, and the Arab Republic of Egypt.

[81] Euro-Mediterranean Association Agreement establishing an Association between the European Communities and their Member States, and the Hashemite Kingdom of Jordan, signed on 24 November 1997 and entered into force on 1 May 2002.

[82] Interim agreement on trade and trade-related matters between the European Community, and the Republic of Lebanon.

— EU–Morocco FTA[83] (2000): Morocco must join UPOV (1991 Act) and accede to Budapest Treaty by 2004.
— EU–Palestinian Authority FTA[84] (1997): Palestinian Authority must implement the 'highest international standards' of IPR protection.
— EU–South Africa FTA[85] (1999): South African must also implement 'highest international standards' of IPR protection and undertake to go beyond TRIPS standards of IPR protection.
— EU–Tunisia FTA[86] (1998): Tunisia must join UPOV (1991 Act) by 2002.
— US–Bahrain FTA[87] |(2004) (signed):Bahrain must join UPOV upon entry into force.
— US–Jordan FTA[88] (2000): Jordan must implement and join UPOV within one year of entry into force and partially implement Budapest Treaty
— US–Morocco[89] FTA (2004) (signed): Morocco must also ratify UPOV Convention (1991)
— US–Sub-Saharan Africa (African Growth & Opportunities Act)[90] (2000): US trade benefits to 38 AGOA-eligible countries are unilaterally gauged on extent to which they go beyond TRIPS standards of IPR protection.

b) Asia and the Pacific

— EU–Bangladesh FTA[91] (2001): Bangladesh must endeavour to join UPOV (1991 Act) by 2006.
— EU–Sri Lanka FTA[92] (1995): Sri Lanka shall implement the 'highest international standards' of IPR protection.
— Switzerland–Viet Nam IPR Agreement[93] (1999): Viet Nam must join UPOV (1991 Act) by 2002.

[83] Euro-Mediterranean Agreement establishing an association between the European Communities and their Member States, and the Kingdom of Morocco.

[84] Euro-Mediterranean Interim Association Agreement on trade and cooperation between the European Community, and the Palestine Liberation Organization (PLO) for the benefit of the Palestinian Authority of the West Bank and the Gaza Strip.

[85] Agreement on Trade, Development and Cooperation between the European Community and its Member States, and the Republic of South Africa.

[86] Euro-Mediterranean Agreement establishing an association between the European Communities and their Member States, and the Republic of Tunisia.

[87] US–Bahrain Free Trade Agreement.

[88] Agreement Between the United States of America and the Hashemite Kingdom of Jordan on the Establishment of a Free Trade Area.

[89] US–Morocco Free Trade Agreement.

[90] Trade and Development Act of 2000, s B.211.5.b.ii.

[91] Cooperation Agreement between the European Community and the People's Republic of Bangladesh on partnership and development.

[92] Council Decision of 27 March 1995 concerning the conclusion of the Cooperation Agreement between the European Community and the Democratic Socialist Republic of Sri Lanka on Partnership and Development.

[93] Abkommen zwischen dem Schweizerischen Bundesrat und der Sozialistischen Republik Vietnam über den Schutz des geistigen Eigentums und über die Zusammenarbeit auf dem Gebiet des geistigen Eigentums.

— US–Cambodia IPR Agreement[94] (1996): Cambodia must join UPOV.
— US–Laos Trade Relations Agreement[95] (1997) (concluded, but entry into force pending): US grant of 'normal trade relations' status to Laos, Laos must join UPOV (1978 or 1991 Act) 'without delay'.
— US–Singapore FTA[96] (2003): Singapore must join UPOV (1991 Act) within six months of entry into force or by end 2003, whichever sooner
— US–Viet Nam FTA[97] (2000): Viet Nam must implement and make best effort to join UPOV

c) Latin America and the Caribbean

— EFTA–Chile FTA[98] (2003): Chile must join the UPOV Convention (1978 or 1991 Act) by 2007
— EFTA–Mexico FTA[99] (2000): Mexico must join UPOV by 2002.
— EU–Mexico FTA[100] (2000): Mexico shall also provide 'highest international standards' of IPR protection.
— US–Andean countries (Andean Trade Preferences Act 1991):[101] US trade benefits to Bolivia, Ecuador, Colombia and Peru unilaterally gauged on extent to which they go beyond TRIPS standards of IPR protection.
— US–Caribbean countries (Caribbean Basin Trade Partnership Act—2000):[102] US trade benefits to up to 24 eligible countries unilaterally gauged on extent to which they go beyond TRIPS standards of IPR protection.
— United States–Dominican Republic–Central America Free Trade Agreement[103] (2004) (signed): Costa Rica, Dominican Republic, El Salvador, Guatemala, Honduras and Nicaragua must join UPOV (1991 Act) or provide patents on plants.
— US–Chile FTA[104] (2003): Chile must join UPOV (1991 Act)
— US–Ecuador IPR Agreement[105] (1993) (signed but not in force due to non-ratification by Ecuador's Parliament): Ecuador must conform with UPOV if it does not grant patents on plant varieties.

[94] Agreement between the United States of America and the Kingdom of Cambodia on Trade Relations and Intellectual Property Rights Protection.
[95] Agreement between the United States of America and the Lao People's Democratic Republic on Trade Relations.
[96] US–Singapore Free Trade Agreement.
[97] Agreement between the United States of America and the Socialist Republic of Vietnam on Trade Relations.
[98] EFTA-Chile Free Trade Agreement, Art 46.
[99] EFTA-Mexico Free Trade Agreement.
[100] Economic Partnership, Political Coordination and Cooperation Agreement between the European Community and its Member States, and the United Mexican States.
[101] Andean Trade Preferences Act.
[102] US–Caribbean Trade Partnership Act of 2000.
[103] Central American Free Trade Agreement, 2004.
[104] US–Chile Free Trade Agreement, 2003.
[105] Agreement between the Government of the United States of America and the Government of Ecuador Concerning the Protection and Enforcement of Intellectual Property Rights.

— US–Nicaragua IPR Agreement[106] (1998): Nicaragua must join UPOV.
— US–Trinidad & Tobago IPR Agreement[107] (1994): Trinidad & Tobago must implement and make best effort to join UPOV.
— North America Free Trade Agreement[108] (1994): Mexico must implement and join UPOV within two years of entry into force.

Free Trade Area of the Americas[109] (under negotiation): Actual negotiating text contains many references to UPOV.

3. Risks to developing countries brought about by UPOV

As a consequence of the strengthening of the international trade in agricultural products in the post II World War, the high costs involved in the development of new plant varieties, the time devoted to the development of a new variety, the dexterity of reproducing self-pollinating plants, the need to reward and protect the investments made in the breeding field, the technical hardship of applying the traditional patent system to plant varieties, the unavailability of an international system of protection of plant varieties, the French government convened an ad hoc diplomatic meeting in December 1961 in Paris.[110] At this occasion, some European States adopted the International Convention for the Protection of New Varieties of Plants (UPOV), establishing the Union for the Protection of New Varieties of Plants.[111] The regime widely known as Plant Breeders' Rights (PBR) is a result, therefore, of the adoption of the UPOV Convention in 1961.

Until the early 1970s, when the US passed the Plant Varieties Protection Act, PBRs were considered a 'West European phenomenon'.[112]

The original UPOV Convention of 1961 was revised twice: in 1978 and in 1991. In the last revision, the breeder's rights over the propagating material of the plant variety was extended to the harvest as well as the spectrum of application of PBR. 'The main goal of the revision was to strengthen the breeder's rights. The reasons were 'the costs of deploying new technologies and the costs of developing and producing new varieties' of plants had 'caused the public

[106] Agreement between the Government of the United States of America and the Government of the Republic of Nicaragua Concerning Protection of Intellectual Property Rights.

[107] Memorandum of Understanding between the Government of the United States of America and the Government of Trinidad and Tobago Concerning Protection of Intellectual Property Rights.

[108] North America Free Trade Agreement, Chapter 17.

[109] Free Trade Area of the Americas, Third Draft Agreement, 21 November 2003, Chapter on Intellectual Property Rights.

[110] Soares, Guido Fernando Silva. Direito internacional do meio ambiente: emergência, obrigações e responsabilidades. São Paulo:Atlas, 2001, págs 524 e ss.

[111] UPOV is an intergovernmental organisation based in Geneva. Because of the common interests between WIPO and UPOV, in 1982 both organisations reached an agreement, being since then UPOV under the administration of the WIPO.

[112] B Dhar, above fn 68, p 3–4.

authorities in the UPOV member states to ask themselves if the plant breeder's rights system was adequate and strong enough to secure the maintenance of the enormous, costly breeding work'. It was argued that the authorities of the members states were convinced of the need to have a strong plant breeding industry, backed by a strong Plant Breeders' Rights System'.[113] The European countries and the USA took advantage of the success of the inclusion of IPRs in the negotiating mandate of the GATT Uruguay Round, revising the UPOV 1978 Act and aiming at an optimised model of protection of plant varieties before the end of the Uruguay Round. This model, known as UPOV 1991, was set forth to the States engaged in the negotiation for the establishment of the WTO as the most efficient and suitable regime of protection of plant varieties.

a) Key differences between the UPOV 1978 Act and the UPOV 1991 Act

The main differences between the UPOV 1991 Act and the UPOV 1978 Act relate to:

(a) the coverage of varieties qualifying for protection,
(b) criteria for protection;
(c) forms of protection;
(d) breeders' rights and essentially derived varieties;
(e) exceptions to breeders rights;
(f) farmers privilege;[114]
(g) duration of protection;
(h) exhaustion of breeders rights.

(i) Coverage of varieties qualifying for protection

1978: article 4.4: certain genera and species may be excluded from the scope of protection for special economic or ecological conditions prevailing in that State.
1991: article 3: all plant genera and species shall be protected. The protection, nevertheless, may be accorded progressively, reaching all genera and species within ten years.

(ii) Criteria for protection

1978: the plant variety must be new, distinct, uniform and stable.
For a plant variety to be protected it must be phenotypically different from others, based on guidelines designed by UPOV.[115] The conventional flexibility non-explored by States in an appropriate manner is the possibility of restricting those parameters for each species in line with agricultural, economic and nutrition concerns. The finer the differentiation, the more varieties can be protected.

[113] B Dhar, above fn 68, p 11.
[114] The right of farmers to freely replant and exchange farm-saved seeds.
[115] Features that identify the plant variety and differentiate it from the others, based upon certain parameters.

More general parameters allow lesser plant varieties that may be deemed protectable. Hence the developing and least developed countries can facilitate or hamper the grant of breeder's rights, depending on how wide or narrow are the descriptors locally adopted. In the specific case of UPOV, its guidelines entail certain minimum parameters that have to be followed by the Member States, and another list that is optional. Accordingly, 'developing countries might consider raising the threshold, in particular so that protection is only given for significant or important innovations with particular characteristics that are deemed socially beneficial (for example, yield increases, or traits of nutritional value). Thus the criteria for distinctness may be strengthened, and also criteria formulated defining utility in terms of the objectives of agricultural policy. Alternatively, countries may decide to retain lower standards for certain categories of plant in order to facilitate access by nascent domestic breeding industries to PVP protection from which may flow commercial and export benefits'.[116] The choice of descriptors shall take full consideration of the variety and the local interest. We will take as an example the case of Brazil. The Decree n 2366/1997 defines descriptors as the morphological, physiological, biochemical or molecular characteristic which is genetically inherited and is utilised to identify the plant variety. The definition of descriptors adopted by the Brazilian legislation is conducive to the wide granting of plant breeder's rights. This stand may be very favourable for soy, provided that Brazil, by virtue of the EMBRAPA (a Brazilian governmental research centre specialised in local farming needs), is the most important soy breeder. Accordingly there is an interest in commercially realising and exporting these varieties. Nevertheless, in the case of varieties in relation to which there is no local expertise developed, a sophisticated definition of descriptors is harmful to the local interests. The widespread practice of adopting the same descriptors set out in Europe is unadvisable.

The criteria for protection are these:

Novelty: The variety shall be commercially new, that is, the variety must not have been commercialised or offered for sale, with the consent of or by the breeder, prior to the filing of the application for a breeders right in the territory of the State where protection is sought. The 1978 act allows the Parties to deem as new, plant varieties that have been commercialised within their territory for up to one year.

Uniformity: The plant variety must horizontally retain the expected characteristics with the least variation possible, that is, this criterion implies that samples of a variety retain the important characteristics that qualify them as protectable.

Stability: the variety must retain, vertically, the relevant characteristics that qualify it for protection, that is, after repeated reproductions the variety must retain the relevant characteristics.

[116] CIPR report, above fn 70, p 70.

1991: the same four criteria for protection are maintained, but with some important variations.

Novelty: All member States have to grant in their laws a one-year grace period.

According to Art 5.2 UPOV 1991, it is not possible the set out further or different conditions of protection, that is, it is not legally possible, for instance, the adoption of the 'disclosure of origin' requirement as to genetic resources that were utilised in the breeding process of the new plant variety or to adopt differential conditions of protection for varieties bred by traditional communities.

Distinctiveness:

1978: Art 6.1.a—A plant variety must be clearly distinguishable from any other variety whose existence is a matter of 'common knowledge' in order to be eligible for protection, besides meeting the other three criteria of protection. 'Common knowledge' *may* be established by reference to various factors such as: cultivation or marketing already in progress, entry in an official register of varieties already made or in the course of being made, inclusion in a reference collection, or precise description in a publication. The mere suggestive definition of 'common knowledge' allows the recognition of traditional plant varieties as part thereof, germ plasm stored in gene banks avoiding the granting of plant breeder's rights over traditional plant varieties. This is, at least, a tool that may mitigate bio-piracy locally.

1991: Art 7—A variety shall be deemed distinct if it is clearly distinguishable from any other variety whose existence is a matter of 'common knowledge' at the time of the filing of the application. The issue here is the definition of 'common knowledge': only plant varieties that are contained in the official registers of varieties, in any country of the Union, may be deemed part of the common knowledge, that is, traditional varieties, bred and selected by traditional farmers are not part of the 'common knowledge', even if object of specialized publications. The meaning of 'common knowledge' adopted by the UPOV 1991 Act favours bio-piracy of traditional plant varieties.

(iii) Forms of protection

1978: Art 2—Each member State of the Union may recognise the right of the breeder either by the grant of a special title of protection or patents. The cumulative approach is prohibited.

1991: UPOV 91 allows simultaneous cumulative protection, in line with article 27.3.b of TRIPS.

(iv) Breeders' rights and essentially derived varieties

1978: Art 5—the breeder's prior authorisation shall be required for:

- (i) the production for purposes of commercial marketing;
- (ii) the offering for sale;
- (iii) the marketing of the reproductive or vegetative propagating material of the variety.

1991: Art 14—the following acts require the prior authorisation of the breeder:

- (i) production or reproduction (multiplication) of the propagation material;
- (ii) conditioning for the purposes of propagation;
- (iii) offering for sale;
- (iv) selling or other marketing;
- (v) exporting; importing;
- (vi) stocking for any of the purposes mentioned above.
- (vii) According to Art 14.2—the breeder has also rights over the harvested materials obtained directly from the protected variety, provided that the breeder has not had reasonable opportunity to exercise his right in relation to the said harvested material;
- (viii) the acts referred to in items i) to vii) in respect of products made directly from harvested material of the protected variety through the unauthorised use of the said harvested material shall require the authorization of the breeder;
- (ix) according to Art 14.4, the Contracting Parties may also provide that acts other than those referred to in items i) to vii) shall also require the authorisation of the breeder;
- (x) the commercial exploitation of varieties which essentially derive from the protected variety or which are not clearly distinguishable from the protected variety (article 14.5): For the purposes of assessing if a given plant variety is essentially derived, the analysis will either be based upon the ostensive essential characteristics that result from the genotype[117] and the combination of genotypes of the initial variety. Therefore, the ostensive features of the new plant variety will be compared with the ones retained by the alleged initial variety, and if it is not enough to prove if the alleged essentially derived variety derives or not from a given plant variety, then it may be necessary to carry out a molecular, genetic analysis of the germ plasm to identify if the new variety presents certain characteristics by chance or as a result of the non-authorised use of protected germ plasm. Basically, both varieties have to be compared, in terms of DNA, assessing the levels of homogeneity between them. The concept of essentially derived varieties is not easily understandable; it is a task left to the court.

(iv) Exceptions to breeders rights

1978: Art 5.3—Authorisation by the breeder shall *not* be required either for the utilisation of the variety as an initial source of variation for the purpose of creating other varieties or for the marketing of such varieties, as long as the protected variety is not used repeatedly for the commercial production of the new variety. In this case, the authorisation of the breeder is required.

[117] The Wikipedia encyclopedia defines genotype as the specific genetic makeup (the specific genome) of an individual, usually in the form of DNA. It codes for the phenotype of that individual.

Art 9—The States may establish restrictions to the exercise of the rights accorded to the breeder for reasons of public interest (general clause). Under the circumstance of widespread distribution of the variety, the Member State of UPOV shall take measures necessary to ensure that the breeder receives equitable remuneration. This last obligation was established to ensure the enforcement of plant breeders rights against medium and large farms that replant the propagation materials resulting from their harvest or that commercialise such material on a great scale. Thus, the farmer's privilege is narrowed in cases of 'widespread distribution of the variety'. Those medium and large farms shall be charged reasonable royalties fees[118] in favour of the plant breeder rights holders.

1991: Art 15: i) acts done privately and for non-commercial purposes; ii) acts done for experimental purposes; ii) acts done for the purposes of breeding other varieties, as long as the resulting variety is not an essentially derived one.

(v) Farmers privilege

1978: There are no limitations to the farmer's privilege. The farmer's privilege is contained in Art 5 of UPOV 1978. The authorisation of the breeder is only required in cases of reproduction of the propagation material for commercial purposes. The reproduction of the propagation material for exchange with the aim of diversifying the genetic variability of the plant varieties and re-planting do not require the authorisation of the breeder.[119]

1991: Art 15.2—farmer's rights are optional. Each Contracting Part *may, within reasonable limits*[120] and subject to the *safeguarding of the legitimate interests of the breeder*, restrict the breeder's right in relation to any variety in order to permit farmers to use for propagating purposes, *on their own holdings*, the product of the harvest which they have obtained by planting, *on their own holdings*, the protected variety or a variety essentially derived.

There is a clear limitation to the farmer's privilege: first, it is now optional and requires the express recognition through a national law, meaning that only

[118] The meaning of reasonable royalties fees is not standardised, even within the European Community. Taking as an example the license fee charged for the sale of certified winter wheat seeds within the EC in 2003/2004, we can realise that there is a huge variation from country to country. While the license fees charged in the Netherlands can amount up to 9,25 euros/100kg, in Spain the fee charged amounts to 0,3 euros/100kg. Therefore, the meaning of 'reasonable fees' may be set case-by-case, according to the local social-economic development and reality.

[119] N Pires de Carvalho. The Trips Regime of Patents. Kluwer Law International. 2002, The Hague, p 182.

[120] B Dhar quotes the interpretation of the Association of Plant Breeders for the Protection of Plant Varieties (ASSINSEL) as regards the boundaries of 'within reasonable limit' expression. ASSINSEL interprets that 'farmer's privilege' should not go 'beyond the provision of the 1991 Act of the UPOV Convention, ie, within the reasonable limits in terms of acreage, quantity of seed and species concerned and subject to the safeguarding of the legitimate interests of the breeders in terms of payment of a remuneration and information'. Any national legislation authorising farm saved seed without reasonable limits and without safeguarding the legitimate interests of the breeders, ASSINSEL argue, 'would not be an effective sui generis system in the meaning of Art 27.3(b) of the TRIPS Agreement'. Above fn 68, p 15.

what is explicitly regulated is legally allowed; second, the scope of the privilege was narrowed. The farmer can only sow the result of its own harvest, and can no longer exchange with or sell these materials for other farmers/neighbours—a practice that has maintained alive, hitherto, the variety of germ plasm available in agriculture. Finally, in the light of the UPOV 1991, only small farms may reap benefits from this rule.

Yet there are other legal and technical restrictions that debilitate the farmer's privilege, besides those resulting from UPOV: i) the breeding of hybrids, ii) patents, iii) purchase agreements, and iv) Genetic Use Restriction Technologies.[121]

It is important to remember that hybrids rapidly lose their hybrid vigour from one generation to the next, making seed-saving unattractive to farmers. Breeding companies, especially in the US, are entering in contracts with farmers, informing them that they will only be allowed to use the protected seeds/propagating materials for feed or processing and that they may not be used or sold for sowing, breeding or any improvement purposes. If the contract obligations are not observed, the use of breach of contract claims in local courts is more easily enforceable.[122] Important plant biotechnology companies in the US add to agreements of commercialisation of seeds and even to the bag where the seeds are stored, a standard clause[123] known as 'bag-tag' or 'seed-wrap' licenses,[124] obliging farmers to buy on an annual basis fresh seeds, circumventing the farmer's privilege.[125]

(vi) Duration of protection

1978: **Art** 8—Not shorter than 15 years from the date of the grant of the breeder's right (general rule). For vines, forest trees, fruit trees and ornamental trees, the period of protection may not be less than 18 years.

1991: Art 19—Not shorter than 20 years from the date of the grant of the breeders right (general rule). For trees and vines, the duration of the breeders right shall not be shorter than 25 years from the said date.

[121] Technology that produces infertile seeds.

[122] J van Wijk. How Does Stronger Protection of Intellectual Property Rights Affect Seed Supply? Early Evidence of Impact. Natural Resources Perspectives, number 13, November 1996. Available at: http://www.odi.org.uk/nrp/13.html

[123] An example of a Pioneer bag-tag license states as follows: 'if the tag indicates this product or the parental lines used in producing this product are protected under one or more US patents, Purchaser agrees that it is granted a limited license thereunder only to produce forage, or grain for feeding or processing. Resale of this seed or supply of saved seed to anyone, including Purchaser, for planting is strictly prohibited under this license.'

[124] MD Janis and JP Kesan, Intellectual property protection for plant innovation: unresolved issues after *JEM v Pioneer*, p 3. Available at: http://www.bioethics.iastate.edu/retreat_2005/Janis.pdf

[125] A Mannan, Intellectual Property as a Tool of Social Repression, p 16. Available at: https://www.kent.ac.uk/law/undergraduate/modules/ip/resources/PlantDissertationDec2002.doc

(vii) Exhaustion of the breeders right
1978: There is no reference to the subject.[126]
1991: Art 16—the breeder's right to prohibit potential propagation (nationally or internationally) of the variety is never exhausted.

b) The myth of sustainable development and UPOV

To conclude, from the preliminary comparative analysis between the UPOV 1978 Act and UPOV 1991 Act, the latter (now imposed to developing and least developed countries through bilateral and regional trade agreements) is harmful to countries where agriculture plays an important socio-economic role as well as in those where the biological and cultural diversity in agriculture must be protected and rewarded for their commercial benefits. In summary, the UPOV 1991 Act restricts:

- — the farmer's privilege, making it optional;
- — the propagation materials exchange is vetoed, leading to genetic erosion and jeopardizing the world food security;
- — the local plant varieties, for their biological diversity, do not meet the stability, distinctness and uniformity requirements, and may not be protectable. And for not being deemed part of the conventional definition of 'common knowledge', bio-piracy is facilitated;
- — long lasting monopoly over plant varieties hampers the free flow of germ plasm;
- — the extension of PBR to essentially derived varieties discourage investments in R&D;
- — the widening of the spectrum of application of PBR to all genera and species of plants prevents the States from keeping important crops in the public domain;
- — there is the trend of replacing traditional plant varieties for industrialised ones, stimulating, thus, the genetic uniformity and, as a consequence, the genetic erosion.

An important feature of UPOV membership is the 'high proportion of countries with relatively low shares of their economically active population in agriculture. Most of the early members of UPOV have less than 5 per cent of their economically active population engaged in agriculture. There seems to be a strong correspondence between adoption of Intellectual Property Protection in agriculture and low shares of economically active population in this sector'.[127] It can be stated that wealthy countries in terms of breeding technologies and industry sponsor the adoption of internationally higher standards of protection in the field of PBR because the impact of the implementation of these provisions will

[126] About exhaustion of rights see M Basso, O direito internacional da propriedade intelectual, Porto Alegre, Livraria do Advogado Editora, 2000, p 181.
[127] B Dhar, above fn 68, p 8.

be very marginal for their own farmers, as the share of population working in the agricultural field is very low.

At the same time that the European countries were developing their economies during the second half of the 20th century, and their populations moved from the countryside to the cities, the regimes of protection of PBR became stricter. However, developed countries that have important agricultural policies—such as Canada and New Zealand—are still members of the UPOV 1978 Act, a version much more flexible, according more protection to farmers to the detriment of PBR holders.

Consequently, countries with an important share of their populations still engaged in the agricultural sector, especially in small and medium sized family properties engaged in harvesting food crops for local markets and with incipient breeding industry will find it disadvantageous to join the UPOV 1991 Act and should develop genuine *sui generis* regimes of protection of plant varieties. The UPOV 1991 Act model is not bad per se, but is a system designed by industrialised countries for the needs of and commercial challenges faced by industrialised countries. UPOV 1991-like systems may play an important role in developing countries with emerging and thriving breeding industries, allowing the local commercial farmers to have access to better commercially marketed varieties. The UPOV system, in this specific case, may play an important role, in terms of access to markets, in order to avoid the imposition of non-tariff barriers to agricultural products by industrialised countries. If a developing country does not protect certain commercially important varieties, a breeder may enforce his/her rights over the harvested material overseas to the detriment of the exporter from the developing country that sowed non-authorised propagating materials. Nevertheless, PBR may still pose a non-tariff barrier. 'In 1994, Argentinean strawberry plant producers were denied permission to export strawberry plants to Europe by the American breeder and European licensees, because the Latin America plants competed directly with plants produced in Europe. PBR protection granted in Europe proved to be an effective non-tariff trade barrier'.[128]

c) The myth of promoting R&D

There is no doubt that industrialised countries defend the strengthening of regimes of protection of plant varieties in developing and least developed countries, considering such a tool as a condition *sine qua non* for protecting foreign direct investment as well as to raise the agricultural productivity, protect the environment and foster the achievement of a ever lasting solution of hunger.[129]

[128] J van Wijk, Plant Breeders' Rights Create Winners and Losers, Biotechnology and Development Monitor, No 23, 1995, pp 15–19.

[129] GRAIN. Plant Variety Protection to Feed Africa? Rhetoric versus Reality. October, 1999. Available at: http://www.grain.org/briefings/?id=126

Jeroen van Wijk, when analysing countries with a tradition in protecting PBR, concluded that PBR regimes 'may help the domestic seed industry in LDCs to restrict the trade in seed saved from their varieties and to increase their income. There is little evidence, however, that this additional income leads to the availability of more and better varieties for farmers (. . .) Despite the claims of the seed industry, the positive effect on R&D investment of the US Plant Variety Protection Act (PVPA), has been limited. It has stimulated new varieties of wheat and soya bean, but it has scarcely affected R&D in other self-pollinating crops. (. . .) In Argentina, where PVP has been enforced from 1990 onwards, it has enabled domestic wheat and soya bean companies to increase their sales and royalty income and to survive difficult economic periods but has not stimulated additional R&D expenditure'.[130]

Dwijen Rangnekar, in a recent study[131] assessing the economic impact of the implementation of PBR in the United Kingdom and in the United States, analysed the impact of PBR on R&D on the number of varieties introduced into the market and on market concentration. His conclusions can be summarised as follows:

— There is an indication of increasing levels of private investment in plant breeding, however, the clear influence of PBR on the level of investment is not theoretically convincing;
— Private investment appears to concentrate on selected crops, suggesting that the profitability of the crop is more crucial in bringing forth private investment;
— There is no uncontroversial proof that PBR caused changes in the number of new varieties;
— Seed companies, as a commercial strategy, constantly replace the portfolio of varieties. The withdrawal of new varieties in the market cannot be claimed a direct positive outcome arising out of the adoption of PBRs;
— The evidence clearly indicates that the merger and acquisition drive in the seed industry was fostered by the availability of PBR.[132]

D. Rangnekar concludes 'based on the review completed here it would be very difficult to recommend the generalisation and harmonisation of PBR across developing countries'.

One of the major outcomes accruing from PBR is the shift of investment from food crops to commercial crops. PBRs are very important to provide the breeding industry with some certainty regarding the stability of consumer markets, enabling them to design investment strategies in the long term. However, as already mentioned, those investments are devoted to commercial crops. Since

[130] J van Wijk, above fn 125, pp 2–7.

[131] D Rangnekar. Intellectual Property Rights and Agriculture: An Analysis of the Economic Impact of the Plant Breeder's Rights. Study commissioned by Actionaid. March 2000, pp 53–5. Available at: http://www.actionaid.org.uk/793/trips.html

[132] D Rangnekar, above fn 128, p 48.

the early 1990s, the expenditures on R&D in public research centres have been stagnant, and not many resources were left to carry out public-oriented plant breeding. Then, the commercial crops are seen by public researchers as a potential source of revenues that may sustain the maintenance of plant breeding activities related to non-commercial varieties. But, even so, the interests of public funded research institutions shifted, and the problem of using public funds and facilities to develop purely commercial crops remains. Even if this strategy of developing commercial varieties is well managed within the institution, the public institutions, generally speaking, are not aware of the requirements for reaping the benefits of IPR. IPR are not valuable in itself. It is mandatory to have good varieties and markets for them, reliable producers to multiply and distribute them, and means to enforce contracts. It is also necessary to have available resources to bear the costs of accessing third party rights; skilled negotiators and staff in charge of calculating the risks of IP-infringement in all research projects in the pipeline. This whole structure is resource-draining, and most of public institutions certainly are not ready to manage IPR adequately. As far as public research in plant breeding is concerned, the major role played by IPR is to prevent third parties to misappropriate the results of public research and to avoid the risk of being prevented to freely explore and distribute the innovation.

d) Issues related to food security and hunger

As to the issue of food security, Brazilian economic studies point out that the solution for the world hunger problem is not the mere introduction of new plant varieties in developing and least developed countries. The argument of higher productivity of new plant varieties raised by the defenders of the Green Revolution ignores the utterly huge environmental and social costs underlying the introduction of those varieties in the environment and still have not resolved the hunger problem. Raising some Brazilian examples, we will see that from 1970 through 1985 the rise of productivity of basic crop varieties amounts to 20 per cent, while the typical crops sown for export (cocoa, soya, etc.) rose between 119 and 1.112 per cent. Brazil is the fourth biggest food exporter today and still has a population of over 50 millions of undernourished. With the implementation of the agricultural model defended by the Green Revolution, at the same time that the productivity of the biggest 15 per cent crop varieties rose about 17 per cent, the intensive use of fungicides, insecticides and herbicides rose about 584 per cent, 233 per cent and 5414 per cent, respectively. The concentration of land possession and the consequent rural exodus caused an unplanned growth of the Brazilian cities and shantytowns.[133]

Finally, PBR regimes keep a deep and close relationship with genetic erosion. The larger the diversity of a system, the more stable it is. The monoculture is, therefore, a factor of unsustainability of the system, requiring compensation by

[133] JM Gusman Ferraz. A insustentabilidade da revolução verde. Informativo Meio Ambiente e Agricultura—ano VII nº 26 abr/mai/jun 1999.

means of chemicals which trigger serious environmental contaminations. A study carried out by Gusman Ferraz reveals that the unsustainability comes up in different forms, such as the reduction of genetic variability of crop varieties as a result of the use of a few commercial varieties, selected by their potentially high yields when cultivated under ideal circumstances. A sad example is the one that took place in the South East Asia where out of the 30 000 varieties of rice, only a dozen are still widely cultivated. This tendency also takes place in relation to others crop varieties, causing genetic vulnerability. In the US, 96 per cent of the production of peas encompasses only two different varieties, and six varieties of corn are responsible for 71 per cent of the total production. In Canada those figures are very akin, where four varieties of rye, four of wheat and four of canola represent, respectively, *80,5; 75,9 e 95,8 per cent* of the local production of those crops. This tendency means a huge risk to food security, leaving the humanity at the mercy of a much reduced number of biological materials. This genetic erosion is fruit of the need of international standardisation. Those are some of the responsible factors for the large dissemination of such a model of production. Furthermore, it is also important to highlight the growing tendency of concentration of breeding companies, which, in their turn, acquire smaller companies that coincidently are also producers of chemicals and genetically modified organisms that require the exclusive use of those chemicals.[134]

V. CONCLUDING REMARKS

As it does not appear possible to avoid the establishment of legal frameworks for the protection of plant varieties, it is recommended that developing and least developed countries should avoid the adhesion to the UPOV 1991 model and, therefore not accept the insertion of chapters regulating IPR in bilateral and regional trade negotiations.

Recommended are less burdensome alternatives that result in regimes of protection of plant varieties that are genuinely *sui generis*, reflecting the local needs and interests, and harmonisation with the obligations accruing from the CDB and the FAO ITPGRFA. Swap access to markets for a new TRIPS-plus regime is a mistaken choice in short, medium and long terms. The ideal is the establishment of a system that accords differentiated levels of protection to the varieties, according to their purpose. Weak protection should be accorded to major crops, benefiting smallholders; sufficient protection of breeding for commercial farmers, protecting food security; and strong protection for export commodities. Then, the States may adopt the UPOV 1991 Act alike provisions for the protection of highly commercial crops, preventing, for example, the granting of farmer's privileges as regards the latter crops, but, at the same time, adopt more flexible provisions for the protection of food crops of national importance,

[134] JM Gusman Ferraz, above fn 130.

fostering food security. Brazil and Kenya, on the one hand, could restrict, respectively, the grant of farmer's privileges over soya beans and flowers, which are purely commercial crops, harvested in these countries for international markets, as well as adopt a more detailed array of descriptors, strengthening the number of potential varieties to be protected, and, on the other hand, could grant farmer's privilege to the varieties that concern local food security. The adoption of a regime of protection of plant varieties should not be simply seen, as by some developing and least developed countries, as a mere tool to comply with WTO obligations and to show to developed countries that these countries are modern and ready to play in the international trade arena. It may be a very relevant instrument for the achievement of higher social and economic standards, and accordingly should not be a mere reproduction of models adopted by industrialised countries.

Prior to the draft of any piece of legislation for the compliance with TRIPS, it is a prerequisite that the State sets an agricultural/innovation policy, enumerating what are the goals to be pursued by means of the new framework, the local deficiencies and advantages for reaching them. Innovation, foreign direct investment, establishment of a plant breeding sector, protection of landraces, farmer's rights and agro-biodiversity, freer flow of germ plasm, wider access to new plant varieties, conservation and sustainable use of genetic resources, amongst others, are possible goals that may be pursued by States, and therefore the new framework has to be adjusted to the effective achievement of these objectives.

There are feasible options for complying with the obligations taken on under the auspices of WTO, without jeopardising the local small and medium farmers, the genetic biological diversity, food security and the balance of the social and environmental tissue.[135] As to themes related to the commercial use of living materials, the rationale of the system must concentrate on their protection for the future generations and their use in a sustainable fashion. IPRs should be a peripheral aspect, provided that the fundamental interests value above purely private ones.[136]

On the understanding that the needs and interests that drive developing and least developed countries to enter into negotiations with developed countries for establishing bilateral and regional free trade areas are very particular, it would be naïve to simply advocate against the negotiation of any free trade agreement that involves IPRs. Not being possible to rule IPR out of the negotiating man-

[135] Some examples of alternative frameworks regulating the protection of plant varieties: i) The Protection of Plant Varieties and Farmer's Rights Act, 2001 (India).One of the most appealing features of the Indian legislation is the protection of farmer's varieties and those which are in the public domain ('extant varieties'), avoiding then the misappropriation of these varieties by the private sector. Available at: http://www.grain.org/brl_files/india-pvp-2001-en.pdf; ii) Legislation modele africaine pour la protection dês droits communautes locales, des agriculteurs et des obtenteurs pour lês regles d'acces aux resources biologiques, Available at: http://www.grain.org/brl_files/oau-model-law-fr.pdf; iii) the draft of plant varieties act of Bangladesh, available at: http://www.grain.org/brl_files/bangladesh-pvp-1998-en.pdf.

[136] Art 16.5 of the CBD.

date, it is recommended that developing and least developed countries adopt new strategies that encompass concrete proposals such as: to propose that industrialised countries require from the applicants for biotechnological patents/PBR to present a pedigree of the materials used, disclosure of the origin of the genetic resources as well, evidence of prior informed consent and adherence to a Material Transfer Agreement.[137]

In summary, it is suggested that developing and least developed countries maintain IPR negotiations in multilateral forums only. If it is considered to use IPR, in bilateral and regional negotiations, as a trade-off currency, it is mandatory to elaborate a socio-economic assessment study prior to any concession involving stricter IPR obligations. Even so it is decided to negotiate free trade agreements that encompass obligations related to IPR, developing and least developed countries must adopt a proactive trading stance, making specific proposals in areas of vital interest for those countries. And, if per chance, those proposals are not successful, there is the possibility of implementing the obligations emerging from the adhesion to UPOV 1991, in a manner conducive to the protection of the local interests, by virtue of setting out more general descriptors for important food crops, restricting the possibilities of distinction and, consequently, the number of protectable plant varieties and more detailed descriptors for those varieties that may interest the international trade-oriented farmers. Nevertheless, for the successful implementation of this flexibility, developing and least developed countries shall heavily invest in *independent* capacity building programs.

[137] NP Louwaars, 'Sui Generis Rights: From opposing to complementary approaches.' Biotechnology and Development Monitor, No 36, p 13–16, 1998.

Part IV

FTAs and Copyrights

Chapter 8

Exporting the DMCA through Free Trade Agreements

ANDREW CHRISTIE, SOPHIE WALLER
AND KIMBERLEE WEATHERALL[1]

I. INTRODUCTION

SINCE THE NEGOTIATION of the Agreement on Trade Related Aspects of Intellectual Property Rights (TRIPS Agreement) at the Uruguay round of the WTO in 1995, IP has been linked with trade negotiations.[2] The US was one of the most influential countries in the negotiation of the TRIPS agreement, and has shown a continued interest in its linkage of IP with trade in the form of the IP Chapters it now includes in the free trade agreements (FTAs) that it negotiates. As will be discussed below, such IP Chapters are often based closely on the equivalent legislation in the US, and this is exemplified by the *Digital Millennium Copyright Act* (DMCA) provisions which the US now routinely includes in its FTAs.

This paper begins by examining the IP provisions that now routinely appear in FTAs negotiated by the US, including in particular the provisions that emulate the US DMCA legislation. The paper then considers two examples of how the US is exporting the DMCA into the national law of other countries, by analysing two of its recently-negotiated FTAs—one with Singapore, and the other with Australia. The analysis considers the extent of the similarities and the differences between the DMCA provisions in those two FTAs, as well as the similarities and differences of those provisions and the provisions in the national US legislation. It also includes an analysis of the extent to which the DMCA provisions become exported into the national law of the other country. The reasons why the US might be exporting DMCA provisions through FTAs are also explored—does the US have benign reasons, such as cost effectiveness in mind, or are its intentions more insidious? Finally, this paper discusses how the US's

[1] The assistance of Laura Petersen is gratefully acknowledged.
[2] See, for example, Peter Drahos 'Global property rights in information: The story of TRIPS at the GATT' (13) *Prometheus* (1995) 6.

export of the DMCA provisions interacts with international trade law, and the consequences of this interaction.

II. FREE TRADE AGREEMENTS AND THE DMCA

1. IP Provisions of US FTAs

The US export of DMCA provisions using FTAs has occurred in the context of the intellectual property Chapters (IP Chapters) that are included in FTAs negotiated by the US. Between late-2000 and mid-2007,[3] the US concluded FTAs with 17 countries[4]—14 of those in the last 3 years. A common feature of the most recent FTAs is a phenomenal increase in the length of the IP Chapters compared with earlier times—as illustrated by Table 1.

Table 1—Size of IP Chapters in US FTAs (1985–2007)

Year of Agreement	Agreement	Number of pages in IP Chapter[5]	Number of words in IP Chapter[6]
1985	US–Israel FTA	1/3 page	81
1992	North American FTA	7.5 pages	3,605
October 2000	US–Jordan FTA	8 pages, plus a Memorandum of Understanding (approx. 1 page)	2,438
May 2003	US–Singapore FTA	23 pages plus 2 side letters (12 pages)	8,737 (plus side letters)
June 2003	US–Chile FTA	32 pages (no relevant side letters)	11,105
February 2004	US–Australia FTA	30 pages plus 3 side letters (5 pages).[7]	11,581 (plus side letters)

[3] This paper was completed in Sept 2005 and updated in June 2007.

[4] Jordan (October 2000), Singapore (Jan 2003), Chile (Jun 2003), Australia (February 2004), Morocco (Jun 2004), the Central American Countries (Costa Rica, the Dominican Republic, El Salvador, Guatemala, Honduras and Nicaragua) (Aug 2004), Bahrain (Sept 2004), Oman (Jan 2006), Peru (Apr 2006), Columbia (Nov 2006), Panama (Jun 2007), Korea (Jun 2007).

[5] The length referred to here is the length of the Chapter and side letters, as presented on the US Trade Representative Website in PDF format. The figures are approximate. However, the Agreements are presented in a consistent way, with consistent-sized text (underlining the template approach used by the US). Thus presenting the information by page length is not, in our view, significantly misleading.

[6] This is an approximate word count undertaken by cutting and pasting the pdf document into a word document, and then using the word count function.

[7] In the case of the US-Australian FTA, there was also a further exchange of letters in Nov 2004, outlining in further detail the way in which Australia would implement the IP Chapter, and the US response:

Year of Agreement	Agreement	Number of pages in IP Chapter	Number of words in IP Chapter
June 2004	US–Morocco FTA	37 pages plus 3 side letters (4 pages)	10,536 (plus side letters)
August 2004	US–Central American FTA	32.5 pages plus 1 common side letter (1/2 page)[8]	12,251 (plus side letter)
September 2004	US–Bahrain FTA	23.5 pages plus 3 side letters (5.5 pages)	10,729 (plus side letters)
January 2006	US–Oman FTA	25 pages plus 3 common side letters (19.5 pages)	11,447 (plus side letters)
April 2006	US–Peru TPA[9]	33 pages plus 3 side letters (5 pages)	12,430 (plus side letters)
November 2006	US–Columbia TPA	31 pages plus 1 Memorandum of Understanding (1 page), 3 common side letters (12 pages), 1 side letter (1 page)	11,367 (plus side letters)
June 2007	US-Panama TPA	28 pages plus 1 common side letter (2 pages)	11,625 (plus side letters)
June 2007	US-Korea FTA	35 pages plus 3 common side letters (6 pages)	12,908 (plus side letters)

IP was a relatively minor part of the US-Israel FTA (1985) and of the North American FTA (1992), consisting of only one-third of a page and 7.5 pages, respectively. Even though it was concluded after the finalisation of the TRIPS Agreement (1994) and the WIPO Copyright Treaties (1996), the FTA with Jordan (2000) contains IP provisions that are relatively simple, amounting to approximately 8 pages. However, since then the IP provisions in US FTAs have expanded very substantially. An IP chapter (including side letters) of at least 30 pages is now standard. This expansion is due to both an increase in the number

see <http://www.ustr.gov/Trade_Agreements/Bilateral/Australia_FTA/Section_Index.html.> While these are not designated 'side letters' by the parties, there appears to be little difference between these letters and the official 'side letters'. Arguably we could add another 8 pages to the Australian total in the table.

[8] There is a further side letter between the US and the Dominican Republic on IP enforcement measures (1 page).

[9] The agreement with Peru is called a 'Trade Promotion Agreement' rather than being called a 'Free Trade Agreement' despite having the same effect. This is also the case for Columbia and Panama.

of IP provisions in the FTAs and an increase in the amount of detail included in the IP provisions in the FTAs.

IP Chapters in US FTAs typically are structured to deal with three types of matter. First, there are provisions dealing with 'general' matters—such as the international agreements to which each party must accede, the entitlement of the parties to provide more extensive protection, the requirement to apply the principle of national treatment, the way in which the provisions apply to existing subject matter, and the requirement of transparency in national laws and enforcement procedures. Then there are provisions dedicated to individual IP regimes—trade marks and geographical indications, copyright and neighbouring rights, designs, and patents—as well as to regimes which interface with IP regimes (such as use of domain names on the internet, and the regulation of marketing of pharmaceutical products). Finally, there are provisions dealing with the enforcement of IP rights.[10]

It is important to note that individual provisions within the IP Chapters are in a range of categories, in terms of their 'strength'. Some merely repeat a provision from an existing multilateral IP treaty—which, in most cases, is the relevant provision in the TRIPS Agreement. Other provisions, however, are more specific, and either elaborate on the particular means of implementation of the relevant Treaty provision, or provide for a level protection that exceeds the protection mandated by the relevant Treaty provision, or both. These two types of provision—called herein 'Treaty-elaborated' and 'Treaty-plus' provisions, respectively—remove some of the flexibility of interpretation permitted in the relevant Treaty. As can be seen from the table in Appendix 1, quite a number of the IP provisions in recent US FTAs are Treaty-elaborated or Treaty-plus, or both. The specificity of many of the IP provisions means that much of the language of the IP Chapters of recent US FTAs departs significantly from the ordinary form of treaty language in the IP area—which tends, in general, to be quite broad.

2. DMCA Provisions in US FTAs

The DMCA became part of United States copyright law in 1998. The DMCA is a lengthy piece of legislation that is divided into five titles. This paper will focus on the anti-circumvention provisions that are found in Title I.[11] In this paper, these provisions will be referred to as the 'DMCA provisions'.

Title I of the DMCA was enacted in order to comply with two World Intellectual Property Organisation (WIPO) treaties signed by the United States

[10] The general IP provisions and the copyright provisions commonly found in US FTAs are set out in the table in Appendix 1. This table describes the content of these provisions in the Australia-United States Free Trade Agreement (AUSFTA), and identifies the differences, if any, with the equivalent provisions of other US FTAs.

[11] Copyright Act, §1201.

in 1996: the WIPO Copyright Treaty and the WIPO Performances and Phonogram Treaty. However, while compliance with these WIPO treaties is often cited as the basis for the Title I provisions, commentators have argued that the DMCA exceeds the requirements of these treaties.[12] The DMCA has been a highly controversial law, as it has created a new form of copyright liability for breaching technological protections used by copyright owners to prevent copying of and/or access to their works.

The DMCA provisions provide a good illustration of two issues that are relevant to the IP Chapters in the US FTAs more generally. First, they illustrate the increasing complexity of IP Chapters over time. No DMCA provisions are found in the US FTA Jordan (2000),[13] but by the time the Chile FTA (June 2003) was negotiated, DMCA-like provisions had made an appearance. However, the Chilean provisions on anti-circumvention were not an exact match with the US law. Instead, they allow Chile to choose how to implement the relevant ban—whether as an independent offence, or as an aggravating factor to some other offence (like copyright infringement)—and they appear to have a slightly narrower application.[14] Later FTAs, such as those the US negotiated with Singapore (May 2003) and Australia (February 2004), tightened these potential 'loopholes'.

Secondly, the DMCA provisions also demonstrate a move away from the broad language usually used in treaties to far more detailed provisions. The DMCA provisions are both Treaty-elaborated and Treaty-plus in content, and the level of detail strikes the reader immediately. In form, the DMCA provisions look more like a piece of legislation than the text of a treaty.

The FTAs that the US negotiated with Singapore and Australia are good examples. The international obligations of these countries in relation to anti-circumvention are found in the WIPO Copyright Treaty (WCT),[15] Article 11 of which states as follows:

[12] See, for example, Leaffer, *Understanding Copyright Law*, (3rd edn), 373; and Ginsburg, 'Legal Protection of Technological Measures Protecting Works of Authorship: International Obligations and the US Experience' (2005) 29 *Columbia Journal of Law and the Arts* 11.

[13] It should be noted, however, that Art 4.13 does require that Jordan implement anti-circumvention laws, including a ban on 'trafficking' circumvention devices.

[14] For example, the provisions only apply to technological measures that 'restrict unauthorised acts in respect of [copyright owners'] works, performances, and phonograms, *protected by copyright and related rights*' (emphasis added). AUSFTA Art 17.4.7(a) applies to technological measures which 'that restrict unauthorised acts in respect of their works, performances, and phonograms'. Arguably, the text of the Chilean Agreement is slightly narrower in its effect. The definition of 'effective technological measures' in the Chilean Agreement is also arguably narrower, as it only covers measures which 'cannot, in the usual case, be circumvented accidentally': Art 17.7.5(f).

[15] As of September 2005, Singapore was, but Australia was not, a contracting party to the WCT: http://www.wipo.int/treaties/en/ShowResults.jsp?country_id=ALL&start_year=ANY&end_year=ANY&search_what=C&treaty_id=16. According to the recently negotiated Singapore-Australia FTA, however, both parties are required to become contracting parties to the WCT by 28 Jul 2007: art 2.2, Singapore-Australia Free Trade Agreement, available at http://www.austlii.edu.au/au/other/dfat/treaties/2003/16.html.

> Contracting parties shall provide adequate legal protection and effective legal remedies against the circumvention of effective technological measures that are used by authors in connection with the exercise of their rights under this Treaty or the Berne Convention and that restrict acts, in respect of their works, which are not authorized by the authors concerned or permitted by law.

The equivalent obligation in both the Singapore–United States Free Trade Agreement (SUSFTA)[16] and the Australia–United States Free Trade Agreement (AUSFTA)[17] extends for some 2.5 pages and for over 2,000 words.[18] It specifies exactly what is an effective technological measure, what acts are to be prohibited, and what exceptions are to be allowed, in accordance with the model adopted in the US. While this level of detail is also seen in other parts of the IP Chapters, the anti-circumvention provisions stand out as particularly detailed and complex.

III. HOW THE US IS EXPORTING THE DMCA PROVISIONS VIA FTAS

1. Analysis of the DMCA Provisions in the SUSFTA and the AUSFTA

Broadly stated, the US has effectively transplanted the DMCA provisions into recently negotiated FTAs, and from there into the national law of other countries. Below we discuss the case of how this transplant has occurred in respect of the SUSFTA and the AUSFTA.

The DMCA provisions that are effectively transplanted into the FTAs include:

— a general provision prohibiting circumvention of technological measures that control access to works;[19]

— a general provision prohibiting the manufacture, import, sale, provision or trafficking in devices designed to circumvent technological measures that control access to or copying of works;[20]

— a 'fail safe mechanism' allowing the review of the DMCA provisions and the making of additional, time-limited, exceptions;[21]and

— various exemptions to the prohibition in relation to some non-profit organisations, government agencies, reverse engineering, encryption research, minors, personal information collection and security testing.[22]

[16] The full of the SUSFTA is available at http://www.ustr.gov/Trade_Agreements/Bilateral/Singapore_FTA/Final_Texts/Section_Index.html.

[17] The full text of the AUSFTA is available at: http://www.dfat.gov.au/trade/negotiations/us_fta/final-text/index.html.

[18] For a comparison of the anti-circumvention provisions of the DMCA, SUSFTA and AUSFTA see Appendix 2.

[19] Copyright Act, §1201(a)(1)(A).

[20] *Ibid* §1201(a)(2) and §1201(b).

[21] *Ibid* §1201(a)(1)(B)–(E).

[22] *Ibid* §1201(d)–(j).

A number of provisions in the DMCA are not exported into the FTAs. While some of these are definitional, others appear to be of greater importance. §1201(c)(4) of the US Copyright Act, for example, states that certain DMCA provisions do not affect the right to free speech. This exception is not included in either the SUSFTA and the AUSFTA. The DMCA provisions also include an exception in relation to certain analogue devices such as videos,[23] and this exception is also not included in the Singaporean and Australian FTAs.

One other important difference between the DMCA provisions and the equivalent provisions in the SUSFTA and the AUSFTA is that there does not appear to be any knowledge requirement for acts prohibited in the DMCA. The general anti-circumvention provision in the DMCA simply states that: 'No person shall circumvent a technological measure that effectively controls access to a work protected under this title'.[24] In contrast, both the SUSFTA and the AUSFTA state that the prohibition only applies where a person 'knowingly, or having reasonable grounds to know, circumvents without authority' any measure to protect copyright.[25]

2. Comparison of the SUSFTA and the AUSFTA

At first glance, the SUSFTA and the AUSFTA appear almost identical. However, although the two FTAs are very similar, there are some differences between them. The differences are in the detail, and are thus only apparent on a close reading of the two texts. Below we discuss two of the differences between the SUSFTA and AUSFTA, to illustrate the fine level of detail to which one must descend in order to observe any difference between the two sets of provisions.

Both FTAs make it an offence to circumvent 'any effective technological measure that controls access to a work. . .'[26] or to manufacture or distribute any device 'primarily designed' to facilitate 'the circumvention of any effective technological measure'.[27] There is a difference between the definition of 'effective technological measure' in the SUSFTA and the AUSFTA. In the AUSFTA an effective technological measure is one that 'controls access to a protected work . . . or protects any copyright'.[28] In contrast, an effective technological measure under the SUSFTA is one that 'controls access to a protected work . . . or

[23] *Ibid* §1201(k).

[24] *Ibid* §1201(a)(1)(A). Lack of knowledge is, however, a ground for the court, at its discretion, to reduce or remit the damages awarded against the infringer: §1203(c)(5). It should also be noted that some concept of deliberate 'evading' of a technical measure may be implied in the concept of 'circumvention', although the definition of 'circumvent' is relatively neutral: §1201(a)(3)(A). There have been only limited cases in US courts concerning the act of circumvention: see Ginsburg, above n12, at 27–8.

[25] See, for example, SUSFTA Art 16.4.7(a)(i), and AUSFTA Art 17.4.7(a)(i).

[26] AUSFTA Art 17.4.7(a)(i), and SUSFTA Art 16.4.7(a)(i).

[27] AUSFTA Art 17.4.7(a)(ii), and SUSFTA Art 16.4.7(a)(ii).

[28] AUSFTA Art 17.4.7(b).

protects any copyright or *any rights related to copyright*'.[29] Although the meaning of 'any rights related to copyright' is not defined in the SUSFTA, the SUSFTA arguably has a wider scope than the equivalent AUSFTA provision because the phrase 'any rights related to copyright' potentially includes a broader range of rights than 'copyright'.

Both FTAs provide for the same list of exceptions to the prohibition on circumvention of effective technological measures. For example, there are exceptions in relation to encryption research, libraries and software that prevents minors from viewing inappropriate internet content. There is, however, an additional exception in the SUSFTA that does not appear in the AUSFTA. This exception, which occurs by way of a side letter, allows circumvention of a technological protection measure whose sole purpose is to control the market segmentation for legitimate copies of motion pictures[30]—that is, to override regional coding of a DVD.

It is perhaps not surprising that we have ended up with such fine-grained differences between the two FTAs, given that the only tactic open to weaker parties is to attempt to negotiate derogations from a strong template text.[31] It is not clear, however, what are the implications of such fine-grained differences in otherwise very similar treaties. In particular, it is not clear whether the existence of alternative 'versions' will have any impact on the interpretation of any given provision in international law. For example, if the AUSFTA contains more flexible language than the SUSFTA in relation to a particular issue, does that render an attempted flexible reading of the SUSFTA provision less legitimate?

3. National Implementation of the DMCA Provisions

Both Australia and Singapore have implemented the DMCA provisions contained in their FTAs into their national law. DMCA-like anti-circumvention provisions are now found in Division 2A of Part V of the Australian Copyright Act and Part XIIIA of the Singapore Copyright Act. Broadly, the anti-circumvention provisions in the Australian and the Singaporean Acts are based on the related provisions in their FTAs with the US. Thus, at least on the face of it, the general prohibitions on circumvention found in the DMCA have been effectively exported into domestic Australian and Singaporean copyright legislation via the AUSFTA and the SUSFTA, respectively. It should be noted, however, that the 'exportation' is by no means perfect: on translation into domestic law, changes are made. Australia, for example, found space in the treaty provisions to exclude certain technologies from protection: those technologies which enforce region-coding of movies or software, those technologies which seek to

[29] SUSFTA Art 16.4.7(b) (emphasis added).

[30] Letter of May 6, 2003 concerning Optical Disks, cl 7.

[31] See the discussion in section D.I, below, of the negotiating process adopted by the US in relation to FTAs.

control after-markets for spare parts, and any technology which is unrelated to the exercise of copyright rights.[32] Singapore's Minister also retains the power to exclude further technologies from protection at any time.[33] Australian law also gives the Attorney-General the power to prescribe, at any time, a new exception to the ban on circumvention of access control measures: this differs from the US system of holding reviews at fixed, 3 year periods.[34] Detailed as the language of the treaty is, it has not prevented variation.[35]

IV. WHY THE US IS EXPORTING THE DMCA PROVISIONS VIA FTAS

Above we saw how the US is seeking to export its DMCA provisions through the FTAs that it negotiates. In this section we will examine two possible reasons why the US is exporting DMCA provisions.[36]

1. Reason of Pragmatism: Cost-effectiveness and Procedural Certainty

One relatively benign reason why the US is exporting the DMCA provisions through its FTAs is that it may simply be a side-effect of pragmatism. The US negotiates FTAs from a central FTA 'template', with slight variations made as the need arises. This template was developed by the US through a series of trade negotiations, with each agreement acting as a template for the next agreement. As a result, subsequent FTAs become longer and more detailed as new provisions are added to existing texts.

The adoption of the template approach has a number of motivations. Using a template is cost-effective, in that it lowers the cost of bilateral negotiations. Bilateral trade negotiations are expensive processes and it is not surprising that experienced negotiators involved in multiple negotiations will seek to avoid 'reinventing the wheel'. In addition, the use of a template is dictated by the need of the US Trade Representative to ensure that FTAs negotiated by the office will pass through the US Congress. Unlike the process in many countries, where the Executive has the power to conclude treaties without strictly requiring reference

32 Copyright Act 1968 (Australia), s 10 (definitions of 'access control technological protection measure' and 'technological protection measure').

33 Copyright Act (Singapore, ch 63), s 261B (definition of 'technological access control measure').

34 Copyright Act 1968 (Australia), s 116AN(9); Copyright Regulations 1969 (Australia), Regulation 20Z.

35 On the importance of looking in detail at domestic implementation in order to assess whether provisions are in fact effectively 'exported' or laws harmonised, see Robert Burrell and Kimberlee Weatherall, 'Exporting Controversy: The Copyright Provisions of the US-Australia Free Trade Agreement', *forthcoming* (copy on file with authors).

36 A full examination of US motivations—and whether they have been achieved—is beyond the scope of this paper. Issues such as the benefits to be achieved from harmonisation, or the desire actually to raise standards, are not explored. For a more detailed consideration, and a questioning of whether the US strategy makes sense at all, see Burrell and Weatherall, above n 35.

to the Parliament, the US Congress must approve the negotiating objectives before negotiations commence, and must pass legislation approving an FTA before it can take legal effect.

This procedure tends to encourage standardisation of highly complex IP texts for a number of reasons. First, an FTA will have a more realistic chance of obtaining the necessary approval if it follows an already established model. This is because part of the Congressional approval process involves the review of the text by certain Industry Advisory Committees. At least in relation to IP, the relevant committee has a history of drawing very explicit comparisons with prior FTAs. Provisions that are seen to be less IP-protective than provisions in past FTAs attract negative comment.

Secondly, according to the negotiating objectives on IP set out in the US Trade Act of 2002, the US Trade Representative in conducting negotiations is required to ensure 'that the provisions of any multilateral or bilateral trade agreement governing intellectual property rights that is entered into by the United States reflect a standard of protection similar to that found in United States law'.[37] This tends to encourage provisions which match US law—leading to a more detailed, 'legislation-like' set of provisions than one might ordinarily expect in a treaty.

The combined effect of these factors is that the US template for the IP Chapter of its bilateral FTAs is a detailed, complex set of provisions that closely reflects US national legislation. On the other hand, such pragmatism, while it might explain the *continued* inclusion of DMCA-type provisions, does not necessarily explain their initial inclusion in FTAs.

2. Reason of Principle: Entrenching US Law

There is another, perhaps more insidious, reason why the US is currently negotiating FTAs with IP Chapters containing detailed DMCA provisions. It is likely that the US is seeking to entrench the US legislative approach in other countries, so as to counter any moves, whether at home or abroad, to adopt an alternative approach to implementing Article 11 of the WCT. The DMCA has been controversial, not the least in the US. The fact that the US is now obliged under its FTAs with other countries to (continue to) adopt the DMCA approach would seem to provide an additional reason for the US government to not heed any domestic calls for legislative change. In addition, obliging other countries by way of FTAs to adopt the DMCA approach has the effect of preventing them from choosing a less draconian alternative, such as that which has been adopted in Europe.[38]

[37] § 2102(4)(A)(II), Trade Act of 2002. See http://www.sice.oas.org/Trade/tradeact/act7.asp.

[38] See Art 6(4) of the Directive 2001/29/EC of the European Parliament and of the Council of 22 May 2001 on the harmonisation of certain aspects of copyright and related rights in the information society, [2001] OJ L167/10.

The desirability of entrenching DMCA provisions in the domestic law of an ever-increasing number of nations is highly questionable. Copyright law attempts to balance the rights of copyright owners and users. The approach to implementation of WCT Article 11 found in the DMCA and, now, in many US FTAs 'shifts the balance significantly in favour of copyright owners' or, at least, adopts a one-size-fits-all approach which may not be suitable for every country.[39]

V. THE IMPACT OF THE US EXPORTING DMCA PROVISIONS

The US negotiation of FTAs such as the SUSFTA and the AUSFTA, and the attendant export of the DMCA provisions into other countries' national legislation, has occurred within a framework of international trade law. Although a comprehensive discussion of trade law and its interaction with FTAs is beyond the scope of this paper, we will discuss the most relevant provision for our purposes, which is Article 4 of the TRIPS Agreement.

In part, Article 4 of the TRIPS Agreement states that:[40]

> With regards to the protection of intellectual property, an advantage, favour, privilege or immunity granted by a Member to the nationals of any other country shall be accorded immediately and unconditionally to the nationals of all other Members.

Article 4 effectively applies the 'most favoured nation' (MFN) principle to IP law specifically. The MFN principle is often noted as being a 'cornerstone' of WTO law.[41] The MFN principle is enshrined in Article 1 of the General Agreement on Tariffs and Trade 1994 (GATT) and Article 2.1 of the General Agreement on Trade in Services (GATS). In respect of these agreements, the MFN principle prevents discrimination amongst WTO members in relation to tariffs and some other taxes. However, although the MFN principle is a core principle of these WTO agreements, both the GATT and GATS allow members to avoid the application of the MFN principle in respect of FTAs with other members. This is spelt out in Article XXIV of GATT 1994 and Article V of GATS. As parties to an FTA provide tariff and other benefits solely to each other, this means that FTAs are effectively an exception to the MFN principle.

However, there is no exception for FTAs under TRIPS, and thus the MFN principle in Article 4 will apply to IP provisions in FTAs. The effect of Article 4

[39] Emma Caine and Kimberlee Weatherall 'Australia-US Free Trade Agreement—circumventing the rationale for anit-circumvention?' (7) *Internet Law Bulletin* (2004/2005) 121, 122.

[40] Art 4 also lists certain exemptions to this principle, none of which are relevant here. However, it is worth noting that Art 4 does not apply to FTAs which entered into force before 1995: Art 4(d).

[41] See The Most Favoured Nation Obligation, Executive Branch GATT Studies, No 9, The Most-Favoured-Nation Provision, p 133, Subcomm on Intl. Trade, Senate Comm on Finance, 93rd Cong, 2nd sess (1974), cited in Alan O Sykes 'Toward a positive theory of the most favored nation obligation and its exception in the WTO/GATT system' 16 (1996) *International Review of Law and Economics* 27.

is that when parties enter into a bilateral agreement that provides advantages in IP provisions, these advantages must be given to all WTO members. This is the case even if only one party of the bilateral agreement is a WTO member. Thus, when Singapore or Australia implements the DMCA provisions it must extend the operation of these provisions to all WTO members.

There are a number of consequences of the interaction of Article 4 of the TRIPS Agreement with US FTAs containing DMCA provisions. First, if the US continues to negotiate FTAs that contain DMCA provisions, those provisions may well become the de facto international standard for implementation of WCT Article 11. This is because the greater the number of countries that have DMCA provisions in their national legislation, the greater the number of other countries whose copyright owners receive the benefit of those provisions under the operation of the MFN principle. When the MFN principle is considered in light of the large number of US FTAs that recently have been or currently are being negotiated, it can be seen that a significant proportion of copyright owners worldwide now receive the additional protection provided by the DMCA provisions.

Secondly, even if the US does not negotiate more FTAs with DMCA provisions, those provisions may still become the de facto international standard for implementation of WCT Article 11 by virtue of the activities of the countries with which the US already has such FTAs. Once a country is obliged by an FTA to provide DMCA protection in its national legislation, there could be at least some incentive to seek to have other countries' legislation contain similar provisions. This is because, under the MFN principle, a country with DMCA provisions must give the benefit of those provisions to the copyright owners of other WTO members, including copyright owners in other countries that do not have DMCA provisions and hence that do not provide a reciprocal benefit to the copyright owners of the country with the FTA. The giving of this benefit to foreign copyright owners without the receiving of this benefit by domestic copyright owners would seem to make it more likely for countries with US FTAs containing DMCA provisions to seek to include such provisions in the IP Chapters of the FTAs that *they* subsequently negotiate with other countries.

However, the chances of this occurring may be slim, given the nature of the horse-trading that goes on when trade agreements are negotiated. In approaching a trade agreement negotiation, a country will have a set of priorities. They may want better access for agricultural goods, a harmonisation of sanitary and phytosanitary standards, a reduction in tariffs on certain manufactured goods—or intellectual property provisions. Exporting DMCA provisions may not rank high on the list of priorities for a country like Australia or Chile, compared with getting access to markets where a comparative advantage is enjoyed. It may, therefore, be one of the first things Australia or Chile is prepared to give up in order to achieve more important aims. Thus, while the US's intention might be to enlist other countries into a coalition fighting the battle in favour of the

DMCA approach to implementation of WCT Article 11,[42] in practice the coalition—like certain other coalitions of the willing—may be small, and its non-US partners committed only in the most token way.

VI. CONCLUSION

It will be appreciated from the discussion in this paper that the US has been successful to some extent in exporting its DMCA provisions into the national laws of other countries through the mechanism of FTAs. In particular, the US has succeeded in including in the treaties provisions that are almost a 'cut-and-paste' of its own domestic enactment. Although there may be a benign reason for doing this, it is likely that there is also a more insidious motive at work. The export of the DMCA through FTAs is most likely an attempt to entrench this particular approach to implementing Article 11 of the WCT at home and abroad, and at the expense of less draconian alternatives. In due course, the US could achieve its aim of making the DMCA the de facto international standard for implementation of the anti-circumvention provision of the WCT. Given the persuasiveness of the argument that the DMCA in practice results in an undue shift in the balance within copyright law in favour of copyright owners, such an outcome is not to be celebrated.

We have, however, raised some doubts in the course of this chapter sufficient to sound a note of caution: the long-term impact of this exportation of US national law through FTAs remains to be seen. In particular, it is an open question whether the US's exportation of DMCA provisions through treaties will lead to countries such as Australia and Chile onward-forwarding those provisions in their subsequent FTAs. It is likely that the success, or failure, of the US method will only be seen in the long term.

[42] Whether this is a coalition of the willing or the unwilling depends on one's view as to the extent to which the country exercised free will in entering the US FTA with the DMCA provisions.

APPENDIX 1—COMPARISON OF THE GENERAL IP AND THE COPYRIGHT PROVISIONS OF RECENT US FTAS

AUSFTA provision	Area of Law	Details of provision and differences between the FTAs	Countries having provision	Variations
17.1.1	**General** Minimum standards only	Provision stating that Chapter provides minimum standards only—that parties can enact higher levels of protection if they wish	All countries	Some minor variations in language (see, eg, Singapore)
17.1.2–17.1.5	**General** Treaties	Provision setting out multilateral treaties to which countries already belong, promise to join	All countries	Some variations exist
17.1.6–17.1.8	**General** National treatment	Provision requiring parties to accord national treatment to nationals of other party	All countries	
17.1.9–17.1.11	**General** Application to existing matter	Provision requiring that obligations in the Chapter apply equally to already existing subject matter (but not to acts done before entry into force)	All countries	
17.1.12 and 17.11.2–17.11.4	**General** Transparency	Requirement that parties make the 'protection and enforcement of intellectual property rights transparent', publishing laws and decisions in writing.	Australia, Singapore, Bahrain, Chile, CAFTA, Morocco, Columbia, Oman, Korea, Peru, Panama	No provision: Jordan
–	**General IP:** technical assistance	Provisions requiring the provision of technical assistance/cooperation	Provisions exist: Chile, CAFTA	No such provisions: Australia, Singapore, Bahrain, Morocco, Jordan, Columbia, Oman, Korea, Peru, Panama

AUSFTA provision	Area of Law	Details of provision and differences between the FTAs	Countries having provision	Variations
17.4.1	**Copyright** Reproduction	Reproduction right including all temporary copies	Australia, Singapore, Bahrain, Chile, CAFTA, Jordan, Columbia, Oman, Korea, Peru, Panama	Jordan language is different—refers to reproduction right 'as envisaged in' the WCT.
17.4.2	**Copyright** Making available	Exclusive right to make copies of copyright works available	Australia, Singapore, Bahrain, Chile, CAFTA, Jordan, Columbia, Oman, Korea, Peru, Panama	AUSFTA has a footnote preserving right to determine when exhaustion occurs (ie, Australia can ban parallel importation)—no other agreement has this qualification. Jordanian Agreement includes explicit ban on parallel importation
17.4.3	**Copyright** No hierarchy	No hierarchy between rights of authors and rights of performers/producers: permission of both required to exercise copyright rights	Australia, Bahrain, Chile, CAFTA, Columbia, Oman, Korea, Peru, Panama	No such provision: Singapore, Jordan
17.4.4	**Copyright** Term	Copyright term of 'life of the author plus 70 years'	Australia, Singapore, Bahrain, Chile, CAFTA, Columbia, Oman, Korea, Peru, Panama	Jordan has no provision on copyright term. Oman: term for 'other than the life of a natural person' is 95 years, or if no publication within 25 years, term is 120 years
17.4.5	**Copyright** Berne Art 18	Extends rights in 17.4–17.6 to material existing at the time the provisions are brought into being	Australia, Singapore, Bahrain, Chile, CAFTA, Columbia, Oman, Korea, Peru, Panama	Jordan has no such provision

AUSFTA provision	Area of Law	Details of provision and differences between the FTAs	Countries having provision	Variations
17.4.6(a)	**Copyright** Free transferability	All economic rights, including those arising from contracts of employment, must be freely transferable	CAFTA, Morocco, Jordan, Singapore, Australia, Bahrain, Columbia, Oman, Korea, Peru, Panama	**Exceptions allowed:** Chile: Chile may provide 'reasonable limits' to the provision which allows transfer of economic rights through employment agreements, 'to protect the interests of original right holders' (Article 17.7.2(b))
17.4.6(b)	**Copyright** *Droit de suite*	Party is allowed to create *droit de suite* as specified by Berne Article 14*ter*	Australia only	No such provision: Singapore, Jordan, Morocco, Bahrain, Chile, CAFTA, Columbia, Oman, Korea, Peru, Panama. But note that every agreement expressly allows countries to provide *higher* levels of protection than are provided in the FTA
17.4.7	**Copyright** Anti-circumvention law	Detailed anti-circumvention provisions based on the *Digital Millennium Copyright Act* 1998 (US), including: —A ban on both the act of circumvention, and the trafficking in circumvention devices;	Australia, Singapore, Bahrain, CAFTA, Morocco, Columbia, Oman, Korea, Peru, Panama	Unusual provisions: Chile.[43] No detailed provisions: Jordan (requires only that WCT/WPPT be

[43] Includes different definition of TPM (see below); also allows Chile to exempt from both criminal *and civil* liability acts by a non-profit library, archive, or educational institution: Art 17.

AUSFTA provision	Area of Law	Details of provision and differences between the FTAs	Countries having provision	Variations
		—An exhaustive list of exceptions similar to that included in the DMCA with limited flexibility only.		enacted to include a ban on trafficking in circumvention devices)
17.4.7 (a)(i)	**Copyright** Anti-circumvention law	Liability for circumventing a technological protection measure applies where circumvention is done knowingly, or having reasonable grounds to know	Australia, Singapore, CAFTA, Korea	Knowingly: Chile. No knowledge requirement specified: Bahrain, Morocco, Columbia, Oman, Peru, Panama. No requirement of a ban on circumvention: Jordan
7.4.7(b)	**Copyright** Anti-circumvention law	Definition of technological protection measure includes access controls and copy controls	Australia, Singapore, Bahrain, CAFTA, Morocco, Columbia, Oman, Korea, Peru, Panama	Chile: unusual definition which confines the concept to measures which 'cannot, in the usual case, be circumvented accidentally'. Jordan: no definition
117.4.7(d)	**Copyright** Anti-circumvention law	Parties must provide that 'violation of a measure implementing this paragraph is a separate civil or criminal offence and independent of any infringement that might occur under the Party's copyright law'	Australia, Bahrain, Morocco, CAFTA, Singapore, Columbia, Oman, Korea, Peru, Panama	Jordan has no such provision. Chilean provision allows that *either* the circumventing party is criminally or civilly liable, *or the conduct is an aggravating circumstance of another offense* (Article 17.7.5(a))

AUSFTA provision	Area of Law	Details of provision and differences between the FTAs	Countries having provision	Variations
17.4.7(e)	Copyright: Anti-circumvention law	Specific exceptions in addition to those provided under US law: exception to allow importation and sale of device that does not render effective TPMs 'whose sole purpose is to control market segmentation for legitimate copies of motion pictures, and is not otherwise a violation of law'	Singapore has specific exception. Jordan has no limits on the exceptions it may create (lacks detailed anti-circumvention provision)	Australia, Bahrain, Chile, Morocco, CAFTA, Columbia, Oman, Korea, Peru, Panama
17.4.7(e) (viii)	Copyright: Anti-circumvention law	Country may create exceptions to the ban on circumventing TPMs in addition to those listed, by a judicial or administrative process, *which do not have an expiry date*	Do not expire: Australia (review after 4 years), Columbia (review after 4 years), Peru (review after 4 years), Panama (review at 4 year intervals). Jordan has no limits on the exceptions it may create (lacks detailed anti-circumvention provision)	Exceptions expire every 3 or 4 years: Singapore, Chile, Bahrain, CAFTA, Morocco, Oman (renewable), Korea (renewable). Note also variation in language: AUSFTA requires that 'actual or likely adverse impact on those non-infringing uses is credibly demonstrated in a legislative or administrative review or proceeding'; CAFTA requires demonstration of actual or likely adverse impact by 'substantial evidence', with *continuing* actual or likely adverse impact

AUSFTA provision	Area of Law	Details of provision and differences between the FTAs	Countries having provision	Variations
				demonstrated by substantial evidence every 4 years thereafter, Columbia, Oman, Korea, Peru and Panama have a similar requirement of 'substantial evidence'
17.4.8	**Copyright** Rights Management Information	Ban on removing rights management information (RMI); distributing removed RMI, knowingly distributing copies of works with RMI removed	Australia, Singapore, Bahrain, Chile, CAFTA, Columbia, Oman, Korea, Peru, Panama	No such provision in Jordan agreement
17.4.9	**Copyright** Government use of non-infringing software	Government agencies to use non-infringing computer software; measures to be taken to ensure this occurs	Australia, Singapore, Bahrain, Chile, CAFTA, Jordan, Morocco, Columbia, Oman, Korea, Peru, Panama	
17.4.10	**Copyright:** Exceptions	Provision that nothing in the Agreement affects the availability of exceptions allowed under multilateral treaties	Australia only	Singapore, Bahrain, Jordan, Chile, CAFTA, Columbia, Oman, Korea, Peru, Panama: Simple re-affirming of TRIPS Art 13; Berne Art 9 (3 step test)
17.5	**Copyright** Making available online	Exclusive right to communicate works to the public, including making available online, by wire or wireless means	Australia, Singapore, Bahrain, Chile, CAFTA, Columbia, Oman, Korea, Peru, Panama	Jordan contains no provision (although note that Jordan is required to comply with WCT and WPPT which include this right).

AUSFTA provision	Area of Law	Details of provision and differences between the FTAs	Countries having provision	Variations
17.6.1	**Copyright** Performers and Producers' rights	Performers and producers to be given national treatment	Australia, Singapore, Bahrain, Chile, CAFTA, Columbia, Oman, Korea, Peru, Panama	Australian obligation subject to side letter. No provision in the Jordan agreement
17.6.2–17.6.5	**Copyright** Performers and producers' rights	Exclusive rights to performers: broadcast and fixation of unfixed performances. Exclusive rights to performers and producers: to broadcast/communicate to public; exceptions for free to air broadcasting and other non-interactive broadcasting.	Australia, Singapore, Bahrain, Chile, CAFTA, Columbia, Oman, Korea, Peru, Panama	Some rights in the Jordan Agreement, but less detailed
17.7	**Copyright** Encrypted satellite signals	Criminalisation of providing satellite decoders, and wilfully making use of illegally decoded satellite signals. Civil remedies	Australia, Singapore, Bahrain, CAFTA, Columbia, Oman, Korea, Peru, Panama	Chile has the option of making the offences *civil* rather than criminal, and can apply a 'sole purpose' rather than primary purpose test. Jordan FTA has no provision at all
17.11.29	**Copyright:** ISP liability	Detailed provisions on ISP liability under the FTA modelled on the *Digital Millennium Copyright Act* 1998 (US)	Australia, Singapore, Bahrain, Chile, CAFTA, Columbia, Oman, Korea, Peru, Panama	No such provisions: Jordan
	Side Letter on ISPs	Provisions setting out what counts as a notice and counter-notice	Yes (have the side letter): Singapore, Australia, Bahrain, Morocco, Columbia, Oman, Korea, Peru	No side letter: Chile, Jordan, CAFTA, Panama

AUSFTA provision	Area of Law	Details of provision and differences between the FTAs	Countries having provision	Variations
		Side Letter on Optical Disks Provisions on the manufacture, and registration of optical disk manufacturers	Yes: Singapore, Bahrain, Oman	No: Australia, Chile, Jordan, Morocco, CAFTA, Columbia, Korea, Peru, Panama

APPENDIX 2—COMPARISON OF DMCA PROVISIONS IN SUSFTA AND AUSFTA

DMCA provision	SUSFTA	AUSFTA	Comments
§1201(a)(1)(A) 'No person shall circumvent a technological measure that effectively controls access to a work protected under this title.'	Art 16.4.7(a)(i) '. . . knowingly, or having reasonable grounds to know, circumvents without authority any effective technological measure that controls access to a protected work, performance, phonogram, or other subject matter . . .'	Art 17.4.7(a)(i) '. . . knowingly, or having reasonable grounds to know, circumvents without authority any effective technological measure that controls access to a protected work, performance, or phonogram, or other subject matter . . .'	No knowledge requirement under the DMCA, *cf* AUSFTA and SUSFTA. 'w/o authority'—AU & S USFTA
§1201(a)(1)(B)–(E) '(B) The prohibition contained in subparagraph (A) shall not apply to persons who are users of a copyrighted work which is in a particular class of works, if such persons are, or are likely to be in the succeeding 3-year period, adversely affected by virtue of such prohibition in their ability to make noninfringing uses of that particular class of works under this title, as determined under subparagraph (C).'	Art 16.4.7(f)(iii) '. . . noninfringing uses of a particular class of works when an actual or likely adverse impact on such noninfringing uses with respect to such particular class of works is credibly demonstrated in a legislative or administrative proceeding, provided that any exception adopted in reliance on this clause shall have effect for a period of not more than four years from the date of conclusion of such proceeding.'	Art 17.4.7(e)(viii) '. . .non-infringing uses of a work, performance, or phonogram in a particular class of works, performances, or phonograms, when an actual or likely adverse impact on those non-infringing uses is credibly demonstrated in a legislative or administrative review or proceeding; provided that any such review or proceeding is conducted at least once every four years from the date of conclusion of such review or proceeding.'	Fail safe mechanism. DMCA allows the Librarian of Congress to review the operation of the DMCA and make additional time limited exemptions for certain acts. Note –this fail safe provision only applies to where a person circumvents a measure NOT to where a person produces a manufactures an item designed to circumvent such measures.

DMCA provision	SUSFTA	AUSFTA	Comments
§1201(a)(2) 'No person shall manufacture, import, offer to the public, provide, or otherwise traffic in any technology, product, service, device, component, or part thereof, that— (A) is primarily designed or produced for the purpose of circumventing a technological measure that effectively controls access to a work protected under this title; (B) has only limited commercially significant purpose or use other than to circumvent a technological measure that effectively controls access to a work protected under this title; or (C) is marketed by that person or another acting in concert with that person with that person's knowledge for use in circumventing a technological measure that effectively controls access to a work protected under this title.'	Art 16.4.7(a)(ii) '. . . manufactures, imports, distributes, offers to the public, provides, or otherwise traffics in devices, products, or components or offers to the public or provides services, which: (A) are promoted, advertised, or marketed for the purpose of circumvention of any effective technological measure, or (B) have only a limited commercially significant purpose or use other than to circumvent any effective technological measure, or (C) are primarily designed, produced, or performed for the purpose of enabling or facilitating the circumvention of any effective technological measure . . .'	Art 17.4.7(a)(ii) '. . . manufactures, imports, distributes, offers to the public, provides, or otherwise traffics in devices, products, or components, or offers to the public, or provides services that: (A) are promoted, advertised, or marketed for the purpose of circumvention of any effective technological measure; (B) have only a limited commercially significant purpose or use other than to circumvent any effective technological measure; or (C) are primarily designed, produced, or performed for the purpose of enabling or facilitating the circumvention of any effective technological measure . . .'	Although the wording between the DMCA and the FTAs is slightly different, they appear to be similar in substance.

DMCA provision	SUSFTA	AUSFTA	Comments
§1201(a)(3)(A) '. . . to 'circumvent a technological measure' means to descramble a scrambled work, to decrypt an encrypted work, or otherwise to avoid, bypass, remove, deactivate, or impair a technological measure, without the authority of the copyright owner . . .'	No such definition.	No such definition.	DMCA provides a definition for 'to circumvent a technological measure', this is not present in either of the FTAs.
§1201(a)(3)(B) '. . . a technological measure 'effectively controls access to a work' if the measure, in the ordinary course of its operation, requires the application of information, or a process or a treatment, with the authority of the copyright owner, to gain access to the work.'	Art 16.4.7(b) '. . . effective technological measure means any technology, device, or component that, in the normal course of its operation, **controls access** to a protected work, performance, phonogram, or other subject matter, or **protects any copyright or any rights related to copyright.**'	Art 17.4.7(b) 'Effective technological measure means any technology, device, or component that, in the normal course of its operation, **controls access** to a protected work, performance, phonogram, or other protected subject matter, or **protects any copyright.**'	Although different terms are defined in the DMCA and the FTAs, the effect appears to be similar.
§1201(b)—equivalent to §1201(a)(2), but protects against circumvention measures that copy protected works.	Covered by 16.4.7(a).	Covered by 17.4.7(a).	N/A.
§1201(c) 'OTHER RIGHTS, ETC, NOT AFFECTED— (1) Nothing in this section shall affect	No equivalent provision.	No equivalent provision.	Exclusion of this provision from the FTAs is probably not a substantive difference— although may effect

DMCA provision	SUSFTA	AUSFTA	Comments
rights, remedies, limitations, or defenses to copyright infringement, including fair use, under this title.			ability to use defences in relation to DMCA provisions.
§1201(c) 'OTHER RIGHTS, ETC, NOT AFFECTED . . . (2) Nothing in this section shall enlarge or diminish vicarious or contributory liability for copyright infringement in connection with any technology, product, service, device, component, or part thereof.'	No equivalent provision.	No equivalent provision.	Exclusion of this provision from the FTAs is probably not a substantive difference.
§1201(c) 'OTHER RIGHTS, ETC, NOT AFFECTED . . . (3) Nothing in this section shall require that the design of, or design and selection of parts and components for, a consumer electronics, telecommunications, or computing product provide for a response to any particular technological measure, so long as such part or component, or the product in which such part or component is integrated, does not	Art 16.7.4(c) 'Paragraph 7(a) obligates each Party to prohibit circumvention of effective technological measures and does not obligate a Party to require that the design of, or the design and selection of parts and components for, a consumer electronics, telecommunications, or computing product provide for a response to any particular technological measure. The absence of a requirement to respond affirmatively	Art 17.4.7(c) 'In implementing sub-paragraph (a), neither Party shall be obligated to require that the design of, or the design and selection of parts and components for, a consumer electronics, telecommunications, or computing product provide for a response to any particular technological measure, so long as the product does not otherwise violate any measures implementing sub-paragraph (a).'	DMCA and FTA provisions appear to be similar in effect.

DMCA provision	SUSFTA	AUSFTA	Comments
otherwise fall within the prohibitions of subsection (a)(2) or (b)(1)'.	shall not constitute a defense to a claim of violation of that Party's measures implementing paragraph 7(a)'.		
§1201(c) 'OTHER RIGHTS, ETC, NOT AFFECTED . . . (4) Nothing in this section shall enlarge or diminish any rights of free speech or the press for activities using consumer electronics, telecommunications, or computing products.'	No equivalent provision.	No equivalent provision.	The fact that there is no equivalent in the FTAs could be interpreted as meaning that free speech could be impacted by the DMCA provisions.
§1201(d) 'EXEMPTION FOR NONPROFIT LIBRARIES, ARCHIVES, AND EDUCATIONAL INSTITUTIONS.—(1) A nonprofit library, archives, or educational institution which gains access to a commercially exploited copyrighted work solely in order to make a good faith determination of whether to acquire a copy of that work for the sole purpose of engaging in conduct permitted under this title shall not be in	Art 16.4.7(f)(i) '. . . access by a non-profit library, archive, or educational institution to a work not otherwise available to it, for the sole purpose of making acquisition decisions . . .'	Art 17.4.7(e)(vii) '. . . access by a non-profit library, archive, or educational institution to a work, performance, or phonogram not otherwise available to it, for the sole purpose of making acquisition decisions . . .'	DMCA and FTA provisions appear to be similar in effect. However SUSFTA possibly more restrictive than AUSFTA as exception only applies to works.

DMCA provision	SUSFTA	AUSFTA	Comments
violation of subsection (a)(1)(A) . . .' **Note—** §1201(d)(2)–(5) provides detail as to the operation of this provision.			
§1201(e) 'LAW ENFORCEMENT, INTELLIGENCE, AND OTHER GOVERNMENT ACTIVITIES—This section does not prohibit any lawfully authorized investigative, protective, information security, or intelligence activity of an officer, agent, or employee of the United States, a State, or a political subdivision of a State, or a person acting pursuant to a contract with the United States, a State, or a political subdivision of a State. For purposes of this subsection, the term 'information security' means activities carried out in order to identify and address the vulnerabilities of a government computer, computer system, or computer network'.	Art 16.4.7(g) 'Each Party may also provide exceptions to the prohibited conduct referred to in paragraph 7(a) for lawfully authorized activities carried out by government employees, agents, or contractors for the purpose of law enforcement, intelligence, national defense, essential security, or similar government activities.'	Art 17.4.7(e)(vi) '. . . lawfully authorised activities carried out by government employees, agents, or contractors for law enforcement, intelligence, essential security, or similar governmental purposes . . .'	DMCA and FTA provisions appear to be similar in effect.

DMCA provision	SUSFTA	AUSFTA	Comments
§1201(f) 'REVERSE ENGINEERING.—(1) Notwithstanding the provisions of subsection (a)(1)(A), a person who has lawfully obtained the right to use a copy of a computer program may circumvent a technological measure that effectively controls access to a particular portion of that program for the sole purpose of identifying and analyzing those elements of the program that are necessary to achieve interoperability of an independently created computer program with other programs, and that have not previously been readily available to the person engaging in the circumvention, to the extent any such acts of identification and analysis do not constitute infringement under this title.' **Note**— §1201(f)(2)–(4) provides for further detail on the operation of this section.	16.4.7(e)(i) '. . . non-infringing reverse engineering activities with regard to a lawfully obtained copy of a computer program, carried out in good faith with respect to particular elements of that computer program that have not been readily available to the person engaged in such activity, for the sole purpose of achieving interoperability of an independently created computer program with other programs . . .'	17.4.7(e)(i) '. . . non-infringing reverse engineering activities with regard to a lawfully obtained copy of a computer program, carried out in good faith with respect to particular elements of that computer program that have not been readily available to the person engaged in those activities, for the sole purpose of achieving interoperability of an independently created computer program with other programs . . .'	DMCA and FTA provisions appear to be similar in substance.

DMCA provision	SUSFTA	AUSFTA	Comments
§1201(g)(2) 'ENCRYPTION RESEARCH . . . Notwithstanding the provisions of subsection (a)(1)(A), it is not a violation of that subsection for a person to circumvent a technological measure as applied to a copy, phonorecord, performance, or display of a published work in the course of an act of good faith encryption research if— (A) the person lawfully obtained the encrypted copy, phonorecord, performance, or display of the published work; (B) such act is necessary to conduct such encryption research; (C) the person made a good faith effort to obtain authorization before the circumvention. . .' **Note**—further detail as to the application of this section is found in §1201(g)(1) and §1201(g)(3)–(5).	16.4.7(e)(ii) '. . . non-infringing good faith activities, carried out by an appropriately qualified researcher who has lawfully obtained a copy, performance, or display of a work, and who has made a good faith effort to obtain authorization for such activities, to the extent necessary for the sole purpose of identifying and analyzing flaws and vulnerabilities of technologies for scrambling and descrambling of information . . .'	17.4.7(e)(ii) '. . . non-infringing good faith activities, carried out by an appropriately qualified researcher who has lawfully obtained a copy, unfixed performance, or display of a work, performance, or phonogram and who has made a good faith effort to obtain authorisation for such activities, to the extent necessary for the sole purpose of identifying and analysing flaws and vulnerabilities of technologies for scrambling and descrambling of information . . .'	DMCA and FTA provisions appear to be similar in substance.

DMCA provision	SUSFTA	AUSFTA	Comments
§1201(h) 'EXCEPTIONS REGARDING MINORS.—In applying subsection (a) to a component or part, the court may consider the necessity for its intended and actual incorporation in a technology, product, service, or device, which— (1) does not itself violate the provisions of this title; and (2) has the sole purpose to prevent the access of minors to material on the Internet'.	16.4.7(e)(iii) '. . . the inclusion of a component or part for the sole purpose of preventing the access of minors to inappropriate online content in a technology, product, service, or device provided that such technology, product, service or device itself is not prohibited under the measures implementing paragraph 7(a)(ii) . . .'	17.4.7(e)(iii) '. . . the inclusion of a component or part for the sole purpose of preventing the access of minors to inappropriate online content in a technology, product, service, or device that itself is not prohibited under the measures implementing subparagraph (a)(ii) . . .'	DMCA and FTA provisions appear to be similar in substance.
§1201(i) 'PROTECTION OF PERSONALLY IDENTIFYING INFORMATION.— (1) CIRCUMVENTION PERMITTED.—Notwithstanding the provisions of subsection (a)(1)(A), it is not a violation of that subsection for a person to circumvent a technological measure that effectively controls access to a work protected under this title, if— the technological measure, or the	16.4.7(f)(ii) '. . . non-infringing activities for the sole purpose of identifying and disabling a capability to carry out undisclosed collection or dissemination of personally identifying information reflecting the online activities of a natural person in a way that has no other effect on the ability of any person to gain access to any work . . .'	17.4.7(e)(v) '. . . non-infringing activities for the sole purpose of identifying and disabling a capability to carry out undisclosed collection or dissemination of personally identifying information reflecting the online activities of a natural person in a way that has no other effect on the ability of any person to gain access to any work. . .'	DMCA and FTA provisions appear to be similar in substance.

DMCA provision	SUSFTA	AUSFTA	Comments
work it protects, contains the capability of collecting or disseminating personally identifying information reflecting the online activities of a natural person who seeks to gain access to the work protected . . .' **Note**—further detail as to the operation of this section is found in §1201(i)(1)(B)–(D) and §1201(i)(2).			
§1201(j) 'SECURITY TESTING.— (1) DEFINITION.— For purposes of this subsection, the term 'security testing' means accessing a computer, computer system, or computer network, solely for the purpose of good faith testing, investigating, or correcting, a security flaw or vulnerability, with the authorization of the owner or operator of such computer, computer system, or computer network.' Note—further detail as to the operation of this section is found in §1201(j)(2)–(4).	Art 16.4.7(e)(iv) '. . .non-infringing good faith activities that are authorized by the owner of a computer, computer system, or computer network for the sole purpose of testing, investigating, or correcting the security of that computer, computer system, or computer network'.	Art 17.4.7(e)(iv) '. . .non-infringing good faith activities that are authorised by the owner of a computer, computer system, or computer network for the sole purpose of testing, investigating, or correcting the security of that computer, computer system, or computer network . . .'	DMCA and FTA provisions appear to be similar in substance.

DMCA provision	SUSFTA	AUSFTA	Comments
§1201(k) 'CERTAIN ANALOG DEVICES AND CERTAIN TECHNOLOGICAL MEASURES.' **Note**—this provisions appears to prohibit tampering with certain copyright protection found in analogue devices such as video recorders.	No equivalent provision.	No equivalent provision.	Omission from the FTAs would not appear to have any great impact.

Chapter 9

Copyright and Free Trade—A Korean Perspective

BYUNGIL KIM

I. GLOBAL TREND TOWARDS FREE TRADE AGREEMENTS

IN RECENT YEARS, the proliferation of Free Trade Agreements (FTA) has become a global trend. In comparison to other regions such as Europe and the Americas, it is true that Asia manifested only nominal interest in regional economic integration until the recent past. However, in the aftermath of the Asian financial crisis in 1997, North East Asian countries became aware of the need for closer regional economic cooperation. Observing the great economic benefits that a FTA may bring with it, countries in Asia, notably Japan and Korea, have been pursuing FTAs in earnest.

In the case of Korea, Korea is one of the greatest beneficiaries of the liberalised global trade regime. The roots of her fundamental trade policies are therefore embedded in supporting a strong multilateral trading system represented by the World Trade Organization (WTO). Recent endeavours to pursue FTAs on the part of Korea do not imply a shift of the focus of her foreign economic policies. Korea, as major global trading nation, attaches great importance to the complementary nature of FTAs in promoting global trade liberalisation and the multilateral trading system as a whole.

Korea signed its first FTA with Chile in October 2002. Korea officially signed a FTA on 4th August 2005 with Singapore. Korea has also signed a FTA with European Free Trade Association (EFTA) which took effect in July 2006. Korea is also currently pursuing FTA negotiations with EU, ASEAN, China, Japan and Mexico, etc. Furthermore, Korea is exploring the feasibility of concluding a trilateral FTA among Japan, Korea, China. Recently, Korea and the United States (US) officially announced the conclusion of negotiations on a FTA that will be binding on both countries subject to parliamentary approval that was still outstanding as of April 2007.

In fact, intellectual property issues have not been a major problem in the Korea–Chile/Korea–Singapore/Korea–EFTA bilateral trade relationships. However, the Korea–EFTA FTA sets a high standard for the protection of intel-

Table 1. Example of FTAs by Korea (4/2007)

FTAs	Progress				
	Discussion	Joint Study	Negotiation	Conclusion	Implementation
Korea-Chile Korea-Singapore Korea-EFTA					O
Korea-US				O	
Korea-Asean Korea-Canada Korea-China Korea-EU Korea-India Korea-Japan Korea-Mercosur Korea-Mexico			O		

lectual property rights, covering areas such as patents, trademarks and copyrights, and goes, in certain areas (for example, geographical indications) beyond what is provided for under the WTO Agreement on Trade-Related Aspects of Intellectual Property Rights (TRIPS Agreement) and other international conventions and treaties.

Furthermore, on 2 April 2007, Korea and the United States officially announced the conclusion of negotiations on a bilateral FTA between the two countries. The US requests Korea to implement a higher level of IPR protection than required by international standards, such as a copyright term extension by 20 years, stronger sanctions on circumvention of technical measures(access control), monitoring temporary storage, statutory damages, rights management information, JSP liability, etc. Like some developing countries,[1] Korea worries about the curtailment of its policy space in an important area of economic development, because the Korean intellectual property regime has often been the target of trade policy measures of the United States. This article outlines copyright issues pertinent to the negotiated Korea–US FTA.

II. INTELLECTUAL PROPERTY PROTECTION AND FTA

Intellectual property rights (IPRs) are a crucial economic and political issue for trans-national corporations in particular and industrialised country govern-

[1] Pedro Roffe, The US–Chile FTA: Intellectual Property Issues, No 7/July–August 2004/www.ictsd.org/ p 17 (last visited 11 Dec 2005).

ments in general. The TRIPS Agreement signalled a major change in international economic relation as it established a link between adequate protection of intellectual property and international trade. The TRIPS Agreement introduces minimum standards of protection and offers some flexibilities, but recent developments suggest a growing trend towards much more strict standards.[2] This 'TRIP-plus' phenomenon seeks to harmonise intellectual property regimes with those of economically and technologically more advanced countries as the US and the European Union. The phenomenon is happening not only through multilateral fora such as the WTO and the World Intellectual Property Organization (WIPO), but also through unilateral, bilateral and regional agreements.[3] Through FTAs and other forms of direct agreements between countries, the economically and technologically more advanced countries are insisting that the partner country adopt their standards of IPR protection and enforcement.

1. Copyright Provisions of the TRIPS Agreement

The TRIPS Agreement builds upon the existing framework of copyright conventions established under World Intellectual Property Organization (WIPO).[4] With respect to copyrights, the TRIPS Agreement grants protection for computer programmes as literary works under the Berne Convention.[5] Databases were granted similar protection.[6] Copyright rules were expanded to cover rental rights whereby authors of computer programmes and producers of sound recordings were ensured the right to prohibit the commercial rental of their works to the public and films were granted similar protection. [7] Performers were also ensured of the right to prevent unauthorised recording, reproduction and broadcast of live-performances for at least 50 years.[8]

2. Treatment of Copyright in Free Trade Agreements

a) In General

In recent years, the tendency has been for new FTAs to extend beyond tariff-cutting exercises, to include a much broader range of products and issues,

[2] *Ibid.*

[3] http://www.bilaterals.org/rubrique.php3?id_rubrique=33 (last visited Dec 22, 2005)

[4] The Berne Convention for the Protection of Literary and Artistic Works, 1971, covering copyrights (although the TRIPS Agreement notably did not incorporate its provisions on moral rights); The Rome Convention for the Protection of Performers, Producers of Phonograms and Broadcasting Organizations, 1961 (although the TRIPS Agreement did not incorporate a general requirement to comply with the substantive provisions of the Rome Convention).

[5] TRIPS Agreement Art 10(1).

[6] TRIPS Agreement Art 10(2).

[7] TRIPS Agreement Art 11.

[8] TRIPS Agreement Art 14.

including intellectual property. According to the TRIPS Agreement, the Members of the WTO may implement in their law more extensive copyright protection than the minimum required under the agreement, provided that this does not contravene the agreement.[9] Furthermore, the strengthening and harmonisation of IPRs under such regional groupings as NAFTA and the EU substantially exceeded the new IPR requirements resulting from TRIPS Agreement.

FTAs generally affirm provisions of the TRIPS Agreement, either by explicit reference or implicitly by echoing at least some of its content. While varying in the extent of their coverage of IPR issues, the FTAs often include one or more provisions going beyond the strict requirements of the TRIPS Agreement. The spread of requirements for IPR protection in FTAs has provided a means to move beyond the provisions of the TRIPS Agreement. However, this has not necessarily led to a greater divergence in requirements. To the extent that these requirements are centred on widely accepted international accords, they may facilitate greater harmonisation in the treatment of copyright.

The States that are parties to FTAs have often mutually agreed to include IPR provisions in addition to those under the TRIPS Agreement or in advance of the timing foreseen in that agreement. Although the FTAs surveyed are broadly consistent with the TRIPS Agreement, they do not always extensively address IPR issues or make reference to the TRIPS Agreement. IPRs are included in different ways, depending on the agreement. For example, the Korea–Chile FTA makes little reference to IPRs, particularly geographical indications. Certain FTAs make reference to the TRIPS Agreement with respect to specific issues, but have no separate chapter or section on IPRs.[10] Other FTAs provide more extensive treatment of intellectual property with respect to one or more issues. Under the Korea–EFTA FTA, the Agreement addresses primarily geographical indications, but touches on other IPR issues only briefly.[11] Coverage of IPRs is much deeper under the NAFTA or EU, which devote substantial attention to a broad range of issues.[12] While the TRIPS Agreement provides a basic standard IPR protection, certain FTAs clearly go beyond minimum protection of IPRs. As already known, the strengthening and harmonisation of IPRs under not only such regional groupings as NAFTA and the EU, but the US–Singapore/US–Australia FTAs substantially exceeded the new IPR requirements resulting from the TRIPS Agreement. This 'TRIPS-plus' trend is clearly noticeable in bilateral, regional and new multilateral initiatives.[13] A prime statement of such phenomenon can be found under the 'Digital Trade Agenda of the US'.[14]

[9] This is stated in the Uruguay Round Final Act, Annex 1c (TRIPS), Art 1.1, available at: http://www.wto.org/english/docs_e/legal_e/27-trips.pdf (last visited 11 Dec. 2005).

[10] For example, the Canada–Chile FTA briefly cites the TRIPS Agreement in two articles.

[11] http://secretariat.efta.int/Web/News/koreasigning/view (last visited 15 Dec.2005).

[12] See, details: TD/TC/WP(2002)28/Final (http://www.oecd.org/trade)(last visited 11 Dec 2005).

[13] Pedro Roffe, *supra* n 1, p 17.

[14] For details see Sacha Wunsch-Vincent, The Digital Trade Agenda of the US: Parallel Tracks of Bilateral, Regional and Multilateral Liberalization, Aussenwirtschaft, 58. Jahrgang (2003), Heft I, Zürich: Rüegger, pp 7–46.

b) Provisions on copyright and related rights

Generally, the FTAs reflect the TRIPS Agreement with respect to copyrights and related rights or omit specific mention of this topic. Several FTAs go beyond the TRIPS Agreement in mandating accession or compliance with subsequent international accords, particularly the WIPO Copyright Treaty (WCT) and the WIPO Performances and Phonogram Treaty (WPPT).[15] Among other issues, these treaties take into account issues related to the development of new technologies such as those related to the Internet.

Some FTAs go beyond the TRIPS Agreement with respect to specific copyright issues. For example, bracketed text in the US–Australia FTA makes reference to respect for moral rights (ie authors' rights to object to certain modifications and derogatory actions), which would go beyond the TRIPS Agreement which explicitly excludes article 6bis of the Berne Convention that refers to moral rights. NAFTA clarifies that the use of decoding devices for intercepting satellite transmissions is illegal.[16] Within the EU, the Commission has sought harmonisation and enhanced protection for copyrights through a number of directives dealing with computer programmes and databases, satellite broadcasting and cable transmission, rental and lending rights, and duration of protection, among others[17]. The EU has also become party to the WCT and WPPT. Steps are now underway to further harmonise the national and EU systems.

3. The US'FTA Strategy: Stronger, Longer Copyright

The United States has recently entered into a number of Free Trade Agreements with Australia, Chile, Singapore, and other trading partners. Negotiations are currently ongoing with respect to the establishment of additional FTAs. It is clear that US frustration with multilateral negotiations has caused it to pursue FTAs and so win concessions on items that have been hard to win in multilateral fora.[18] One objective of forming the FTAs is to establish a standard of intellectual property protection similar to that found in United States law'.[19] As a

[15] The WCT entered into force on 6 Mar 2002. The WPPT entered into force on 20 May 2002(eg both are required under EFTA, US–Australia FTA, EU–Mexico FTA, US–Jordan FTA, etc).

[16] NAFTA Art 1707.

[17] For more information, see Council Directive 91/250/EEC of 14 May 1991 on the legal protection of computer programmes; Directive 96/9/EC of the European Parliament and of the Council of 11 Mar 1996 on the legal protection of databases; Council Directive 93/83/EEC of 27 Sept 1993 on the co-ordination of certain rules concerning copyright and rights related to copyright applicable to satellite broadcasting and cable retransmission; Council Directive 92/100/EEC of 19 Nov 1992 on rental right and lending right and on certain rights related to copyright in the field of intellectual property; and Council Directive 93/98/EEC of 29 Oct 1993 harmonising the term of protection of copyright and certain related rights.

[18] RB Zoellick, Our credo: free trade and competition, The Wall Street Journal, 7 Oct 2003, at http://www.ustr.gov/speechtest/zoellick/2003-07-10_WSJ.htm(last visited 11 Dec 2005)

[19] See, the congressional directive established in the Bipartisan Trade Promotion Act of 2002, Public Law 107–210.

result, most of the FTAs stipulate minimum levels of protection with respect to copyrights, data protection, patents, trade marks, and other forms of intellectual property. These standards relate to such provisions as the term of protection, scope of rights, and mechanisms by which these intellectual property rights are acquired and enforced. The different FTAs vary in their comprehensiveness and level of detail. Each of these agreements has nonetheless been drafted in a manner that complies with current US law. As a result, the effect of each FTA is to obligate signatories to such agreements to amend their intellectual property laws to match or resemble those of the United States.[20]

Under 'the Digital Trade Agenda of the US', a set of rules and trade concessions are called for that concern the elimination of tariffs on physical media carrier, the liberalisation of trade in telecommunication, computer, entertainment and other electronically deliverable services, free trade chapters on e-commerce, and a strong protection of intellectual property rights (IPRs)—especially copyrights—in an online environment. [21] The agenda is aimed to update trade agreements so that new treaties deal with trade-related aspects of intellectual property protection in the digital trade age. Moreover, the agenda recognises that intellectual property disciplines (especially copyright and related rights) are jeopardised by the emergence of the internet and electronic commerce.[22] The US digital trade policy extends the 'TRIPS standards' so that trade partners should ratify the two new WIPO treaties and that these new obligations shall be linked to existing or new trade agreements. At times, the US will also ask for country-specific improvements of IPR laws.[23]

FTA negotiations thus provide the most effective approach currently available to the United States for improving global intellectual property protection. The negotiation of an individual FTA provides the opportunity to deal with specific intellectual property concerns that US industry may have in the particular negotiating partner.[24] In 2004, the USTR reached a final agreement on a Free Trade Agreement with Bahrain and Jordan, and the FTAs include a chapter on intellectual property rights and enforcement that sets the highest levels of copyright protection and enforcement. The strong copyright and enforcement standards of this FTA followed closely those developed in the FTA with Morocco, etc. This FTA sets important precedents that we Koreans expect to follow in an FTA with the US.

[20] JR Thomas, Intellectual Property and the Free Trade Agreements: Innovation Policy Issues, http://www.bilaterals.org/article.php3?id_article=3398(last visited 21 Dec 2005).

[21] Sacha Wunsch-Vincent, *supra* n 14, p 18.

[22] See WIPO, A primer on Electronic Commerce and Intellectual Property Issues, Report NoWIPO/OLOA/EC/PRIMER, Geneva: World Intellectual Property Organization (2000) pp 27 *ff*; Sacha Wunsch-Vincent, *supra* n 14, p 18

[23] Sacha Wunsch-Vincent, *id*, p 18–19.

[24] Industry Functional Advisory Committee on Intellectual Property Rights for Trade Policy Matters (IFAC-3), The US–Australia Free Trade Agreement (FTA): The Intellectual Property Provisions, Report of the Industry Functional Advisory Committee on Intellectual Property Rights for Trade Policy Matters (IFAC-3), 12 Mar 2004, pp 45, available at http://www.ustr.gov/new/fta/Australia/advisor/ifac03.pdf (last visited 11 Dec 2005).

IV. THE US–KOREAN FTA AND KOREAN COPYRIGHT LAW

The 'TRIPS-plus' phenomenon corresponds to the view that the TRIPS Agreement does not adequately reflect the high standards of intellectual property protection needed to promote global trade to respond to the requirements of the digital age. Accordingly, the US has recently followed an explicit bilateral trade policy of going beyond the TRIPS Agreement by including TRIPS-plus provisions in its FTAs. Especially the FTA between US and Jordan constituted an important precedent for future negotiations regarding IPRs. Korea has been well aware of the US position on trade liberalisation and intellectual property issues. Thus, at least in terms of intellectual property protection, particularly copyright protection, the Korea–US FTA definitely adopts 'TRIPS-plus' provisions.

The Korea-US FTA will also introduce some new rights and schemes that previously did not exist in Korean copyright law. The agreement will require that the copyright term be extended to life of the author plus 70 years for works, and to 70 years from the date of publication for films and sound recordings. The agreement will also include an obligation to provide for criminal procedures and penalties to be applied at least in cases of wilful copyright infringement or related rights piracy on a commercial scale. The most significant changes include:

1. Accession to the WCT and WPPT

For the protection of copyright in the internet age, the WIPO convened a diplomatic conference in Geneva and produced the WCT and the WPPT in 1996. The new features of the WCT included, amongst others, a Right of Communication to the Public, Obligations concerning 'Technological Protection Measures (TPMs)' and Obligations concerning 'Rights Management Information'.

Korea was a signatory to the WCT, but has not acceded to the WPPT. The Government has, however, taken steps to put Korea in a position to accede to the WPPT. Korea has implemented the main features of the WCT in her Korean Copyright Act (KCA) and Korean Computer Program Protection Act (KCPPA), either voluntarily or by the pressure of the United States, even before the ratification of the treaty. In 2000, the KCA was updated to expand the coverage of the author's right of transmission. Besides this and in order to comply with the WPPT, a right of transmission was also granted to performers and phonogram producers in 2005. Indeed, it seems to make sense to expand the right of transmission of authors/ performers and phonogram producers also to the stage of making transmittable.

But also the users of copyrighted works should not be ignored in the digital environment. The interests of copyright holders and users of copyrighted works need to be aligned properly. Recent copyright legislation around the world, in particular the DMCA and the European Copyright Directives, tend to strengthen, or expand the exclusive rights of copyright owners. It is understandable that copyright holders should be able to keep their share of the copyright pie in the face of new technologies. However, stronger protection of copyright is not always good because it may result in unfairly diminished public access to copyrighted materials. Therefore, it is the most important issue in the digital economy to achieve the balance of the interests of copyright holders and users of copyrighted works.[25]

At present, the fair use doctrine, in particular, is a hot issue because the Korean copyright system is taking into consideration the adoption of the US fair use doctrine into both the KCA and the KCPPA. It should be noted that the scope of copyright limitations is wider in the United States than in Korea, and that the United States may apply copyright limitations flexibly to facts or to unexpected situations such as the internet.[26] The KCA and KCPPA are currently being reviewed by the Government, particularly those required under the US–Korean FTA such as temporary reproductions and online service provider liability.

2. Temporary storage

Under the Korean Copyright Act, owners of copyright in works (literary, dramatic, musical and artistic works) have the exclusive right to reproduce the work in tangible form.[27] 'Reproduction' is defined to include 'the fixation of works or the reproduction of works in tangible media of expression by means of printing, photographing, copying, sound or visual recording or other means'. What is at issue is whether or not temporary copies in a computer should or could be considered as act of use under copyright law.[28]

In order to meet the international standards embodied in Art 9.1 TRIPS Agreement [incorporating Art 9(1) Berne Convention] and referenced in footnote 1 of the WCT and footnote 9 of the WPPT, the reproduction right accorded to works and sound recordings should be made clearer and more comprehensive, by including within the scope of the reproduction right (1) direct or indirect reproduction; (2) temporary or permanent reproduction; (3) reproduction by any means or in any form; and (4) reproduction in whole or in part.

In the network digital environment, the right to make and use temporary copies of all kinds of works is attaining ever-increasing economic significance, and indeed in some cases will become the primary means of legitimate exploita-

[25] Kyong-soo Choe, 'Temporary Storage' and Limitation and Exception, in Korean Copyright Law in the digital environment, (ed) Seokin Huang, Samjiwon, p 56(2004).

[26] Dae-Hee Lee, Comparative Analysis of Software Copyright Limitation in the US and Korea, vol 2 No 1 Journal of Digital Property Law pp 200–1 (2002).

[27] Section 16 of the Copyright Act.

[28] Kyong-soo Choe, *supra* n 25, p 61.

tion of copyrighted material. Korean law, which stands nearly alone in the world in its rejection of protection for temporary copies, must spell out that this right is encompassed within the copyright owner's exclusive control over reproduction. However, such legislative revision could in fact require a fundamental change in the structure of copyright law, since new effort to achieve a balance among different interest and consideration may need to follow.[29]

3. Term of protection

The period of copyright protection in Korea is generally the life of the author plus 50 years, or 50 years from first publication. The US argues that the new global standard is life plus 70 years as in the US and the European Union.

The US extended their copyright terms recently after intense lobbying by a group of powerful corporate copyright holders, most notably Walt Disney, which faced the expiry of its copyright on Mickey Mouse and other famous cartoon characters. We Koreans are a small country that consumes enormous amounts of information. The US, on the other hand, is an exporter of copyright material. In its free trade agreements with Singapore and Chile, the US achieved a commitment to extend the term of copyright protection. The US is urging Korea to accelerate its effort on the term of protection issue. However, it is noted that the free trade deal will lead to huge increases in copyright licence fees paid by Korean for use of copyrighted works, including novels, poems, films and songs. Korea has taken the view that the global standard is that required by the multilateral treaties: life plus 50 years. However, the Korean Copyright Act in the future will provide that where the term of copyright protection is to be calculated on the basis of the life of a natural person, the term shall be no less than the life of the author and 70 years after the author's death.

4. The Law on Anti-Circumvention and Digital Rights Management

On 28 October 1998, the DMCA was signed into law, as an amendment to the Copyright Act. As a signatory to the WCT, the US was obligated to provide legal protection for authors 'against the circumvention of effective technological measures . . . that restrict acts . . . which are not authorized by the authors concerned or permitted by law.' However, the DMCA went much further than what the WCT required. The DMCA does contain some provisions exempting libraries and law enforcement from liability.[30] It also offers limited protection to certain reverse engineering and encryption research activities.[31] In addition,

[29] *Ibid*, p 62.
[30] 17 USC § 1201 (d).
[31] 17 USC § 1201 (f), (g).

it explicitly states that its anti-circumvention provisions shall not affect substantive copyright rights and defences to infringement, including fair use.[32] Nevertheless, it sweeps far more broadly than did the prior copyright law that preceded it. For one thing, despite its statement that fair use is preserved, it appears to prohibit circumventing access control measures even on public domain works. At least one decision construing the DMCA prohibits access control circumvention with the intent of 'fair use,' as opposed to copyright infringement.

The Korean Copyright Act also includes civil remedies and criminal penalties relating to circumvention of technological protection measures. These are intended to be consistent with the requirements of the WCT and the WPPT. Article 11 of the WCT and article 18 of the WPPT oblige the contracting parties to provide adequate legal protection and effective legal remedies against the circumvention of effective technological measures that are used by authors, performers or producers of phonograms in connection with the exercise of the rights under the WCT, WPPT and the Berne Convention and that restrict acts, in respect of their works, which are not authorised by the right holders concerned or permitted by law. At the Diplomatic Conference, countries have not agreed upon the exact definition of 'effective' technological measures, 'adequate' legal protection or 'effective' legal remedies, for copy/access control technology was still premature in 1996[33] and most of the participants had no concrete idea about it.[34]

However, the DMCA prohibits the circumvention of technological measures that effectively control access to a copyrighted work. The DMCA additionally prohibits the manufacture of, and trafficking in, such software—and other types of technology that are 'primarily designed or produced for the purpose of circumventing a technological measure' controlling access to a copyrighted work. Therefore, the US–Australia FTA negotiation, the US will definitely raise concerns about the level of protection:

- the definition of 'technological protection measure' covers measures intended to inhibit infringement of copyright ('copy controls'), but not measures intended to control access to copyright material ('access controls');
- the provisions relate to the manufacture, importation and supply, but not use, of circumvention devices and services; and
- the provisions allow supply for certain 'permitted purposes', including library use, educational use, government use and de-compilation of computer programs.[35]

[32] 17 USC § 1201 (c).

[33] Pamela Samuelson, The US Digital Agenda at WIPO, 37 Va Int'l LJ 369 (1997).

[34] Naoki Koizumi, Protection of Technological Measures under Japanese Law, Vol 2 No 1 Journal of Digital Property Law, pp 97–8 (2002).

[35] Libby Baulch, Copyright issues for the proposed Australia/US Free Trade Agreement, http://www.copyright.org.au/publications/pdf/articles/A03n05.pdf (last visited 11 Dec 2005).

With regard to technical protection measures (TPMs) against the manufacture and distribution of programmes or devices meant to overcome or circumvent copyright management systems, the Korean Copyright Act was amended in 2003 to implement anti-circumvention measures.[36] Unlike the Japanese Copyright Act,[37] the 2003 Copyright Amendment and the 2006 Copyright Amendment did not make certain reproductions for private use by use of circumvention measures subject to liability. However, the USTR pointed out that although the KCA contains provisions regarding TPMs, these fall short of full compliance with the WCT and WPPT in some critical respects, namely, coverage of access control and act of circumvention. It should be noted that the 2006 Copyright Amendment does not include access control but only provides copy control. The Government (MOCT) thought that the term 'in connection with the exercise of their rights under this Treaty or the Berne Convention' in the Article of WCT does not require implementation on access control. However, the Korea–US FTA will require that KCA must provide that any person who circumvents without authority any effective technological measure that controls access to a protected work, performance, phonogram, or other subject matter, shall be liable and subject to the remedies.

5. Safe Harbour scheme for Online Service Providers

There have been several decisions around world about the legitimacy of P2P file sharing. In Korea, a Korean court held that the operator of P2P file sharing system, *Soribada*, infringed copyright law.[38] These decisions are all about exchanging music files in the MP3 format via a peer-to-peer network with a central server. As a general rule, the operator of the central server seems to be liable for the operation of the network.

There is a case that a P2P service provider does not know about illegal works that are exchanged through its service. It is absurd that these kinds of services are considered illegal, just because there is a possibility of an infringement of copyright. There is a concern that imposing too much responsibility on an online service provider might lead to stymie the industry itself, which is a conflict of the general public's interest. Relating to this, the 2003 Copyright Amendment contains regulations on liability limitations for an online service

[36] Section 124 of the Copyright Act; See also Section 30 of the Computer Program Protection Act.

[37] Section 30 of the Japanese Copyright Act.

[38] Suwon District Court (Sungnam branch), 7 Sept 2002, 2002kahab77 decision—oribada. Even if after 22 months and hearings before three different judges, the case was dismissed in May 2003 on the grounds that the charges were defective, in civil cases, the Seoul High Court on appeal (1 Dec 2005, 2003Na21140 & 2003Na89798) & the Supreme Court (25 Jan 2007, 2005Da11626) held the centralised server operators and distributors of P2P file-sharing software liable for infringement of copyright.

However, the Seoul District Court on appeal (1 Dec 2005, 2003No4296) held that the operator of centralised server is not criminally liable for infringement. The final decision of the Supreme Court is pending.

provider. An online service provider is 'the one who provides the service that allows to copy and transmit works, performances, records, broadcasting, or databases of others through wire or wireless communications'.[39] Therefore, the operator of *Soribada* falls under the category of an online service provider. According to Section 102 of the 2006 Copyright Amendment, in order for this kind of online service provider to be exempted from or to have less degree of the liability regarding infringements of the copyright and related rights, the provider should fulfil at least one of the following requirements: First, the provider knows copyrights and related rights could be infringed through the reproduction and transmission of others' works, and prevents or interferes the concerned reproduction and transmission.[40] Second, the provider knows copyrights and related rights could be infringed through the reproduction and transmission of others' works, and tries to prevent or interfere the concerned reproduction and transmission, but it is impossible in a technical way.[41]

The FTA requires Korea to make clear that—

— In all cases, including cases in which liability is 'exempted' under Section 102, the courts retain the authority to issue appropriate injunctions;
— No liability limitations should apply to a case in which the ISP has the right and ability to control infringing activities on its network and in which it derives a direct financial benefit from such activities;
— Any liability limitations are inapplicable when the infringement is carried out by an employee or agent of the ISP, or by any other affiliated party, or when the ISP has any other direct involvement in the infringement;
— The provision should not be applicable to an ISP who refuses to cooperate in combating online piracy, such as by refusing to terminate the accounts of subscribers or customers who repeatedly use the system to commit infringements.

Furthermore, Korea shall establish an administrative or judicial procedure enabling copyright owners who have given effective notification of claimed infringement to obtain expeditiously from a service provider information in its possession identifying the alleged infringer.

V. CONCLUSION

Korean copyright law has recently undergone several reforms, with more to follow, in order to give effect to our obligations under the WCT and WPPT. These reforms have passed both Parliaments in 2006. The majority of the copyright reforms relate to performers rights. Furthermore, the FTA requires Korea to rat-

[39] Section 2 No. 22 of the Copyright Act.
[40] Section 102(2) of the Copyright Act.
[41] *Ibid.*

ify or accede to the WPPT. Korea is not currently a signatory to the Rome Convention and the WPPT imposes higher standards.

Implementation of the comprehensive obligations in these WCT, WPPT and FTA will strengthen copyright law in Korea, and will also improve the legal tools available there for enforcement of copyright. However, the implementation of the international treaties would tie both the judiciary's and Congress's hands to protect consumers' long-established right to fair use. The beneficiaries of these improvements include creators and consumers of copyrighted works in Korea. A comprehensive instrument for regulation of the global marketplace for copyrighted materials can only be achieved if all interests involved, namely those of creators, performer and users, are taken into account. A reform of the Korean Copyright Act should consider all these interests.

The inclusion of the Intellectual Property Chapter in FTA recognises the importance of a strong intellectual property regime to economic growth through trade and investment. Koreans will benefit through closer harmonisation of our already strong intellectual property regime with that of the largest intellectual property market in the world. Intellectual Property Rights is an essential element for economic and cultural development. I think that the IPR-related provisions in the Korea–US FTA should comply with the existing treaties on copyrights of which both sides are members, including the Berne Convention, particularly regarding the principles of the most-favoured nation and national treatment. The Korean government should make more efforts to enforce its IPR regime. In addition, the Korean agree that the greater efforts of the Korean government to enhance the IPR protection would contribute to attracting more foreign investments and increasing the trade of products related to cultural industries between the countries.

The intellectual property system of Korea–US FTA should be able to prevent a breach of intellectual property obligations whereas it should not be overly restrictive to hamper free transfer of knowledge and innovation. Successful internationalisation inevitably leads to a harmonisation of different values. That means that the Korean Copyright Act should be fundamentally overhauled in the near future, so that certain formal minimum standards to protect not only interests of creators and performer, but those of users. I can only hope that the new Copyright Act will remove the defects of the current Copyright, contain fair use clause and be enacted out of the need for a legal policy to prohibit infringement of copyright and related rights.

Part V

FTAs and Antitrust

Chapter 10

International Antitrust and Intellectual Property

ANDREAS HEINEMANN

I. INTRODUCTION

THE RELATIONSHIP BETWEEN antitrust and intellectual property law (the 'interface problem') has always been highly controversial. Nevertheless, there has been a considerable change of concepts in the last decades.[1] Whereas in former times the conflict between the two fields of law has been emphasised, today the complementarity between the constitution of exclusive rights on the one hand and the protection of undistorted competition on the other hand is underlined. No longer, intellectual property rights (IPRs) are seen as monopolies or dominant positions on relevant markets, but as exclusive rights similar to tangible property. The short-term exclusion of competition is opposed to the long-term promotion of innovation and new competition. An abundant literature has focused on the economic and ideological foundations of the interface question.[2]

In our context, the main stress shall be put on the *international* aspects of the subject. The term 'international' can be grasped in different ways which will all be followed here. In the first place it can comprise the rules on the interface problem in international law, particularly in the TRIPS Agreement of the WTO (B). Second, it can allude to substantive application problems which are of international importance, especially the abuse of dominant positions based on IPRs

[1] For an overview see Heinemann, Immaterialgüterrecht und Kartellrecht: Konflikt oder Koexistenz?, in Baudenbacher/Simon, Neueste Entwicklungen im europäischen und internationalen Immaterialgüterrecht, 2003, p 179 *et seq*.

[2] See eg Anderman, EC Competition Law and Intellectual Property Rights, 1998; Anderson/Gallini (Ed), Competition Policy and Intellectual Property Rights in the Knowledge-Based Economy, 1998; Govaere, The Use and Abuse of Intellectual Property Rights in EC Law, 1996; Heinemann, Immaterialgüterschutz in der Wettbewerbsordnung, 2002; Tom/Newberg, Antitrust and Intellectual Property: From Separate Spheres to Unified Field, 66 Antitrust Law Journal 167–229 (1997); OECD, Competition Policy and Intellectual Property Rights, Series Roundtables on Competition Policy No 18, DAFFE/CLP(98)18, 1998; UNCTAD—Trade and Development Board, Competition Policy and the Exercise of Intellectual Property Rights, TD/B/COM.2/CLP/22/Rev.1, 19 Apr 2002.

(C), and third, there are international aspects directly linked to the general subject of this book, ie Free Trade Agreements and the tendency towards regional integration (D).

II. ANTITRUST LAW IN THE TRIPS AGREEMENT

The principal aim of the TRIPS Agreement is to reduce obstacles to international trade by setting minimum standards for the protection of intellectual property. Usually, national IP statutes define scope and internal boundaries of IPRs, but they do not contain antitrust rules. The same is true for the international IP conventions like the Paris or Berne Convention. An exception is Art 17 of the Berne Convention which clarifies that the Convention does not prohibit the application of national administrative control. Although antitrust law did not exist at the time of adoption of the Berne Convention, it is today generally accepted that the reservation made in Art 17 covers, inter alia, the application of national competition law.[3] Therefore, boundaries of IP law set by national (or *supra*national) competition law do not violate the requirements of international IP law. The TRIPS Agreement goes one step further. In the preamble as well as in Arts 8, 31 and 40 it contains rules on competition law control of IPRs.[4] Thus, the TRIPS agreement is the first international IP convention that explicitly recognises the necessity of submitting IPRs to competition law control.

1. Preamble and Art 8(2) TRIPS

a) Principles

According to the TRIPS preamble, it has to be ensured 'that measures and procedures to enforce intellectual property rights do not themselves become barriers to legitimate trade'. By this general statement it is recognised that the protection of intellectual property—albeit an important condition for optimal trade—might itself become an obstacle to 'legitimate trade' if it is not embedded in a system of general rules.

[3] Ricketson, The Berne Convention for the Protection of Literary and Artistic Works: 1886–1986, 1987, p 546 et seq.; Nordemann/Vinck/Hertin/Meyer, International Copyright, 1990, p 160. This result applies also to those conventions which do not provide for a general reservation clause as in Art 17 Berne Convention. Eg Art 10[bis] of the Paris Convention only concerns unfair competition not antitrust law. Nevertheless, see the special reservation clause in Art 5A(2) of the Paris Convention which allows the countries of the Paris Union to provide for compulsory licenses 'to prevent the abuses which might result from the exercise of the exclusive rights conferred by the patent'.

[4] For an analysis of the TRIPS competition law rules see UNCTAD/ICTSD, Resource Book on TRIPS and Development, 2005, p 539 *et seq* (available at: http://www.iprsonline.org/unctadictsd/docs/Part3_Update.pdf) with further references. See also Ullrich, Expansionist Intellectual Property Protection and Reductionist Competition Rules: A TRIPS Perspective, 7 JIEC 401 (2004).

The general warning in the preamble is taken up again in Art 8(2) which allows WTO members to provide for 'appropriate measures [. . .] to prevent the abuse of intellectual property rights by right holders or the resort to practices which unreasonably restrain trade or adversely affect the international transfer of technology'. By this article which is still of a very general nature, it is recognised that WTO members are allowed to control IPRs by a national legislation against anti-competitive practices.[5] It is important to notice that this rule (like the other TRIPS provisions on anti-competitive behaviour) was introduced into the TRIPS agreement on initiative of the developing countries. Antitrust law was supposed to counterbalance the power of IP right holders whose position would be considerably strengthened by the TRIPS agreement.[6] It is worth mention that there has been an important change in the developing countries' position. In the discussion about the need to introduce a general competition law into the WTO system, developing countries have become very reluctant. The competition law subject which is one of the so-called 'Singapore issues' has been removed from the agenda of the Doha Round. Developing countries want to prevent that a WTO competition law will be used to dismantle their public monopolies. Moreover, there is the fear of cross retaliation in case of violation of WTO competition rules.[7]

Even if there will not be a WTO antitrust agreement in the near future, the TRIPS competition rules will serve as a reminder that many subjects of the WTO system are in urgent need of a general competition law agreement.

b) Function of the TRIPS competition rules

The TRIPS agreement does not *oblige* the Members to take action against the abuse of intellectual property rights, it just *allows* such measures. This follows from the careful wording of Art 8(2) TRIPS according to which appropriate measures 'may be needed' and of the function of this article as an exception clause. It is not intended to establish minimum standards for national competition law. It is just clarified that national competition law—under certain conditions—does not infringe international IP law.

[5] For a general description of the relationship between the TRIPS-Agreement and competition law see Fikentscher, Historical Origins and Opportunities for Development of an International Competition Law in the TRIPS Agreement of the World Trade Organization (WTO) and Beyond, in: Beier/Schricker (ed), From GATT to TRIPS, 1996, p 226 *et seq*; E Fox, Trade, Competition, and Intellectual Property—TRIPS and its Antitrust Counterparts, 29 Vanderbilt Journal of Transnational Law 481 (1996); Ullrich, TRIPS: Adequate Protection, Inadequate Trade, Adequate Competition Policy, 4 Pacific Rim Law & Policy Journal 153 (1995).

[6] See Drexl, Entwicklungsmöglichkeiten des Urheberrechts im Rahmen des GATT, 1990, p 365 *et seq*; Pacón, What Will TRIPS Do For Developing Countries?, in: Beier/Schricker (ed), From GATT to TRIPS, 1996, p 329 et seq.; Gervais (in this volume). Generally on the interests behind the TRIPS Agreement see Koury Menescal, Those behind the TRIPS Agreement, Intellectual Property Quarterly 2005, 155 with further references.

[7] However, these worries can be dispelled or at least reduced, see Heinemann, La nécessité d'un droit mondial de la concurrence, RIDE 2004, 293 (315 *et seq*).

c) Consistency requirement

According to Art 8(2) TRIPS, appropriate measures against the abuse of IPRs are only permissible if 'they are consistent with the provisions of this Agreement'. Such a consistency requirement is quite striking in the context of an exception clause. Art 8(2) allows exceptions to the general rules. At the same time, the exceptions shall be consistent with the general rules. A convincing interpretation is hardly possible. The unclear wording is due to conflicting interests during the TRIPS negotiations:[8] The special rule on prevention of an abuse of IPRs had been introduced by the developing countries. In return, the industrialised countries wanted to prevent an 'abuse of the abuse'. Therefore, the sense of the consistency requirement is to prevent an excessive invocation of the exception clause which could lead to an uncontrolled intrusion into the substance of IP protection. The minimum sense of the consistency requirement is that the application of national competition law has to be consistent with the basic TRIPS rules, eg national and MFN treatment: national competition law must not be applied in a discriminatory manner.[9]

2. Art 31 TRIPS

a) Compulsory licences

Art 31 TRIPS concerns the subject of compulsory licences. This is not a specific antitrust rule because it covers in a general way cases in which use of the patent without authorisation of the right holder might be ordered. However, a strong relationship to antitrust law exists which is even explicitly made in Art 31(c) and (k) TRIPS. Therefore, the scope of article 31 TRIPS is sufficiently large to qualify it as a rule having at least partly an antitrust character. Like Art 8(2) TRIPS the adoption of a rule on compulsory licences was subject to a very controversial debate. Protection of intellectual property on the one hand and the establishment of boundaries in the public interest on the other hand were the two opposites of the debate. The result is: There is a rule on compulsory licences, but that the authorisation of such compulsory licences is subject to *twelve* (!) conditions. In addition, Art 5A of the Paris Convention (applicable via Art 2 TRIPS) has to be taken into account.[10]

[8] See the in-depth analysis in UNCTAD/ICTSD, Resource Book on TRIPS and Development, 2005, p 460 *et seq* (available at: http://www.iprsonline.org/unctadictsd/docs/RB2.5_Patents_2.5.8_update.pdf).

[9] See UNCTAD/ICTSD (*supra* n 4), p 553.

[10] Art 5A of the Paris Convention reads (in extracts):

> (2) Each country of the Union shall have the right to take legislative measures providing for the grant of compulsory licenses to prevent the abuses which might result from the exercise of the exclusive rights conferred by the patent, for example, failure to work. [. . .]
> (4) A compulsory license may not be applied for on the ground of failure to work or insufficient working before the expiration of a period of four years from the date of filing of the

b) Predominant supply of the domestic market?

The importance of Art 31 TRIPS for antitrust law can be made clearer by referring to the most famous of the twelve conditions, Art 31(f) TRIPS. According to this condition, the compulsory licence must predominantly serve the purpose of supplying the domestic market of the state in which such use was authorised. In the discussion on TRIPS and public health this rule has been criticised because WTO members without production capacities of their own can—because of this restriction—hardly solicit the importation of drugs produced under a compulsory licence in another country.[11] This problem was solved by the waiver of the WTO General Council of August 2003[12] in which the obligations of WTO members under Art 31(f) TRIPS were suspended according to certain conditions. In December 2005, the General Council decided to transform this temporary exception into an amendment of the TRIPS-Agreement.[13] The new Art 31bis TRIPS constitutes the first modification of a WTO text and is supposed to enter into force on 1 December 2007. The EU has already adapted its legislation.[14]

Another way which does not require the reform or the waiver of existing WTO law is Art 31(k) TRIPS: Members are not obliged to apply Art 31(f) TRIPS 'where such use is permitted to remedy a practice determined after judicial or administrative process to be anti-competitive.' Therefore, if the compulsory licence is ordered by an antitrust authority, the requirement of a predominant supply of the domestic market of the country ordering the compulsory licence is not applicable. Certainly, the conditions for an antitrust violation have to be met, eg there has to be an illegal monopolising or the abuse of a dominant position. Moreover, the legal consequence of this violation has to be a compulsory licence and not only the obligation to pay damages. Nevertheless, WTO members are—to a large extent—free in designing their national competition laws. Therefore it is up to national law to determine what is 'anti-competitive'. Restrictions of the discretionary power of WTO members follow eg from Art 8(2) TRIPS: The application of national competition law

patent application or three years from the date of the grant of the patent, whichever period expires last; it shall be refused if the patentee justifies his inaction by legitimate reasons. Such a compulsory license shall be non-exclusive and shall not be transferable, even in the form of the grant of a sub-license, except with that part of the enterprise or goodwill which exploits such license.

11 At least if the exporting country does not use more than 50 % of the drugs produced under the compulsory licence for its domestic market. See Kampf, Patents versus Patients?, 40 Archiv des Völkerrechts 90 (2002).

12 Available at: http://www.wto.org/english/tratop_e/TRIPS_e/implem_para6_e.htm.

13 *WTO General Council*, Amendment of the TRIPs Agreement, WT/L/641, 6.12.2005. See *Matthews*, From the Aug 30, 2003 WTO Decision to the Dec 6, 2005 Agreement on an Amendment to TRIPS, 10 Intellectual Property Quarterly 91–130 (2006).

14 Regulation (EC) No 816/2006 of the European Parliament and of the Council of 17 May 2006 on compulsory licensing of patents relating to the manufacture of pharmaceutical products for export to countries with public health problems, OJ 2006 L 157/1.

must not violate the consistency requirement, that is mainly the requirement of national and most-favoured-nation treatment.

3. Art 40 TRIPS

a) Antitrust law of licensing agreements

The most detailed article on the interface between antitrust and intellectual property law is Art 40 TRIPS. This article deals with the problem which has the greatest practical importance that is anti-competitive practices in contractual licences. Art 40 TRIPS does not oblige WTO members to adopt competition rules against anti-competitive licensing clauses, but clarifies that such rules do not violate the TRIPS agreement.[15] This clarification is of utmost importance because many countries in the world have special competition law rules on IP licensing or at least apply their general rules thereto.

Art 40(2) allows WTO members to specify 'in their legislation licensing practices or conditions that may in particular cases constitute an abuse of intellectual property rights having an adverse effect on competition in the relevant market.' Examples are given like exclusive grant back conditions, conditions preventing challenges to validity and coercive package licensing. At the same time, it is made clear that there is considerable scope for the national legislature: The details have to be determined in national law. The three examples of anti-competitive clauses in licensing agreements are by no means exhaustive. The national legislature may provide for other examples or may forego examples of anti-competitive licensing clauses instead of a general clause. Art 40 TRIPS does not interfere with this liberty.

b) National (or supranational) rules on anti-competitive licensing contracts

Specific antitrust rules on licensing contracts exist in many countries.

(i) The US

In the US, eg, the subject is governed by the 1995 *Antitrust Guidelines for the Licensing of Intellectual Property* jointly issued by the two federal antitrust agencies, ie the Antitrust Division of the Department of Justice and the Federal Trade Commission.[16] The Guidelines start from three basic assumptions: For the purpose of antitrust law, antitrust law is applied to intellectual property in the same way as to other forms of tangible or intangible property. Second, there is no presumption that IPRs as such confer market power. And third, there is no longer a presumption that licensing contracts are anti-competitive: on the

[15] For a different opinion see UNCTAD/ICTSD (*supra* n 4), p 555: Art 40 (1) TRIPS (in conjunction with Art 7 TRIPS) 'may well be understood as imposing an obligation on Members to address certain forms of anticompetitive practices in licensing agreements'.

[16] Available at http://www.usdoj.gov/atr/public/guidelines/ipguide.htm.

contrary, according to the guidelines, licensing is generally pro-competitive because it allows firms to combine complementary production factors.

This is a revolution compared eg to the *Nine No-No's* of the 70s and the early 80s where certain licensing clauses were held to be anticompetitive regardless of their economic context in the particular case. The most important statement of the guidelines in this respect is: 'The Agencies will focus on the actual effects of an arrangement, not on its formal terms.'[17] Therefore, in the US, it is not the abstract wording of a licensing contract but its effects in the real word which are analysed. There are only some *per se* prohibitions left, eg price-fixing or market division among competitors. Outside these *per se* prohibitions, there is a 'safe harbour': If the agreement does not involve markets on which the joint market share of the parties exceeds 20 per cent, the licensing arrangement is not challenged. Beyond a joint market share of 20 per cent, a case-by-case analysis on the basis of the *rule of reason* is preferred.

(ii) The European Union

The European Union has followed the US-American development to a large extent.[18] Since 1996 the European Commission has adopted an 'economic approach'. Under European competition law, it is not any longer the wording of an agreement which is relevant for antitrust scrutiny but the complete economic (and legal) context. This is of special importance for the block exemption regulations. In the past, these block exemptions contained long lists of contract clauses which were allowed or forbidden ('white' and 'black' and even 'grey' lists). The result was the so-called 'strait-jacket'-effect: Enterprises had to choose for their licensing agreements exactly the clauses white-listed in the block exemption regulations. Otherwise they ran the risk that the exemption would not apply. With the 1999 block exemption regulation on vertical agreements[19] the European Commission for the first time applied the 'economic approach' to a block exemption regulation: The exemption is granted not for certain clauses but in general for certain types of contract. There are no more white lists, yet still a black list, ie there is a transition to the principle: 'Everything which is not forbidden is allowed'.

In 2004, this approach has been applied to licensing agreements. The new block exemption regulation on technology transfer agreements[20] does not contain white lists but simply states in its Art 2 in a general manner 'that Article 81(1) of the Treaty shall not apply to technology transfer agreements entered into between two undertakings permitting the production of contract products'.

[17] Licensing Guidelines at n 3.1.

[18] For a comparison see Feil, The New Block Exemption Regulation on Technology Transfer Agreements in the Light of the US Antitrust Regime on the Licensing of Intellectual Property, 36 IIC 31 (2005).

[19] Commission Regulation (EC) No 2790/1999 on the application of Art 81(3) of the Treaty to categories of vertical agreements and concerted practices of 22 Dec 1999, OJ L 336/21.

[20] Commission Regulation (EC) No 772/2004 on the application of Art 81(3) of the Treaty to categories of technology transfer agreements of 27 Apr 2004, OJ L 123/11.

Further conditions are provided for in the following articles of the regulation. For example, the exemption is not valid for certain hardcore restrictions like price fixing or certain measures of territorial protection, as well as for exclusive grant-back-obligations or no challenge clauses. Different rules apply depending on whether the parties to the agreement are competitors or not.

A strong link to the economic context is made in Art 3 of the regulation regarding market-share thresholds. In case of competing undertakings, the regulation applies up to joint market shares of 20 percent. For non-competitors the 'safe harbour' is 30 percent. If these thresholds are exceeded, the behaviour in question is not necessarily forbidden. It is always possible to resort to the general exception stipulated in Art 81(3) EC. Since the 1st May 2004, this provision is directly applicable. Another 'safe harbour' is provided for in the guidelines to the technology transfer regulation.[21] According to the European Commission, 'Article 81 is unlikely to be infringed where there are four or more independently controlled technologies in addition to the technologies controlled by the parties to the agreement that may be substitutable for the licensed technology at a comparable cost to the user.' In many cases, it may be easier to determine substitutable technologies instead of calculating market shares.

(iii) Japan

The Japanese Fair Trade Commission adopted new Licensing Guidelines in 1999.[22] The Guidelines share the same principles as the US–American Guidelines or the European Block Exemption Regulation. Licensing agreements are considered basically as pro-competitive. At the same time, the guidelines state that competition law has to prevent an anti-competitive use of licensing contracts. In every single case, the question has to be asked if the use of the IPR in the single case corresponds to the purpose of the IPR system or if it deviates from it. Specific examples are given. Restrictions on the licensee on the scope of the patent, like eg the separation of licenses to manufacture, to use or to sell a protected product are not considered to violate competition law. The same is true for field of use restrictions, for the limitation of the time period within the life of the patent rights or for a limitation to a certain territory within Japan. Restrictions 'that are not considered to be an exercise of rights under the Patent Act', will be assessed 'on a case-by-case basis, in light of their effect on competition in a market.'[23] The Guidelines give detailed advice which licensing clauses or practices are harmless and which ones raise competitive concerns. As in the US-American guidelines, preference is given to a case-by-case analysis following the rule of reason. Some *per se*-prohibitions exist, eg for price fixing.

[21] European Commission, Guidelines on the application of Art 81 of the EC Treaty to technology transfer agreements, OJ 2004 C 101/2.

[22] Fair Trade Commission of Japan, Guidelines for Patent and Know-how Licensing Agreements under the Antimonopoly Act, Jul 30, 1999; available at: http://www2.jftc.go.jp/e-page/legislation/ama/patentandknow-how.pdf.

[23] Guidelines, p 20.

(iv) Conclusions

The antitrust law of licensing agreements moves away from strict prohibitions towards a case-by-case analysis taking into account the whole economic context. This new approach leads to more efficient results. This improvement has to be paid by a loss of legal certainty. For an enterprise, it is not so simple any longer to evaluate the lawfulness of a licensing contract because not only the text of the contract, but all the surrounding facts have to be included into the analysis. On the other hand, legal certainty is strengthened by the fact that many countries, following the example of the US, the EU and Japan have adopted legal texts which give guidance on practical questions in this field. Thus, these countries have made use of the possibility offered in Art 40 of the TRIPS agreement.

III. PARADIGM OF AN INTERFACE PROBLEM: THE *MICROSOFT* CASE

Problems at the interface of Intellectual Property and Antitrust law have become more frequent because of the high IP density in information technology. Problems in this context vary considerably and concern constellations like refusal to licence, essential facilities, monopoly leveraging, de facto-standards, computer interfaces and so forth. The most exemplary case in this context is certainly *Microsoft*.[24]

1. Basic Facts

Microsoft has a dominant position on the market for PC operating systems, based on a market share for the different versions of the *Windows*-program above 90 per cent and on high barriers to entry caused by network effects. The dominance of *Windows* is so much established that it has to be called a de facto standard. Different business strategies of *Microsoft* came into conflict with competition law. Several competition authorities in the world opened proceedings. The US-American and the European antitrust authorities did not undertake parallel efforts but focused on different subjects. Whereas the American case focuses on the browser and the Java problem, the European Commission left this part to the American authorities and picked up instead the problem of server software markets and of integration of the media player into the operating system. In both cases, business strategies are in question which tend to perpetuate the dominant position on the market for operating systems. Both in the US and in the EU, *Microsoft* was held to infringe antitrust law. However, the outcome was different. Whereas the American case was closed by a consent

[24] The following analysis of the Microsoft case draws on Heinemann, Compulsory Licences and Product Integration in European Competition Law, 36 IIC 63 (2005).

decree, the European Commission preferred to make a unilateral decision giving certain orders to *Microsoft* accompanied by a record fine.[25]

2. Conflict of IP and Antitrust in the *Microsoft* Case

In our context, the interface aspect of the case is in the centre of interest. In the US-American case, *Microsoft* invoked IP protection to legitimate its anti-competitive behaviour. The US Court of Appeals for the District of Columbia Circuit rejected this argument and reduced it *ad absurdum*:

> Microsoft's primary copyright argument borders upon the frivolous. The company claims an absolute and unfettered right to use its intellectual property as it wishes: "[I]f intellectual property rights have been lawfully acquired," it says, then "their subsequent exercise cannot give rise to antitrust liability." [. . .] That is no more correct than the proposition that use of one's personal property, such as a baseball bat, cannot give rise to tort liability. As the Federal Circuit succinctly stated: "Intellectual property rights do not confer a privilege to violate the antitrust laws".[26]

In the European case, the IP-antitrust conflict is stronger. The case has two components, ie a 'product integration' and a 'refusal to licence' part. On the one hand, the European Commission saw an antitrust violation in the bundling of *Windows* and Microsoft's media player ('Windows Media Player', a software necessary to present audio and video content on a computer). Because of the joint shipping of operating system and media player competing media players are impeded. The Commission imposed on *Microsoft* the duty to offer a full-functioning *Windows* version which does not incorporate the media player.

On the other hand, according to the findings of the Commission, the firm abused its dominant position on the market for client PC operating systems to conquer the market for work group server operating systems by creating compatibility problems between competing server software and the *Windows* client PC operating system. The Commission obliged *Microsoft* to make interoperability information available to all interested undertakings, and to allow them the use of the information 'on reasonable and non-discriminatory terms'.[27]

A representative of *Microsoft* said that the European Commission's decision 'amounts to the broadest compulsory licensing of intellectual property rights since the European Community was founded'.[28] Indeed, the decision raises the general question under which conditions an IP holder can be obliged to give a

[25] European Commission, 24.3.2004, Case COMP/C-3/37.792—*Microsoft*; provisional version available at http://europa.eu.int/comm/competition/antitrust/cases/decisions/37792/en.pdf.

[26] US Court of Appeals for the District of Columbia Circuit, 28.6.2001, *United States v Microsoft Corp*, http://cnnfn.cnn.com/2001/06/28/microsoft_file/decision.pdf, S. 33.

[27] European Commission (*supra*, n 25), Art 5 (at the end of the decision).

[28] Brad Smith, News Teleconference, 24.3.2004, available at: http://www.microsoft.com/presspass/legal/european/03-24steveballmer-us.asp.

licence to a third party. Case law of the European Court of Justice (ECJ) exists on this subject, the two most important cases being *Magill* and *IMS Health*.

3. Case Law of the ECJ: *Magill* and *IMS Health*

a) Magill

In *Magill*, TV broadcasters refused to license copyright-protected program listings to an enterprise which wanted to edit the first weekly TV guide in Ireland. The ECJ said in a famous citation, 'that the exercise of an exclusive right by the proprietor may, in exceptional circumstances, involve abusive conduct.'[29] In European competition law, as in US antitrust law, IP rights are not immune against the application of antitrust law. In *Magill*, the ECJ had given three criteria for the existence of an abuse pursuant to Art 82 EC. First, by the refusal to license his copyright the copyright owner prevents the appearance of a new product (*in casu* a comprehensive weekly TV guide for Ireland) which constitutes an abuse according to Art 82 b) EC; second, there is no justification for such refusal; and third, the copyright owners 'reserved to themselves the secondary market of weekly television guides by excluding all competition on that market [. . .] since they denied access to the basic information which is the raw material indispensable for the compilation of such a guide.'[30] There has been an intense discussion about the exact meaning of these criteria. Does an abuse in the sense of Art 82 EC presuppose that all three conditions are simultaneously met? Or do they stand in an alternative relationship, ie is it sufficient that there is an artificial restraint on production *or* the abusive conquest of a secondary market?

b) IMS Health

The ECJ itself has answered this question in its *IMS Health* preliminary ruling.[31] The Court clarifies that the three conditions of the *Magill* decision have to be construed as cumulative, and adds a further condition coming from the essential facilities-context of the *Bronner* judgment.[32] Henceforth, all of the following conditions have to be met to impose a compulsory licence based on European competition law:[33]

[29] ECJ, 6.4.1995, Joined Cases 241 and 242/91 P, *Magill*, [1995] ECR I-743, n 50.

[30] ECJ, *Magill* (*supra* n 29), point 54–6. See Anderman, Does the *Microsoft* Case offer a New Paradigm for the 'Exceptional Circumstances' Test and Compulsory Copyright Licenses under EC Competition Law?, (2004) 1(2) CompLRev, available at: http://www.clasf.org/CompLRev/assets/Vol1Issue2Article1.pdf.

[31] ECJ, 29.4.2004, Case C-418/01, *IMS Health/NDC Health*, not yet published in ECR.

[32] ECJ, *IMS Health* (*supra* n 31), point 37–8.

[33] The general conditions of Art 82 EC are added in order to get a complete list.

(1) The owner of an IP right has a dominant position within the common market or in a substantial part of it; trade between member states is affected.
(2) The IP right gives access to a product or service indispensable for carrying on a particular business (***essential facilities***-test).
(3) There are two separate markets, ie an upstream market for the indispensable product and a downstream market for the dependent business (***two markets***-test).
(4) The refusal to grant a licence prevents the emergence of a new product not offered by the IP owner and for which there is a potential consumer demand (***limiting of production***-test in the sense of Art 82 b) EC).
(5) The refusal is not justified by 'objective considerations'.
(6) The refusal excludes all competition on a secondary market (***leveraging-*****test**).

The cumulation of these tests leads to an extremely restrictive compulsory licences regime in Europe.[34] Only in situations which combine a leveraging situation with the limiting of production in the sense of Art 82 b) EC is there an abuse pursuant to Art 82 EC. To put it another way: In intellectual property cases—according to the ECJ—leveraging itself does not constitute an abuse under Art 82 EC. In addition, there has to be the prevention of a new product, ie of a product that the IP owner does not offer himself. Thus, the conditions for compulsory licensing are more restrictive than those for a general obligation to contract.[35]

c) Application of these criteria to the Microsoft *case*

The ECJ's decision in *IMS Health* came one month after the European Commission's *Microsoft* decision. Therefore, the European Commission could not take into account the Court's new requirements regarding compulsory licences. However, the Commission's decision has been attacked by Microsoft and will be controlled by the European courts. Therefore, it is necessary to analyse if the *Microsoft* decision is compatible with the different tests developed by the ECJ in *IMS Health*.[36] Very problematic in this respect is the *limiting of production*-test: Does the refusal of *Microsoft* to deliver interface information prevent the emergence of a new product not offered by *Microsoft*? It is precisely the strategic goal of *Microsoft* to become the leading supplier of server software.

[34] In this respect, the *IMS Health* judgment is comparable to the *Trinko* decision in which the US Supreme Court defined very narrowly the obligation of a monopolist to deal with competitors, see *Verizon Communications Inc. v Law Offices of Curtis V Trinko*, 124 S. Ct. 872 (2004).

[35] For a critique of a different antitrust treatment of intellectual and tangible property see C Ritter, Refusal to Deal and 'Essential Facilities': Does Intellectual Property Require Special Deference Compared to Tangible Property?, 28 World Competition (No 3, Sept 2005, not yet published).

[36] In this respect see Killick, *IMS* and *Microsoft* Judged in the Cold Light of *IMS*, (2004) 1(2) CompLRev, available at: http://www.clasf.org/CompLRev/assets/Vol1Issue2Article2.pdf.

Microsoft already offers its own server software with increasing success. If we assume that the *Microsoft* product has a quality comparable to competing products, there would be no limiting of production to the prejudice of consumers, hence no obligation to make available protected interface information. The mandatory licensing part of the *Microsoft* decision is therefore very problematic against the backdrop of the recent case law.

d) Critique

In our opinion, the starting point of the ECJ is not correct. It is not appropriate to cumulate the *limiting of production*-test with the *leveraging*-condition. These are two distinct forms of abuse because—inter alia—the leveraging abuse requires two distinct markets whereas the typical case of a limiting of production abuse concerns only one independent market. The cumulation of both conditions implies the abolition of the *leveraging* doctrine in IP law because it is the very intention of dominant enterprises to become active on neighbouring markets and to achieve there a dominant position as well. This result is not convincing: The existence of a separate leveraging abuse should be accepted also in an IP context. The owner of an IPR gets a certain reward in the form of an exclusive right. However, the exclusive right does not confer absolute power. Neighbouring markets should be attributed to the IP owner only if he is successful by competition on the merits. The mere use of economic power cannot be justified by the existence of IP rights. The ECJ should therefore rethink its *IMS Health*-decision. The *Microsoft* case is a good occasion to clarify under which conditions a market dominant owner of an IPR abuses his position.

4. General Conclusion: No 'Fine-Tuning' of IPRs by Competition Law

The discussion of the ECJ's case law applying Art 82 EC to IPRs shows that the main task of competition law is to keep markets open. Even if on certain main markets a natural monopoly will prevail for a longer period of time (because of IP protection and the network effect) there is at least the possibility to protect *neighbouring* markets from anti-competitive strategies of the monopolist. Even more important is the task of keeping the monopolised markets themselves open for competition. Strategies which tend to strengthen even further the network effect by eliminating system competition from the outset should be thoroughly scrutinised by the competition authorities. The role of competition law in this context is not to correct or to fine-tune national IPR's.[37] Competition law does not assess IPR's as such but its specific use on certain markets. The case law of

[37] Ullrich, Intellectual Property, Access To Information, And Antitrust: Harmony, Disharmony, And International Harmonization, in: Dreyfuss/Zimmerman/First (ed), Expanding the Boundaries of Intellectual Property—Innovation Policy for the Knowledge Society, 2001, p 365 (378).

the ECJ makes this point perfectly clear: Certainly, in the *Magill* and—in our opinion—also in the *IMS Health* case national copyright is defined rather (too?) broadly (in the *Magill* case, there is national copyright for TV program lists; at the centre of *IMS Health* is copyright protection for a mere geographical structure).[38] But the *Microsoft* case shows that the same problems may arise when IPRs are designed appropriately. The connection between IP overprotection and competition law is rather of a statistical nature: The more extensively IP rights are defined, the more probable a conflict with competition law will be. Therefore it is an essential task of the national legislature to proceed to a 'wise' definition of IPRs avoiding at the same time under- and overprotection.[39] But even if legislature succeeds in doing so will there be problems at the interface of the two fields of law. In order to solve these problems, the common goal of IP law and competition law has to be underlined: The ultimate goal should be the promotion of innovation. It is not IP protection in itself which can achieve this goal, but the use of IPRs on certain markets. On these markets, however, antitrust law has to guarantee the absence of anti-competitive behaviour. Therefore, an equilibrium between IP protection and antitrust law has to be found.

IV. IP ANTITRUST LAW IN CUSTOMS UNIONS AND FREE TRADE AREAS

There is another subject of IP antitrust with has a special link to our general subject, ie to regional integration via customs unions and free trade areas. One of the goals of regional integration is the free movement of goods and services. IP protection may conflict with this goal, eg when IPRs are used to prevent cross-border trade of IP protected products. In Europe, the concept of EU-wide (respectively EEA-wide) exhaustion has been developed to resolve this conflict. Once a protected product has been marketed somewhere in the EU (or in the EEA) with the consent of the IP owner (or another authorised person like eg a licensee), the product in question is allowed to circulate in the EU (or EEA). The IP owner cannot prevent further transactions. His right of distribution is exhausted.

1. European Competition Law and the Rules on Free Movement

One of the functions of European Competition law is to protect the free movement of goods and services against private restraints. The abolition of *state*

[38] For a critique see Leenen, Urheberrecht und Geschäftsmethoden, 2005.

[39] See Hilty, Entwicklungsperspektiven des Schutzes Geistigen Eigentums in Europa, in Behrens (Hrsg.), Stand und Perspektiven des Schutzes Geistigen Eigentums in Europa, 2004, p 139 (177); for reflections on how to define better metes and bounds of copyright see Hilty/Peukert (Hrsg.), Interessenausgleich im Urheberrecht, 2004.

barriers must not be contradicted by *private* restraints wrecking the concept of the internal market. Therefore, private agreements which contain territorial restrictions have to be examined as to their compatibility with Art 81 EC.

a) Parallel Imports

Distinguished rules have been developed by the European legislature and the courts. The most important distinction is that between parallel imports and direct sales. Parallel imports concern goods that have already been marketed in the EU triggering exhaustion of the distribution rights. The right owner has no longer the legal power to prevent further sales of the product in question. Art 81 EC prevents enterprises to circumvent this effect by a private agreement in which they agree on restrictions on further circulation of these goods. Therefore, private export restrictions for 'exhausted' goods are absolutely forbidden.[40]

b) Territorial Restrictions in Distribution and Licensing Agreements

Contrary to such 'absolute' territorial protection, certain 'relative' territorial restrictions may be allowed. In vertical distribution agreements, a supplier may allocate exclusive territories to his buyers. The block exemption regulation on vertical agreements[41] contains specific rules on the legality of such restrictions. According to the regulation the supplier may (if market shares do not exceed 30 per cent) agree with the buyer on a restriction of *active* sales into the exclusive territories of other enterprises. Active sales are all measures targeted at customers in another distributor's exclusive territory like eg direct mail, visits, specific advertising or the establishment of an outlet in that territory. On the other hand, passive sales cannot be excluded. A sale is 'passive' when it responds to unsolicited requests from individual customers.[42]

These rules apply to simple distribution agreements in which intellectual property only plays a minor role. For genuine licensing contracts, the block exemption regulation on technology transfer agreements[43] is applicable which—in the interest of IP protection—allows larger restrictions of competition. If the parties of a licensing contract are not competitors (and if the market share does not exceed 30 per cent), even passive sales into territories allocated to other licensees may be excluded for a period of two years. But also in licensing contracts, parallel imports cannot be excluded.[44]

[40] For more recent cases see CFI, 13.1.2004, Case T-67/01—JCB, especially point 85 *et seq*; European Commission, 26.5.2004—*Pokémon stickers*, Press Release IP/04/682.

[41] Supra, n 19.

[42] For a definition of active and passive sales see European Commission, Guidelines on Vertical Restraints, OJ 2000, C 291/1, n 50.

[43] Supra, n 20.

[44] Conde Gallego (Handelsbezogene Aspekte des Lizenzkartellrechts, 2003, p 225) appreciates the maintenance of free parallel imports as the main task of international IP antitrust law.

2. Dual Pricing

Agreements on export restrictions outside the mentioned exceptions are prohibited by Art 81 EC. This is not only valid for clear-cut export prohibitions, but also for more subtle forms of export impediments. E.g. in the *Glaxo Wellcome* case, the *European Commission* prohibited a system of dual pricing according to which dealers in Spain had to pay a higher price for goods going to be exported than for goods that were sold on the Spanish market.[45] The Court of First Instance (partly) annulled the Commission's decision.[46] According to the Court, the Commission did not sufficiently examine the question if dual pricing improves innovation. Therefore, the Commission has to re-examine the application of Art 81(3) EC.

The CFI's decision is not convincing. Dual pricing goes against the goal of market integration. Differences in national health care systems are not a sufficient reason to partition national markets. The Commission in the *Glaxo* case rightly uses a special IP argument: As drugs are patent protected, parallel imports are often the only alternative source of supply. Therefore, they must not be made more difficult or more expensive.[47] The argument of the CFI according to which the additional revenues from dual pricing can be invested in R&D could be equally applied to hard core price cartels. Moreover, it is highly questionable to what extent the CFI may replace economic considerations of the Commission by its own. The Court rightly states that 'complex economic assessments' are subject only to a confined control,[48] but then demands a detailed examination of all economic aspects.[49] The question may be asked if there should not be more judicial self-restraint concerning economic expertise.[50] It should be added that in the case of dual pricing the market integrating function of European competition law becomes perfectly clear. In the same way public customs duties on imports and exports are prohibited (see Art 23, 25 EC), private 'export taxes' should be forbidden. Otherwise the frontiers abolished by the internal market project (Art 14 EC) would be reintroduced by private agreements. It is the very goal of European competition law to prevent such strategies. Therefore, a clear interdiction of dual pricing should be established, which cannot be overruled by Art 81(3) EC.

[45] European Commission, 8.5.2001, Decision 2001/791/EG—*Glaxo Wellcome*, OJ 2001 L 302/1.

[46] CFI, 27.9.2006, T-168/01—*GlaxoSmithKline* (subject to an appeal before the ECJ as case C-462/06).

[47] For the general rules on parallel imports of drugs see European Commission, Commission Communication on parallel imports of proprietary medicinal products for which marketing authorisations have already been granted, COM(2003) 839 final of 30.12.2003.

[48] CFI (*supra* n 46), n 241 *et seq.*

[49] *Ibid*, n 277.

[50] See the critique by *Gerber*, Courts as Economic Experts in European Merger Law, in: *Hawk* (ed), Annual Proceedings of the Fordham Corporate Law Institute—International Antitrust Law & Policy, 2004, p 475–94, who calls for a specialized competition court and for economic consultants assigned to the judges. He equally wants to oblige the judges to give a detailed reasoning for placing their economic assessment over that of the Commission.

3. Quantitative Restrictions

Similar problems arise in the case of quantitative restrictions in private agreements. Fixing of quotas in distribution or licensing contracts may pursue the aim of eliminating the other party's export potential. By limiting supply the other party may get just the number of products necessary to satisfy the demand on the domestic market. Thus, no quantities are left which could be exported. Therefore, quantitative restrictions in private agreements have to undergo antitrust scrutiny.

a) Vertical Agreements in General

(i) Starting point
Starting point is the fact that everyone is free in deciding how much he wants to sell to a certain buyer. Normal sales contract as such do not violate competition law. However, a conflict with competition law arises when the contracting parties agree that the buyer is not allowed to export the supplied goods. The rules on vertical agreements—as described above—apply. In the case of output restrictions the question has to be asked if the quantitative restriction hides a territorial segmentation agreed upon in an open or at least implied manner by the two parties. The most important question in this respect is if the quantitative restriction was imposed unilaterally, or if the buyer gave—albeit reluctantly—his consent.

(ii) The Adalat *Case*
This is exactly the subject of the *Adalat* case. The German pharmaceutical company *Bayer* limited the supply of its product *Adalat* to the Spanish and French wholesalers in order to prevent parallel imports to the UK where the price for *Adalat* is much higher.[51] The Commission came to the conclusion that the quantitative limitation was not a unilateral conduct, but followed from an agreement between supplier and buyer. The Court of First Instance and the ECJ did not share this view and annulled the Commission's decision. The mere coexistence of a sale's contract and a unilaterally imposed limitation of supply does not—according to the courts—constitute a restrictive agreement in the sense of European Competition Law.[52]

(iii) Agreement or Concerted Practices?
In our view, although the starting point of the European courts is correct, its application in the specific case is doubtful. According to the findings of the European Commission, *Bayer* limited supplies to a certain buyer when he had

[51] European Commission, 10.1.1996, IV/34.279/F3—*Adalat*, OJ 1996 L 201/1.

[52] CFI, 26.10.2000, T-41/96—*Bayer/Commission*, ECR 2000, II-3383; ECJ, 6.1.2004, Joined Cases C-2/01 P and C-3/01 P—*Bundesverband der Arzneimittel-Importeure*. For a positive view of the court decisions in this case see Brown, ECLR 2004, 386.

been identified as a source of parallel imports. Thus, the shortening of supply had a penal character aiming at eliminating parallel imports. The buyers reacted to this threat by stopping or at least hiding their parallel imports. This very evident connection of stimulus and response leads to a coordination of behaviour for which in European competition law the category of 'concerted practices' exists. Therefore, even if there is not an 'agreement' between *Bayer* and its wholesalers, there is at least a concerted practice which is explicitly covered by Art 81 EC. Unfortunately, the European courts did not examine the question if there is such a concerted practice. In our view, it should be sufficient for the application of the European cartel interdiction if the supplier—explicitly or implicitly—expresses certain behavioural expectations to the buyer, and if the buyer then complies or at least pretends to comply with the declared intentions of the supplier. Otherwise, it would be possible for the supplier to circumvent the cartel interdiction by a system of seemingly unilateral measures leading in the end to a segmentation of the internal market.

b) Licensing Contracts

The situation is different for licensing contracts. In European competition law—under the old 1996 block exemption regulation on technology transfer agreements—quantitative restrictions in licensing contracts were blacklisted. The licensee should be free to produce as much of the protected goods as he wanted. This was due to the idea that quantitative restrictions in licensing contracts might have the same effect like export bans. By limiting the quota to the level required for supplying the domestic market, no goods would be left for export.

In the 2004 block exemption regulation on technology transfer agreements,[53] the regime of quantitative restrictions in licensing contracts was relaxed. Output restrictions are only prohibited in certain situations.[54] For the rest they are allowed. According to the European Commission, the pro-competitive aspects (dissemination of the technology in question) outweigh the anticompetitive risks (reduced intra-technology competition).[55]

It is true that the block exemption applies only to market shares below 30 per cent. On the other hand, the context of restrictions in licensing contracts has to be taken into account. As already pointed out, the block exemption regulation allows a far-reaching exclusion of direct sales in the territories of other suppliers. The possibility of output restrictions goes one step further: Thus, even parallel imports may be prevented. The danger of partitioning national markets has become very high.[56]

[53] See *supra* n 20.

[54] Ie for the specific case of reciprocal output restrictions between competitors, see Art 4(1)(b) of the group exemption regulation.

[55] See European Commission, Technology Transfer Guidelines (*supra* n 21), point 175 *et seq*.

[56] See the warning of the European Commission in the Technology Transfer Guidelines (*supra* n 21), point 98.

4. The Role of IP Antitrust Law in Regional Integration

a) Back-up of Market Integration

The examples make perfectly clear the predominant role of IP antitrust law in the context of regional integration. Free interchange across borders is to be guaranteed. IPRs must not be used to establish absolute territorial protection within the integrated territory. A difficult balance has to be found: On the one hand, restrictive agreements in distribution or licensing contracts may be necessary to encourage the dissemination of innovations. On the other hand, contract clauses may not have simply the goal to partition markets. The first sale doctrine (principle of exhaustion) is of great importance in this respect. If the rules on free movement allow the import of protected goods, this result must not be destroyed by excessively restrictive contract clauses. Therefore, one of the tasks of IP antitrust law is to back-up market integration.

It has to be stressed that the integrative function of competition law is not a specific feature of European integration but it is necessary for all attempts to establish Free Trade Agreements (FTA's). The free movement of goods and services can only be achieved if public *and* private restraints of trade are abolished. Apart from the EU, NAFTA may be mentioned here:[57] Art 1501(1) explicitly recognises the integrative function of competition law.[58]

b) Obligation to Adopt Competition Law?

Of course, also in regional integration, competition law keeps its general function of securing workable competition by prohibiting restrictive agreements and the abuse of economic power. Similar to Art 8(2) TRIPS, FTAs often contain provisions which make it clear that the application of competition law to IPRs does not violate the IP obligations undertaken in the respective agreement. The recently concluded CAFTA-DR may be cited in this respect.[59] In its IP chapter, it is stated that the IP obligations do not prevent the parties from prohibiting anticompetitive practices.[60] Like Art 8(2) TRIPS, such a rule leaves it to the states in question to adopt and to implement competition rules or not. Certainly, it is a very useful clarification to state that the application of competition law to IPRs is not a violation of IP protection standards. On the other

[57] North American Free Trade Agreement.

[58] Art 1501 (1) NAFTA reads: 'Each Party shall adopt or maintain measures to proscribe anticompetitive business conduct and take appropriate action with respect thereto, recognizing that such measures will enhance the fulfillment of the objectives of this Agreement [. . .]'.

[59] Central America–Dominican Republic–United States Free Trade Agreement ('CAFTA-DR'). See also Art 1704 NAFTA.

[60] Art 15.15 CAFTA-DR reads: 'Nothing in this Chapter shall be construed to prevent a Party from adopting measures necessary to prevent anticompetitive practices that may result from the abuse of the intellectual property rights set out in this Chapter, provided that such measures are consistent with this Chapter'.

hand, the question arises if states should not be obliged to introduce such competition rules. If it is essential for the efficient functioning of a market economy to have a competition law framework, why should there be no binding rules on this subject? For the world level, the Draft International Antitrust Code (DIAC) proposed by a private group explores this avenue. The DIAC is conceived as a plurilateral agreement to be integrated into the WTO system.[61] The DIAC contains in Art 6 a specific rule on the antitrust law treatment of IPRs.

WTO has put the topic of transnational antitrust on the agenda as one of the so-called Singapore issues, but after the failure of the 2003 Ministerial Conference, the subject has been removed.[62] Especially from the IP perspective, it seems necessary to continue with the efforts towards a binding competition law agreement. The obligation to protect IP has to be complemented by the general framework on using these rights in the market.

c) Competition Law in FTAs

The same is true for the adoption of competition law rules within regional or bilateral FTAs.[63] The constitution of property rights by inserting IP chapters into these agreements must be accompanied by rules which indicate the limits of these rights. Certainly—as has already been mentioned—developing countries are nowadays rather reluctant to accept binding competition rules.[64] However, the fears could be attenuated by providing for special rules on public monopolies and renouncing on cross retaliation.

This leads to the question of implementation of such rules. In the NAFTA agreement for example, the special dispute settlement mechanism does not apply to the competition law rules, Art 1501(3) NAFTA. In the context of WTO, even the supporters of a WTO competition law agreement sometimes think that the dispute settlement mechanism is not appropriate for competition law because it should not interfere with individual decisions of national competition authorities. This is for example the case of the EU.[65] In our view however, this reserve is not justified. Very often, international agreements like the WTO Agreement or FTAs are not recognised as self-executing or directly applicable.

[61] The DIAC is published for example in Fikentscher/Immenga (ed), Draft International Antitrust Code, 1995, p 53 *et seq*. On the DIAC see eg Fikentscher, Competition Rules for Private Agents in the GATT/WTO System, Aussenwirtschaft 1994, p 281; Petersmann, Proposals for Negotiating International Competition Rules in the GATT-WTO World Trade and Legal System, Aussenwirtschaft 1994, p 231.

[62] See Drexl, WTO und Kartellrecht, Zeitschrift für Wettbewerbsrecht 2004, 191; Heinemann (*supra* n 7), p 303.

[63] For a survey on the insertion of competition rules into bi- and multilateral free trade or investment agreements see UNCTAD, International Investment Agreements: Key Issues, vol III, 2005, p 75 *et seq*.

[64] See *supra* B I 1.

[65] See the Communication from the European Community and its Member States, 14 May 2003, WTO-document WT/WGTCP/W/229, available at: http://docsonline.wto.org:80/DDFDocuments/t/WT/WGTCP/W229.doc.

Consequently, private parties cannot invoke these agreements before national courts or authorities. Therefore, in order to ensure the effectiveness of such rules, at least an international mechanism should be available to guarantee the implementation of the rules in question. Accordingly, competition law rules in FTAs should be subject to the same dispute settlement mechanism which applies to the other parts of the agreement. The extent of control exercised by the competent organ depends on the substantive law adopted. If sufficient flexibility (discretion, exceptions) is given to the national authorities the dispute settlement organ will not function as a court of appeals in individual procedures. Its task will be to control if national authorities and courts effectively implement the competition law rules provided for by the FTA.[66]

V. CONCLUSION

The Asian Development Outlook 2005, published by the Asian Development Bank (ADB),[67] contains an entire chapter on the importance of competition policy for long-term development. The text deals among other things with our subject, ie the relationship between competition law and IP protection. The view is taken that there is no genuine contradiction between competition law and IP law because both policies seek to promote innovation and consumer welfare.[68] IP law strives for this aim by giving incentives to invest in research and development. Competition law strengthens innovation because enterprises are more likely to invest in innovation if they act on contested and therefore competitive markets.

This starting point reflects the approach universally shared today, that IP protection and competition policy do not conflict, but complement each other, at least in the long run.[69] Complementarity does not mean harmony, though. In the real world there will always be tensions between both fields of law, eg in case of patent pooling, of licensing contracts containing restricting clauses or of abuse of an IP protected dominant position. One strategy for the legislature to minimise interface problems is the appropriate definition of IP rights, eg in duration and scope. Two extremes have to be avoided. On the one hand, *overprotection* increases conflicts with competition law. On the other hand, *underprotection* jeopardises innovation. But even if IPRs are tailored appropriately, conflicts will persist.

In the context of regional integration the general interface problem is complicated by the goal of market integration. IPRs must not be used to maintain

66 See more in detail Heinemann (*supra* n 7), p 312 *et seq*.

67 Asian Development Bank, Asian Development Outlook 2005, 2005, available at: http://www.adb.org/documents/books/ado/2005/default.asp.

68 Asian Development Outlook 2005 (*supra* n 64), p 283 *et seq*.

69 See eg UNCTAD—Trade and Development Board, Competition Policy and the Exercise of Intellectual Property Rights, TD/B/COM.2/CLP/22/Rev.1, 19 Apr 2002, point 32.

market segmentation. Therefore, special attention has to be paid that the abolition of state borders is not contravened by anticompetitive IP strategies. The adoption of universal IP antitrust rules in the TRIPS agreement has underlined the special importance of this field of law. However, a real balance in the WTO between IP protection on the one hand and competition law on the other hand could only be achieved by the adoption of a WTO competition law agreement. The resistance against such a transnational antitrust code is still strong, as the 2003 WTO Ministerial Conference in Cancún has shown. Perhaps it is the field of IP antitrust law which most clearly demonstrates that such rules are necessary. Thus, the issue of 'International Antitrust and Intellectual Property' has a dimension which goes far beyond its original limits.

Index

www.ingramcontent.com/pod-product-compliance
Ingram Content Group UK Ltd.
Pitfield, Milton Keynes, MK11 3LW, UK
UKHW020135290926
15471UKWH00003B/496